PUBLIC ADMINISTRATION

PUBLIC ADMINISTRATION AND PUBLIC POLICY

A Comprehensive Publication Program

Executive Editor

NICHOLAS HENRY

Center for Public Affairs
Arizona State University
Tempe, Arizona

Publications in Public Administration and Public Policy

1. Public Administration as a Developing Discipline (in two parts)
   by Robert T. Golembiewski

2. Comparative National Policies on Health Care
   by Milton I. Roemer, M.D.

3. Exclusionary Injustice: The Problem of Illegally Obtained Evidence
   by Steven R. Schlesinger

4. Personnel Management in Government: Politics and Process
   by Jay M. Shafritz, Walter L. Balk, Albert C. Hyde, and David H. Rosenbloom

5. Organization Development in Public Administration (in two parts)
   edited by Robert T. Golembiewski and William B. Eddy

6. Public Administration: A Comparative Perspective
   Second Edition, Revised and Expanded
   by Ferrel Heady

Other volumes in preparation

Developmental Editors

PUBLIC ADMINISTRATION

A Comparative Perspective

Second Edition
Revised and Expanded

FERREL HEADY

The University of New Mexico
Albuquerque, New Mexico

Marcel Dekker, Inc.   New York and Basel

Library of Congress Cataloging in Publication Data

Heady, Ferrel.
    Public administration : a comparative perspective.

    (Public administration and public policy ; 6)
    Includes bibliographical references and indexes.
    1. Public administration. I. Title.
II. Series.
JF1351.H4 1979   350   79-590
ISBN 0-8247-6802-7

MARCEL DEKKER, INC.
270 Madison Avenue, New York, New York 10016

Originally published under the title *Public Administration: A Comparative
Perspective* by Ferrel Heady, ©1966 by Prentice-Hall, Inc., Englewood Cliffs,
New Jersey.

Current printing (last digit):
10 9 8 7 6 5 4

PRINTED IN THE UNITED STATES OF AMERICA

To the memory
of my parents

FOREWORD

Ferrel Heady's presentation between these covers invites comparison but does not, meaningfully, permit it. That is, although there is a large literature in the various areas addressed—public administration, bureaucracy, comparative politics, "development," and others—there is no work that much resembles this in its synoptic aim and its synthetic accomplishment. It is a major scholarly achievement.

Some books purport to tell us *What Is Happening in the World* (as one was titled) but in fact mostly display the prejudices, moods, or idiosyncracies of their authors. But this book, modestly titled and modest in tone, tells us much of importance about what is happening in the world. In fact, a large fraction of what is reported in the news media on any day would be illuminated by the facts and opinions here gathered, sifted, and balanced.

The subject of the study is by many standards a narrow or specialized one: the "higher" public bureaucracy of the nation-state. But the examination of the public bureaucracy ranges chronologically from prehistoric man to the latest dispatches, and geographically around the world, encompassing (in the most common terminology) the developed and the developing countries.

Searching for words to characterize the presentation, *comprehensiveness* and *balance* come into prominence. We do not start with a model, a paradigm, a theory, and proceed to fit the data to it, or conversely, proceed to "inexorable" conclusions from a welter of data. Rather, we start with a review of the treatment of the subject of comparative administration, of the related subject of comparative politics, and of the methods and significance of comparison itself. We proceed to a searching inquiry of such matters as "development" and "system transformation" with note taken of the changing and controversial nature of opinion on these matters. We proceed in turn to develop an understanding of public administration in terms of history, and in relation to its political, social, and economic context. Only then is the task of comparing public bureaucracies on a world-wide basis undertaken. In all, critical and opposing views are presented accurately and fairly. If there is prejudice, it escapes my eyes because I see the world much as does the author.

Closer than any book that has come to my attention this book resembles the "picture" of the ideal introductory book for public administration that has been in my mind for three decades. This ideal introductory book would put the subject into a context of both history and contemporary affairs; it would provide orientation and the beginnings of a "philosophy"; it would supply a framework within which either further scholarly probing or the development of professional competence could be placed.

But this book was not written primarily to serve as an introductory book in public administration, a "textbook." It is addressed, I believe it is correct to say, to persons of knowledge and experience in the several areas it treats. And although the novice can no doubt read it with benefit, I can and do testify that I learned much from it though I have given much time and attention to the matters it treats for now more than four decades.

Dwight Waldo

PREFACE

The first edition of this book was published, in a shorter version, over a decade ago. At that time, I commented that some readers might consider it overdue and that others might regard it as premature. Recognition that in a sense each view was correct led me to assert both a claim and a disclaimer. The claim was that I was making the first comprehensive effort to assess the state of the comparative study of public administration and to characterize the administrative systems in a wide range of present-day nation-states. The disclaimer was that the book did not attempt to provide a definitive treatment in such a brief compass for a field probably not yet ready for the task to be performed. My modest objective was to respond to an existing need felt by many students, teachers, and researchers who had chosen to explore the fascinating problems of comparison among national systems of public administration.

This objective has not altered substantially, nor have the difficulties of trying to meet it. During the intervening years, no similar comprehensive treatment has appeared, although the volume of literature on comparative public administration has expanded tremendously and much of it has been made more accessible. Likewise, diversities of approach have continued to characterize the field, leading to numerous recent assessments expressing disappointment in actual accomplishments when contrasted to earlier promise.

In the revision, I have had several aims in view. The most obvious is updating of materials to take into account developments in recent years in various national systems of administration. Another is to discuss fully the recent debate as to the current condition of this field of study. In doing this, I have drawn extensively in Chapter 1 on my article "Comparative Administration: A Sojourner's Outlook," which appeared in the *Public Administration Review* (Vol. 38, No. 4, July/August 1978, pp. 358-65). Cursory mention of system transformation concepts and historical antecedents has been expanded in Chapters 3 and 4 into much fuller treatment of each of these topics. The classification system for dealing with political regime types in developing countries has been revamped and applied with more case study examples in Chapters 8 and 9. Overall, the opportunity afforded by removal of a strict limitation on length has been used to introduce additional topics and provide more adequate coverage.

The basic approach chosen for this study continues, as before, "to bring within the range of consideration administrative systems that have wide variations among them, and to make the task manageable by focusing on public bureaucracies as common governmental institutions and by placing special emphasis on relationships between bureaucracies and political regime types."

Although wanting to acknowledge contributions from several sources for whatever merits the book may possess in either its original or revised form, I do not intend to expose any of the contributors to blame for its defects. I am grateful to the Horace H. Rackham School of Graduate Studies at the University of Michigan and to the East-West Center at the University of Hawaii for providing funds, facilities, and time which allowed me to plan and complete the original manuscript, and to the Division of Public Administration at the University of New Mexico for facilitating the work of revision and expansion. Many professional colleagues—particularly those with whom it has been my good fortune to associate at Michigan, New Mexico, and the East-West Center, and in the Comparative Administration Group and the Section on International and Comparative Administration of the American Society for Public Administration—have given me the benefit of their help. I am especially indebted to the late Wallace S. Sayre, and to William J. Siffin, Edward W. Weidner, and Alfred Diamant for detailed comments and suggestions, which were often but not always followed. To students in comparative public administration at both Michigan and New Mexico, I owe much for their willingness to offer constructive criticism of working drafts of the manuscript.

Sybil L. Stokes, then a member of the Michigan Institute of Public Administration staff, provided expert editorial assistance and advice when the first edition was being prepared. Bruce H. Kirschner, a graduate assistant in the Division of Public Administration at New Mexico, has been equally helpful in working on the revision. In addition, Mr. Kirschner has collaborated closely with me in the analysis of bureaucratic elite regimes and the presentation of case examples contained in Chapter 8 of this edition. I am grateful for his keen interest, diligent pursuit of relevant materials, and perceptive suggestions.

Finally, I appreciate the genial willingness of my wife, Charlotte, to put up with an author trying to meet a deadline, so soon after we had jointly contended with the vicissitudes of a university presidency during the most turbulent years on campus.

Ferrel Heady

CONTENTS

1

COMPARISON IN THE STUDY OF PUBLIC ADMINISTRATION

Public administration as an aspect of governmental activity has existed as long as political systems have been functioning and trying to achieve program objectives set by the political decision-makers. Public administration as a field of systematic study is much more recent. Advisers to rulers and commentators on the workings of government have recorded their observations from time to time in sources as varied as Kautilya's *Arthasastra* in ancient India, the Bible, Aristotle's *Politics*, and Machiavelli's *The Prince*, but it was not until the eighteenth century that cameralism, concerned with the systematic management of governmental affairs, became a specialty of German scholars in Western Europe. In the United States, such a development did not take place until the latter part of the nineteenth century, with the publication in 1887 of Woodrow Wilson's famous essay, "The Study of Administration," generally considered the starting point. Since that time, public administration has become a well-recognized area of specialized interest, either as a subfield of political science or as an academic discipline in its own right.

Despite several decades of development, consensus about the scope of public administration is still lacking, and the field has been described as featuring heterodoxy rather than orthodoxy. A recent text reviews the intellectual development of the field under the heading of public administration's "eighty years in a quandary."[1] This may be a strength rather than a weakness, but such a feature does rule out a short, precise, and generally acceptable definition of the field. The identification of tendencies and of shared subjects of concern is more feasible, and is all that is necessary for our purposes.

Public administration is presumably an aspect of a more generic concept—administration, the essence of which has been described as "determined action taken in pursuit of conscious purpose."[2] Most efforts to define administration in general add the element of cooperation among two or more individuals and view it as cooperative human effort toward reaching some goal or goals accepted by those engaged in the endeavor. Administration is concerned with means for the achievement of prescribed ends. Administrative activity can take place in a variety of settings, provided the crucial elements are present: The cooperation of human beings to perform tasks that have been mutually accepted as worthy of the joint effort. The institutional framework in which administration occurs may be as diverse as a business firm, labor union, church, educational institution, or governmental unit.

Public administration is that sector of administration found in a political setting. Concerned primarily with the carrying out of public policy decisions made by the authoritative decision-makers in the political system, public administration can be roughly distinguished from private, or nonpublic, administration. Of course, the range of governmental concern may vary widely from one political jurisdiction to another, so that the dividing line is wavy rather than clear-cut.

In the United States, actual usage in the past somewhat narrowed the range of administrative action dealt with in most writings on public administration, with the result that the term came to signify primarily "the organization, personnel, practices, and procedures essential to effective performance of the civilian functions assigned to the executive branch of government."[3] This was acceptable for purposes of emphasis but was unduly restrictive as a definition of the scope of public administration. Consequently, in recent years the tendency has been to move away from such a restricted range of concerns, even though no consensus has emerged as to the exact boundaries of the field. One indication is the gradual abandonment of the sharp dichotomy between politics and administration made by earlier writers such as Frank J. Goodnow and Leonard D. White. Paul H. Appleby, whose career combined varied experiences both as a practitioner and an academic, was one of the first to stress the interrelationships rather than the differences between the policy-making and policy-execution aspects of governing, in his influential book *Policy and Administration*, published in

1949.[4] Since then, the dominant view has come to be that students
of administration cannot confine themselves to the implementation
phase of public policy. Indeed, one of the current basic textbooks
states that "the core of public administration is politics and public
policy," and that "public administration can be defined as the
formulation, implementation, evaluation, and modification of public
policy."[5] One way of stressing this linkage has been the widespread
use of case studies in the teaching of public administration. These
case studies are narratives of the events constituting or leading to
decisions by public administrators, taking into account "the personal, legal, institutional, political, economic, and other factors that
surrounded the process of decision," and trying to give the reader
"a feeling of actual participation in the action."[6]

A second line of questioning of earlier assumptions appeared
as a by-product of the unrest centering on university campuses
during the late 1960s and early 1970s, and found expression in the
teaching, writing, and professional activities of younger public
administrators both on the campus and in government. Generally
labeled the "new" public administration, this movement not only
reaffirmed the breakdown of the politics–administration dichotomy
but also challenged the traditional emphasis on techniques of administration, and stressed the obligations of public administrators to be
concerned with values, ethics, and morals, and to pursue a strategy
of activism in coping with the problems of society. Whether or not
the "new" public administration will have a lasting and forceful
impact remains to be seen.[7]

Finally, the inadequacies of a narrow culture-bound definition
of public administration became apparent early to those who were
interested in the comparative study of administration across national
boundaries. As we shall see, the comparative administration movement inevitably had to turn to a more comprehensive view concerning the scope of public administration than had been generally
accepted in the United States before World War II.

These summary statements about the focus of public administration hide a host of knotty problems—conceptual, definitive,
semantic—that do not have to be explored here. Sharp differences
of opinion do indeed exist among students of public administration
on important issues of approach and emphasis, but should not
obscure basic agreement on the central concerns in administrative
studies. These concerns include (1) the characteristics and behavior
of public administrators—the motivations and conduct of the
participants in the administrative process, particularly those who

are career officials in the public service; (2) the institutional arrangements for the conduct of large-scale administration in government—
organizing for administrative action; and (3) the environment or
ecology of administration—the relationship of the administrative
subsystem to the political system of which it is a part and to society
in general. This combination of concerns, proceeding from the more
circumscribed to the more comprehensive, provides a basic framework both for the analysis of particular national systems of public
administration and for comparisons among them.

Significance of Comparison

The purpose of this study is to offer an introduction to the comparative analysis of systems of public administration in the nation-states
of today. This is not an entirely new venture, but comparison has
certainly not been the main thrust in most of the literature on public
administration, particularly that produced in the United States.[8]
Pioneers such as Woodrow Wilson and Ernst Freund drew upon
European experience in their efforts to understand and improve
American administration, but most subsequent writers concentrated
on the local scene, with only incidental references to other systems
of administration. The limitations and hazards of such parochialism
have now been recognized, and we have started a new era in administrative studies that stresses comparative analysis.

  Persuasive reasons for such an effort lie behind this reorientation. Those who are attempting to construct a science of administration recognize that this depends, among other things, on success in
establishing propositions about administrative behavior which
transcend national boundaries. This requirement was pointed out
by Robert Dahl in his influential 1947 essay, "The Science of Public
Administration," when he said

... the comparative aspects of public administration have largely been ignored;
and as long as the study of public administration is not comparative, claims for
"a science of public administration" sound rather hollow. Conceivably there
might be a science of American public administration and a science of British
public administration and a science of French public administration; but can
there be a "science of public administration" in the sense of a body of generalized principles independent of their peculiar national setting?[9]

  Formulating general principles concerning public administration
in the United States, Great Britain, and France may be difficult

enough, but this would be quite inadequate in a world having the great number and diversity of national administrative systems that must now be included in our field of interest. Administration in Communist countries and in the multitude of newly independent nations scattered around the globe must also be taken into account. Even cursory observation brings home the complexities involved in describing and analyzing the administrative variations and innovations that have developed in these settings.

Aside from the demands of scientific inquiry, there are other advantages to be gained from a better understanding of public administration across national boundaries. The increasing interdependence of nations and regions of the world makes comprehension of the conduct of administration of much more importance than in the past. The success of Zaire, Bolivia, and Indonesia in organizing for administrative action is no longer just a matter of intellectual curiosity; it is of immense practical significance in Washington, Moscow, and London, not to mention Manila, Cairo, and Peking.

Various administrative devices developed abroad may also prove worthy of consideration for adoption or adaptation at home. The influence of Western patterns of administration in the newly independent countries is well known and easily understandable. Less obvious is the growing interest in larger countries concerning administrative machinery originated in smaller nations. An example is the Scandinavian office of Ombudsman, designed for protection of the public against administrative abuse or inadequacy, which has been widely studied and in several instances transplanted in the United States, countries of the British Commonwealth, and some of the new states.[10] The laboratories for administrative experimentation provided by the emergence of many new nations should in the future offer numerous instances of innovations in administration worthy of attention in the more established countries. Some of the most extensive and crucial use of government corporations, for example, is now occurring in the developing nations.

Problems of Comparison

Recognizing the need for comparison is much easier than coping with some of the problems posed by efforts to compare on a systematic basis.

To begin, any attempt to compare national administrative

systems must acknowledge the fact that administration is only one aspect of the operation of the political system. This means inevitably that comparative public administration is linked closely to the study of comparative politics, and must start from the base provided by the current stage of development of comparative studies of whole political systems.

Comparative politics has been through a transition that deserves to be called revolutionary. This resulted from a combination of dramatic expansion of the range of coverage of the subject and a drastic reorientation of approach, both occurring mainly during the last three decades. A field that was largely confined to consideration of the political institutions of a handful of countries in Western Europe and North America, plus at most a scattering of other countries such as selected members of the British Commonwealth and Japan, suddenly confronted the urgent need to account in its comparisons for a welter of additional nations which had emerged on the world scene, with the resulting problem of numbers and diversity. The United Nations now has almost 150 member states, and there are others waiting to get in, excluded from membership, or not wanting to be included. Moreover, their diversity is more of a complication than their number, since they range so widely in area, population, stability, ideological orientation, economic development, historical background, governmental institutions, future prospects, and a host of other relevant factors. The student of comparative politics must undertake to provide a framework for comparison that can cope with such complexity.

The response of students of comparative politics to these needs has been impressive, with substantial, although not complete, agreement on new means of fulfilling them.[11] The common objectives are that the purview of comparative studies must be capable of including all existing nation-states, that comparison to be significant must be based on the collection and evaluation of political data in terms of definite hypotheses or theories, and that some alternative to a simple institutional basis for comparison must be found.[12]

The insistence on inclusion of the nations of Asia, Latin America, and Africa signifies recognition of the fact that these countries occupy approximately 63 percent of the land area of the earth and contain over 75 percent of the world's population. These statistics are particularly significant in view of the waning age of imperialism and colonialism, the "revolution of rising expectations" among the people of these countries, and the battleground they furnish for rivalry among competing world powers and political ideologies. As Ward and Macridis remark, it is essential that "the discipline of comparative politics keep abreast of such developments and expand its frames of reference and concern so as to include the political systems of these emergent non-Western areas. This is easy to say, but hard in practice to do."[13]

Heroic efforts have been made to define key concepts and formulate hypotheses for systematic testing. Attempts to define "political system" had first priority, with the result that a political system is now generally described as that system of interactions in a society which produces authoritative decisions (or allocates values) that are binding on the society as a whole and are enforced by legitimate physical compulsion if necessary. The political system, in Almond's words, is "the legitimate, order-maintaining or transforming system in the society."[14] Government is the official machinery by which these decisions are "legally identified, posed, made, and administered."[15] This formulation is intended to include a variety of states—developed and developing, totalitarian and democratic, Western and non-Western. It also embraces types of primitive political organizations that do not qualify as states in the sense used by Max Weber, that they monopolize the legitimate use of physical force within a given territory. Other key concepts that have received much attention but are the subject of more disagreement are political modernization, development, and change. Further consideration of some of the issues involved in these concepts is given in Chapter 3.

The most influential of the comprehensive efforts to substitute a functional approach for the more traditional institutional or structural approach to comparative politics has been made by Gabriel A. Almond.[16] As to the advantage of this approach, the basic claim is that it attempts "to construct a theoretical framework that makes possible, for the first time, a comparative method of analysis for political systems of all kinds."[17] The indictment against comparisons on the basis of specialized political structures such as legislatures, political parties, chief executives, and interest groups is that such comparisons are of only limited utility because similar structural features may not be found in different political systems, or they may be performing significantly different functions. Almond concedes that all political systems have specialized political structures, and that the systems may be compared with one another structurally. Almond, however, sees little to be gained from this, and a serious danger of being misled. Instead, the correct functional questions should be asked. He asserts that "the same functions are performed in all political systems, even though these functions may be performed with different frequencies, and by different kinds of structures."[18]

What are these functional categories? Let us begin by saying they are derived from consideration of the political activities that take place in the most complex Western political systems. Thus, the activities of associational interest groups led to derivation of the function of interest articulation, and the activities of political parties, to the function of interest aggregation. In its revised form, this scheme of analysis suggests a sixfold functional breakdown for the internal conversion processes through which political systems transform inputs into outputs. These functions are (1) interest articulation (formulation of demands); (2) interest aggregation (combination of demands in the form of alternative courses of action); (3) rule-making (formulation of authoritative rules); (4) rule application (application and enforcement of these rules); (5) rule adjudication (adjudication in individual cases of applications of these rules); and (6) communication (both within the political system and between the political system and its environment). The innovation in this list is clearly in the functions that have been traditionally related to policy-making rather than policy execution, which detracts considerably from the usefulness of this analytical framework to those principally interested in the administrative aspects of comparative study.

Despite the generally favorable reception given to the Almond functional approach, it has not escaped sharp criticism. Leonard Binder acknowledges that it is an advance over institutional description, but dismisses it with the curt observation that it "may be praised as interesting or perceptive, without compelling further attention." He concedes that the categories can be universally applied, but this is because they are broad and ambiguous. The scheme claims to facilitate the analysis of whole political systems, but Binder feels that it will be accepted "only if it lends itself to the analysis of specific systems as well as to problems of comparison, and only if the implicit assumptions of the scheme accord with the theoretical assumptions of individual researchers." The root defect that Binder sees is that these functions, having been located by "the device of generalizing what appeared to the theorist to be the broad classes of political activity found in Western political systems," are "derived neither logically nor empirically." He asks why these functions should be selected and not others, and he challenges the supposition that "a limited number of functions . . . comprise the political system." Further, he argues that the weakness of the scheme is evidenced by the fact that the authors who attempted to apply the Almond scheme in the volume it introduced "judiciously avoided remaining within its limiting framework or, in the case of the 'governmental functions,' made it clear how insignificant has been the effort to apply the traditional categories of Western political science."[19]

Another critic of Almond's input-output model is Fred W. Riggs, who admits that it is useful for the study of developed political systems, but finds it inadequate for the analysis of transitional systems, such as that of India, which is, of course, precisely the kind of system to which Almond thought it would be most applicable. Riggs feels that a different model is needed for such a polity, which has "inputs which do not lead to rule-making, and rules which are often not implemented." What is required is "a two-tiered model, a system which distinguishes between 'formal' and 'effective' structures, between what is prescribed ideally and what actually happens."[20] Riggs suggests as more appropriate for such political systems his own "prismatic model," which we explore in more detail in Chapter 2.

Another attack on the structural–functional approach comes from critics who associate this school of thought with a basic philosophical bias favoring the political systems which have evolved in liberal Western capitalist societies, and who argue that analytical schemes such as Almond's operate in practice to justify and perpetuate the status quo in developing countries to the benefit of the advanced industrialized societies and to the detriment of the countries subjected to study by social scientists using this methodology. This judgment is made particularly by the dependency development theorists whose views are examined in Chapter 3.

In summary, the problems of comparison are formidable. First, some way must be found for singling out the administrative segment of the political system as a basis for specialized comparison. This cannot be done without involvement in issues related to the comparison of whole political systems, where there is ferment and progress but no consensus. The dominant tendency in comparative politics is to substitute a functional approach to comparison for one emphasizing political structures and institutions. Insofar as the functional approach receives exclusive or even preferred recognition as the proper basis for comparisons of less than whole political systems, a dilemma is created for the comparative study of administration, because the full range of concerns of public administration as a field of academic inquiry is less easily identified with one or more functions in a framework such as Almond's than with particular familiar institutions in Western political systems.

Postwar Evolution of Comparative Studies

A sustained effort to undertake comparative analysis in public administration did not begin until after the end of World War II. Since that time, a comparative administration "movement" has gained momentum, with enthusiastic and industrious devotees whose efforts have evoked praise from some quarters for impressive accomplishments and criticism from others for what are regarded as pretentious claims.[21]

The timing and vigor of this movement resulted from a combination of factors: the rather obvious need for this extension of range in public administration as a discipline; the exposure of large numbers of scholars and practitioners of administration to experience with administration abroad during wartime, postwar occupation, and subsequent technical assistance assignments; the stimulation of the largely contemporary revisionist movement in comparative politics which has already been summarized; and the rather remarkable expansion of opportunities during the 1950s and 1960s for those interested in devoting themselves to research at home or field experience abroad on problems of comparative public administration.

Manifestations of these developments were numerous during the first two decades after the end of World War II. A growing number of colleges and universities offered courses in comparative public administration, and some of them made it a field of specialization for graduate study. Professional associations extended recognition, first through the appointment in 1953 of an ad hoc committee on comparative administration by the American Political Science Association, and later by the establishment in 1960 of the Comparative Administration Group affiliated with the American Society for Public Administration. The latter group, usually abbreviated as CAG, grew vigorously with the help of generous support from the Ford Foundation. The CAG, under Fred W. Riggs as chairman and leading spokesman, mapped out and entered into a comprehensive program of research seminars, experimental teaching projects, discussions at professional meetings, special conferences, and exploration of other ways of strengthening available resources, such as through the expansion of facilities for field research.

The most tangible product of these early endeavors was an

output of published writings on comparative public administration which soon reached voluminous proportions[22] and led, despite the short span of time, to several attempts at review and analysis of the literature produced by the early 1960s.[23] Classification of this literature is best done by subject matter or focus of emphasis rather than chronological order, since it appeared in a variety of forms more or less simultaneously. I have suggested as a useful scheme of classification one which divides this literature as follows: (1) modified traditional, (2) development-oriented, (3) general system model-building, and (4) middle-range theory formulation.

The modified traditional category showed the greatest continuity with earlier more parochially oriented literature. The subject matter was not markedly different as the focus shifted from individual administrative systems to comparisons among them, although there was often a serious effort to utilize more advanced research tools and to incorporate findings from a variety of social science disciplines. This literature may be further subdivided into studies made from a comparative perspective of standard administrative subtopics, and those which undertook comparisons of entire systems of administration. Topics in the first subcategory included administrative organization, personnel management, fiscal administration, headquarters–field relations, administration of public enterprises, regulatory administration, administrative responsibility and control, and program fields such as health, education, welfare, and agriculture.

The second subcategory included a number of studies that were basically descriptive institutional comparisons of administration in Western developed countries, with special emphasis on administrative organization and civil service systems.[24] Also worthy of mention is an outline for comparative field research formulated by Wallace S. Sayre and Herbert Kaufman in 1952, and later revised by a working group of the American Political Science Association subcommittee on comparative public administration. This research design suggested a three-point model for comparison, focusing on the organization of the administrative system, the control of the administrative system, and the securing of consent and compliance by the administrative hierarchy.[25]

Advocates of a focus on "development administration" sought to concentrate attention on the administrative requisites for achieving public policy goals, particularly in countries in which these goals involve dramatic political, economic, and social transformations.[26] "Development," according to Weidner, "is a state of mind, a tendency, a direction. Rather than a fixed goal, it is a rate of change in a particular direction. . . . The study of development administration can help to identify the conditions under which a maximum rate of development is sought and the conditions under which it has been obtained."[27] He contended that existing models for comparison were of limited use because "they make inadequate provision for social change; characterize modern bureaucracy in very inaccurate ways; are unduly comprehensive, all-inclusive and abstract; and fail to take account of the differences in administration that may be related to the goals that are being sought." Hence, he urged the adoption of development administration as a separate focus for research, with the end object being "to relate different administrative roles, practices, organizational arrangements, and procedures to the maximizing of development objectives. . . . In research terms, the ultimate dependent variable would be the development goals themselves."[28] Although work with a development administration emphasis need not be normative, in the sense of a choice among development goals by the researcher, much of it has had a prescriptive coloration.

Dwight Waldo, among others, was intrigued by this approach and argued that a concentration on the theme of development might "help to bring into useful association various clusters of ideas and types of activity that are now more or less separate and help clarify some methodological problems," even though he admitted that he found it impossible to define development, as used in this connection, with precision.[29] Although the term does raise serious questions about what it means and what is included and excluded, development administration has continued as a focus of attention because it has the virtue of consciously relating administrative means to administrative ends, and of deliberately spotlighting the problems of administrative adjustment faced by emerging countries seeking to achieve developmental goals. As Swerdlow remarks, "poor countries have special characteristics that tend to create a different role for government. These characteristics and this expanded or emphasized role of government, particularly as it affects economic growth, tend to make the operations of the public administrator significantly different. Where such differences exist, public administration can be usefully called development administration."[30]

The remaining two groups were more typical of the dominant mood among students of comparative public administration during this period, and indeed of comparative politics as well. In contrast to the first two categories, the emphasis here was much more self-consciously on the construction of typologies or models for comparative purposes, and there was a strong concern to keep these value-free or value-neutral. The word "model" was used here, as by Waldo, to mean "simply the conscious attempt to develop and define concepts, or clusters of related concepts, useful in classifying data, describing reality and (or) hypothesizing about it."[31] Interdisciplinary borrowing was extensive, primarily from sociology, but to a considerable extent also from economics, psychology, and other fields. This emphasis on theory and methodology was repeatedly noted, often praised as indicative of sound preparation for future progress, as well as frequently disparaged as a preoccupation diverting energies that might better have been devoted to the conduct of actual field studies of administrative systems in operation. Any attempt to classify this plethora of models must be somewhat arbitrary, but the most useful distinction was made by Presthus, who distinguished between theorists attempting broad, cross-cultural, all-encompassing formulations and those advancing more modest and restricted "middle-range" theories.[32] Diamant likewise discerned "general system" models and "political culture" models among contributions in comparative politics.[33]

Among those who preferred the general system approach to comparative public administration, Fred W. Riggs was clearly the dominant figure. As I have said elsewhere, "mere acquaintance with all of his writings on comparative theory is in itself not an insignificant accomplishment."[34] Drawing essentially upon concepts of structural–functional analysis developed by sociologists such as Talcott Parsons, Marion Levy, and F. X. Sutton, Riggs, in a series of published and unpublished writings, over a period of years formulated and reformulated a cluster of models or "ideal types" for societies, designed to contribute to a better understanding of actual societies, particularly those undergoing rapid social, economic, political, and administrative change. This work culminated in his book, *Administration in Developing Countries: The Theory of Prismatic Society*,[35] which continues to be probably the most notable single contribution in comparative public administration.

Another prominent source of comprehensive model-building was equilibrium theory, postulating a system with inputs and outputs as a basis of analysis. John T. Dorsey outlined an approach to theory of this type in his "information-energy model," which he believed might be useful in the analysis of social and political systems in general as well as for a better understanding of administrative systems.[36] Dorsey later used this scheme in an analysis of political development in Vietnam.[37]

As Waldo observed, the central problem of model construction in the study of comparative public administration is "to select a model that is 'large' enough to embrace all the phenomena that should be embraced without being, by virtue of its large dimensions, too coarse-textured and clumsy to grasp and manipulate administration."[38]   The alleged gap between such "large" models and the empirical data to be examined led Presthus and others to stress the need for middle-range theory rather than theory of "cosmic dimension," to use his phrase. He advised social scientists working on comparative administration to "bite off smaller chunks of reality and . . . research these intensively." Similar expressions of preference for middle-range theories were made at about the same time in the field of comparative politics.[39]

By the early 1960s, the most prominent and promising middle-range model available for comparative studies in administration had already been established as the "bureaucratic" one, based on the ideal-type model of bureaucracy formulated by Max Weber but with substantial subsequent modification, alteration, and revision. Waldo found the bureaucratic model useful, stimulating, and provocative, its advantage and appeal being that this model "is set in a large framework that spans history and cultures and relates bureaucracy to important social variables, yet it focuses attention upon the chief structural and functional characteristics of bureaucracy."[40]   He correctly pointed out that not much empirical research had actually been done using the bureaucratic model. However, this deficiency applied to other models as well, and there was at least a base of such studies upon which to build, with others on the way. The most notable such research, despite substantial flaws in execution, was Morroe Berger's *Bureaucracy and Society in Modern Egypt*,[41] but there were a number of other partial treatments of bureaucracy in particular countries, either in separate essays or as parts of analyses of individual political systems. The entire subject of the role of bureaucracy in political development had been explored in depth in papers prepared for a conference sponsored in 1962 by the Committee on Comparative Politics of the Social Science Research Council and published the following year in a volume edited by Joseph LaPalombara.[42]   The bureaucratic perspective for comparison was thus already well rooted during the formative period of the comparative public administration movement.

This review of the literature during the emergence of comparative studies in public administration provides a base for describing the flowering of the movement during the decade beginning in the

early 1960s. Trends which continued into this period of expansion
had already been identified and encouraged by Fred Riggs in an essay
published in 1962.[43]   He discerned three trends which have been
generally accepted as important and relevant. The first was a shift
from normative toward more empirical approaches—a movement
away from efforts to prescribe ideal or better patterns of administration toward "a growing interest in descriptive and analytic information for its own sake."[44]   This consideration has already been
mentioned, but it should be noted that the popular development
administration theme often had a strong prescriptive motivation.
The second trend was a movement from what Riggs called idiographic
toward nomothetic approaches.   Essentially this distinguished
between studies "which concentrate on the unique case" and those
seeking "generalizations, 'laws,' hypotheses that assert regularities
of behavior, correlations between variables."[45]   Model-building, particularly of the general system type, showed this nomothetic inclination. The third trend was a shift from a predominantly nonecological
to an ecological basis for comparative study. Riggs described the
first trend as being fairly clear by the time he wrote, but considered
the other two as "perhaps only just emerging."[46]   Obviously, he
approved of these trends and was trying to encourage them. Indeed,
he stated that his personal preference would be "to consider as
'truly' comparative only those studies that are empirical, nomothetic,
and ecological."[47]

The Heyday of the Comparative Administration Movement

"The time of greatest vitality, vigor, influence, etc." is the dictionary
definition of heyday, describing accurately the comparative administration movement during the period of about a decade beginning in
1962, the year in which the Comparative Administration Group
received initial funding from the Ford Foundation through a grant
to the American Society for Public Administration, CAG's parent
organization.

During these years, students of comparative public administration demonstrated an amazing productivity, and their field of interest
grew rapidly in glamor and reputation. At the core of all this activity
was the Comparative Administration Group, with a membership
composed of academics and practitioners, including a considerable
number of "corresponding members" from countries other than the
United States, reaching a total in 1968 of over 500. Fred W. Riggs

was chairman of CAG from its inception in 1960 through 1970, when Richard W. Gable succeeded him. The principal source of financial support was the Ford Foundation, which made grants to CAG of about half a million dollars in all, beginning in 1962 with a three-year grant which was extended for a year and then renewed in 1966 for five additional years. In 1971 this support was not renewed again, and after that CAG resources were much reduced, with a corresponding curtailment of programs. The primary focus of interest of the Ford Foundation was on the administrative problems of developing countries, and the CAG was expected to analyze these problems in the context of societal environmental factors found in the developing countries. The Foundation had a strong development administration orientation and was eager to see a transfer of knowledge from CAG programs to practical applications through technical assistance projects and domestic developmental undertakings within the target countries.

The CAG spun an elaborate network for carrying out its obligation to stimulate interest in comparative administration, with special reference to development administration problems. The primary device chosen initially was a series of summer seminars, held two per year over a three-year period at different universities, involving in each instance about a half dozen senior scholars who prepared papers on a common theme, plus graduate research assistants and visiting consultants. Later, special conferences and seminars were scheduled on various topics both in the United States and abroad. In addition, a number of small subgrants were made for experimental teaching programs.

A committee structure evolved under CAG auspices as areas of interest became identified. Several had a geographical orientation, relating to Asia, Europe, Latin America, and Africa. Others had a subject matter focus, including committees on comparative urban studies, national economic planning, comparative educational administration, comparative legislative studies, international administration, organization theory, and systems theory. These committees were not equally active or productive.

The work of CAG was reflected principally in publications which it spawned, either directly or indirectly. A newsletter was issued regularly as a means of internal communication. More than 100 occasional papers were distributed in mimeographed form. After editing and revision, many of these were later published under various auspices. The primary outlet was provided by the Duke University Press, which published seven volumes in cooperation with

CAG from 1969 through 1973, including general collections on political and administrative development and "frontiers" of development administration, volumes on development administration in Asia and in Latin America, studies of temporal dimensions and spatial dimensions of development administration, and a comparative analysis of legislatures. For a five-year period, from 1969 to 1974, the quarterly *Journal of Comparative Administration* was issued by Sage Publications in cooperation with CAG. There were also, of course, numerous articles published in other scholarly journals in the United States and abroad which were written by CAG members.

Paralleling these research efforts, a corresponding growth was taking place in the teaching of courses in comparative and development administration in the United States, as evidenced by a 1970 report of a CAG survey which enumerated a proliferation of offerings beginning in 1945 at one institution and growing to over thirty by the time of the survey, but it also revealed very little uniformity as to approach, emphasis, or level of presentation. This interest in comparative aspects of administration was also reflected in the curricula and publications of numerous schools and institutes of public administration scattered around the world, usually as products of technical assistance projects, although the record was uneven as to the quantity and quality of these efforts.

The record of this "golden era" in comparative public administration is basically a continuation and expansion of what had already begun during the postwar period. The sheer bulk and great diversity of the output make generalizations hazardous. Nevertheless, it is possible to identify some characteristic features which not only show what was accomplished but also foreshadow some of the current predicaments faced by the comparative administrative movement.

One obvious enduring influence can be traced to the large-scale postwar effort to export administrative know-how through unilateral and multilateral technical assistance programs. The CAG inherited the then favorable reputation and shared many of the attitudes associated with the public administration technical assistance efforts of the 1950s. Experts in public administration, not only from the United States but from several European countries as well, were scattered around the world, engaged in similar projects to export administrative technology, largely drawn from American experience, to a multitude of developing countries. Looking back, one of these experts describes the scene as follows: "The 1950s was a wonderful period. The 'American Dream' was the 'World Dream'—and the best and quickest way to bring that dream into reality was through the mechanism of public administration. . . . The net result of all of this enthusiastic action was that in the 1950s public administration was a magic term and public administration experts were magicians, of a sort. They were eagerly recruited by the United States' aid-giving agencies and readily accepted by most of the new nations, along with a lot of other experts as well."[48] Another well-informed participant observer takes 1955 as the baseline year, and describes it as "a vintage year in a time of faith—faith in the developmental power of administrative tools devised in the West. It was a sanguine year in a time of hope—hope that public administration could lead countries toward modernization. It was a busy year in a brief age of charity— the not-unmixed charity of foreign assistance."[49]

Members of the CAG, many of whom had been or still were active participants in such programs, shared as a group most of the assumptions of the public administration experts, at least initially. Siffin has provided an accurate and perceptive analysis of the orientations which marked this era, noting several major features. The first was a tool or technology orientation. The best developed and most widely exported of these processes were in the fields of personnel administration and budgeting and financial administration, but the list included administrative planning, records management, work simplification, tax and revenue administration, and at least the beginnings of computer technology. Part of the tool orientation was a belief that use of the tools could be essentially divorced from the substance of the governmental policies which they would be serving.

Second, there was a structural orientation which placed great emphasis on the importance of appropriate organizational arrangements, and assumed that organizational decisions could and should be based on rational considerations. For the most part, organizational forms then popular in the West were thought of as the most fitting, and organizations recommended for the developing countries usually emulated some model familiar to the expert at home.

Underlying these administrative manifestations were certain value and contextual orientations which helped explain the specifics of technical assistance recommendations. The instrumental nature of administration was the core value, with related supportive concepts of efficiency, rationality, responsibility, effectiveness, and professionalism. Education and training projects, including the sending of thousands of individuals to developed countries and the establishment of about seventy institutes in developing countries, were designed to inculcate these values as well as transmit technical know-how in specific subjects. Probably most important of all, these normative elements, particularly the commitment to responsibility as a basic value, were in Siffin's words "predicated upon a certain kind of socio-political context—the kind of context which is distinguished in its absence from nearly every developing country in the world."[50] This context included economic, social, political, and intellectual aspects drawn mainly from U.S. experience and to some extent from other Western democratic systems. Politically, for example, these systems operated "within reasonably stable political frameworks, with limited competition for resources and mandates. In this milieu, administrative technologies provided *order* more than *integration*. The political context of administration was generally predictable, supportive, and incrementally expansive." In this and other respects, Siffin concludes that "the radical differences between the U.S. administrative context and various overseas situations were substantially ignored."[51]

It would be unfair to infer that misconceptions prevalent in the technical assistance efforts of the 1950s were accepted without question by students of comparative public administration during the 1960s. As a matter of fact, many of them voiced doubt and skepticism about approaches being used and opposed particular reform measures in countries with which they were familiar. Nevertheless, the comparative administration movement at its height can accurately be described as imbued with a pervasive overall mood of optimism about the practicality of utilizing administrative means to bring about desirable change. Commentators who disagree on other assessments agree on this. In a review of several of the major books produced by the CAG, Garth N. Jones remarks that they "make a case for positive intervention into the affairs of men. Men can take destiny in their hands, control, and mold it." Noting that many of the papers under review systematically eviscerate "past approaches and efforts in planned development in public administration," Jones points out that even so "scarcely a word is mentioned that questions the approach of positive intervention. The main task is to find a better way by which to do this."[52]

Peter Savage, who served as editor of the *Journal of Comparative Administration*, observes that the study of administration from a comparative perspective "possesses a peculiar quality; a concern for the management of action in the real world, for creating organizational and procedural arrangements that handle specified and identifiable problems in the public realm." Indigenous to the comparative administration movement, in his opinion, has been " a belief in the possibility of managing change by purposive intervention by administrative institutions."[53]

Even more than before, during the 1960s development administration became a term often used in the titles of books and articles with a comparative thrust. No doubt this reflected in part the faith in positive results just discussed and behind that the desire to assist developing countries in meeting their overwhelming problems. It was also responsive to the core interest of the Ford Foundation as chief financial benefactor in directing CAG programs toward developmental topics. Furthermore, it proved attractive to leaders in the developing countries themselves by highlighting an intent to assist in reaching domestic goals. From a more strictly scholarly point of view, strong arguments were made as to the benefits to comparative studies of a developmental focus. Whatever the motivations, development administration largely displaced comparative administration in the labeling of CAG output. This is shown most significantly in the Duke University Press series of books, each of which has in its title either the word "development" or "developmental," and none of which has "comparative."

Despite the trend toward greater usage, little progress appeared in defining more precisely what development administration meant. Riggs, in his introduction to *Frontiers of Development Administration*,[54] says that no clear answer can be given as to how the study of development administration differs from the study of comparative administration or the study of public administration generally. He does identify two foci of attention—the administration of development and the development of administration. In the first sense, development administration "refers to the administration of development programs, to the methods used by large-scale organizations, notably governments, to implement policies and plans designed to meet their developmental objectives."[55] The second meaning involves the strengthening of administrative capabilities, both as a means to enhance the prospects for success in carrying out current development programs, and as a by-product of prior programs such as in education.[56] Writings under the heading of development administration have indeed explored both of these facets, but have not by any means been confined to one or the other of these subjects of inquiry. As a matter of actual practice, development administration came in the 1960s to be synonymous with, or at least not clearly distinguishable from, comparative public administration. The two terms became virtually interchangeable. This usage was in part an affirmation of the faith in positive intervention for societal reform held by most of those identified with the comparative administration movement.

Among the middle-range models for comparative studies, bureaucracy continued to be widely preferred. Ramesh K. Arora has identified the construct of bureaucracy drawn from the work of Max Weber as "the single most dominant conceptual framework in the study of comparative administration."[57] A large proportion of the literature dealt in one way or another with bureaucracies— refining what was meant by the term bureaucracy, describing particular national or subnational bureaucratic systems, classifying bureaucracies as to type on the basis of dominant characteristics, debating the problem of relationships between bureaucracies and other groups in the political system, and so forth. Lacking, however, was any outpouring of field studies on the current operations of developing bureaucracies, in part because of the scarcity of financial support for the substantial costs involved.

The most conspicuous trait of the comparative administration literature during this period, nevertheless, was an extension of the search for comprehensive theory, with contributions from a wide range of social scientists, not just from students of public administration and political science. Savage notes the production of much "grand theory," and comments that if one envisions a high and a low road to science, then certainly comparative administration "tended to travel loftily,"[58] and undervalued the approach of systematic inquiry directed toward reducing indeterminacy. James Heaphey found "academic analysis" to be the foremost among a few "dominant visions" in his analysis of characteristics of comparative literature.[59] Jamil E. Jreisat also concluded that the research orientation leading in influence has been macro-analysis of national administrative systems, with emphasis tending to be at "the level of grand theory in the sociological tradition."[60] All those who have surveyed the output of the comparative administration movement during its peak seem to agree on this pervasive, but not dominant, characteristic.

When all of these partially overlapping and partially competing forces have been taken into account, the overwhelming impression is that diversity has been the hallmark of this movement, recognized as such by both its enthusiasts and its detractors. Fred Riggs, acknowledging that "dissensus prevails," with no agreement on "approach, methodology, concept, theory, or doctrine," considered this "a virtue, a cause for excitement," normal in a preparadigmatic field.[61] As Peter Savage puts it, comparative administration "started with no paradigm of its own and developed none." No orthodoxy was established or even attempted. "The net result has been paradigmatic confusion, as much a part of Comparative Administration as it is held to be of its parent field, Public Administration."[62] This failure to draw the boundaries and set the rules of comparative administration as a field of study has become, as we shall see, a main complaint of those disenchanted with accomplishments made by the CAG.

Retrenchment and Reappraisal

Recent years have been for the comparative administration movement a period of lessened support and lowered expectations. The exuberance of CAG's heyday has been replaced by a mood of introspection. Individuals long identified with CAG have joined earlier detractors and younger scholars in a reassessment of the accomplishments, and the outlook for the future, of comparative administration as a focus of study and action.

Foreshadowing these trends in the comparative administration movement itself came a downshift in the attention devoted to public administration as a category for technical assistance efforts. Siffin has supplied some of the relevant statistics. Emphasis on these programs continued into the mid 1960s, but declined rapidly and sharply beginning about 1967. Funding by the U.S. government for such projects dropped from $18 million that year to $11.4 million in 1970 and $9.8 million in 1972. By the early 1970s the annual rate of support from the United States for public administration aid was less than half what it had been during the decade from the mid 1950s to the mid 1960s. International as well as U.S. technical assistance agencies shifted their attention from administrative reform efforts to complex programs with an economic orientation designed to foster indigenous economic growth through policies jointly worked out by domestic and international agencies. As Jones dramatically puts it, the public administration technicians, the POSDCORB types of the 1950s, were exterminated by a new animal "as fearsome and aggressive as the ancient Norsemen—the new development economists."[63] Projects high on the priority list of the experts in development economics largely displaced the administrative know-how export projects favored earlier. This transition not only reduced the number of practitioners in technical assistance agencies affiliated with the CAG, it also sharply curtailed even the theoretical possibilities of bringing the work of CAG to bear directly on technical assistance programs.

The 1970s have brought several direct alterations and reductions in the scope of activities of the comparative administration movement itself. The end of Ford Foundation support has already been mentioned. No substitute financial sponsor has materialized with help approaching the level provided during the 1960s. Even during those years, the CAG was turned down in its search for funds to support field research in developing countries on any substantial, systematic, and planned basis. The *Journal of Comparative Administration*, after only five years of existence as the primary vehicle for scholarly research in the field, ceased publication in 1974. Although this move involved merger into a new journal, *Administration and Society*, rather than outright extinction, it clearly meant a more diffused focus with no assurance that the broader scope would assure success either. Publications in the Duke University Press series continued to appear as recently as 1973, but these were products of work done several years earlier. Reports from university campuses indicated a falling off of student interest in comparative administration courses, and there was evidence that fewer doctoral dissertations were being written in the field.

Perhaps most symbolically if not substantively important, the Comparative Administration Group itself went out of existence in 1973, when it merged with the International Committee of the American Society for Public Administration to form a new Section on International and Comparative Administration (SICA). SICA has continued with much the same membership, and engages in many of the same activities as CAG, such as participation in professional meetings, issuance of a newsletter, and distribution of occasional papers, but all at a somewhat reduced level.

These indications of decline have been accompanied, and probably stimulated, by a series of critiques of the comparative administration movement made during the last few years, usually in the form of papers presented at professional meetings, several of which were subsequently published. These deserve our attention, not only for what they have to say about shortcomings and disappointments, but also about prescriptions and predictions.

The usual takeoff point is that the comparative administration movement has now had over twenty-five years, including a decade of rather lavish support, in which to prove itself, and should now be scrutinized for results.

Peter Savage takes as his point of reference the propositions that any "fresh ideas, theories, and perspectives in Political Science have about a decade to 'make it' before they are dropped and replaced by even fresher ones," and that the first few years are the easiest. During that time, the "honey-pot syndrome" emerges, with money and professional rewards accorded the progenitors of the new movement. After that, "orthodoxy begins and the crucial test is then upon the innovation, namely to produce some results. If this does not happen, the pot is assumed not to contain honey, or not the right kind of honey, and it is quietly and sometimes abruptly abandoned in favor of an even newer one."[64] He thinks comparative administration is no exception, and that the time for testing the honey in the pot has come.

Whatever the worth of this notion, comparative public administration certainly is now well enough established to become one target of the general tendency to question older orthodoxies which surfaced dramatically at the turn of this decade. No doubt linked to campus unrest, in turn stemming from reaction to the unpopular war in Vietnam, this revolt against the establishment appeared in one form or another in all the social sciences and in some of the natural sciences. In the form of what was usually called the "new" public administration movement, this combination of attack and reform proposals reached its peak about 1970, just as comparative public administration was facing straitened circumstances and completing its period of scholarly probation. Comparative administration turned out to be attractive to some of the leaders of the "new" public administration because of its own relative newness, and also the subject of their skeptical questioning.

However stimulated, the tone of the appraisers has been essentially negative, and they have expressed generally unfavorable judgments. A few sample quotations will suffice to illustrate: "The auguries for Comparative Administration are not good."[65] Described as a declining and troubled field which has made only minimal progress, it is charged with lagging "far behind the fields to which it is most closely related in its application of systematic research technologies."[66] Comparative public administration is "floundering at a time when other social scientists have finally come to appreciate the central role bureaucracy and bureaucrats play in the political process."[67] Development administration as an academic enterprise appears ill-prepared to meet the challenge it faces at a critical juncture. "Need and opportunity beckon; performance falls short."[68]

Like the writers in comparative public administration whose work they are analyzing, the evaluators do not by any means fully agree with one another as to what is wrong and what ought to be done about it, but there are some readily identifiable common themes.

The most frequent complaint is that comparative public administration has now had time enough but has failed to establish itself as a field of study with a generally accepted restricted range of topics to be addressed, and that despite the inclination to theorize no consensus has been achieved permitting primary attention to be given to empirical studies designed to test existing theories about cross-national public administration.

Keith Henderson, writing in 1969 about the "identity crisis" in the field, asked what was *not* within the scope of comparative public administration. Calling attention to the diversity of titles in CAG publications, he observed that although "there are certain dominant themes (the developing countries, the political system, etc.) it is hard to know what the central thrust might be and equally hard to find anything distinctly 'administrative' in that thrust. Seemingly, the full range of political science, economic, sociological, historical, and other concerns is relevant."[69] Lee Sigelman made a content analysis of the entire output of the *Journal of Comparative Administration* as the primary vehicle for scholarly publication in the field, and found that in comparative public administration "no single topic or set of questions came close to dominating." Among substantive categories, he placed the highest percentage of articles (14.6 percent) under the heading "policy administration," followed by categories such as concepts (of bureaucracy, institution-building, etc.), structural descriptions of organizations in various national settings, and studies of bureaucratic values and behavior. His residual category of "other" has the most entries (22 percent), "embracing an astounding array of topics, e.g., communication models for social science, time, the ombudsman, law, problems of causal analysis, the nature of the political process, party coalitions, and anti-bureaucratic utopias." To Sigelman, this suggests that "students of administration have not narrowed their interests to a manageable set of questions and topics. A substantial amount of their effort continues to be spent in activity that can best be characterized as 'getting ready to get ready'—exploring epistemological matters, debating the boundaries of the field, and surveying the manner in which concepts have been used."[70] Jones has remarked even more acidly that the CAG movement "never got much beyond the researching of the definition stage of the subject. Some would say it did not even reach that stage."[71]

Similar concerns are reiterated elsewhere, often by commentators who observe that the prospects for integration seemed promising only a few years ago but have not materialized. For example, Jreisat believes that "the absence of integrative concepts and central foci in comparative research and analysis" is a critical problem, manifested in recent CAG literature indicating a "wide range of seemingly independent concerns." He explores the reasons for the "kaleidoscopic development" of comparative research, such as the movement from culture-bound to cross-cultural studies, the diverse backgrounds and interests of social scientists from a variety of disciplines, the absence of cumulativeness in acquiring administrative knowledge, and particularly the lack of an identifiable core that would enable scholars "to distinguish an administrative phenomenon when they see one and to sift out its critical aspects from the uncritical ones." Recognizing that there were reasons initially for sacrificing conceptual rigor for substantive breadth and methodological experimentation, Jreisat asserts that such justification "is less convincing after more than two decades of research in the comparative field and because prospective evolution toward consolidation and synthesis is not emerging."[72]

The indictment basically is that students of comparative administration have simultaneously shown an unseemly addiction to theorizing and a lack of ability to offer theories which can win acceptance and be tested empirically. Savage says that the literature "displays a melange of idiosyncratic theoretical formulations and organizing perspectives, many of which have more to do with academic or personal fancy than with any generally acceptable cumulative purpose." Using an illustration from Riggs, he suspects that the proposals "were often not so much theories, in any scientific sense of the word, as they were fantasies."[73] J. Fred Springer claims that development administration is "starved for theories which will guide the pooling of empirical knowledge, orient new research, and recommend administrative policy."[74] Sigelman likens the plight of comparative public administration to that of the Third World nations being studied, in the sense that like them the field is caught in a vicious circle. Reliable data must be brought to bear on theoretically significant propositions for research to be meaningful, but Sigelman believes that comparative administration has been sorely lacking in both reliable data and testable propositions, resulting in theoretical and empirical underdevelopment, and presenting the strategic problem to students in the field of how to break out of the circle of stagnation.[75]

Explanations for this plight are not obvious, but one suggestion offered is that students of comparative administration have not kept pace with progress in closely related fields, and that this helps account for the lag in accomplishment. Sigelman makes an unfavorable contrast of the analytic techniques employed in the comparative administration literature against those used in research in comparative politics. According to his content analysis of the *Journal of Comparative Administration*, less than one-fifth of the articles published were at all quantitative in their techniques, and only half of these used what he defined as "more powerful" measurement techniques. Most of the works published consisted of essay-type theoretical or conceptual pieces, or were empirical but nonquantitative, such as case studies. On the other hand, three out of every four articles published in *Comparative Political Studies*, representing comparative politics research, have been empirical in character, with the preponderance of these falling into the "more powerful" quantitative category. Linked to this fault, Sigelman also found that cross-national studies were the exception rather than the norm, with 70 percent of the studies which focused on national or subnational units examining administration in only one national setting, 15 percent comparing a pair of national settings, and only 15 percent undertaking comparisons on a larger scale.

Taking a different tack, Jong S. Jun faults comparative public administration for not keeping pace with its own parent field of public administration, and suggests that revival in comparative studies must incorporate recent developments in the broader discipline, particularly with regard to organization theory. He finds that the literature of comparative public administration "does not deal with the comparison of methods and strategies of organizational change and development in a cross cultural context," and recommends the utilization in comparative studies of research findings having to do with problem-solving capabilities of organizations and their ability to cope with external environmental changes.[76]

Turning to another theme, the term development administration has been a frequent target, but from different angles of attack. Garth Jones bluntly scolds the CAG for appropriating and then obfuscating this concept. He views development administration as "a polite way to talk about administrative reform, and this in all cases means political reform." After commending the CAG writers for recognizing that political reform must precede administrative reform and that the two cannot be separated, he finds little else to say by way of approval of how the CAG has dealt with development administration. To start with, he accounts for the shift in CAG usage from comparative public administration to development administration in a very simple fashion, calling it a device to secure money for research. By changing the name of the "game" to development administration, the CAG seized upon a term more marketable to the Ford Foundation. Besides being more exciting, the term was also more difficult to define, but not as difficult as the CAG tried to make it. Jones states that he can understand some of the earlier writing on development administration, but that the CAG volumes under review raise the question of whether the concept is all that complex, and whether after twenty-five years we still need to be talking about "frontiers" of development administration. As he sees it, development administration is a subject that has been "captured by a few political scientists." He examines the biodata of the CAG authors, and classifies nearly all of them as "pure-blood" academes, with only a few having extensive administrative experience or government service. Moreover, he thinks their work falls more properly in the area of development politics than development administration, and that they have very little to offer of practical utility to those who want to know how to "reform an archaic accounting system, integrate new national planning methodology within a dynamic administrative program, organize and administer a new national family-planning effort, or design management operations for a new irrigation system." In sum, he accuses the CAG of adopting the term development administration for its own advantage, without actually contributing much to the solution of development administration problems. The CAG stayed in its ivory tower and away from the field of action.[77]

A quite different complaint comes from Brian Loveman, who raises questions about assumptions in the development administration literature concerning the ability of governments to strengthen administrative capabilities and carry out plans for meeting developmental objectives.[78] He groups CAG members with others labeled liberal democratic theorists who are alleged to share these assumptions, which are similar to ideas about development and development administration held by Marxist-Leninist theorists as well. His summary conclusion is that both the liberal democratic and socialist models of development cost more than they are worth to developing societies. These models, in his judgment, call for an "administered society" which is antagonistic to the important value of expanded human choice as an alternative to the extension of intervention by government administrators. In short, development cannot, or at least should not, be administered.

Loveman's criticism thus contrasts with the one made by Jones. He accuses CAG of overidentification with the aims of development administrators, and overinvolvement in development administration programs. He quotes Milton Esman, a CAG spokesman, as writing that much of the change desired today must be induced, and therefore managed. He identifies the CAG as sharing the assumption that development can be administered and that it requires administration by a politico-administrative elite. The quest for such an elite has led often to the military as a stabilizing or modernizing force. "By the 1970s," according to Loveman, "administrative development and development administration had become euphemisms for autocratic, frequently military, rule that, admittedly, sometimes induced industrialization, modernization, and even economic growth. But this occurred at a great cost in the welfare of the rural and urban poor and a substantial erosion if not deletion of the political freedoms associated with liberal democracy."[79] He mentions Brazil, Iran, and South Korea as "showcases." The CAG role, in his interpretation, was both to elaborate an academic ideology of development and to encourage participation by its members in programs to induce development.

Ambivalence also shows up in related evaluations of the "relevance" of the comparative administration movement. CAG documents have frequently expressed the desire to have the work of CAG prove useful to technical assistance experts and to officials in developing countries, and this was one of the explicit expectations from the Ford Foundation grants.

However, except for agreement on somewhat peripheral matters such as the establishment of links among scholars from various countries, the usual judgment has been negative as to the success of CAG in achieving relevancy.

Disappointment on this score was conceded by Fred Riggs in a 1970 CAG newsletter when he noted that CAG had an ivory tower image and had failed to form a bridge between academic life and practice. Others have agreed, and some have tried to explain why. Jones finds little in CAG writings "that will contribute to social technologies related to the burning issues of the day such as population control, environmental protection, and food production. These authors undoubtedly have something to say here, but it is best that they start all over again."[80] Savage concurs that CAG did not produce much in the way of socially useful knowledge. It was not a matter of producing "bad medicine," but "no medicine." These judgments may be overly severe in what was expected of CAG, but whatever the worth of CAG efforts, there was another problem of getting attention and acceptance. Jones, speaking as a former practitioner, has this comment which he no doubt intended not to be restricted to one individual: "As much as I admire Fred Riggs, and I do, his thinking had little relevance for my kind of problems. Certainly the AID bureaucracy was not willing to accept it."[81] B. B. Schaffer wrote that CAG members "had their conferences and wrote their papers, but the practitioners did not seem to take much notice and changes in developing countries did not seem to be directly affected."[82]

These are typical common assessments, focused on the question of relevance to developing countries. Jreisat adds an unusual fillip by pointing out that comparative studies have so concentrated on emerging countries and their problems that little is offered of theoretical or practical utility in Western, particularly American, contexts.

Some critics, on the other hand, seem to view the comparative administration movement as all too relevant. In opposing the outcomes of technical assistance and development administration programs in recipient countries, they directly or implicitly chastise the CAG for participation by some of its members, and for its desire to be supportive to practitioners. Loveman, as part of his argument that development cannot be administered, repeatedly speaks of "United States–AID–CAG" models, doctrines, or programs of development administration. He credits the CAG with providing "an intellectual grounding for American foreign policy in the 1960s." According to his version, the failure of liberal democratic regimes to "develop" gradually made it clear that "United States policy and the CAG would have to make ever more explicit the relationship between growth, liberal democracy, anti-Marxism, and a strategy giving first priority to political stability." For this to occur, the problem of administrative development had to be resolved. "Administrative development had to precede effective development administration; any concern for constraints on bureaucratic authority had to be subordinated to the need to create effective administrative instruments." Hence the CAG and United States policy-makers turned to programs intended to build up administrative elites, often military elites. Recommendations of CAG spokesmen such as Esman "to be less concerned with control of the development administrators and more concerned with the capabilities of these elites to carry out developmental objectives" were heeded by officials making U.S. government policy, with the unfortunate consequences, as seen by Loveman, already mentioned.

The point in connection with the relevancy issue is that Loveman, far from viewing the CAG as detached from and ignored by governmental technical assistance policy-makers, evidently pictures CAG members as closely allied with these officials and highly influential in crucial policy decision-making.[83]

The relevancy issue, then, has received plenty of attention, with quite a spread of opinion on it. Few regard CAG as achieving the degree of relevancy desired by its members or its sponsors, but the explanations for the deficiency vary. As Jreisat puts it, "although the cry of non-relevance is common, it comes to us from different sources for different reasons and, consequently, the remedial suggestions are not always consistent."[84] With measures of relevancy as uncertain as they are, and with such inconsistency in assessing the situation and what ought to be done about it, probably the only certain conclusion is that not all the commentators can be right, but those who report a close working collaboration between the CAG as a group entity and official policy-makers have so far produced little evidence to support this interpretation.

Prospects and Options

The prospects for comparative public administration are obviously not as bright as they once seemed to be. The period of massive technical assistance in public administration which helped launch the movement is over. The Comparative Administration Group which was the organizing force during the years of greatest activity has lost its separate identity and the programs it initiated have been ended or cut back. As a source of action-oriented programs for dealing with problems of development administration, the movement has generally been judged disappointing, and, at any rate, whatever impact it had has now lessened. Moreover, earlier optimistic expectations about the possibilities of transferring or inducing change in developing societies have come into question as many of these nations have suffered from increasing rather than decreasing problems of economic growth and political stability. As an academic or intellectual enterprise, comparative administration has moved from a position of innovation and vitality to a more defensive posture, reacting to charges that the promises of its youth have not been fulfilled and to advice from various quarters as to remedial measures.

For our purposes, having reviewed the retrenchment evidence

and the critical reappraisals, it is now even more important to examine analyses and recommendations about the future. Before doing so, however, it should be noted that even the more severe critics of the CAG and its record (such as Jones, Jreisat, and Jun) acknowledge the impressive productivity of the 1960s and the vast accumulation of knowledge in comparative public administration which resulted. Others who were more closely identified personally with the CAG (such as Savage and Siffin) are even more apt to temper their criticism with reference to specific accomplishments. Savage emphasizes that the intentions were commendable, despite flaws in priorities and methods, and that overall the legacy of the CAG can be viewed with considerable satisfaction. He mentions, for example, that comparative studies have "shed a bright light on the existence and importance, in many settings, of the public bureaucracy," and have called attention insistently to the importance of the administrative factor in political analysis. At the same time, he believes that the comparative administration movement has made a dent in "the myth of managerial omnipotence" by its increasing recognition and exploration of the cultural shaping of administrative techniques, and by identifying factors that must be taken into account when making prescriptions for administrative reform. More generally, he credits the movement with building bridges with comparative politics and other subfields in the discipline of political science, and providing a kind of "demonstration effect" of the attractions of venturing into unfamiliar territory. He thinks a lot of underbrush has been cleared out by the pursuit of false leads which other scholars need not now pursue. He also makes the point, often overlooked, that the failure of the movement to achieve some of the early promises "has more to do with the complexities and intractabilities in its chosen domain than with faulty purpose."[85]

Siffin, more directly concerned with efforts to export administrative technology, gives credit to students of comparative administration for inquiring into the reasons for technology transfer failures, and commends their attention to environmental factors as inhibitors in attaining developmental administration objectives.

The most often recurring complaint, as already indicated, has been that comparative public administration has never been able to reach paradigmatic consensus. As might be anticipated from this, the most common recommendation is that this deficiency must be remedied if this field of study is to achieve intellectual standing and academic maturity. Repeatedly, the point is stressed that an adequate paradigm must be sought to bring coherence, purpose, and progress. The following statement from Jreisat is typical: "The achievement of higher levels of integration and relevance of administrative concepts is critical for the viability and utility of the comparative approach as well as for the emergence of theory."[86]

Given the urgency of the need expressed, one naturally looks hopefully for suggestions as to what the basis for consensus should be. On this score, most critics are embarrassingly silent or vague. Some immediately qualify the call for an accepted paradigm by disavowal of any intention to establish a paradigmatic orthodoxy in comparative public administration. "The search for common ground," to quote Jreisat again, "is not necessarily a call for the establishment of precise and rigid boundaries."[87] The main disappointment, however, is that when it comes to specifics, the suggestions made are strongly reminiscent of those voiced much earlier, near the beginning of the movement's heyday. We find repeated the caution expressed in 1959 by Robert Presthus against "cosmic" theory and the advice to seek instead "middle-range" theory. Jreisat asserts, for instance, that "a higher degree of synthesis and relevance of comparative analysis may be attained through conceptualization of critical administrative problems at the 'middle range' level and involving institutions rather than entire national administrative systems."[88] Lee Sigelman describes his views as representing "a meaningful middle ground between the present state of affairs and unrealistically optimistic schemes for improving it." Also in line with a preference already established by the early 1960s, Sigelman states as his conviction that the future of comparative public administration lies in studies of bureaucracies, in "examinations of the backgrounds, attitudes, and behaviors of bureaucrats and those with whom they interact."[89]

Even though there are to date no drastically new departures suggested to improve comparative studies, recent commentators have provided a number of thoughtful, useful, and helpful suggestions.

Most of these have to do with methodologies to be used, data to be gathered, or subjects to be studied—all rather persistent concerns of comparative administration students. However, one recent analyst, Jong S. Jun, has argued that methodological considerations have received too much attention, and that the problem is essentially one of epistemology rather than methodology. That is, he wants to raise questions as to the limits and validity of human knowledge as it is brought to bear on the comparative study of systems of administration. He presents a critique of the structural–functional and bureaucratic models, which he regards as the dominant models up to now, that is essentially an epistemological one.

Jun argues that both models "fail to explore the subjective meaning of social action, to provide a mechanism for organizational change, and to consider the renewal effects of conflict-induced disequilibrium. Both. . .stress the structural pattern of social action, with an emphasis on orderliness, roles, and organizational norms. . . . both models are not comprehensive enough to explain social phenomena that vary from system to system, or from country to country." A common tendency is for the researcher to superimpose "his perspective and method onto a culture not his own." Given a tendency to imitate natural science methodologies, social scientists have had inadequate tools to cope with the incredible variety of data from the world's political and administrative systems and have been unable to generate a suitable comparative perspective.

Jun's suggestion for a different conceptual framework, which he does not elaborate, is that scholars should adopt a phenomenological approach to comparative study to provide a new perspective for analyzing other cultures. He quotes Robert B. MacLeod that this calls for "the bracketing of all presuppositions and the description of immediate experience in terms of its essential structures and attributes." He then goes on to observe that with the phenomenological approach, "the need becomes apparent to bracket one's own feelings and separate them from one's perceptions." He maintains that this perspective is "a useful way of standing aside from our presuppositions and cultural biases, and looking at someone else a good deal more in their own terms."[90] He does not illustrate specifically how this perspective would be applied although he does indicate some foci for attention which are referred to later.

On the themes of scope and method rather than psychological approach, several related points are made. Sigelman deplores the loss of focus on *administration* in comparative public administration, and believes that advice that students of administration should study unrelated or loosely related substantive fields is equivalent to institutionalizing that loss of focus. Continuing "the seemingly never-ending quest for an all-inclusive analytic framework" seems to him "positively perverse." He quotes as applicable to comparative public administration Jorgen Rasmussen's supplication "O Lord, deliver us from further conceptualization and lead us not into new approaches." In his view, scholars in the past "have spent so much time and energy debating issues of comparison, putting forth general analytic frameworks, and sketching out the environment of administration that we have been diverted from the study of administration itself."[91]

Both Peter Savage and J. Fred Springer call attention to choices in comparative studies among different levels of analysis. Although their terminology differs somewhat, they both are referring to a range of options running from whole social systems through descending levels of inclusiveness to units such as institutions, organizations, and even individuals. Springer argues that reliance on one level of analysis decreases the prospects for understanding complex systems. He stresses the use of concepts, such as those from role theory, which will have utility "in relating phenomena at different levels of analysis, and in sensitizing the analyst to contextually specific patterns of interaction and behavior." He cites a number of recent studies which "penetrate into the structure of national bureaucracies to identify important contextual effects within the organization," including role analyses of public officials in Indonesia and Thailand, and a cross-national multilevel study of the administration of rice production projects in Indonesia, the Philippines, and Thailand.[92]

The problem of data for research is another serious matter. The growth of availability of data from a multitude of countries is evident, but magnitude of data does not equate with comparability and reliability of data. Sigelman addresses this problem, stressing the importance of new strategies of data collection and maintenance. He examines the matter at both the macro or system level of research, and the micro level. In both instances, he concentrates on comparative studies involving bureaucracies, which he considers should be the core of future research endeavors.

Sigelman is quite pessimistic about the availability of data for systematic testing of hypotheses in system level studies, concluding that "there is little hope, even in the long run, for the appearance of reliable data on bureaucracy in any historical depth for even a moderate number of nations." This leaves the testing of macro-level theory to be done primarily with judgmental data derived from experts considered to be knowledgeable. Despite problems such as how the experts are chosen and how many, how their advice is weighted, how discrepancies among them are reconciled, how to avoid comparisons that are static rather than active, and how to deal with the matter of cultural bias, Sigelman feels that such studies have promise. He specifically recommends use of a method, call the Delphi technique, for soliciting and aggregating the forecasts of a group of experts on some issue, to obtain a presumably unbiased consensus on predictions of future events. He suggests that the technique can be used to *post*dict as well as *pre*dict, and cites as an example a Delphi exercise conducted in 1971 by the National Academy of Public Administration on developments in the American public service, which included an element of retroactive assessment as well as prognostication. Sigelman then outlines in some detail how the Delphi technique might be used as a tool for historical research to produce usable data on bureaucracy. Although the cost would be considerable, such an approach "could produce a badly-needed body of macro-level longitudinal data on several aspects of bureaucracy—data which would facilitate theory-building and testing in comparative public administration."[93]

Sigelman believes that many potentially significant micro-level research studies on bureaucracy have already been undertaken, but that many have never been published or have appeared in journals devoted to specific geographical areas that are not noticed by comparative administration students. Besides the problem of inaccessibility, he identifies two other acute deficiencies. Only occasionally has the research been cross-national in scope, and the literature is scattered and diffuse. "Different scholars with different research perspectives use different instruments to interview different types of bureaucrats in examinations of different problems in different nations."[94]   In short, micro-level research is non-cumulative.

Riggs and others have advocated without success the establishment of a comparative administration research center to plan and organize large-scale cross-national research projects. Sigelman is doubtful that such a project of data collection is feasible, both because of the resources required and the poor record of social scientists in group work. He proposes as less costly and more beneficial a large-scale data maintenance project by the establishment of an archive of comparative administration research along the lines of the Inter-University Consortium for Political Research, for the purpose of "disseminating information on existing data sets and making the data sets themselves available for secondary analysis." This would involve an up-to-date listing of micro-level studies, including, where possible, information about research instruments used.   Such an institutionalized mechanism for data maintenance, he argues, "could go far toward bringing some order to the chaos of microlevel administrative studies."[95]

As to the subject matter focus for research, certainly there is no consensus beyond the dominant view that the choice of substantive topic should be designed to test middle-range theory. Indeed, if anything, the range of suggestions has been broadened recently rather than narrowed. Bureaucracy as a common institution in political systems continues to be most frequently recommended as the target with the greatest promise for research efforts, although as we will discover in the following chapter, different people have different ideas even as to what bureaucracy means, not to mention how it ought to be studied on a comparative basis.

A persistent strain in the recommendations of recent commentators is that new advances in the area of organization theory can be brought to bear fruitfully in the analysis of organizational units of interest to comparative administration researchers, whether these are whole national bureaucracies or bureaucratic subunits. Springer calls for supplementing earlier work aimed at individual or systemic levels with increasing attention to conceptual and empirical work at the organization level. Jun, although objecting to certain elements which he considers to be usually included in the bureaucratic model, over-stressing continuity and conformity, advocates the introduction of concepts and hypotheses from modern organization theory which will focus attention on organizational change and development in a cross-cultural context. He refers particularly to experiments in industrial democracy or self-management, involving various manifestations of a philosophy of participation by organizational employees in organizational decisions, which he contrasts with the traditional bureaucratic model. He mentions the Workers' Self-Management Movement in Yugoslavia as the most famous such experiment, but also lists other industrial democracy efforts in West Germany, Israel, France, the United States, Peru, and Scandinavian countries. Jun believes that comparisons among such experiments "will provide a new avenue for learning about the effectiveness of different organizations in different cultural settings."[96]

Jorge I. Tapia-Videla also asserts that research and writing in comparative public administration have not been much influenced by theoretical progress in the area of organizational theory.[97] Comparative politics has provided most of the theoretical constructs applied in comparative administration, which as a consequence has suffered from some of the same shortcomings. With a few exceptions, such as *Bureaucratic Politics and Administration in Chile* by Peter Cleaves,[98] Tapia-Videla finds that the potential benefits of blending organization theory into the comparative study of administration have not been realized. Tapia-Videla himself examines the characteristics of public bureaucracies in Latin America, and the relationships between these bureaucracies and the "corporate-technocratic" state which has emerged in several Latin American countries as well as elsewhere in the Third World.

Jreisat concurs that cross-cultural comparisons at the organizational level have rarely been attempted, even though studies of formal organizations within one cultural setting such as the United
States, with stable environmental influences, are advanced and so-
phisticated. He regards the few ventures which have been made toward comparative organizational theory as not representing genuine
cross-cultural comparisons and as "not seriously concerned with the
various possible patterns of human interaction which may be prevalent outside the limits of customary Western styles of behavior."[99]

Public policy-making is another subject which has received
much attention in recent years, with attempts made on one hand to
analyze the process of policy-making in a descriptive way, and on the
other to analyze outputs and effects of policy in a fashion which is
more prescriptive and aims to improve both the process and the
content of public policy.[100] Again, with few exceptions, policy-
making studies have not been comparative across countries, leading
Jun to urge comparative policy analysis as an additional field for
pioneering work which might serve both scientific and practical
purposes.

Among those having basically a development administration
orientation, the tendency has been to talk about what William
Siffin calls a "developmental design strategy," and to focus on the
process of "institution-building," a term associated especially with
the work of Milton Esman. Siffin notes that traditional administrative technology transfer efforts have aimed more at *maintenance*
needs than *developmental* needs. Although maintenance activities
are essential in developing countries as well as elsewhere, Siffin
stresses that the essence of development is not to maintain, but to
create effectively. Development administration is required when
"the need for ability to design and implement arrangements involving
technologies is greater than the need for the technologies." In the
"design approach" of development administration, "innovative
problem analysis and 'definition' logically precede the specification
of solutions." Although the problem-defining capabilities within
developing countries have grown considerably during the last twenty
years, usually in planning agencies and finance ministries, ability is
still limited to take acount of organizational and managerial factors.
More knowledge needs to be marshalled about organizational design
and the effects of alternative organizational arrangements, with
special attention to environmental factors not intrinsic to the organizations themselves. .Siffin cites as an excellent example of design
strategy a comparative study by John D. Montgomery on the effects

of alternative organizational approaches to land reform, in which twenty-five cases were examined. The organizational arrangements were classified into three categories—centralized, decentralized, and "devolved"—and the findings dealt with how each of these arrangements affected bureaucratic power and peasant security, political power, and income. The study showed that alternative designs do have alternative consequences, and demonstrated how "design can be rooted in analysis of the prospective effects of known alternatives, prior to the basic decisions about implementation.[101]

The institution-building model is intended to systematize the cross-cultural analysis of institutions as appropriate units for comparison. Jreisat describes this model, as developed and applied earlier by Esman and his associates in the Inter-University Research Program in Institution Building, and suggests a modification of it intended to focus less exclusively on developing societies, place more emphasis on cross-cultural comparison, and draw more heavily on research in organization theory for propositions regarding organizational structure, behavior, leadership, goals, and so forth. Jreisat presents four reasons for the increasing interest in institutional analysis.[102] First, institutions are crucial in political and administrative development because they are "fundamental instruments for conversion of demands into policy or action." Second, institutions are more manageable units of research than total national systems, so that it is feasible methodologically to achieve "vigor, verifiability, relevance, and comparability" in analyzing them. Third, means of measurement or evaluation of the effectiveness of performance by institutions can be achieved. Fourth, the institutional perspective places greater emphasis on the environment than do other organizational models which focus more on technical requirements for reaching specific goals.

The institution-building process, as defined by the Esman group and accepted by Jreisat, is "the planning, structuring, and guidance of new or reconstituted organizations which (a) embody changes in values, functions, physical and/or social technologies; (b) establish, foster, and protect normative relationships and action patterns; and (c) attain support and complimentarity in the environment."[103] Three categories of variables are used for institutional description and analysis, having to do with organizational behavior, linkages, and transactions. Five major variables are included in the organizational behavior category: leadership (the group of persons who are actively engaged in the formulation of the doctrine and program of the institution and who direct its operation and relationships with the environment); doctrine (the specification of values, objectives, and operational methods underlying social action); program (the performance of functions and services constituting the output of the institution); resources (physical, human, and technological inputs of the institution); and structure (the processes established for the operation and maintenance of the institution). Measurement indicators are provided for each of these variables.

Linkages are defined as the interdependencies which exist between an institution and other relevant parts of the society. Four types are identified: enabling (with organizations and social groups which control the allocation of authority and resources needed by the institution); functional (with organizations performing functions and services which are complementary in a production sense); normative (norms and values which are relevant to the doctrine and program of the institution); and diffused (diffused support or resistance in the immediate environment).

The transactions concept denotes "the exchange of goods and services and the exchange of power and influence between the institution and the social organizations with which it has linkages." The purposes of transactions include "gaining support, overcoming resistance, exchanging resources, structuring the environment, and the transferring of norms and values."[104]

Jreisat claims for the institution-building model that it "provides openness to external influences without sacrificing intra-institutional variables and interactions. The search for patterns in the linkages between the environment and administrative institutions and the cross-cultural comparisons of such patterns reveal common as well as distinguishing features of administrative settings and their performance."[105]

Beyond whatever advantages this model may have in theory, it has the added attraction that it has been tested. During the 1960s empirical data were collected and analyzed for a number of countries, among them Yugoslavia, Venezuela, Nigeria, Jordan, and Ecuador.[106] Undoubtedly, it will continue to be used and improved.

It should be clear by now that no new path has been plainly mapped out for the comparative administration movement by those who feel that its bearings have been lost. Many suggestions echo those made a decade or more ago. Others are tentative and incomplete recommendations to draw more heavily on recent advances in related fields such as organization theory or public policy analysis. A few urge follow-up or replication of research projects which have already been completed. The unevenness and lack of reliability of data for comparison are often noted. If comparative administration has been and is in a preparadigmatic state as a field of study, it seems likely to remain so for some time to come. No consensus appears to be emerging which will bring the coherence, purpose, and progress sought by Ilchman and others. Diversity continues to be more descriptive of comparative studies in administration than does uniformity or orthodoxy. Those whose aim is the scientific testing of precisely stated hypotheses as a basis for prediction remain frustrated and unhappy about the rate of progress. On many points, then, earlier expectations or at least hopes of pioneers in comparative public administration have not materialized, making it understandable that we are in a period of reassessment.[107]

Some perceptive observers have recently suggested that the reassessment ought to include a reappraisal of objectives for comparative administrative studies, including even such widely shared aims as the search for scientific predictability and the attainment of separate disciplinary recognition.

The first issue is touched on perceptively by Jonathan Bendor in a discussion of developmental versus evolutionary theories, in which he admits that evolutionary theory does have lower predictive power, but notes that this is not the only criterion of theoretical merit. Predictions from inadequate hypotheses may be precise but inaccurate. Explanatory power and predictive power are not the same; adequate explanation is not dependent on the capacity to predict correctly. He mentions that biologists consider evolutionary theory adequate for the explanation of evolutionary processes, despite the fact that the theory generates only weak predictions, and suggests that social scientists might also settle for understanding rather than foresight.[108]

On the second issue, Savage, Jun, and Riggs all question the virtue and feasibility of trying in the future to emphasize the separate identity of comparative public administration as a field of study. Savage argues that the impact of the comparative administration movement has been significant and lasting enough that we no longer need any "movement," because its concerns and perspectives have become a part of the broader discipline of political science and public administration. Hence dissolution of the CAG does not necessarily mean the end of its legacy. Savage draws a parallel with the effect of the behavioral movement on political science, with both movements exerting significant influence and sharing "the quality of presenting beliefs, assumptions, perspectives and concerns which came to be regarded as unique or as, in an important way, identifying

each movement." He regards the influence of comparative administration as supplementary rather than revolutionary, having a "round-
ing-out" rather than a transformational effect. In summary, he says:
"The movement's ten years are up and it passes. I judge that while it
did not produce in sufficient ways to forestall its decline as a movement, its legacies are being absorbed into the larger Political Science
and Public Administration. . . . The problems which spawned the
movement have not gone away. If anything, they have become
exacerbated."[109]

Jun approaches the issue from the less complimentary point of
view that comparative administration as an isolated field has served
its purpose and should become an integral part of the larger field of
public administration, which can be enriched by placing it in a world
context.[110] Riggs also foresees convergence, but in the sense that
comparative administration will become the master field within
which American public administration will be only a subfield.[111]

However expressed, I concur with the cardinal point that it is
neither necessary nor feasible to strive for restoration of the degree
of autonomy and separatism once characteristic of the burgeoning
comparative public administration movement. The time has now
come to blend the comparative perspective with the traditionally
parochial national emphasis of study and research in public administration. This promises to remedy some of the deficiencies in depth
of analysis attributed to comparative efforts, but it also will enrich
general public administration by widening the horizon of interest
in such a way that understanding of one's own national system of
administration will be enhanced by placing it in a cross-cultural
setting.

Also, I agree with the point of view that the comparative phase
of study and research in public administration does not require
escape from the kind of paradigmatic uncertainties which have long
been characteristic of the parent discipline. Coercive superimposi-
tion of a feigned consensus would be futile and stifling. A real consensus will emerge if and when work done in the field leads to it in
a cumulative fashion, but premature urging of it as the top priority
would be counterproductive.

Meanwhile, an overview of public administration from a comparative perspective cannot be undertaken without deciding upon
a framework for presentation. It should be clear from this historical
review of the evolution of comparative studies that systems of public administration in existing nation-states can only be treated com-
paratively after a choice of focus has been made among numerous

and partially conflicting alternatives. The task of selecting a focus for comparison is faced in Chapter 2.

Notes

1. Nicholas Henry, *Public Administration and Public Affairs* (Englewood Cliffs, N.J.: Prentice-Hall, Inc., 1975), Chapter 1, pp. 3-32.
2. Fritz Morstein Marx, ed., *Elements of Public Administration*, 2nd ed. (Englewood Cliffs, N.J.: Prentice-Hall, Inc., 1963), p. 4.
3. *Ibid.*, p. 6.
4. Paul H. Appleby, *Policy and Administration* (University, Ala.: University of Alabama Press, 1949).
5. James W. Davis, Jr., *An Introduction to Public Administration: Politics, Policy, and Bureaucracy* (New York: The Free Press, 1974), p. 4.
6. Harold Stein, ed., *Public Administration and Policy Development* (New York: Harcourt, Brace, and Company, 1952), p. xxvii. This case book, supplemented by other cases published by the Inter-University Case Program, has been the primary source of public administration cases used in the United States.
7. The main source book, containing papers presented at a conference in 1968, is Frank Marini, ed., *Toward a New Public Administration: The Minnowbrook Perspective* (Scranton, Pa.: Chandler Publishing Company, 1971). See also Dwight Waldo, ed., *Public Administration in a Time of Turbulence* (Scranton, Pa.: Chandler Publishing Conpany, 1971).
8. See Fred W. Riggs, "The American Tradition in Comparative Administration," prepared for the 1976 National Conference of the American Society for Public Administration, mimeographed, 28 pp.
9. Robert A. Dahl, "The Science of Public Administration: Three Problems," *Public Administration Review* 7, No. 1 (1947): 8.
10. Donald C. Rowat, *The Ombudsman Plan: Essays on the Worldwide Spread of an Idea* (Toronto: McClelland and Stewart, 1973).
11. Among numerous summaries of these developments, some of the most useful are Alfred Diamant, "The Relevance of Comparative Politics to the Study of Comparative Administration," *Administrative Science Quarterly* 5, No. 1 (1960): 87-112; Bernard E. Brown, *New Directions in Comparative Politics* (New York: Asia Publishing House, 1962); and Harry Eckstein and David E. Apter, eds., *Comparative Politics: A Reader* (New York: Free Press of Glencoe, Inc., 1963), pp. 3-32.
12. "Comparison is significant only if it seeks to interpret political data in terms of hypotheses or theories. Interpretation must deal with institutions as they really function—which sometimes differs radically from the way in which they are supposed to function. It is also desirable that agreement be reached on the frame within which research is to be pursued. The comparative method thus requires an insistence on the scientific nature of

inquiry, a focus on political behavior, and orientation of research within a broad analytic scheme." Brown, *New Directions*, pp. 3-4.

13.   Robert E. Ward and Roy C. Macridis, eds., *Modern Political Systems: Asia* (Englewood Cliffs, N.J.: Prentice-Hall, Inc., 1963), pp. 3-4.

14.   Gabriel A. Almond and James S. Coleman, eds., *The Politics of the Developing Areas* (Princeton, N. J.: Princeton University Press, 1960), p. 7.

15.   Ward and Macridis, *Modern Political Systems*, p. 8.

16.   Almond and Coleman, "Introduction: A Functional Approach to Comparative Politics," *Politics of the Developing Areas*, pp. 3-64. For a reformulation and elaboration that does not basically alter this analytical scheme, see Gabriel Almond, "A Developmental Approach to Political Systems," *World Politics* XVII, No. 2 (1965): 183-214; and Gabriel Almond and G. Bingham Powell, Jr., *Comparative Politics: A Developmental Approach* (Boston: Little, Brown and Company, 1966).

17.   Almond and Coleman, *The Politics of the Developing Areas*, p.v.

18.   *Ibid.*, p. 11.

19.   Leonard Binder, *Iran: Political Development in a Changing Society* (Berkeley, Calif.: University of California Press, 1962), pp. 7-10.

20.   Fred W. Riggs, *Administration in Developing Countries—The Theory of Prismatic Society* (Boston: Houghton Mifflin Company, 1964), pp. 456-457.

21.   An informative general treatment of the evolution of comparative administration studies is available in Ramesh K. Arora, *Comparative Public Administration* (New Delhi: Associated Publishing House, 1972), Chapter 1, pp. 5-29.

22.   The best comprehensive bibliographical sources are Ferrel Heady and Sybil L. Stokes, *Comparative Public Administration: A Selective Annotated Bibliography*, 2nd ed. (Ann Arbor, Mich.: Institute of Public Administration, The University of Michigan, 1960); Allan A. Spitz and Edward W. Weidner, *Development Administration: An Annotated Bibliography* (Honolulu: East-West Center Press, 1963); and the bibliographical entries on comparative public administration by Nimrod Raphaeli which appeared in the *American Political Science Review* from 1963 through 1966. The most up-to-date bibliography, which concentrates primarily on public bureaucracies but includes much of the recent comparative administration literature, is Manindra K. Mohapatra and David R. Hager, *Studies of Public Bureaucracy: A Select Cross-National Bibliography* (Monticello, Ill.: Council of Planning Librarians, Exchange Bibliography #1385-1386-1387, 1977).

23.   These included Dwight Waldo, *Comparative Public Administration: Prologue, Problems, and Promise* (Chicago: Comparative Administration Group, American Society for Public Administration, 1964), and Ferrel Heady, "Comparative Public Administration: Concerns and Priorities," in Ferrel Heady and Sybil L. Stokes, eds., *Papers in Comparative Public*

Administration (Ann Arbor, Mich.: Institute of Public Administration, The University of Michigan, 1962). Earlier treatments are cited in these essays.

24. Poul Meyer, *Administrative Organization: A Comparative Study of the Organization of Public Administration* (London: Stevens & Sons, 1957); Brian Chapman, *The Profession of Government* (London: George Allen & Unwin, 1959); the parts dealing with administration in Herman Finer, *Theory and Practice of Modern Government*, rev. ed. (New York: Holt, Rinehart & Winston, Inc., 1949); Fritz Morstein Marx, *The Administrative State* (Chicago: University of Chicago Press, 1957).

25. This research design is discussed in Fred W. Riggs, "Relearning an Old Lesson: The Political Context of Development Administration," *Public Administration Review* 25, No. 1 (1965): 72-75.

26. Leading early expositions of this view are found in Edward W. Weidner, "Development Administration: A New Focus for Research," in Heady and Stokes, *Papers*, pp. 97-115; Irving Swerdlow, ed., *Development Administration Concepts and Problems* (Syracuse, N.Y.: Syracuse University Press, 1963); and Milton J. Esman, "The Politics of Development Administration," in John D. Montgomery and William J. Siffin, eds., *Approaches to Development: Politics, Administration and Change* (New York: McGraw-Hill Book Company, 1966), pp. 59-112. Copyright © 1966. A recent valuable contribution, focusing on the developmental role of the civil service in India, is V. A. Pai Panandiker and S. S. Kshirsagar, *Bureaucracy and Development Administration* (New Delhi: Centre for Policy Research, 1978).

27. In Heady and Stokes, *Papers*, p. 99.

28. *Ibid.*, pp. 103, 107.

29. Waldo, *Comparative Public Administration*, p. 27.

30. Swerdlow, *Development Administration*, p. xiv.

31. Waldo, *Comparative Public Administration*, p. 15.

32. Robert V. Presthus, "Behavior and Bureaucracy in Many Cultures," *Public Administration Review* 19, No. 1 (1959): 25-35.

33. Diamant, "The Relevance of Comparative Politics," pp. 87-112.

34. Heady and Stokes, *Papers*, p. 4.

35. See Note 20.

36. "An Information-Energy Model," in Heady and Stokes, *Papers*, pp. 37-57.

37. John T. Dorsey, "The Bureaucracy and Political Development in Viet Nam," in Joseph LaPalombara, ed., *Bureaucracy and Political Development* (Princeton, N.J.: Princeton University Press, Copyright 1963), pp. 318-359.

38. Waldo, *Comparative Public Administration*, p. 22.

39. See, for example, Brown, *New Directions*, pp. 10-11.

40. Waldo, *Comparative Public Administration*, p. 24.

41. Morroe Berger, *Bureaucracy and Society in Modern Egypt* (Princeton, N.J.: Princeton University Press, 1957).

42. LaPalombara, *Bureaucracy and Political Development*.

43. Fred W. Riggs, "Trends in the Comparative Study of Public Administration," *International Review of Administrative Sciences* 28, No. 1 (1962): 9-15.

44. *Ibid.*, p. 10.

45. *Ibid.*, p. 11.

46. *Ibid.*, p. 9.

47. *Ibid.*, p. 15.

48. Garth N. Jones, "Frontiersmen in Search for the 'Lost Horizon': The State of Development Administration in the 1960s," *Public Administration Review* 36, No. 1 (1976): 99-110, at pp. 99-100.

49. William J. Siffin, "Two Decades of Public Administration in Developing Countries," *Public Administration Review* 36, No. 1 (1976): 61-71, at p. 61.

50. *Ibid.*, p. 64.

51. *Ibid.*, pp. 65-66.

52. Jones, "Frontiersmen in Search," pp. 105-6.

53. Peter Savage, "Optimism and Pessimism in Comparative Administration," *Public Administration Review* 36, No. 4 (1976): 415-23, at pp. 419-20.

54. Fred W. Riggs, *Frontiers of Development Administration* (Durham, N.C.: Duke University Press, 1970). Copyright 1971 by Duke University Press.

55. *Ibid.*, p. 6.

56. *Ibid.*, pp. 3, 6, 7.

57. Arora, *Comparative Public Administration*, p. 37.

58. Savage, "Optimism and Pessimism," p. 419.

59. James Heaphey, "Comparative Public Administration: Comments on Current Characteristics," *Public Administration Review* 29, No. 3 (1968): 242-49, at pp. 242-43.

60. Jamil E. Jreisat, "Synthesis and Relevance in Comparative Public Administration," *Public Administration Review* 35, No. 6 (1975): 663-71, at p. 667.

61. Riggs, *Frontiers of Development Administration*, p. 7. Paradigm is used here in the meaning suggested by Thomas S. Kuhn, in *The Structure of Scientific Revolution*, 2nd ed. (Chicago: University of Chicago Press, 1970). He says that a paradigm is "what the members of a scientific community share, and conversely, a scientific community consists of men who share a paradigm." He regards social sciences generally as in a pre-paradigmatic stage, as compared to the physical sciences.

62. Savage, "Optimism and Pessimism," p. 417.

63. Jones, "Frontiersmen in Search," p. 101.

64. Savage, "Optimism and Pessimism," p. 415.

65. *Ibid.*

66. Lee Sigelman, "In Search of Comparative Administration," *Public Administration Review* 36, No. 6 (1976): 621-25, at p. 623.

67. *Ibid.*, p. 625.

68. J. Fred Springer, "Empirical Theory and Development Administration: Prologues and Promise," *Public Administration Review* 36, No. 6 (1976): 636-41, at p. 636.

69. Keith Henderson, "Comparative Public Administration: The Identity Crisis," *Journal of Comparative Administration* 1, No. 1 (May 1969): 65-84, at p. 75.
70. Sigelman, "In Search of Comparative Administration," p. 622.
71. Jones, "Frontiersmen in Search," p. 102.
72. Jreisat, "Synthesis and Relevance," p. 655.
73. Savage, "Optimism and Pessimism," p. 417.
74. Springer, "Empirical Theory and Development Administration: Prologues and Promise," p. 636.
75. Sigelman, "In Search of Comparative Administration," p. 623.
76. Jong S. Jun, "Renewing the Study of Comparative Administration: Some Reflections on the Current Possibilities," *Public Administration Review* 36, No. 6 (1976): 641-47, at p. 645.
77. Jones, "Frontiersmen in Search," pp. 101-5.
78. Brian Loveman, "The Comparative Administration Group, Development Administration, and Antidevelopment," *Public Administration Review* 36, No. 6 (1976): 616-21.
79. *Ibid.*, p. 619.
80. Jones, "Frontiersmen in Search," p. 103.
81. *Ibid.*, p. 102.
82. B. B. Schaffer, "Comparisons, Administration, and Development," *Political Studies* 19, No. 3 (September 1971): 327-37, at p. 330.
83. Loveman, "The Comparative Administration Group," pp. 618-19.
84. Jreisat, "Synthesis and Relevance," pp. 666-67.
85. Savage, "Optimism and Pessimism," pp. 420-22.
86. Jreisat, "Synthesis and Relevance," p. 664.
87. *Ibid.*, p. 665.
88. *Ibid.*, p. 663.
89. Sigelman, "In Search of Comparative Administration," p. 624.
90. Jun, "Renewing the Study of Comparative Administration," pp. 643-44.
91. Sigelman, "In Search of Comparative Administration," p. 623.
92. Springer, "Empirical Theory and Development Administration," pp. 639-40.
93. Sigelman, "In Search of Comparative Administration," pp. 623-24.
94. *Ibid.*, p. 624.
95. *Ibid.*, p. 625.
96. Jun, "Renewing the Study of Comparative Administration," pp. 645-46.
97. Jorge I. Tapia-Videla, "Understanding Organizations and Environments: A Comparative Perspective," *Public Administration Review* 36, No. 6 (1976): 631-36.
98. Peter Cleaves, *Bureaucratic Politics and Administration in Chile* (Berkeley, Calif.: University of California Press, 1975).
99. Jreisat, "Synthesis and Relevance," p. 668.
100. For important examples of this literature, see Yehezkel Dror, *Public Policymaking Reexamined* (San Francisco: Chandler Publishing Company, 1968), and Thomas R. Dye, *Understanding Public Policy* (Englewood Cliffs, N.J.: Prentice-Hall, Inc., 1972).

101.   Siffin, "Two Decades of Public Administration," pp. 68-70.

102.   Jreisat, "Synthesis and Relevance," pp. 668-69.

103.   *Ibid.*, p. 669.

104.   *Ibid.*, p. 670.

105.   *Ibid.*

106.   W. Blase, *Institution Building: A Source Book* (Beverly Hills, Calif.: Sage Publications, 1973).

107.   For a fuller discussion of these reassessment efforts, see my article, "Comparative Administration: A Sojourner's View," *Public Administration Review* 38, No. 4 (1978): 358-65.

108.   Jonathan Bendor, "A Theoretical Problem in Comparative Administration," *Public Administration Review* 36, No. 6 (1976): 626-30.

109.   Savage, "Optimism and Pessimism," pp. 419-20, 422.

110.   Jun, "Renewing the Study of Comparative Administration," p. 647.

111.   ". . . the new paradigm for 'public administration' must be 'comparative,' i.e., global, since the solution of the problems to which it addresses itself will require increasing communication between scholars and practitioners in all countries. The American dimension of these problems will surely come to be seen as a 'subfield' or a parochial aspect of the broader subject." Fred W. Riggs, "The Group and the Movement: Notes on Comparative and Development Administration," *Public Administration Review* 36, No. 6 (1976): 648-54, at p. 652.

2

A FOCUS FOR COMPARISON

Bureaucracy as a Focus

Of the many ways to organize a survey of the existing state of knowledge concerning administration in various countries, I have chosen the institution of the public bureaucracy as the means for comparison.

In view of the preference of many leading students of comparative politics for a functional or nonstructural approach, it is certainly legitimate to ask why the structure or institution of bureaucracy should be selected as the subject for comparative administrative analysis rather than a function such as Almond's rule application. The answer does not lie in a general judgment that a functional approach to comparative study of whole political systems is inferior to a structural approach; rather, it is a decision that the bureaucracy as a specialized political structure offers a better basis for treatment than would a choice of one or more functional categories. Our objective is comparison of public administration across polities, not the comparison of whole political systems. Such a narrowing of interest forces us to choose the most promising basis for comparison for the particular purpose (in this case public administration)—a basis that will simultaneously include enough, but not too much, and can promise data for comparison in the polities covered. For the student of public administration, the structure of bureaucracy has some advantages over the function of rule application, or any functional alternative that has been suggested.

The major objections made by Almond and others to comparative studies that have a structural emphasis are that structures may
vary substantially from system to system, and like structures in
different systems may have significant functional differences that
are overlooked. These cautions do not seem to vitiate the utility
of a structural approach in the comparative study of public administration. Apparently bureaucracy as a specialized structure is
common to all contemporary nation-states, as is explained later.
On the second point, to focus on the public bureaucracy is not
automatically to ignore the probability that it performs functions
other than rule application. Indeed, if all structures are multifunctional, as Almond hypothesizes, it may be just as valuable for
comparative studies to focus on a universally existing structure and
to investigate the differing functions it performs as it is to focus on
one function and identify the structures that perform it. Tracing a
given function through a multitude of structures would appear to
present problems of conceptualization and research at least as great
as singling out one structure and analyzing the functions it performs.[1] Whether the approach is through structure or function in
structural–functional analysis, the central question, as Landau has
pointed out,[2] is always some form of "What functions are performed
by a given institution, and how?" Siffin has explored the issue as to
whether the structural bureaucratic perspective deserves continued
use and concludes that it does merit further reliance in traveling what
he calls the "low road" to science, equivalent to what others have
referred to as "middle-range" theory. Even though he concedes the
limited capacity of structuralism as a tool, Siffin argues that abandoning it will not help the situation much.[3]

Any partial comparative analysis of political systems presents
a dilemma, whether the approach is functional or institutional. This
may not be serious in Western countries where there is a high degree
of correlation across systems between structures and corresponding
functions, but either approach runs into serious difficulties in the
developing countries. Comparison by function may be more difficult
in practice than in theory, since we have had very little of it, and it
calls for identification of vaguely formed or strange structures
through which the function under study may be carried out. On the
other hand, structural comparison has hazards more easily identifiable, including the absence or precarious existence of comparable
institutions, and the danger of assuming that similar structures will
always have equivalent functions.

A structural basis of comparison is feasible if the institution or institutions being studied actually exist in corresponding form in the political systems under study, and if notice is taken of variations in the functional role of these institutions in different systems.

From another angle, it might be argued that comparison of bureaucratic structure and behavior is deficient because it offers only partial coverage of topics traditionally dealt with in books on public administration in particular countries, such as administrative organization and management, fiscal and personnel administration, relations between levels of government and levels of administration, and administrative law. One response is that a common framework for treatment is less observable now than was the case a few years ago, so that variation in perspective is more acceptable. The more compelling reason, however, is that a sweeping comparison across national boundaries requires some organizing concept to avoid burial under an avalanche of data about a multitude of diverse administrative systems. Bureaucracy provides such an organizing concept, one which certainly is at the core of modern administration even though public administration and public bureaucracy are not synonymous, and which has impinging upon it all the other forces that have in the past interested students of public administration.

Before proceeding, we need to examine with care and in some detail how the term bureaucracy has been used by different people, the confusions of meaning and understanding that have resulted, and the meaning given to bureaucracy as used here.

Concepts of Bureaucracy

The term bureaucracy has often been attacked as contrived, ambiguous, and troublesome. All of these charges are accurate. Nevertheless, bureaucracy is a word that has demonstrated great staying power. Even most of its critics have concluded that there is more to be gained by keeping it (provided it is given the meaning they prefer) than by abandoning it. And that is essentially the position taken here.

The origins of the word are not entirely clear. Morstein Marx gives it a French pedigree, identifies a Latin ancestor of long ago, calls it a hideous example of teaming French with Greek, and counts it as among the notorious words of our age.[4] He points out that it was first used in the French form *bureaucratie* by a French minister of commerce in the eighteenth century to refer to the government in operation, spread to Germany during the nineteenth century as

Burokratie, and has since found its way into English and many other languages. As a subject for scholarly inquiry, the term is primarily associated with the German social scientist Max Weber (1864–1920), whose writings on bureaucracy have stimulated a flood of commentary and further research.[5]

What is probably the most common usage of bureaucracy may distract us, but it need not detain us. In popular language, bureacracy is most often employed as a "political cussword," and is cast in the role of villain by opponents of "big government" or "the welfare state." Sometimes this meaning appears in academic writings as well, two often quoted examples being Harold Laski's definition in the 1930 edition of the *Encyclopedia of the Social Sciences*, and the treatment by Von Mises in his book, *Bureaucracy.*[6]

Most social scientists define bureaucracy in a way intended to identify a phenomenon associated with large-scale complex organizations, without any connotation of approval or disapproval. A usage that is value-neutral, it identifies bureaucracy as neither hero nor villain, but as a form of social organization with certain characteristics.

The confusion in bureaucratic theory comes from differences in approach in describing these characteristics, and failure to distinguish among these approaches.[7] The ambiguity can be traced to Weber's own formulations, and despite a high degree of agreement and consistency concerning some essential earmarks of bureaucracy, it continues down to the present.

The dominant tendency is to define bureaucracy in terms of an organization's basic structural characteristics. The most compact formulation is that of Victor Thompson, who characterizes bureaucratic organizations as composed of a highly elaborated hierarchy of authority superimposed upon a highly elaborated division of labor.[8] From Weber on, most writers on bureaucracy have enumerated the structural dimensions of bureaucracy, with minor variations in their formulations, both in content and breakdown of items, but with substantial agreement among them. Richard H. Hall has tabulated characteristics of bureaucracy as listed by a number of authors, including Weber, Litwak, Friedrich, Merton, Udy, Heady, Parsons, and Berger.[9] From the longer roster of characteristics, Hall picked six dimensions of bureaucracy for special attention. These were (1) a well-defined hierarchy of authority, (2) a division of labor based on functional specialization, (3) a system of rules covering the rights and duties of positional incumbents, (4) a system of procedures for dealing with work situations, (5) impersonality of interpersonal relationships, and (6) selection for employment and promotion based on technical competence. This list can serve very well as a summary of the most commonly mentioned structural earmarks of bureaucracy.

A second tendency has been to define bureaucracy in terms of behavioral characteristics, or to add these to the structural character- istics, the result being a pattern of behavior or related patterns of behavior presumed to be bureaucratic. Opinion varies considerably on what kind of behavior deserves to be so labeled. One option is to emphasize normal, desirable, functional traits positively associated with attainment of the objectives of bureaucratic organizations. Friedrich, for example, stresses traits such as objectivity, precision and consistency, and discretion. He describes these traits as "clearly and closely related to the measure-taking function of administrative officials."[10] They "embody rules defining desirable habit or behav- ior patterns of all the members" of such a bureaucratic organization, and they were originated by "men of extraordinary inventiveness who were laying the basis of a rationalized society by these inven- tions."[11] Eisenstadt speaks approvingly of a type of dynamic equi- librium that a bureaucracy may develop in relation to its environ- ment, in which the bureaucracy maintains its autonomy and distinc- tiveness by behavior retaining its structural differentiation from other social groups but recognizing the claims of those legitimately entitled to exercise supervisory controls over the bureaucracy.[12]

A more common emphasis, which shows up in the work of many other authors, highlights behavioral traits which are basically negative, "dysfunctional," pathological, or self-defeating, tending to frustrate the realization of the goals toward which the bureaucracy is supposed to be working. Robert Merton has made the classic statement of this point of view.[13] He is concerned with the fact that "the very elements which conduce toward efficiency in general pro- duce inefficiency in specific instances" and "also lead to an over- concern with strict adherence to regulations which induces timidity, conservatism, and technicism." Stress on "depersonalization of relationships" leads to conflict in relations with bureaucratic clientele. Specific behavioral orientations often mentioned are "buck passing," red tape, rigidity and inflexibility, excessive imper- sonality, oversecretiveness, unwillingness to delegate, and reluctance to exercise discretion. Behavior of this sort is typical of the "trained incapacity" of the bureaucrat. The implication is that behavior which is most typically bureaucratic is behavior emerging from overemphasis on the rationality of bureaucratic organization and dysfunctional in its effects, suggesting a model for bureaucratic behavior which would stress these contradictory or self-defeating traits. This continues to be a common orientation. Morstein Marx talks of such traits as "ailment of organization," explained by the fact that "the bureaucratic type of organization gives rise to certain tendencies that pervert its purpose. Some of its strength—and in extreme cases all of it—is drained off constantly by vices that paradoxically spring from virtues."[14]   Michel Crozier describes his valuable study, *The Bureaucratic Phenomenon*, as a scientific attempt to understand better this "malady of bureaucracy." He explains that the subject to which he refers in speaking of the bureaucratic phenomenon "is that of the maladaptations, the inadequacies, or, to use Merton's expression, the 'dysfunctions,' which necessarily develop within human organizations."[15]

Either of these paths toward defining bureaucracy in terms of behavior leads to distinctions between patterns of behavior that are "more" or "less" bureaucratic, with the meaning of such descriptions being uncertain unless the kind of behavior that has been labeled "bureaucratic" is clearly understood. This approach may also result in identifying the "process of bureaucratization" with a pronounced inclination toward a patterned combination of behavioral traits, usually pathological, such as Eisenstadt's use of the word bureaucratization to mean "the extension of the power of a bureaucratic organization over many areas beyond its initial purpose, the growing internal formalization within the bureaucracy, the regimentation of these areas by the bureaucracy, and in general a strong emphasis by the bureaucracy on the extension of its power."[16]

A third method for dealing with bureaucratic behavior has been suggested by Peter Blau, who defines bureaucracy in terms of achievement of purpose, as "organization that maximizes efficiency in administration or an institutionalized method of organized social conduct in the interests of administrative efficiency."[17]   In modern society, with its necessities for large-scale operation, this probably requires that certain basic organizational characteristics be present, including hierarchical arrangements, specialization, professionalization to some degree, a set of operational rules, and a basic commitment to rational adaptation of means to ends. Although Blau recognizes the tendencies for bureaucracies to develop behavior patterns which detract from the attainment of legitimate objectives, he does not accept the view that all behavior that deviates from the formal expectation or seems irrational is in fact dysfunctional. He suggests a category of behavior of a somewhat different kind, which he terms "irrational but (perhaps) purposeful."[18]   Behavior having its source in undercommitment to rationality may be dysfunctional, but this must be judged by results rather than by reference to a preconceived set of behavioral traits which are assumed to accompany the structural components of bureaucracy. The test as to the propriety of behavior would be its contribution to fundamental bureaucratic goals. Behavior which is pathological in one bureaucracy may be healthful in another. This would seem to make both structural and behavioral characteristics of bureaucracy somewhat variable, since the test for whether or not an organization is a bureaucracy is whether it is achieving its purpose, and the elements of structure and behavior that this requires may shift from time to time and place to place.

As indicated by this resumé, considerable agreement exists as to the basic organizational characteristics of bureaucracy, but there is much less certainty as to the behavioral traits associated with it. Three alternatives have been presented for designating a pattern of behavior as "bureaucratic." One points toward normal, functional, desirable behavior to be expected and accepted as natural in bureaucratic operations. Another stresses dysfunctional behavior which is likely to develop from the rationalistic orientation of bureaucracy and the structural features designed to maintain it. The third alternative relates the propriety of behavior to the bureaucratic environment and results in a more flexible standard as to what behavior is bureaucratic in the sense of being functional.

Of course, all of these considerations are important, and the selection of any one of these aspects as critical to the definition of bureaucracy is quite justifiable. It is crucial to clarity of understanding, however, to make an explicit choice.[19] I have argued elsewhere[20] that Morroe Berger's pioneering study, *Bureaucracy and Society in Modern Egypt*, is flawed by a failure to do this, and that this affects his conclusion that theories of bureaucracy developed in the West have serious shortcomings for the analysis of bureaucracies both in Western and non-Western settings.[21] His view as to the inadequacy of existing theory is based mainly on the fact that responses to the questionnaire which he used in his study did not conform to his expectations. In his research he made certain assumptions about "Western norms" of bureaucratic behavior, and he discovered upon analysis of the questionnaire data that the Egyptian civil servants most highly exposed to Western influences did not, as he had anticipated, come closest to what he had assumed to be the Western norms. Berger pays relatively little attention to the structural side of bureaucratic theory, but he implicitly assumes that a model of bureaucracy would combine structural and behavioral features. As to behavioral attributes, he quotes Merton and seems to imply that on the behavioral side a model for bureaucracy would stress dysfunctional or pathological tendencies, along the lines of the second alternative discussed earlier. Nevertheless, he combines traits generally considered pathological or dysfunctional with others usually viewed as functional or desirable, in constructing his research tools for measuring "typical" or "Western" bureaucratic behavior. In short, his assumptions as to "the bureaucratic pattern of behavior," which he apparently equates with "the Western bureaucratic pattern of behavior," seem not to conform with his own citation from bureaucratic theory as to the behavioral components of bureaucracy. The hybrid or bifurcated model of bureaucracy which he uses results in confusion which might have been avoided by greater consistency in the approach used for identifying behavioral components, or by defining bureaucracy in a way which avoids attaching the label of "bureaucratic" to any particular pattern of behavioral traits.

My choice of the most useful way to view bureaucracy is as an institution defined in terms of basic structural characteristics.[22] Bureaucracy is a form of organization. Organizations either are bureaucracies or they are not, depending on whether or not they have these characteristics. Regarding bureaucracy as characteristic of the structure of an organization does not mean that all bureaucracies are identical as far as structure is concerned. Some promising efforts have been made to conceptualize elements that can be considered dimensions of organizational structure, the objective being to rate organizations on a continuum for each of the dimensions, with the position of a particular organization on all these dimensions jointly forming a profile of its structure. This structural profile can then be used, it is hoped, to characterize the organization for purposes of comparison.[23]

A principal advantage of selecting a structural focus in defining bureaucracy, rather than incorporating a behavioral component as well, is that it allows us to consider all patterns of behavior that are actually found in bureaucracies as equally deserving to be called bureaucratic behavior. One pattern of behavior is not singled out as somehow entitled to be labeled bureaucratic, leaving other behavior patterns, also found in existing bureaucracies, to be described as nonbureaucratic or less bureaucratic. This practice has been the source of much confusion that can be eliminated.

The approach suggested does not ignore or de-emphasize differences in behavioral tendencies in bureaucracies. On the contrary, it facilitates the identification and classification of these patterns, which are extremely significant and should be primary objects for analysis and comparison. Behavioral traits, more than structural elements, are what distinguish one bureaucracy from another. These patterns can be expected to vary from bureaucracy to bureaucracy and from time to time in a given bureaucracy, but other than that we know very little about this highly complicated subject. As Friedrich has pointed out, the problems presented by the behavioral aspects of bureaucracy are considerably more complex than those associated with the structural aspects. He observes that "although a certain similarity is observable, the behavior of bureaucrats varies widely in time and place without there being any clear-cut pattern of development. Nor is this fact to be wondered at. The behavior of all persons in a particular cultural context is bound to be moulded by the values and beliefs prevalent in that culture. Thus the Chinese official, motivated by the doctrine of Confucius and his followers, will be much more concerned with good manners than the Swiss official, while the latter, motivated by the teachings of Christianity and more especially (typically) by a Protestant and Pietist version of Christian beliefs, will be more concerned with honesty and duty."[24] A theory of bureaucracy and techniques of comparative study which will facilitate exploration of these problems is an objective of the highest priority. "Intuitively . . . people have always assumed that bureaucratic structures and patterns of action differ in the different countries of the Western world and even more markedly between East and West. Men of action know it and never fail to take it into account. But contemporary social scientists . . . have not been concerned with such comparisons."[25] A structural characterization of what constitutes bureaucracy will not in itself accomplish much along this line, but it should at least clear away part of the debris so as to make progress somewhat easier.

The Prevalence of Public Bureaucracy

What are the generally accepted organizational features common to all bureaucracies? Do bureaucracies with these essential features exist in all or nearly all of the political systems of the world, so that they afford an actual basis for comparison of public administration across national boundaries? If bureaucracies are uniformly found to be in operation in modern polities, what points about their structure and behavior should be selected as most productive for purposes of comparative study?

As has already been mentioned, there are almost as many

formulations of the essential characteristics of bureaucracy as there are writers on the subject (and they have been plentiful). Nevertheless, the area of agreement on the structural or organizational features that are central is substantial. The variations come mostly in the way the structural aspects are expressed and in the divergence that comes when behavioral traits are added.

The pivotal structural characteristics can be reduced to three: (1) hierarchy, (2) differentiation or specialization, and (3) qualification or competence.[26] Hierarchy is probably the most important because it is so closely associated with the effort to apply rationality to administrative tasks. Max Weber viewed this effort as explaining the origin of the bureaucratic form of organization. He refers to hierarchy as involving principles and levels of graded authority that ensure a firmly ordered system of superordination and subordination in which higher offices supervise lower ones. Such a formal scheme of interlocking superior–subordinate relationships is intended to provide direction, cohesion, and continuity. Specialization in organization is a result of division of labor, which in turn is a requirement for accomplishment in cooperative human endeavor to master the environment and reach complex goals. Specialized allocation of tasks means differentiation within the organization of what sociologists refer to as roles. The structure of organization must provide for a functional relationship of these roles. Qualification "refers to these functions or roles and requires that the person playing a certain role must be qualified for it, typically in highly developed bureaucracies by adequate preparation and education."[27] Such intensive preparation might justify referring to professionalism in connection with this aspect, but competence and qualification are preferable because these terms hint at fitting the official to the role as it is conceived in the particular context. Competence might or might not require what would be considered professionalized training in a highly specialized society.

Other features of a structural sort are also frequently mentioned, but these are somewhat more peripheral, or are closely related to those already mentioned, such as a body of rules governing the behavior of members, a system of records, a system of procedures for dealing with work situations, and size sufficient at least to assure a network of secondary group relationships.

It should be noted that this treatment of bureaucracy differs substantially from Weber's formulation of an "ideal-type" or a "fully developed" bureaucracy. His "ideal-type" was not intended to represent reality but was an abstraction that highlighted certain features, a "mental construct" which, in his words, "cannot be found empirically in reality."[28]   As Arora observes, Weber "seemed to be clear in his mind that the ideal-type does not represent 'reality' *per se*, but is only an abstraction weaving an exaggeration of certain elements of reality into a logically precise conception."[29]   Such an "ideal-type" is based on a combination of inductive and deductive analysis, and hopefully has heuristic value even though it does not match any existing instance of the phenomenon being studied.

This formulation, on the other hand, is intended to identify actual organizations as bureaucracies if they have the specified characteristics. Moreover, Weber's formulation combined organizational with behavioral aspects, whereas this one confines the definition of bureaucracy to a minimal number of key structural characteristics.

There seems to be little doubt that a viable polity in the world of today must have a public service that meets these criteria for a bureaucracy.[30]   The necessities of governmental operation require large-scale organization of a bureaucratic type, with a definite internal hierarchical arrangement, well-developed functional specialization, and qualification standards for membership in the bureaucracy. This does not mean that uniformity, even of these structural features, is assumed. Certainly, variations in operating characteristics are anticipated among bureaucracies in different political settings. Bureaucratic adaptation and innovation should be expected, particularly in the newer nations.

In order to compare the public bureaucracies of the entire range of existing political entities, on what parts of these bureaucracies and on what aspects of bureaucratic activity should we concentrate to make the attempt manageable and to take into account realistically the available stock of reliable information?

To begin, let us use what LaPalombara calls "an accordion-like conceptualization of the bureaucracy."[31]   The bureaucrats of major interest to us will generally be "those who occupy managerial roles, who are in some directive capacity either in central agencies or in the field, who are generally described in the language of public administration as 'middle' or 'top' management."[32]   This is the higher civil service as the term is used by Morstein Marx to mean "the relatively 'permanent' top group composed of those who share, in different degrees, in the task of directing the various agencies," including "administrative," "professional," and "industrial" categories, "staff" as well as "line" personnel, and "field service" as well as "headquarters" officials.[33]   In relation to the total number of people in the public service, this will be a small proportion, probably not more than 1 or 2 percent. This more restricted concept of the bureaucracy is most relevant when the concern is bureaucratic participation in the formation of public policy.

The usual convention in public administration literature has been to concentrate on the civil, rather than the military, bureaucracy. This has been an understandable and for the most part acceptable emphasis for the study of administration in Western democratic systems. However, neglect of the military bureaucracy would be a serious omission in making comparisons on a global basis, in view of the numerous instances of nation-states in which the military has not consistently in the past conformed, or does not now conform, to a role of subordination to civilian political leadership. This role for the military has been common in many Latin American countries since independence, and currently is on the rise. A large proportion of the newly independent countries have started with or turned to military or semimilitary regimes, and the frequency seems to be increasing. Sporadically, such regimes have appeared elsewhere in long established polities. In such circumstances, where the higher military leadership has collaborated with or dominated the civil bureaucracy in making major public policy decisions, this participation in political rule will be of direct interest to us, although we will not deal with the military bureaucracy as it operates within the sphere of conventional military activity.

This perspective for a comparative survey of public administration, focusing on the institution of bureaucracy as it adapts to environmental conditions (particularly to the degree of social and economic development and to the configuration of the political system) does not claim to be the only one, or even necessarily the best of possible perspectives. It has been picked because it is relatively manageable, because it can rely upon a fairly adequate accumulation of basic data, and because it offers the promise of leading to future comparative research that will be both more exact and more comprehensive.

A focus on bureaucracy also has the advantage that it has already been recognized as the most commonly accepted basis for comparative studies. As early as 1964, Dwight Waldo found the bureaucratic model useful, stimulating, and provocative.[34] Writing several years later, Arora identified the construct of bureaucracy drawing upon the work of Max Weber as "the single most dominant conceptual framework in the study of comparative administration."[35] More recently, Jong Jun and Lee Sigelman have reaffirmed this preference. Although Jun finds it not comprehensive enough to explain societal differences among social phenomena, he concedes that the bureaucratic model has been considered more manageable for comparative study than its alternatives, as indicated by the abundance of literature using it, including the majority of empirical studies and single country analyses which have appeared in the last twenty years, and he calls for continued study of "the structures, functions, behaviors, and environments of bureaucracy."[36] Sigelman states as his conviction that the future of comparative public administration lies in studies of bureaucracies, in "examinations of the backgrounds, attitudes, and behaviors of bureaucrats and those with whom they interact."[37]

With this background, recognizing that the subject matter is highly complicated and that available information sources are limited, we will seek to compare the higher civil and, where relevant, military bureaucracies in a variety of existing political systems, taking the following questions as the most pertinent ones for our purposes:

1. What are the dominant internal operating characteristics of the bureaucracy reflecting its composition, hierarchical arrangements, pattern of specialization, and behavioral tendencies?

2. To what extent is the bureaucracy multifunctional, participating in the making of major public policy decisions as well as in their execution?

3. What are the principal means for exerting control over the bureaucracy from sources outside it, and how effective are those external controls?

As these questions indicate, our interest is not confined to a comparison of structural variations, but extends to an exploration of differences in behavioral patterns among bureaucracies.

Before trying to answer these questions in particular polities or types of political systems, let us consider two general background factors that can be expected to influence markedly the characteristics of bureaucratic systems. One is a relatively immediate and easily discernible factor—the overall formal organizational pattern for the system of public administration in which the bureaucracy operates. The other, less tangible and more complex, but of much greater significance, is the political, economic, and social environment in which the bureaucracy functions, often referred to as the "ecology of administration." At a minimum, we must identify those environmental features that have the greatest impact in shaping and reshaping the bureaucracy.

Organizational Patterns for Administration

A necessary consequence of hierarchy and specialization in large-scale organization is an orderly arrangement of units into successively larger and more inclusive groupings. This process of departmentalization has occurred in a remarkably uniform way in countries that vary greatly in their political orientations and other aspects of their administrative systems. The basic unit is the department or ministry, with each one representing a major organizational subdivision of administration. Brian Chapman identifies five "primordial fields of government"—foreign affairs, justice, finance, defense and war, and internal affairs—represented in Europe's past by primary ministries with origins dating back to the Roman system of administration.[38] With the growth of governmental responsibilities and services, new ministries emerged from what had been the residual category of internal affairs, adding new ministries in such fields as education, agriculture, transport, trade, and more recently, social security and health.[39] The contours of the sphere of governmental activities in each country will certainly affect the number and missions of the central ministries, but the impression one gets from reviewing rosters of ministries in many countries is one of uniformity or close similarity rather than of wide variation.

Central government ministries normally range from around twelve to about thirty, depending on the degree to which the country concerned prefers specialized or composite units, and the range of governmental program areas. Switzerland has only seven central government departments, reported by Chapman as a record low number, and presumably reflecting the country's small size, restricted scope of government intervention, and confederative constitutional arrangements emphasizing autonomy for the member cantons.[40] A more usual figure is around twelve, found in countries as separated in size, location, political configuration, and level of development as the United States, Madagascar, Panama, Portugal, Thailand, Japan, Turkey, Colombia, Burundi, and the Netherlands. Another cluster occurs around twenty, including Indonesia, South Africa, South Korea, Morocco, Jamaica, Canada, Greece, Burma, and Uganda. Also in this group are several countries, among them Iran, Israel, Mexico, and the Philippines, which had fewer units a decade ago, indicating a tendency toward gradual proliferation. Among countries having a higher number and more short-range fluctuation in the total are several with parliamentary governments such as Italy, Great Britain, and former or current members of the

British Commonwealth, as well as the USSR, the People's Republic of China, Poland, Cuba, and other Communist countries. For the first group the explanation is probably the ease of making changes by action of the cabinet in some parliamentary systems, and in the second group the extensive sweep of direct state responsibility for economic and industrial enterprises. The USSR probably is a record setter both as to fluctuation and current total number of ministries. Fainsod gives the tally at intervals during the thirty-year period from the mid 1920s to the mid 1950s, showing only ten at the start, moving up to fifty-nine in 1947, hovering around fifty for several years, and then dropping sharply to twenty-five in 1953.[41] However, in the last twenty-five years the total has moved up again dramatically to sixty-two in 1976.

Organizational features other than the lineup of core ministries or departments are likely to have a greater impact on the bureaucracy. In most countries, an outcropping of administrative agencies has developed that does not fit within the ministerial system. These may be units that have split off from parent ministries and are on their way to becoming full-fledged ministries but have not yet arrived. They may be agencies, such as the independent regulatory commissions in the United States, that have deliberately been given an autonomous status because of the nature of the controls they wield over private interests. The most common form of incremental organization in recent decades is the government corporation, which has been popular in many countries displaying wide differences in the role of government in the economy. The corporate form has had a special appeal in the newer nations struggling toward industrialization under governmental auspices. The autonomy often accorded to these public corporations in staffing and related matters may have profound effects not only on that part of the bureaucracy in the corporations but on the remainder of the public service as well.

Variations in the way in which the core ministries and other units of organization are tied to the organs of political leadership are also of obvious significance. These include such differences as those between unitary and federal arrangements for territorial distribution of governmental powers; presidential and parliamentary systems for organizing executive–legislative relationships; single-party, two-party, and multiparty patterns in political party systems; and various procedures for providing interest group representation in the conduct of administration. All of these choices concerning the structure of government machinery and the conduct of government business have direct and traceable effects on the bureaucracy.

The Ecology of Administration

An ecological approach to public administration is usually traced to
the writings of John M. Gaus,[42] who drew upon the work of sociologists during the 1920s concerned with the interdependence of human
life and its surrounding environment, who had in turn borrowed
from botanists and zoologists seeking to explain how plant and
animal organisms adapt to their environments. Such an approach,
in his words, "builds . . . quite literally from the ground up; from
the elements of a place—soils, climate, location, for example—to the
people who live there—their numbers and ages and knowledge, and
the ways of physical and social technology by which from the place
and in relationship with one another, they get their living."[43] Gaus
was primarily concerned with identifying key ecological factors for
an understanding of contemporary American public administration,
and he explored a list of factors which he found to be particularly
useful: people, place, physical technology, social technology, wishes
and ideas, catastrophe, and personality.

If ecological considerations were helpful in studying one's own
administrative system, they would obviously be doubly important in
comparative studies, and this was recognized early by Riggs and
other pioneers in the field.[44] More recently, R. K. Arora has stressed
that cross-cultural administrative analysis "should focus upon the
interaction between an administrative system and its external environment, and also study the dynamics of socio-administrative change
in the context of such interaction."[45] In Arora's judgment, more
success has been achieved in the treatment of the social environmental impact on the administrative system than in the reciprocal
treatment of the bureaucracy's influence on the environment, and
he calls for a more balanced interactional analysis.[46]

We will accept this recommendation that a systematic effort
should be made to relate public administration to its environment, in
much the same way that the science of ecology is concerned with the
mutual relations between organisms and their environment. Of
course, social institutions are not living organisms, so the parallel is
at most suggestive. The point is that bureaucracies, as well as other
political and administrative institutions, can be better understood if
the surrounding conditions, influences, and forces that shape and
modify them are identified and ranked to the extent possible in the
order of relative importance, and if the reciprocal impact of these
institutions on their environment is also explored.

The environment of bureaucracy may be visualized as a series of concentric circles, with bureaucracy at the center. The smallest circle generally has the most decisive influence, and the larger circles represent a descending order of importance as far as the bureaucracy is concerned. We may visualize the largest circle as representing all of society or the general social system. The next circle represents the economic system or the economic aspects of the social system. The inner circle is the political system; it encloses the administrative subsystem and the bureaucracy as one of its elements.

Without undertaking any full exploration of the ecology of public administration, we can try to pick out the environmental factors impinging on bureaucracy that would seem to be most helpful in answering the questions posed earlier regarding bureaucracies. Comparative analysis requires a preliminary classification of the nation-states in which these bureaucracies function, based on the environmental factors that are deemed to be most decisive.

The basic categories employed here are not original; they are already widely known and used. The first classification is "developed" and "developing" societies, referring to clusters of characteristics, primarily of a social and economic nature, that are identified with development as contrasted to underdevelopment or partial development. This is a classification based on the outer environmental circles, with consequences for the bureaucracy that may be considered secondary.

The second classification is one of political systems (using types that have been suggested by students of comparative politics) for both the developed and the developing countries. These political system differences are assumed to encompass environmental factors that have the most direct and consequential effects on bureaucracies. Most of our attention later is devoted to examining the interactions between political regimes of various types and their bureaucracies, within the two broader categories first of developed and then developing countries.

"Development" is admittedly debatable as a criterion for classification, with drawbacks as well as advantages. For these reasons, the following chapter is devoted entirely to a detailed discussion of the concept of development and related concepts such as modernization and change. Pending this review as to various meanings given to development and related terms, and recognizing that such terms in themselves have invidious implications, we can nevertheless capture the essential theme from this statement by Milton Esman: "Development denotes a major societal transformation, a change in system states, along the continuum from peasant and pastoral to industrial organization. The assimilation and institutionalization of modern physical and social technology are critical ingredients. These qualitative changes affect values, behavior, social structure, economic organization and political process."[47]

In terms employed by sociologists such as Talcott Parsons who use a structural–functional approach to study social systems, the more traditional, less developed societies would tend to be predominantly ascriptive, particularistic, and diffuse. In other words, they would confer status based on birth or inherited station rather than personal achievement; they would favor a narrow base rather than more generalized bases for making social decisions; and given social structures would be likely to perform a large number of functions rather than a few. More developed modern societies, on the other hand, would tend to be achievement-oriented, universalistic, and specific.[48]

The word "developing," referring to the countries that are undergoing this process of social transformation, seems preferable to such alternative adjectives as backward, poor, undeveloped, underdeveloped, less developed, emerging, transitional, and even expectant. This profusion of terms has led to the facetious comment that the terminology develops faster than do the developing countries. We shall consider developing, emerging, and transitional as acceptable and more or less interchangeable.

The concept of development does not purport to sort societies into classes of opposites, but only to locate them along a continuum. Our interest is to compare countries that are commonly placed toward the upper end of a scale of development with some of those rated lower on the development scale. The group of countries generally conceded to be highly or fully developed is quite small compared to the total number of existing nation-states, and these countries are geographically concentrated. They include Great Britain and a few members of the British Commonwealth, such as Canada and Australia, most of the countries of western continental Europe, the United States, the USSR, and probably only Japan among the nations of the so-called non-Western world. The overwhelming majority of present-day countries will fall into the "developing" category, although this does not, of course, imply that they are all at a common level of development.

Models of Administrative Systems

Social scientists have suggested using models, corresponding to real world phenomena, to guide investigation and analysis of administrative practices that actually prevail in existing polities. A well-chosen model highlights general characteristics and their interrelationships in a way that facilitates the gathering and interpretation of data about whatever subject matter is being studied. The inevitability of using models of some kind for systematic study of any topic has often been pointed out.[49] The problem lies in choosing a model that matches reality closely enough to aid in comprehending it.

We do have proposed models for the conduct of public administration and the operations of bureaucracy in both the developed and developing countries. The Weberian or "classic" model of bureaucracy applies essentially to the countries of Western Europe, which are the prototypes for developed or modernized polities. For developing countries, the most elaborate model has been formulated by Riggs in his "sala" administrative subsystem in the "prismatic" model for transitional societies. Let us review the main features of these models and comment briefly on their utility in explaining the information we have concerning bureaucracies in a range of developed and developing countries.

The classic model of bureaucracy not only incorporates the essential structural characteristics that have been postulated as definitive of bureaucracy as a form of organization—hierarchy, differentiation, and qualification. It also specifies a network of interrelated characteristics, both structural and behavioral, which identify bureaucracy of this type. An underlying assumption is that the pattern of authority, which lends legitimacy to the system, will be legal–rational rather than traditional or charismatic, and that within the bureaucracy rational means will be used to comply with the commands of the legitimate authority. Bureaucracy is above all a form of organization dedicated to the concept of rationality, and to the conduct of administration on the basis of relevant knowledge. This calls for a series of arrangements. Recruitment is based on achievement as demonstrated competitively rather than on ascription, and similar criteria are to determine subsequent movement within the bureaucracy. Service in the bureaucracy is a career for professionals, who are salaried and have tenured status, subject to discipline or removal only on specified grounds following specified procedures. Administrative roles are highly specialized and differentiated; spheres of competence are well defined and hierarchical relationships are thoroughly understood. The bureaucracy is not an autonomous unit in the political system but is responsive to external controls from legitimized political authority, although there are tendencies within the bureaucracy toward evasion and self-direction.

This simplified model has been widely used to guide descriptions
of, and comparisons among, bureaucracies in modern nation-states,
even though it does not accurately depict any of them. The closeness
of fit varies among political system subtypes in the modernized
polities. The greatest conformity is in such bureaucracies as those
in Germany and France, which we have designated as "classic"
bureaucracies. The model is essentially acceptable when it is applied
to numerous other developed countries with a Western political
tradition, including not only Great Britain and the United States but
also Canada, Australia, New Zealand, and several of the small
European countries. As we move away from these core countries
toward other polities which have been categorized as developed but
which are more removed from the Western European political orbit,
this classic model becomes increasingly less applicable. In the two
cases to be examined here, Japan and the USSR, the divergences are
substantial, but the model is still helpful for purposes of comparison.

When bureaucracies in the developing countries become the
object of attention, however, the inadequacy of the classic model
becomes so apparent that it is nearly always abandoned in favor of
models chosen because they are presumed to correspond much more
closely to actuality in these societies. An outstanding example is the
"prismatic–sala" combination proposed by Riggs.[50] No brief summary can do justice to the intricacies of this model or familiarize
the uninitiated with the specialized vocabulary used in presenting it,
but we can indicate its dimensions and implications.[51]

There is some ambiguity concerning the link Riggs sees between
the prismatic model and existing societies. "Fused" and "differentiated" societies are models constructed deductively from contrasting
assumptions about the relationship between structures and the
number of functions they perform. A structure is "functionally
diffuse" when it performs a large number of functions, "functionally
specific" when it performs a limited number of functions. The
"fused" hypothetical model is of a society in which all component
structures are highly diffuse; in the "diffracted" model component
structures are highly specific.[52] These models cannot be found in
the real world, but they "can serve a heuristic purpose by helping us
to describe real world situations." Some real world societies may
resemble the fused model, others the diffracted.

The "prismatic" model, as originally presented by Riggs, is of
the same hypothetical type as the fused and the diffracted. Designed
to represent a situation intermediate between the fused and diffracted ends of a continuum, it combines relatively fused traits with

relatively diffracted ones. It refers to a social system that is semi-differentiated, standing midway between an undifferentiated fused society and a highly differentiated diffracted society. Although its characteristics are derived deductively also, there may be societies that have characteristics resembling those of the model. Logically speaking, it would seem quite plain that no actual society would be either completely fused or completely diffracted; all would be to some degree prismatic in the sense of being intermediate. On a scale measuring the degree of functional specificity of structures, presumably the pure prismatic model as originally conceived by Riggs represented a society at midpoint between the fused and diffracted models, although this was not made entirely clear.

In *Prismatic Society Revisited*, Riggs complicates matters further by introducing new connotations for "prismatic." He now refers to his original conceptualization as a mistaken "one-dimensional approach," and offers a new definition of prismatic society, based on a "two-dimensional approach." The original dimension was degree of differentiation, ranging from undifferentiated through semidifferentiated to highly differentiated societies, with the fused, prismatic, and diffracted models corresponding to these three stages along the dimension of differentiation.

The second dimension now introduced has to do with the degree of integration among structures in a society that is differentiated. This dimension is insignificant in the fused society model because it is undifferentiated, and the possibility of malintegration among social structures does not arise. With the process of differentiation comes the possibility of malintegration or lack of coordination among social structures. Riggs illustrates by comparing the problem to that of coordinating sounds from the different specialized instruments in a symphony orchestra. When the conductor's baton provides proper direction for coordination, the cacophony of instruments being tuned up or playing out of synchronization is replaced by the sounds of a symphonic performance. Integration has been achieved in the differentiated sounds of the various instruments. Likewise, differentiated social systems can be ranked on a malintegrated–integrated scale.

The problem is not with recognition of the possibility that differentiated societies may differ as to their degree of integration, or that very highly differentiated societies may turn out to be also extremely malintegrated, with dire consequences. The terminological difficulty is that Riggs has chosen to redefine the prismatic model by expanding it to include any society that is differentiated but malintegrated. A corresponding reinterpretation of the diffracted model makes it refer to any society that is differentiated and integrated. Hence prismatic and diffracted are no longer models next to one another on a one-dimensional scale based on degree of differentiation. Instead the usage now suggested for these terms would have them refer to any society that is not fused, at any point along a scale of differentiation, with the distinction being that prismatic societies are malintegrated and diffracted societies are integrated. This in turn leads to the suggestion that prefixes be attached to both the prismatic and diffracted types to indicate stages in the degree of differentiation. These shifts in terminology are indicated by the accompanying illustrations, showing first the one-dimensional and then the two-dimensional approach.[53]

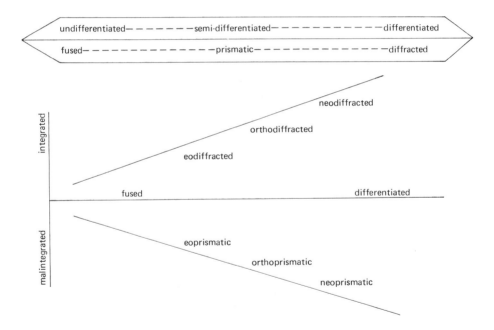

The advantage claimed by Riggs is that the two-dimensional approach recognizes that "prismatic" conditions may occur in societies at any level of differentiation, or to put it in terms of contemporary nation-states, such conditions need not be confined to less developed countries, but may occur in developed countries as well. This enables him to explore recent phenomena in the United States and other developed nations that may manifest increasing malintegration "in the form of urban crises, race riots, student uprisings, popular apathy, the hippy phenomenon, and the profound turbulence wrought by a continuing war in Vietnam."[54]

Our concern, however, is primarily the value of the prismatic model in understanding developing societies, which is what Riggs originally had in mind. Although Riggs has stressed the deductive nature of these models, he has also emphasized their relevance for understanding phenomena in real societies, saying that he has been "fascinated by the prismatic model not only as an intellectual game but also as a device that might eventually help us understand more about administrative behavior in transitional societies."[55]

Despite the shift in usage by Riggs, clearly his claim for relevance is still focused on the type of prismatic society that is semidifferentiated and malintegrated, that is, on what his latest formulation labels orthoprismatic society. For purposes of brevity and clarity, in discussing the prismatic model we will be referring essentially to the societal type which he earlier simply called prismatic and now prefers to call orthoprismatic. This appears to be quite in keeping with his own emphasis, as indicated by this statement: "Since prevalent conditions in third world countries provided the initial impetus and data for creation of the prismatic model, it seems fitting to apply the label 'orthoprismatic' to the characteristic syndrome of the kind of malintegrated differentiated society that we find best illustrated in some, though not necessarily all, the countries of the third world."[56]

The prismatic model in its entirety deals with the full range of social phenomena and behavior, subsuming political and administrative aspects. In other words, it is a model pertaining to the ecology of administration in a type of society. This model is "intrinsically paradoxical."[57] Riggs examines the economic sector (describing it as a "bazaar-canteen" pattern), the elite groupings ("kaleidoscopic stratification"), social structures, symbol systems, and political power patterns. He then turns more specifically to public administration in prismatic society, and evolves the sala model for the administrative subsystem. In line with the general configuration of the prismatic model, administrative functions in such a society "may be performed both by concrete structures oriented primarily toward this function and also by other structures lacking this primary orientation."[58] Such a situation calls for an alternative to conventional ways of thinking about the conduct of public administration, since these are related to experience in Western societies, which are closer

52314

to the diffracted model (or neodiffracted in the more recent formulation).

Riggs is interested in bureaucracies and how they differ in his models. He uses what he calls a "simplified structural definition" of bureaucracy, similar to the one adopted for our purposes, which recognizes wide operational variations among bureaucracies which meet the basic structural requirements. Traditional bureaucracies in societies closer to the fused model were functionally quite diffuse: "each official typically performed a wide range of functions, affecting political and economic as well as administrative functions." In well-integrated differentiated societies approximating the neo-diffracted model, bureaucracies have become much more functionally specific "as the chief—though by no means the only—agents for performing administrative tasks." Indeed, Riggs strongly suggests that such a "functionally narrowed bureaucracy," effectively controlled by other political institutions, "may well be one of the requisite institutional means for achieving integration in a differentiated society."[59] Bureaucracies in the transitional prismatic societies are intermediate as to the degree of their functional specialization, and they contribute to malintegration by not meshing well with other institutions in the political system.

In discussing the locus of bureaucratic action in each of the three principal models, Riggs suggests a choice of terms for each one, as well as a general term to cover them all. He chooses "bureau" for the more comprehensive purpose, and suggests "chamber" to denote the fused bureau, and "office" the diffracted one. For the prismatic bureau, he employs the word "sala," used in Spanish and other languages (including Arabic and Thai) to refer to various kinds of rooms, among them government offices, thus suggesting that "interlocking mixture of the diffracted office and the fused chamber which we can identify as the prismatic bureau."[60]

The profile of administration and the role of the bureaucracy in the sala as drawn by Riggs rest basically on his treatment of the power structure in prismatic society. He finds that the scope of bureaucratic power, in the sense of the range of the values affected, is only intermediate in the prismatic setting, but that the weight of bureaucratic power (referring to the extent of participation in making decisions) is very heavy as compared to either the fused or diffracted models. This is particularly so in polities that have patterned their bureaucratic systems after more diffracted foreign examples. Rates of political and bureaucratic growth are imbalanced in prismatic society. There the bureaucracy has the advantage in competition with the political institutions, which might be better able to control the bureaucracy in more diffracted societies, whether pluralistic or totalitarian. The weight of bureaucratic power in prismatic society tempts bureaucrats to interfere in the political process.

A second and corollary proposition concerning prismatic administration is that the heavy weight of bureaucratic power lowers administrative efficiency, in the sense of cost relative to accomplishment, with the result that such an administration is less efficient than that in either a fused or a diffracted system. The sala is associated with unequal distribution of services, institutionalized corruption, inefficiency in rule application, nepotism in recruitment, bureaucratic enclaves dominated by motives of self-protection, and, in general, a pronounced gap between formal expectations and actual behavior. Administration in the sala model is "basically wasteful and prodigal." Many factors combine in prismatic society to "heighten administrative profligacy." Riggs concedes that this is a "gloomy view" but maintains it is one which "seems to grow out of the logic of the prismatic model."[61]

Influential though it has been, this prismatic–sala model of Riggs has also received much adverse criticism, particularly from those who object to the pessimistic tone admitted to by Riggs himself. R. K. Arora discusses at some length the "negative character" of the prismatic model, claiming that it has a Western bias, and that the terms chosen to describe prismatic traits are value-laden, emphasizing only the negative aspects of prismatic behavior.[62] Michael L. Monroe has described prismatic theory as reflecting standards from a Western frame of reference, and faults Riggs for overlooking evidence of prismatic behavior in countries such as the United States.[63] E. H. Valsan[64] and R. S. Milne[65] have argued that "formalism," meaning in Riggsian terms the gap between what is formally prescribed and actually practiced, may have positive as well as negative consequences, depending on the circumstances. These reactions have undoubtedly influenced Riggs in making the modifications contained in *Prismatic Society Revisited.* It should be noted, however, that Riggs never has made any claim about how well the sala model fits any existing transitional society, and indeed has emphasized a need to research the extent to which the sala attributes actually are to be found in particular developing countries. All he has asserted is that his model-building effort "rests on a substratum of empiricism."[66]

Before exploring the utility of these models, we devote the following two chapters to treatment of two exceedingly important background factors: the concepts of modernization, development, and change; and the historical antecedents of administration in contemporary nation-states.

Notes

1. For a fuller explanation, see Ferrel Heady and Sybil L. Stokes, eds., *Papers in Comparative Public Administration* (Ann Arbor, Mich.: Institute of Public Administration, The University of Michigan, 1962), pp. 10-11.

2. Martin Landau, "On The Use of Functional Analysis in American Political Science," *Social Research* 35, No. 1 (1968): 48-75, at p. 74.

3. William J. Siffin, "Bureaucracy: The Problem of Methodology and the 'Structural' Approach," *Journal of Comparative Administration* 2, No. 4 (1971): 471-503.

4. Fritz Morstein Marx, *The Administrative State* (Chicago: University of Chicago Press, 1957), pp. 16-21.

5. For excellent introductions to this literature, see Robert K. Merton et al., eds., *Reader in Bureaucracy* (New York: Free Press of Glencoe, Inc., 1952); Peter M. Blau, *Bureaucracy in Modern Society* (New York: Random House, 1956); Alfred Diamant, "The Bureaucratic Model: Max Weber Rejected, Rediscovered, Reformed," in Heady and Stokes, *Papers*, pp. 59-96; Henry Jacoby, *The Bureaucratization of the World* (Berkeley, Calif.: University of California Press, 1973).

6. Both Laski and Von Mises are quoted in Wallace S. Sayre, "Bureaucracies: Some Contrasts in Systems," *Indian Journal of Public Administration* 10, No. 2 (1964): 219.

7. Ferrel Heady, "Bureaucratic Theory and Comparative Administration," *Administrative Science Quarterly* 3, No. 4 (1959): 509-25.

8. Victor A. Thompson, *Modern Organization* (New York: Alfred A. Knopf, Inc., 1961), pp. 3-4.

9. Richard H. Hall, "Intraorganizational Structural Variation: Application of the Bureaucratic Model," *Administrative Science Quarterly* 7, No. 3 (1962): 295-308.

10. Carl Joachim Friedrich, *Man and His Government* (New York: McGraw-Hill Book Company, 1963), p. 471. For a fuller presentation of Friedrich's most recent views on bureaucracy, see in particular Chapter 18, "The Political Elite and Bureaucracy," and Chapter 26, "Taking Measures and Carrying On: Bureaucracy."

11. Carl Joachim Friedrich, *Constitutional Government and Democracy*, 4th ed., (Boston: Blaisdell Publishing Company, 1968), pp. 44-45.

12. S. N. Eisenstadt, "Bureaucracy, Bureaucratization, and Debureaucratization," *Administrative Science Quarterly* 4, No. 3 (1959): 302-320. He contrasts this preferred type of equilibrium with two other less desirable main possibilities, which he labels bureaucratization and debureaucratization, each of which results from patterns of aberrant bureaucratic behavior

which overextend the role of bureaucracy, in the first instance, and weaken or subvert it in the second.

13. Robert Merton, "Bureaucratic Structure and Personality," in *Social Theory and Social Structure* (New York: Free Press of Glencoe, Inc., 1949), Chapter 5; reprinted in *Reader in Bureaucracy*, pp. 361-71.

14. Morstein Marx, *The Administrative State*, pp. 25-28.

15. Michel Crozier, *The Bureaucratic Phenomenon* (Chicago: University of Chicago Press, 1964), pp. 4-5, © 1964 by The University of Chicago.

16. Eisenstadt, "Bureaucracy, Bureaucratization, and Debureaucratization," p. 303.

17. Blau, *Bureaucracy in Modern Society*, p. 60.

18. *Ibid.*, p. 58: "To administer a social organization according to purely technical criteria of rationality is irrational, because it ignores the nonrational aspects of social conduct."

19. "Most writers have kept these aspects distinct. . .and have not attempted any rigorous analysis or formal definition of bureaucracy. They have been content to take some selection of structural, behavioral, and purposive aspects as characterizing a bureaucratic organization." D. S. Pugh et al., "A Conceptual Scheme for Organizational Analysis," *Administrative Science Quarterly* 8, No. 3 (1963): 297.

20. Ferrel Heady, "Bureaucratic Theory and Comparative Administration," *Administrative Science Quarterly* 3, No. 4 (1959): 509-25.

21. Morroe Berger, "Bureaucracy East and West," *Administrative Science Quarterly* 1, No. 4 (1957): 518-29.

22. For a fuller discussion, see Ferrel Heady, "Recent Literature on Comparative Public Administration," *Administrative Science Quarterly* 5, No. 1 (1960): 134-54.

23. Pugh et al., "A Conceptual Scheme for Organizational Analysis," pp. 298 ff.

24. Friedrich, *Man and His Government*, p. 470.

25. Crozier, *The Bureaucratic Phenomenon*, p. 210.

26. This formulation of the organizational aspects of bureaucracy has long been identified with Carl J. Friedrich. It was first presented (with Taylor Cole) in *Responsible Bureaucracy: A Study of the Swiss Civil Service* (Cambridge: Harvard University Press, 1932), and appears recently in *Man and His Government*, pp. 468-70.

27. *Ibid.*, p. 469.

28. Quoted by Diamant in Heady and Stokes, *Papers*, p. 63.

29. Ramesh K. Arora, *Comparative Public Administration* (New Delhi: Associated Publishing House, 1972), p. 51. Arora has a fuller explanation of the nature of ideal-type constructs.

30. Fred Riggs, for example, states that "it is clear that all contemporary states recognized by the United Nations have bureaucracies." *Frontiers of Development Administration*, p. 388.

31. Joseph LaPalombara, "An Overview of Bureaucracy and Political Development," in Joseph LaPalombara, ed., *Bureaucracy and Political Development* (Princeton, N.J.: Princeton University Press, 1963), p. 7.

32. *Ibid.*
33. Morstein Marx, "The Higher Civil Service as an Action Group in Western Political Development," *ibid.*, p. 63.
34. Dwight Waldo, *Comparative Public Administration: Prologue, Problems, and Promise* (Chicago: Comparative Administration Group, American Society for Public Administration, 1964), p. 24.
35. Arora, *Comparative Public Administration*, p. 37.
36. Jong Jun, "Renewing the Study of Comparative Administration: Some Reflections on the Current Possibilities," *Public Administration Review* 36, No. 6 (1976): 641-47, at p. 644.
37. Lee Sigelman, "In Search of Comparative Administration," *Public Administration Review* 36, No. 6 (1976): 621-25, at p. 624.
38. Brian Chapman, *The Profession of Government* (London: George Allen & Unwin, 1959), pp. 48-61.
39. For a comprehensive treatment of patterns of organization as they have developed in various countries, see Poul Meyer, *Administrative Organization: A Comparative Study of the Organization of Public Administration* (London: Stevens & Sons, 1957).
40. The current record may be held by Nepal, with only six ministries in 1976.
41. Merle Fainsod, *How Russia Is Ruled*, rev. ed. (Cambridge: Harvard University Press, 1964), p. 333.
42. John M. Gaus, *Reflections on Public Administration* (University, Ala.: University of Alabama Press, 1947).
43. *Ibid.*, pp. 8-9.
44. See, for example, Fred W. Riggs, *The Ecology of Public Administration* (Bombay: Asia Publishing House, 1961); and "Trends in the Comparative Study of Public Administration," *International Review of Administrative Sciences* 28, No. 1 (1962): 9-15.
45. R. K. Arora, *Comparative Public Administration* (New Delhi: Associated Publishing House, 1972), p. 168. The subtitle of Arora's book is *An Ecological Perspective.*
46. *Ibid.*, p. 175.
47. Milton J. Esman, "The Politics of Development Administration," in John D. Montgomery and William J. Siffin, eds., *Approaches to Development: Politics, Administration & Change* (New York: McGraw-Hill Book Company, 1966), p. 59. Copyright © 1966.
48. For a fuller discussion of this application of the structural–functional approach, see Riggs, *Administration in Developing Countries*, pp. 19-27.
49. A favorite statement is that of Karl Deutsch: "We are using models, willing or not, whenever we are trying to think systematically about anything at all." In "On Communications Models in the Social Sciences," *Public Opinion Quarterly* 16, No. 3 (1952): 356.
50. The most complete and comprehensive formulation is in his *Administration in Developing Countries*. A more recent up-dated presentation, including a number of clarifications and modifications, is in *Prismatic Society Revisited* (Morristown, N.J.: General Learning Press, 1973).

51. The following sentence gives a hint about the terminological innovation: "We have seen how the inefficiency of the sala is reinforced by the price indeterminacy of the bazaar-canteen, by pariah entrepreneurship and intrusive access to the elite, by the agglomeration of values, by strategic spending and strategic learning as instruments of elite recruitment, by poly-communalism and poly-normativism, by double-talk, blocked throughputs, bifocalism and equivocacy, by the dependency syndrome, interference complex, and the formalism effect." *Administration in Developing Countries*, p. 284.

52. *Ibid.*, pp. 23-24. This relationship between model name and structural characteristics is given incorrectly on p. 23, correctly on p. 24.

53. Riggs, *Prismatic Society Revisited*, pp. 7-8. These illustrations are adapted from those used by Riggs.

54. *Ibid.*, p. 7.

55. Riggs, *Administration in Developing Countries*, p. 401.

56. Riggs, *Prismatic Society Revisited*, p. 8.

57. Riggs, *Administration in Developing Countries*, p. 99.

58. *Ibid.*, p. 33.

59. Riggs, *Prismatic Society Revisited*, pp. 24-5.

60. Riggs, *Administration in Developing Countries*, p. 268.

61. *Ibid.*, p. 424. These themes are developed primarily in "Bureaucratic Power and Administrative Prodigality," Chapter 8, pp. 260-85.

62. Arora, *Comparative Public Administration*, pp. 121-23.

63. Michael L. Monroe, "Prismatic Behavior in the United States?" *Journal of Comparative Administration* 2, No. 2 (1970): 229-42.

64. E. H. Valsan, "Positive Formalism: A Desideratum for Development," *Philippine Journal of Public Administration* 12, No. 1 (1968): 3-6.

65. R. S. Milne, "Formalism Reconsidered," *Philippine Journal of Public Administration* 14, No. 1 (1970): 21-30. "Given the existence of a divergence between personal goals and organizational goals, it is possible to create institutional arrangements so that the official's pursuit of self-interest may at the same time promote organizational goals." *Ibid.*, p. 27. Although such "positive formalism" cannot be expected to occur very often in developing countries, Milne suggests that it be practiced as much as is practicable.

66. Riggs, *Administration in Developing Countries*, p. 241.

3
CONCEPTS OF SYSTEM TRANSFORMATION

The close linkage between the study of comparative politics and the study of comparative public administration has already been pointed out, as has the fact of disagreement among students of comparative politics concerning key concepts relating to modifications over time in the characteristics of political systems. Because of the extreme importance of these issues to our concerns with the administrative aspects of these systems, this chapter is devoted to an exploration of concepts usually discussed under terms such as modernization, development, or change.

To begin, it must be recorded that the literature on these matters has now grown to be enormous. No attempt at exhaustive treatment of it is made here. Moreover, standardization of terminology has not occurred, so that use of the same words by different commentators may give an appearance of agreement that further analysis shows to be wrong. This lack of standardization also forces upon us a choice as to what terms to use and what meanings to attach to them.

This cluster of concepts does represent, however, a sharing of some basic interests on the part of students of political systems. They are seeking to explain variations on a comparative and chronological basis among nation-states. These concepts have in common the twin goals of comprehensiveness and realism. Comprehensiveness here means global scope with a time dimension, embracing as a minimum political systems which qualify as nation-states, and permitting historical, contemporary, and futuristic treatment of them. Realism means ability to explain what has happened, is happening, or may happen in terms that go beyond a descriptive institutional approach to emphasize the dynamics of political transformation.

Conceptualization along these lines is an integral part of the dramatic revolution in comparative political studies since the end of World War II, and therefore reflects stages in the growth of these studies, with more recent writers building upon or dissenting from what earlier ones have had to say. The focus is on major societal transformations involving a complex of social, economic, and political factors. For our purposes, treatment of these attempts can be grouped, in an order that is chronological to some extent but not completely, under the broad headings of modernization, development, and change.

Modernization

Modernization is in one sense the most comprehensive of these terms, but it is also, as we shall see, the most culture and time bound. Daniel Lerner describes modernization as a "systemic" process involving complementary changes in the "demographic, economic, political, communication, and cultural 'sectors' " of a society.[1] Modernity may presumably be thought of in terms of the society as an entity, or it may be segmented into phases such as economic or political. As Inkeles and Smith have stated, the term "modern" has "many denotations and carries a heavy weight of connotations."[2] The word, taken literally, refers to "anything which has more or less recently replaced something which in the past was the accepted way of doing things." Scholars, in attempting to give the term more specificity with reference to the nation-state, have included as defining features of modernity such manifestations as "mass education, urbanization, industrialization, bureaucratization, and rapid communication and transportation." Inkeles and Smith go on to point out that "the more or less simultaneous manifestation of these forms of social organization *as a set* certainly was not observed in any nation before the nineteenth century, and became really widespread only in the twentieth." Therefore, modernity may be conceived of as "a form of civilization characteristic of our current historical epoch, much as feudalism or the classical empires of antiquity were characteristic of earlier historical eras. Just as feudalism was not present in all the world in the eleventh to the fifteenth centuries, so modernity is not found everywhere on the globe. And just as feudalism did, so modernity varies in accord with local conditions, the history of a given culture, and the period when it was introduced. Within these limits, however, there exists a syndrome of characteristics, readily recognized at both the national and international level, which marks the modern."[3]

Sometimes modernization is described in somewhat more generalized language, but the context makes it clear that the reference point is the same. For example, Monte Palmer states that modernization "refers to the process of moving toward that idealized set of relationships posited as *modern*." However, he also indicates that "the term *modern* will be used to refer to an *idealized* pattern of social, economic, and political arrangements that is yet to be achieved but is approximated by the world's more economically developed states."[4]

In other words, this orientation centers on a relatively recent and still ongoing historical process, whether the word modernization is used or some substitute, such as development, with the same meaning. Whatever may be the hazards of defining modernization generically, there is much less uncertainty about what people who commonly refer to modernization actually do have in mind: the political systems, and the interrelated economic and social systems, that are actually found in a limited number of nation-states. Diamant states that "it should not be necessary to define precisely what is meant by modernization, except to say it is the sort of transformation which we have come to know in Europe and North America and in less complete forms in other parts of the world."[5] As Edward Shils comments, these states of Western Europe, North America, and the English-speaking dominions of the British Commonwealth "need not *aspire* to modernity. They *are* modern. It has become part of their nature to be modern and indeed what they are is definitive of modernity. The image of the Western countries, and the partial incorporation and transformation of that image in the Soviet Union, provide the standards and models in the light of which the elites of the unmodern new states of Asia and Africa seek to reshape their countries."[6] Eisenstadt likewise asserts that political modernization can be equated historically with "those types of political systems which developed in Western Europe from the seventeenth century and which spread to other parts of Europe, to the American continent, and, in the nineteenth and twentieth century, to Asian and African countries."[7]

In this perspective, the evolution of political and administrative institutions in Western Europe becomes of crucial importance not only to the nation-states that have taken shape there, but also to the other countries that have already modernized or developed politically, and to the scores of nations both old and new that strive toward modernization. As Reinhard Bendix says, "today we face a world in which the expansion of European ideas and institutions has placed the task of nation-building on the agenda of most countries, whether or not they are ready to tackle the job."[8] The political system these countries have sought in large measure to emulate is one which had its origins in Western Europe. The principal features connected with modernization in a political system were developed there. Political modernization in this sense (like industrialization) can be initiated only once.[9] Hence the experience continues to be significant to both "developed" and "developing" societies, even though every polity evolves along a path of its own.

Despite the obvious relevance of modernization thus viewed to the actualities of historical events in recent decades, Western scholars have been troubled by the ethnocentric nature of this approach, a feeling which has been more than shared by their non-Western colleagues. This led fairly early to attempts at formulation of models of modernization that were less openly tied to the examples of particular countries in Europe and North America. A notable example from the literature of comparative administration is the essay published in 1957 by Fred W. Riggs, entitled "Agraria and Industria—Toward a Typology of Comparative Administration,"[10] in which he proposed to establish "ideal or hypothetical models of public administration in agricultural and industrial societies"[11] to provide a basis for empirical analysis of administrative systems. Useful as this effort was at the time, Industria turned out to be descriptive of the United States in all significant respects, and Agraria matched closely the characteristics of Imperial China, as Riggs himself later acknowledged. Moreover, the implication was that the process of modernization was unilinear, from Agraria to Industria, with some kind of historical imperative moving actual societies from one model toward the other.[12]

All these, and many other formulations which could be mentioned, share the tendency to equate modernization with emulation of a few existing nation-states. They take as given that the elites of modernizing societies strongly desire to bring about societal transformations that will make them as much as possible like the modern prototype, as soon as possible. Modernization is to be measured by the degree of actual achievement of this objective.

With this treatment in mind, Joseph LaPalombara argued as long ago as 1963 that the concept was a "serious pitfall" and suggested that its use be suspended, at least for the time being. His objections took three forms. First, he was disturbed by the confusion caused by the tendency to substitute economic system or social system for political system, particularly when this leads to the implication that a "modern" political system is one that exists in a highly industrialized society, with high per capita output of goods and services. Second, he argued that the concept is "often implicitly and perhaps unintentionally" normative, using an Anglo-American standard for modernity. Third, he thought that such a term suggests "a deterministic, unilinear theory of political evolution," whereas change in political systems should be viewed as "neither evolutionary nor inevitable."[13]

Going beyond the points mentioned by LaPalombara, note that little attention is given in this approach to speculation, prediction, or prescription as to the future of nation-states that are already considered modernized. How they may evolve in coming years is an unfaced question. The impression might even be that these modernized societies have reached a condition of near perfection which leads to regarding further modification as likely to be harmful and retrogressive. The future lies in limbo or in a state of suspended animation. The only benchmark is the modernized society of today, to be maintained by those societies which have arrived at that point, and to be achieved by those which have not.

Linked with the obvious deficiency of seeming to ignore the inevitable future, modernization so conceived labors under a semantic difficulty. The primary dictionary definition of the word "modern" is "of, pertaining to, or characteristic of the present or most recent past; contemporary." If modernization is defined in terms of the characteristics of certain contemporary societies, this seems to be equivalent to redefinition by confining what is modern to what is characteristic of the present. At the very least, if accepted, this imposes an obligation on coming generations of word coiners to devise a new term for what will be contemporary then rather than now.

Development

A second group of analysts seeks to escape from these dilemmas by avoiding a definition that centers on what is, and instead focuses on a condition or set of conditions that may or may not exist in a particular political system or society at a particular time. Although the term they use is not always the same, I have chosen to discuss this orientation under the label of "development."

Development, like modernization, is widely employed without having acquired an agreed-upon meaning. Uphof and Ilchman refer to it as "probably one of the most depreciated terms in social science literature, having been used vastly more than it has been understood."[14] According to Joseph J. Spengler, development in general takes place "when an index of that which is deemed desirable and relatively preferable increases in magnitude."[15] More than in the case of modernization, development tends not to be discussed in total societal terms, but to be segmented into phases such as economic or political development.

The economists have vigorously pursued the study of "development" or "growth" economics. Economic development is understood to entail "the diversion of a nation's scarce resources and productive powers to the augmentation of its stock of productive wealth and to the progressive enlargement of its gross and net national product of goods and services."[16] The objective may be stated in aggregate or in per capita terms, so that an index of accomplishment is readily available, whatever may be the problems associated with securing accurate economic data or with designing strategy for economic development. Among economists, disagreements have not been so much over the concept of economic development as over the means of accomplishing it, with growing divergence of views as to obstacles to economic development and strategies for overcoming them. The earlier optimistic belief that there is a common road toward economic growth, expressed for example in *The Stages of Economic Growth* by W. W. Rostow,[17] has given way to much more pessimistic explanations and prognostications, illustrated by the work of Raul Prebisch of the Economic Commission for Latin America and numerous other Latin American economists in recent years.[18]

Among political scientists, on the other hand, the very concept of political development has been assigned various meanings and has been a cause of dispute.[19]

As already indicated, political development has sometimes been used as the equivalent of political modernization, subject as a result to the same objections. Most formulations, however, have endeavored to avoid the kind of pitfalls mentioned by LaPalombara, at least by trying to identify characteristics of political development rather than simply pointing to specific nation-states as being politically developed. This is so for nearly all of the ten major meanings of political development enumerated by Pye in 1966, the exception being the one which considers political development to be the same as political modernization, in the sense of Westernization. However, Pye found most of the other meanings to be partial, insufficient, or overly value-laden. His own inclination was to stress the importance of increasing political capability and the interlinkage of political development with other aspects of social change as a multidimensional process.

In their review of the literature on political development from the early 1960s through 1975, Huntington and Dominguez commented that definitions "proliferated at an alarming rate," partly because the term had positive connotations for political scientists. Hence, they "tended to apply it to things that they thought important and/or desirable," using it to perform "a legitimating function rather than an analytical function." According to these authors, the term was used in four different general ways: geographical, derivative, teleological, and functional. Geographical means simply a shorthand way of referring to the politics of developing countries in Asia, Africa, and Latin America, and in this sense political development has no specific content or characteristics except that it has to do with poorer and less industrialized countries. Derivative usage links political development to the broader process of modernization, and often identifies political development with political modernization, as already mentioned. The concern is with "the transition from a traditional, agrarian society to a modern, industrial one." This approach is the one given most attention by Huntington and Dominguez themselves, who state that insofar as any one definitional approach has priority in their treatment, it is "political development conceived as the political consequences of modernization."

In the teleological case, political development is defined as "movement toward one or more goals or states of being for the political system." The goals may be single or multiple. If multiple, attainment of one may have to be at the cost of another. This list is offered as illustrative of the diversity of goals mentioned: "democracy, stability, legitimacy, participation, mobilization, institutionalization, equality, capability, differentiation, identity, penetration, distribution, integration, rationalization, bureaucratization, security, welfare, justice, liberty." Obviously, there is no commonalty among these goals, except that they reflect value preferences of the political scientists who selected them.

The functional approach as understood here is movement toward a certain kind of political system, toward "the politics characteristic of a modern, industrial society." For example, political parties may be considered as a functional necessity in such a society, making the evolution of political parties an important aspect of political development. In this sense, political development is not derivative of the modernization process. It does not consist of "the political consequences of modernization" but rather refers to "the political requisites for an effectively functioning modern society."[20]

As Huntington and Dominguez comment, discussions on political development often "focus more on development *toward* what than on development *of* what."[21] The teleological and functional approaches share in concentrating on the specification of characteristics for a developed political system. Indeed, functional political development seems to be only a special application of the teleological approach.

For our purposes, it will be worthwhile to describe several of the formulations which have been influential as descriptions of the prerequisites of a developed political system. Certainly one of the most fully elaborated of these is the contribution of Almond and Powell.[22] Political development, in their view, is the consequences of events which may come from the international environment, from the domestic society, or from political elites within the political system itself. Whatever the source, these impulses "involve some significant change in the magnitude and content of the flow of inputs into the political system."[23] When the political system as it exists is unable to cope with the problem or challenge confronting it, development occurs if the system has capabilities for successful adaptation to meet the challenge. Otherwise, the result will be retrogression or "negative development."

Four types of problems or challenges are identified which put an existing political system under such a strain. The first is the problem of state-building, referring to a requirement of increased penetration and integration of the system. The second is nation-building, requiring greater loyalty and commitment to the system. Participation is the third problem, calling for response to pressure from groups for a part in decision-making within the political system. The fourth problem of distribution or welfare calls for employment of the coercive power of the political system to redistribute "income, wealth, opportunity, and honor." State-building is essentially a structural problem, whereas nation-building emphasizes the cultural aspects of political development. Participation demands lead to growth of the political infrastructure of political cliques, factions, and parties, and representative legislative assemblies, and to the increase of competence in political bargaining among groups in the system. The problem of distribution leads to an expansion in the control or influence of the political system in the allocation of resources among elements of the population.

Almond and Powell suggest five factors which affect the process of political development and help explain variations among systems. The first is whether the problems come successively or cumulatively. The political systems of Western Europe, as they evolved, met these problems in the sequence listed. "By and large, state and nation building occurred before the nations of Western Europe had to confront the problems of participation and welfare."[24] This contrasts sharply with the predicament of developing nations which must meet several or all of these challenges simultaneously. A second factor is the resources available to the system, and a third is whether or not other systems of the society develop in step with the political system. A fourth is the extent to which the existing system is geared for change and adaptation, which may determine whether it can respond to new demands successfully. Finally, the creativity or stagnation of political elites may be a decisive factor in the ability of the system to accommodate.

These authors stress functionalism in their comparative framework for the study of political systems and use a threefold classification of functions as important for political analysis. These different levels of functioning are capabilities, conversion functions, and system maintenance and adaptation functions. Capabilities have to do with the way a system performs as a unit in its environment, and these are discussed under the headings of extractive, regulative, distributive, symbolic, and responsive capabilities. Conversion functions transform inputs into outputs, according to a sixfold scheme consisting of interest articulation, interest aggregation, rule-making, rule application, rule adjudication, and communication. Finally, system maintenance and adaptation functions consist of the twin concepts of political recruitment and political socialization.

Without trying to trace the analysis in detail, the conclusion of Almond and Powell is that political development, in accordance with these variables, is a cumulative process of (1) role differentiation, (2) subsystem autonomy, and (3) secularization.

In our treatment of political structure we have emphasized role differentiation and subsystem autonomy as criteria of development, and in our treatment of political culture and socialization we have stressed the concept of secularization as a criterion of development. Similarly, in our treatment of the conversion process of politics, the themes of differentiation, structural autonomy, and secularization have served to distinguish the varieties of ways in which these functions are performed. In our treatment of the capabilities of political systems we have argued that particular levels and patterns of system performance are associated with levels of structural differentiation, autonomy and secularization. Finally, our classification of political systems is a developmental one in which the variables of structural differentiation, autonomy, and secularization are related to other aspects of the functioning of particular classes of political systems — their conversion characteristics, capabilities, and system maintenance patterns.[25]

In connection with structural differentiation, these authors predict that "higher capabilities depend upon the emergence of 'rational' bureaucratic organizations. . . .a system cannot develop a high level of internal regulation, distribution, or extraction without a 'modern' governmental bureaucracy in one form or another. . . . Likewise, the development of something like a modern interest-group or party system seems to be the prerequisite to a high development of the responsive capability."[26]

Another influential study is a product of the Committee on Comparative Politics of the Social Science Research Council, growing out of a workshop sponsored by the Committee. *Crises and Sequences in Political Development*, edited by Leonard Binder, with five other contributors, reduces political development to three key concepts: equality, capacity, and differentiation.[27] Collectively, these are called the "development syndrome."[28]

In this schema, differentiation refers to "the process of progressive separation and specialization of roles, institutional spheres, and associations undergoing modernization."[29] The assumption is made that "the more highly developed a political system becomes, the greater will be its structural complexity and the larger the number of explicit and functionally specific administrative and political structures it will have."[30]

The concept of equality in connection with political development has three components: (1) national citizenship (2) a universalistic legal order and (3) achievement norms. Citizenship rights in the nation-state provide basic equality for members of the political community. Realization of the equal rights of citizenship in turn is dependent on the prevalence of universalistic over particularistic norms, which assure equality before the law as to both legal privileges and deprivations. Achievement norms must predominate over ascriptive norms in recruitment for and allocation to political and bureaucratic roles in the system, so that individuals will be assured of equality of initial opportunity and can then demonstrate their fitness for assignment to the more highly valued roles in the stratified society.

Capacity denotes attributes that are "integrative, responsive, adaptive, and innovative," with the ability "not only to overcome the divisions and manage the tensions created by increased differentiation, but to respond to or contain the participatory demands generated by the imperatives of equality."[31] It includes a capacity to innovate, to manage continuous change, and to adapt, but it goes beyond being just a "survival" or "adaptive" capacity. It must be "creative." Such a creative capacity must include the attributes of scope, effectiveness, and rationality. Scope is reflected in a large volume and wide range of decision-making. To be effective, there must be a capability to attain the goals decided upon. Rationality must predominate in governmental decision-making for such performance to be realized. Historically, this rationalization of government has been marked by "the emergence of a centralized civil bureaucracy staffed by personnel whose recruitment and status mobility are governed by achievement norms, and whose decisions reflect what Weber termed *formal* rationality (i.e., procedural formalization and the consistency of principle in decision-making). The peculiarly modern feature of this development is not the existence of centralized bureaucracy. Rather it is the predominance, pervasiveness, and institutionalization of a rational-secular orientation in political and administrative processes. This orientation is an absolutely indispensable ingredient in the creative capacity of a developing polity."[32]

The development syndrome consisting of these three basic dimensions is a combination of congruences and contradictions. The three elements in the syndrome are at the same time congruent and interdependent, and incongruent and potentially conflictive. "Because of these inherent contradictions among the elements of the development syndrome, the process of development and modernization must be regarded as interminable. We cannot logically envisage a state of affairs characterized at once by total equality, irreducible differentiation, and absolute capacity. Moreover, not only is development interminable, but the course it takes in concrete polities is extremely variable and unpredictable."[33]

Patterns of political development in the newly developing countries are of primary concern to this group of scholars, and they direct their main attention to crises of political development faced by these polities with a degree of intensity not imposed on nation-states that emerged earlier. Five of these crisis-type issues are suggested, and then analyzed in the light of the three components of the development syndrome.

The five are crises of identity, legitimacy, participation, penetration, and distribution. Since not all are self-explanatory, some brief commentary is needed. The identity crisis refers to the subjective basis of membership in a political community, to "the tension between the culturally and psychologically determined sense of personal-group identity and the political definition of the community."[34] In the modern polity, subjective identity and objective political identifications need to coincide. "The identity crisis is not the crisis of any country necessarily, but it is a crisis of our era."[35]

The crisis of legitimacy has to do with the change in the nature of the ultimate authority to which political obligation is owed, essentially a shift from the transcendental to the immanent, a decline of the sacred character of political legitimacy and the spread of nation-state claims to legitimacy.

Participation represents "the most apparent and ubiquitous form in which contemporary political change has occurred."[36] It refers to involvement in the political process, appearing with an increase in the number of persons participating. It is manifested not only in extension of the suffrage and the growth of political parties and mass movements, but also in many developing societies through such devices as the politicization of caste and ethnic groups, strikes, and political demonstrations. Mass participation, when citizens have a limited capacity to participate knowledgeably, may reduce the effectiveness of governmental operations. In addition to methods of direct representation, a supplemental method of meeting participation needs is through encouraging the activity of secondary interest associations, which may be helpful by diffusing what would otherwise be detrimental effects of direct participation.

The problem of penetration concerns the relations between the political community and its environment, characterized by growth in recent times in the depth and extent of political control, reaching into social structures that were previously insulated and into geographical areas previously inaccessible.

The crisis of distribution is linked to the so-called revolution of rising expectations, and to the demand for governmental intervention to acccomplish increases in the standard of living and more equitable allocation of available transferable resources. Allocative responsibility of this sort obviously places severe requirements on the planning skills and structures of distribution of the political system.

These categories are efforts to provide a framework for the analysis of potential crises. "They need not become crises, and there need not be five of them, although historically they often do become crises and few of the five are avoided. . . . Each is an area of possible conflict."[37] The bulk of the volume is devoted to separate articles that deal with each of these crises, plus a contribution by Sidney Verba on a sequential model for their occurrence.[38] Verba's essay mainly raises questions which need to be answered before such a model is possible, but he does agree with Almond and Powell that the overlapping or accumulation of problems makes each harder to solve, and that this is the common predicament faced by the newer nations.

The treatment by Binder and his associates is an example of defining political development in terms of the functional requisites of a modern or developed political system. As Binder says, "the idea of political development is that in modern systems identity will be politicized, legitimacy will be based in part on performance, governments will be capable of mobilizing national resources, the majority of the adult population will be participant citizens, political access will be ubiquitous, and material allocations will be rational, principled, and public."[39]

Numerous other authors could be cited who have offered their own variations on the theme of the key characteristics found in developed polities. Harry Eckstein has explored dimensions for ascertaining whether the political performance of a system is adequate.[40] He proposes four that satisfy his criteria: durability, civil order, legitimacy, and decisional efficacy.[41] Roger W. Benjamin also argues that any systematic explanation of political development must employ some method of measurement of system characteristics and performance. However, he chooses different key dimensions of political development as a process: political participation, political institutionalization, and national integration. The process, he believes, "may be viewed as a historically identifiable set of political changes associated with the onset of industrialization in any given society."[42] His own study is a comparative analysis involving Japan, India, and Israel.

Monte Palmer asserts that the challenge of political development is "to create a system of political institutions capable of controlling the state's population, of mobilizing the state's human and material resources towards the ends of economic and social modernization, and of coping with the strain of social, economic, and political change without abdicating its control and mobilization roles. States in which the political system has met this challenge over a substantial period of years will be considered politically developed."[43] The importance of institutions in managing conflict is accorded similar stress by Powelson, who points out that this capacity "requires national consensus on an economic and a political ideology. These ideologies are defined as the ways in which individuals envisage the economic and political systems—how they operate, and how just they are. Ideological consensus in turn is fostered by a popular nationalism, which therefore plays a positive role in growth rather than the negative one usually attributed to it by economists."[44]

Needler views political development from both formal and contemporary substantive aspects. Formally, he regards political development as "the process of transition from one stable equilibrium state of the polity to another, with stability conceived of as the regular functioning of the polity in accordance with the norms it posits for itself." In the contemporary world, political development can be regarded as "the extension of the polity to include the maximum number of participants in political processes on terms of equality." The two dimensions in which political development can take place today are the attainment of constitutional integrity and participation on terms of equality.[45]

Helio Jaguaribe presents one of the most interesting recent comprehensive theories of political development.[46] He reviews the earlier literature in a different way from Huntington and Dominguez, making a twofold classification of it. Writers of his first group understand political development as political modernization. Although their meanings vary considerably, they agree that in terms of a process that is "historically situated," modernization basically designates "the transformation of the Western societies since the eighteenth century and, under the influence of that process, the transformation of other societies, such as the Russian with the enlightened czars and the Communists, the Japanese with the Meiji restoration, and the contemporary societies gradually or suddenly emerging from traditionalism."[47] This description corresponds closely, of course, to our previous review of writings under the heading of "modernization," although Jaguaribe includes in this group some scholars whose work we have referred to in this section on development.

Jaguaribe's second group includes those who understand political development as political institutionalization, again with various interpretations as to meaning. He regards the referents of political institutionalization as political mobilization, political integration, and political representation, but points out that former writers have tended to use only one of them. He includes Pye and Karl W. Deutsch[48] in this group, but regards Huntington as the most noteworthy advocate of political development as "the institutionalization of political organizations and procedures."[49] According to Huntington, institutionalization and hence political development take place when the political process goes in the direction of adaptability, complexity, autonomy, and coherence, as against their polar opposites of rigidity, simplicity, subordination, and disunity.

In his own theory, Jaguaribe attempts to build upon the work of these two schools of thought by proposing a formulation of political development as political modernization plus political institutionalization. He considers that Pye[50] and Apter,[51] although using different terms and categories, substantially share the same conceptual frame, and that Myron Weiner[52] and Irving Horowitz[53] do also at least partially.

This theory, abbreviated PD = M + I, is elaborated on by Jaguaribe in great detail.[54] He defines the component of political modernization as the process of increasing the operational variables of a polity, and identifies three of them: rational orientation, structural differentiation, and capability. For each of these operational variables, he identifies subvariables, suggests measures of quantitative and qualitative variation, and points out resulting variables in the political system. For example, rational orientation as an operational variable is subdivided into decision rationality and implementing rationality. Decision rationality is measurable by the extent, accuracy, and rational use of information by the political system, and by the degree of consistency of decisions. An increase in decision rationality results in more secularization in the political system. Similarly, measures of implementing rationality are given as the degree of consistency of action, of control of results, and of achievement of self-awareness. An increase results in more controllability in the system.

The component of political institutionalization is defined as the process of increasing the participational variables of a polity. Three of them are proposed also: political mobilization, political integration, and political representation. For each, the same analysis is offered of breakdown into subvariables, identification of measures of variation, and indication of resulting variables in the political system from an increase in the participational variable. For instance, under political mobilization, one of the subcategories is political socialization, measured by the degree, accuracy, and congruence of members' participation in the political culture, and resulting in increased politicalization in the political system.

When fully laid out, Jaguaribe's model provides a grid for comparative analyses of political systems, linked to these twin basic components of modernization and institutionalization. The net effect of the modernization increments, in his view, is "an increasing command, by the political system, over its environment and its decreasing dependence on casual favorable circumstances." An evolutionary advance occurs, because the system is better able to exploit utilizable resources for its own ends. The net effect of the institutionalization increments, on the other hand, is "an increasing consensuality in the political system, resulting from an increasing correspondence between individual and collective goals and individual and collective decisions, with a consequent decrease in the necessity for, and actual use of, coercive means in the polity." The consequence of increasing consensus and decreasing coercion is again a better use of available energy and resources for the system's ends, because part of the system does not have to impose itself on the rest.[55]

Another crucial point made by Jaguaribe is that political modernization and political institutionalization are closely interrelated, and that political development requires an appropriate balance between the two. A pronounced imbalance in the form of a high level of modernization and a low level of institutionalization makes the political system dependent on the successful use of violence. He sees this as a characteristic of advanced fascist regimes such as Nazi Germany, as well as of current fascist regimes in semi-colonial and dependent countries and of the "ethnic fascism" of South Africa. An imbalance of the opposite kind, with a high level of institutionalization and a low level of modernization, adversely affects the operational capability of the political system. Participational variables, although indispensable for political development, cannot be sustained without sufficient political modernization. "The increase of the participational variables is not possible without the corresponding and supporting increase of the operational valuables [sic] of the same polity. An insufficiently modernized political system has neither the command of its environment to bear, for instance, high levels of political participation, mass-elite integration, and system legitimacy, nor the politico-juridical means for coordinating the decisions and performing and controlling the services required for such a purpose." In comparison to modern fascist societies, Jaguaribe points out, primitive societies have open and egalitarian regimes of participation for their members, and aristocratic traditional societies also have discriminating regimes of participation, but both types have much lower operational conditions than the fascist regimes.[56]

A final thesis of Jaguaribe's theory has to do with what he terms the three aspects of political development: (1) development of the capability of the political system, (2) development of the contribution of the political system to the overall development of the concerned society, and (3) development of the responsiveness of the political system. Any one of these taken alone, as he sees it, would be too restrictive a view. "Taken together, as cumulative aspects of political development, they correspond to the process as a whole." Capability refers to the effectiveness of the polity as a subsystem of the social system. The second aspect has to do with the development of the whole society by political means. Such promotion, to be feasible, is dependent on the fulfillment of two conditions: the appropriate change must be successfully introduced in the political system and it must be endurable there, and circumstances must be such that through use of the political system congruent changes can be achieved in the other systems of the society. The third aspect, responsiveness, has to do with the development of political consensus and of social consensus by political means.

Of these three aspects, Jaguaribe considers the development of the system's capability as a necessary precondition of the other two, and hence the "most general," and presumably the most basic, aspect of political development. Maximum general political development is achieved "when the concerned polity, besides maximizing its capability . . . , and besides contributing to the overall development of the society . . . , also achieves maximum political consensus and opens the way to maximum social consensus." This stage, however, is one "which no modern political system has ever achieved and which can only be viewed as an ideal type."[57]

Although overlapping in part and differing in part, all of these commentators on political development present versions that identify some combination of characteristics thought to be requisite for classification of a nation-state as politically developed. Many of them give a prominent or even pivotal role (as does Jaguaribe, for example) to a requisite variously labeled with terms such as capacity, capability, or sustained growth potential.

Some authorities have chosen to single out and emphasize this characteristic as itself definitive of political development. In doing this, they have been motivated both by conceptual preferences and by a desire to avoid some of the difficulties of too close an association of political development with the contemporary polities of a few highly industrialized Western societies. In some of his earlier writings, Gabriel Almond used "change" and "development" as synonyms, and formulated a thesis in terms of the performance capabilities of political systems, according to which political systems change or develop "when they acquire new capabilities in relation to their social and international environments." The criterion is "the acquisition of a new capability, in the sense of a specialized role structure and differentiated orientations which together give the political system the possibility of responding efficiently, and more or less autonomously, to a new range of problems."[58]

S. N. Eisenstadt and Alfred Diamant are leading proponents of this approach which equates political development with the ability of a political system to grow or adjust to new demands put upon it. Eisenstadt views sustained political growth as "the central problem of modernization" and says that "ability to deal with continuous change is the crucial test of this growth."[59] Diamant objects to any conception of political development that equates it with the process by which traditional political systems change "into certain forms of democracy as developed in what is loosely called the West," because such a conception "excludes as irrelevant the political experience of a large number of polities and might lead us to conclude that there has been no form of political development in most parts of the world outside Europe and a few sections of the American hemisphere." Hence he defines political development in its most general form as "a process by which a political system acquires an increased capacity to sustain successfully and continuously new types of goals and demands and the creation of new types of organizations."[60]

This formulation is intended to do several things. It avoids the suggestion that there are identifiable stages of political development or that development requires the creation of particular kinds of political institutions. It permits the possibility that traditional symbols and institutions may be successfully utilized for modernization. It implies nothing about eventual success or failure, since the process is not irreversible but can stop even after it has persisted for some time.

Commendably, these ways of understanding political development avoid too pronounced an identification with a Western democratic political system such as that of Great Britain or the United States. A different question may be raised about them, however, because they seem to come extremely close to equating political development with political survival. If political development or modernization is "a generic process of successfully sustaining new demands, goals, and organizations in a flexible manner,"[61] any political system that has managed to maintain its identity over a considerable period of time, particularly under conditions of challenge or stress of any magnitude, would seem to qualify as developed or modernized, whatever might be its characteristics as a political system—other than that it still exists. In other words, somewhat different problems may crop up unless we can distinguish between political modernity or development on the one hand, and political survival on the other. If this is not done, there is the hypothetical possibility, at least, of having to regard as developed political systems such as that of Great Britain, which made drastic political adaptations but responded incrementally over a long period of time; Communist China, which has attempted within a single generation the remolding of a society and its political life by revolutionary means; Ethiopia, which at least until recently[62] has maintained political identity for a very long time against a series of internal and external threats but with little modification of social institutions; and the remnants of a society that might successfully manage to maintain the rudiments of a political system following a nuclear holocaust. These political systems would seem to have in common the attribute of survival, rather than any other more definite characteristics of modernity or development.

Thus far, we have reviewed a variety of attempts to define or explain political development. Generally they have shared what might be called a positive orientation, in the sense that they have indicated what polities have achieved political development and why, or they have pointed toward requirements to be met by polities striving to become politically developed. The stress has been on the potentialities for movement from a less desirable to a more desirable general situation in the political system.

Another train of thought, particularly in more recent writings on political development, has concentrated on the more negative aspects of the subject, either by dealing with the circumstances that lead to movement away from rather than toward development, or by exploring the factors external or internal to political systems that hinder or inhibit development. Some of this attention has been given by scholars who also have discussed political development in general theoretical terms, but much of it comes from skeptics or critics of the bulk of writing on political development.

Samuel Huntington has provided the most penetrating analysis of breakdowns in political development, or "political decay."[63] His concern is to probe the conditions under which societies undergoing social and economic change that is rapid and disruptive can realize political stability. He thinks that the indices of political order or its absence are reasonably clear and even quantifiable, using forms of instability such as violence, riots, and insurrections. The overall record shows that whereas modernity means stability, the process of modernization breeds instability. Since World War II, with only a few exceptions, the modernizing countries of Asia, Africa, and Latin America have been characterized, in his words, by "increasing ethnic and class conflict, recurring rioting and mob violence, frequent military coups d'etat, the dominance of unstable personalistic leaders who often pursued disastrous economic and social policies, widespread and blatant corruption among cabinet ministers and civil servants, arbitrary infringement of the rights and liberties of citizens, declining standards of bureaucratic efficiency and performance, the pervasive alienation of urban political groups, the loss of authority by legislatures and courts, and the fragmentation and at times complete disintegration of broadly based political parties."[64]

Huntington proposes what he calls the "political gap" hypothesis as an explanation. He groups the aspects of modernization most relevant to politics into two broad categories: social mobilization and economic development. Social mobilization means a change in "the attitudes, values, and expectations of people" from those associated with the traditional world to those associated with the modern world, as a consequence of such factors as "literacy, education, increased communications, mass media exposure, and urbanization." Economic development refers to "the growth in the total economic activity and output of a society," measured by per capita gross national product, level of industrialization, and level of individual welfare gauged by indices such as life expectancy and caloric intake. "Social mobilization involves changes in the aspirations of individuals, groups, and societies; economic development involves changes in their capabilities. Modernization requires both."[65]

On the assumption that social mobilization is much more devastating than economic development, Huntington hypothesizes that the gap between these two forms of change furnishes a measure of the impact of modernization on political stability. Traditional man is exposed to new experiences in the process of social mobilization that promote new levels of wants and aspirations which transitional societies have difficulties in satisfying. Because the ability to

respond increases much more slowly than the wants, "a gap develops
between aspiration and expectation, want formulation and want
satisfaction, or the aspiration function and the level-of-living function. This gap generates social frustration and dissatisfaction. In
practice, the extent of the gap provides a reasonable index to political instability."[66]

This gap is manifested in phenomena such as income inequali-
ties, inflation, widespread corruption, and a widening spread between
the city and the countryside which in turn leads to unrest from the
rising urban middle class based on a belief that the society is still
dominated by the rural elite and often to a rural mobilization or
"Green Uprising" due to resentment of urban upthrust.

Although using somewhat different terminology, Huntington
makes the same point as Jaguaribe that political systems can be
distinguished by their levels of political institutionalization and
their levels of political participation, and that the stability of any
given polity is related to a proper relationship between these two
levels. Political stability, he argues, depends on the ratio of institutionalization to participation. "As political participation increases,
the complexity, autonomy, adaptability, and coherence of the
society's political institutions must also increase if political stability
is to be maintained." A crucial distinction must be made between
political systems with low levels of institutionalization and high
levels of participation, and those with high levels of institutionalization and low levels of participation. The latter, with a high ratio
of institutionalization to participation, Huntington terms "civic
polities." The former, he calls "praetorian polities." In these
systems, "social forces using their own methods act directly in the
political sphere." According to this analysis, civic or praetorian
societies may exist at various levels of political participation. One
society may have more highly developed political institutions than
another and also be more praetorian because it has a still higher level
of political participation.[67]

Many new states are institutionally deficient when they are
confronted with rapid social mobilization and increasing demands on
the political system. The expansion of political participation needs
to be accompanied by the development of strong, complex, and
autonomous political institutions, but the usual effect is to undermine traditional and obstruct the development of modern political
institutions. "Most societies, even those with fairly complex and
adaptable traditional political institutions, suffer a loss of community and decay of political institutions during the most intense phase

of modernization."[68] Huntington feels that this tendency toward political decay has been neglected in literature on modernization, and that concepts of modernization or development are as a result not as relevant as they should be to many of the countries that are hopefully considered to be modernizing or developing. In seeking clues as to which societies during the modernization process have better prospects of avoiding political decomposition, Huntington looks to the nature of their traditional political institutions. If these are weak or nonexistent, prospects are poor. If the bureaucratic structure is highly developed and autonomous, the nature of the structure will make adaptation to broader political participation hard, as shown by the highly centralized bureaucratic monarchies of China and France. Societies with more pluralistic feudal systems such as existed in England and Japan proved to be more able to absorb new middle class groups into the political system. These historical examples he considers instructive in assessing the prospects of contemporary modernizing states.

However, even if adaptation to middle class political participation is successful, the ultimate test is the expansion of participation to the urban working class and the rural peasantry to achieve "a fully participant, highly institutionalized modern polity." If institutional adjustment takes place, the result is in Huntington's terms a participant society. Otherwise, the outcome is a mass praetorian society. In either case, the societies have high levels of political participation, but they differ in how their political organizations and procedures are institutionalized. In the mass praetorian society, political participation is "unstructured, inconstant, anomic, and variegated. . . . The distinctive form of political participation is the mass movement combining violent and nonviolent, legal and illegal, coercive and persuasive actions. Mass society lacks organized structures which can relate the political desires and activities of the populace to the goals and decisions of their leaders." Popular involvement at a high level in the participant polity, on the other hand, "is organized and structured through political institutions. Each social force must transform its sources of power and forms of action . . . into those which are legitimate in and institutionalized in the political system. The structure of a participant polity may assume a variety of forms, and power may be dispersed or concentrated. In all cases, however, participation is broad and is organized and structured into legitimate channels." The political institutions of such a polity must be capable of organizing mass participation in politics. The distinctive institution of the modern polity for this purpose is the political party. Other political institutions in modern political systems are adapted or carried over from traditional political systems. Since 1800, political party development has paralleled the development of modern government. Where earlier political institutions continue to be the primary sources of continuity and legitimacy, parties play a secondary and supplemental role. Where the traditional political institutions collapse, or where they are weak or nonexistent, the role of the party is quite different. "In such situations, strong party organization is the only long-run alternative to the instability of a corrupt or praetorian or mass society. The party is not just a supplementary organization; it is instead the source of legitimacy and authority." The prerequisite for stability in these circumstances is "at least one highly institutionalized political party." He cites the examples of the emergence of one strong party in each case from the Chinese, Mexican, Russian, and Turkish revolutions.

From this perspective, modernization is dangerous and traumatic. It is very likely to lead to political breakdown and decay because political institutions are inadequate to respond to the new demands resulting from the expansion of political participation. The political party as an institution is the most promising device for avoiding political decay and gaining political order.[69]

A couple of subpoints in Huntington's presentation are of particular importance to us. One is that he does not equate popular participation in politics with popular control of government. In his definition of participant polities, both constitutional democracies and Communist dictatorships qualify. The United States and the USSR are each participant polities, although they arrived there by different routes, adopted very different forms of government, and assigned widely variant roles to the political party as an institution. Western liberal states and Communist totalitarian states fall in the same category because their polities share characteristics such as "consensus, community, legitimacy, organization, effectiveness, stability," and because their governments really govern. They have avoided political breakdown and have achieved political order.[70]

Related to this point, Huntington notes that one reason for the appeal of Communist and Communist-type movements in modernizing countries is that they can overcome the scarce supply of authority chronic in these societies.

History shows conclusively that communist governments are no better than free governments in alleviating famine, improving health, expanding national product, creating industry, and maximizing welfare. But the one thing communist governments can do is govern; they do provide effective authority.

Their ideology furnishes a basis of legitimacy, and their party organization provides the institutional mechanism for mobilizing support and executing policy. . . . They may not provide liberty, but they do provide authority; they do create governments that can govern. . . . communists offer modernizing countries a tested and proven method of bridging the political gap. Amidst the social conflict and violence that plague modernizing countries, they provide some assurance of political order.[71]

The same basic theme of disenchantment with the prospects of many transitional countries is sounded by Heeger in his recent book, *The Politics of Underdevelopment*.[72] These countries are seeking political order and political stability, but are frustrated because they discover that underdevelopment "threatens to become a permanent condition rather than a transitory stage."[73] Available data indicate that politics in the underdeveloped states is essentially "the politics of faction, coalition, maneuver, and personalism."[74] After exploring the sources of this widespread political instability and explanations given for it, Heeger summarizes by noting that the consistent answer to the question as to why underdeveloped states are unstable politically is that their political institutions lack the capability to deal with the consequences of social and economic change. The usual reaction is to make recommendations as to how the political institutions might improve in their capabilities and eventually provide the means for reaching a stable political equilibrium. Heeger doubts the feasibility of expecting this to happen, and develops the view that in these polities a more likely outcome is that "conflict—factional, communal, oppositional, armed—becomes the norm rather than an aberration."[75] He then examines in some detail what he calls "the politics of instability," giving particular attention to the role of the military when it gains political power, and to relations between the military and the civil bureaucracy. Contrary to other commentators who have found that military regimes might be useful in a transition to greater political stability, Heeger passes a negative judgment, saying that "in their denial of politics, such regimes only exacerbate the fragmentation of the underdeveloped political sytem."[76] Heeger's orientation, therefore, is far removed from those who view development as unilinear and inevitable, or who anticipate that in the future contemporary underdeveloped states will come to resemble closely current models of developed polities, whether they be of the Western liberal or Communist totalitarian varieties.

A sobering but somewhat less pessimistic appraisal is found in John Kautsky's *The Political Consequences of Modernization*.[77] This author also casts doubt on the assumption that there is any single path to political development, and he concurs that the politics of communism need not be divorced from but can be integrated with the broader subject of the politics of modernization. He perceives politics as group conflict, and is primarily interested in the political change that results from conflict. His analysis draws a sharp distinction historically between the processes of political change involved in modernization from within as contrasted with modernization from without. In either case, the politics of traditional societies is transformed, but modernization from within has native origins, is relatively slow, and involves continued predominance of the aristocracy. This is basically the way currently developed countries become modernized, but they are not likely to be models for countries that are now underdeveloped. These countries are caught up in the process of modernization from without, through such agents as colonialism, a modernizing aristocracy influenced from the outside, and foreign and native capital. The impact of modernization from without results in different effects on various segments of the traditional society, but the modernizing elements bring about revolutionary political change. Usually this is followed by postrevolutionary conflict among the modernizers, which often leads to the use of mass terror, regimentation, and persuasion, to the suppression of opposition, to drives for rapid industrialization, and to frequent changes in the group basis of the modernizing regimes. A condition of balance may or may not emerge eventually. If it does, it may be after a second-wave revolution of modernizers. Another prospect is an aristocratic reaction that may usher in a Fascist regime. If a balance that is persistent becomes established, then the prospects of the modernizing country markedly improve. The longer a balance lasts in the polity, the better become its chances for further survival.[78]

The overwhelming importance of external environmental factors forms the basic thesis of a school of social scientists who advocate a dependency theory of development. Originating among economists who were concerned with dependency aspects of economic development, this emphasis on dependency has been extended by sociologists to social development in general and by political scientists to political development in particular. Although they share this common orientation, these dependency social scientists offer a wide spectrum of philosophic backgrounds, geographical interests, and prescriptive recommendations. Some write from what is clearly an orthodox Marxist perspective; some do not. Many leaders in the elucidation of dependency points of view are Latin Americans, but others are social scientists from developing areas elsewhere in the world and some are located in countries considered developed, including the United States and other nations viewed as imposing dependency status abroad. The tendency is for younger social scientists to be well represented, including many from developing countries who were trained in educational institutions of developed countries, so that the movement is obviously in part a rebellion against an older generation of social scientists and against foreign education of domestic scholars.

The dominant note is that what is commonly called under-development is the consequence of a state of dependence by one society on another, and a secondary theme is that this dependency condition is repeated within the affected society by an internal colonialism which one segment of the society imposes on another segment. The net effect is a situation which allows little prospect for improvement without a drastic alteration of both the external environment and the internal system.[79]

In contrast to diffusion concepts which regard development as a positive process of importation or borrowing by less advanced from more advanced societies, dependency theorists believe that the impact of external factors is essentially negative, in the form of pressure and influence from "metropolitan" developed countries on "peripheral" developing countries. The distinguishing feature of the dependency model is that "growth in the dependent nations occurs as a reflex of the expansion of the dominant nations and is geared toward the needs of the dominant economies—i.e., foreign, rather than national needs."[80]

Writers with an orthodox Marxist or neo-Marxist interpretation tend to view this process as the historically inevitable outcome of "capitalistic imperialism," with the United States as the primary imposer of obstacles to autonomous development, and with Latin America as the prime example of a developing area fitting the dependency model. As Bodenheimer puts it, "European and U.S. development and Latin American underdevelopment are not two isolated phenomena, but rather two outcomes of the same historical process, the global expansion of capitalism."[81] Linked to this perspective is often a spirited attack on social science research methodology as it has evolved in the United States, particularly through the structural–functional approach, which is accused of serving as a tool of imperialistic capitalism by supporting the diffusion concept, by advocating the "end of ideology" as a means of promoting Western pluralism, by rationalizing the status quo, and by offering a generally distorted interpretation of the situation in the dependent countries.

Christian Bay claims that modern works in comparative politics, unlike other behavioral literature, "almost always focus on real political problems," but criticizes them for viewing behavior as dysfunctional "in terms of some conception or other of the public good; usually such conceptions are couched in terms of 'modernization' or 'development,' at least if comparisons are cross-cultural as well as cross-national. The point is that developmental perspectives and therefore political purposes are ever-present in this literature, even if they are not often well articulated."[82]

Other supporters of this basic thesis offer as an explanation the emergence since World War II of a new bipolar international system, replacing the international balance of power system stemming from the Napoleonic era. In this emerging "interimperial" system, the United States and the Soviet Union appear as the two superpowers, with the United States in a role of general primacy but with the Soviet Union holding a status in the present world order that is basically the same except that its primacy is less pervasive and more regionally focused. A few other nation-states (including Japan, China, and the nations of Western Europe as a group) at present enjoy autonomy in the sense of being able to make crucial domestic decisions and to resist overt aggression, or in other words, to maintain national viability in the interimperial system. The rest of the world is in a condition of dependency, including the older nation-states in Latin America and scattered here and there elsewhere, and the many newer nation-states of Asia and Africa. Some movement between categories is hypothesized before the end of the century, from autonomy to dependency and vice versa, but this would be quite limited and would not alter the outlook for most dependent countries. Another frequently noted aspect of this analysis is the developmental cleavage in the world between the north, where the superpowers and autonomous nation-states are mostly located, and the south, which has nearly all of the dependent countries. The distinction between capitalism and socialism, on the other hand, is either dropped or muted to secondary status, with both the United States as a capitalist democracy and the USSR as a socialist totalitarianism considered as being more alike than different because despite their ideological and regime variations, both as superpowers in the new imperial situation create conditions of dependency.

Dependency is often divided into subtypes based on substantive and chronological considerations. Historically, dependency began in the form of classic colonialism. After political independence, neocolonialism replaced classic colonialism as the dependency relationship. Jaguaribe describes the sequence this way: "The Iberian countries in the fifteenth century, followed by the Low Countries, England, and France, established, both with force and without, colonies in the Americas, Africa, and Asia. These colonies continued to serve the interests of the metropolitan countries after the industrial revolution, following the classic patterns of supplying raw materials and importing finished industrial goods. Unlike the independence of the American colonies, which was won in the eighteenth and early nineteenth centuries through effective military victories, most of the European ex-colonies in Africa and Asia have recently been granted independence. Far from expressing a process of decolonization, as has been so prematurely advanced, that independence only characterizes a change in the ways of exploitation." The advantages of strict colonial control came to be outweighed by the disadvantages to the colonial power, so neocolonialism replaced classic colonialism, but "the basic colonial relationship—the exchange of low-priced primary products and services for high-priced industrial goods and technical services—was maintained and enhanced."[83] Neocolonialism, according to this view, came first to Latin America, and this explains why the Latin American countries, despite their fairly long period of political independence, have not been able to achieve autonomous development.

Jaguaribe goes on to delineate two other forms of dependency now appearing or projected for the future. Satellite dependency involves first a shift from dependency on the former European colonial power to one of the new superpowers. For countries in the Western Hemisphere, that means dependency on the United States, except in the case of Cuba. For dependent countries elsewhere, the dependency may be on either the United States or the Soviet Union, according to circumstances. The second feature is "a change in the inherent nature of the dependency. It is no longer, basically, an unbalanced exchange of low-priced primary goods and high-priced industrial goods and services. It is, essentially, a financial, cultural, and political dependency. It consists in the growing flux of capital and technology from the metropolis to the satellite, together with the politico-military guardianship that maintains both the internal predominance of the local elite over its own mass and the intra-imperial dependence of the satellite on the metropolis."[84] This dependency transition is likely to occur unless the local elite chooses and is capable of managing autonomous development, as happened in Meiji Japan during the nineteenth century. The prospects for accomplishing this are low with perhaps a few exceptions, such as a semicontinental country like Brazil, or by groupings of Latin American countries.

Satellite dependency varies considerably as between paramount-cy of the United States and of the Soviet Union, as shown by the contrast between Latin America under U.S. hegemony, and Eastern Europe under the Soviet Union. The former "tends to be very broad, all-pervasive, internally co-opted by several domestic groups, but not externally unified, except in moments of crisis or over issues concerning very relevant strategic interests." The latter is "mono-lithic, in the sense of being externally unified and exercised in a basically coherent form, through tight and concentrated lines of command from government to government, and official party to official party. The extent of Soviet internal control, however, over the nonpolitical subsystems and groups of the dominated countries is very small or nonexistent and effectively contained by deliberate nationalist resistance."[85]

In the absence of autonomous development, Jaguaribe sees satellitism as also a self-exhausting process, and forecasts as a final stage what he calls provincial dependency, which does not now exist, but is likely to evolve as the future intraimperial form of depen-dency. In terms of the requirements of the metropolitan imperial power, it means optimizing the use and management of the resources of the "provinces." Drawing a parallel in historical practice from the Roman Empire, this would probably call for the suppression of the former local elites and direct rule by representatives of the imperial superpower. Also, as in the case of the Roman Empire, this process would be at the expense of the unskilled masses in the dependent areas, who would constitute "demographic surpluses" in a society where unskilled labor is not much needed, and would not be incorporated into the modern sectors of the system. Instead, these mass populations would be subjected to policies under provin-cial administration that would lead to their gradual reduction or extermination.[86]

This long-range scenario for the future of the contemporary nation-states of the developing world is a far cry from optimistic earlier prognostications that these societies were embarked on a road that would lead them after a period of trials and tribulations to a situation in which their societies would match very closely the characteristics of the limited number of currently developed countries. The only ray of hope held out is that some countries not enjoying superpower status are today able to pursue a course of autonomous development, and that others of the currently dependent nation-states may be able to achieve that option later, either singly in a few instances or in combination with other nation-states in the same geographical region.

As indicated earlier, the dependency theorists emphasize the overwhelming impact of the external environment on developing societies, and devote their main attention to an examination of the relationships between metropolitan and peripheral countries, but they also explore the resultant domestic societal characteristics within the dependent nations. They reject as myths several prevailing theses concerning the nature of these societies. Stavenhagen describes seven such generalizations: that these are dual societies with a modernized sector and a backward sector that has not yet caught up; that progress will be achieved by diffusion of the products of industrialism to backward and traditional zones; that the existence of traditional rural zones is an obstacle to development; that the new industrial and business elite is interested in breaking the dominant power position of the landholding oligarchy; that development is contingent upon the growth of a nationalistic, progressive, and dynamic middle class; that national integration is the product of racial intermixture; and that progress will be realized by means of an alliance between urban workers and the peasantry of the country-side.[87]

The counterinterpretation proposed consists of several propositions, the most important of which are the concepts of internal colonialism, stagnation, marginality, and denationalization. The notion of internal colonialism is basically that the international relationship of dominance by metropolitan over peripheral countries is repeated internally by a comparable dominance by domestic elitist groups linked to foreign governments and multinational corporations over submerged elements in the society unable to resist being kept in a status of internal dependency. As a result, the limited growth that does take place for the benefit of dominant groups is achieved at the expense of the mass of the population, both in the urban centers and in the countryside.[88]

Stagnation refers to the static character of the economies of Latin America and other underdeveloped areas, to the lack of achievement of a process of self-sustained growth. Underdevelopment, instead of being a temporary condition showing signs of improvement, tends in many countries to become continuing and persistent. Economic explanations offered for this relate to a long-range deterioration in terms of trade between areas such as Latin America and the developed countries, with the prices of the primary agricultural products and minerals being exported falling in relation to the prices of the finished industrial products being imported, creating a steadily decreasing capital-to-product ratio because the amount of exports has had to increase in order to keep imports at the same volume. This has led to a chronic deficiency in domestic capital formation, which has not been adequately compensated for by infusions of foreign capital. In recent years, these economies have tried to become less export-oriented, and the dependence on foreign trade has indeed dropped, but without achieving self-sustained growth within the domestic economy. Stagnation persists, and further deterioration threatens, because the gap separating the developing from the developed countries measured by per capita economic growth is increasing continuously, spurred in part by high rates of population growth.

The concept of marginality has come to mean basically the phenomenon of nonparticipation or very limited participation by large proportions of the people in underdeveloped countries in economic, social, and political activities beyond the most minimal levels. Used originally to refer to the inhabitants of a variety of substandard living quarters on the margins of principal cities, the term has now acquired this more generalized connotation. The situation has numerous aspects which cannot be explored here, but a few of the most important are the continuation of largely self-sufficient subsistence economies among indigenous populations with very little interest in or ability to purchase industrial goods, the extremely low agricultural productivity coupled with incapacity to provide employment to a huge segment of the rural labor force, and the rapidly growing unskilled jobless or underemployed population flooding into the big cities which contain a rising percentage of the total inhabitants. These marginal population groups have very little education, and they for the most part are either in rural areas or have recently been displaced by migration from the countryside to the congested urban centers. Estimates for Latin America as a whole are that countries suffer from having 30 to 80 percent of their populations neutralized by such marginality. In the judgment of Jaguaribe, even large countries such as Brazil and Mexico "are actually reduced to about 20 percent of their size by the marginal condition of most of the population."[89] He and other commentators view the combined phenomena of stagnation and marginality as mutually reinforcing and operating in a process of circular causation to drive the typical dependent country deeper into a corner of underdevelopment.

The process of denationalization is in turn seen as an impending consequence of these other factors. As described by Jaguaribe, it "consists in the actual transfer of control over relevant decisions or factors, and conditions affecting them, from actors loyal or favorable to a nation to actors loyal or favorable to another nation." It is, of course, closely related to his projection summarized earlier of movement from satellite to provincial dependency. "It is not relevant for the process of denationalization whether the processes occur de jure and in an official way (as in the cases of legal transference of control) or as a de facto situation, either in a deliberate or in a spontaneous way. Neither is it important whether the agents obtaining control are formally nationals of another country." What is essential is the effective exercise of control by agents who "are loyal to another nation and/or proceed in a way that actually tends to favor that nation." He discusses at some length three varieties of denationalization: economic, cultural, and politico-military. The economic aspect he links to suffocation of national mechanisms for generating free-floating resources, with transference of that crucial function to nonnational agents. In connection with cultural denationalization, special stress is placed on reliance upon foreign sources for scientific and technological knowledge. The politico-military dimension is related to the rise of military-controlled or -dominated governments, partly because of the failure to evolve viable and capable political systems, which governments have then chosen to combine authoritarianism with a policy of economic liberalism, thus accentuating economic and cultural denationalization as well.[90]

Aside from economic aspects, these hypotheses concerning dependency have not been the subject of much comparative empirical study. An exception is an examination by Sofranko and Bealer of the relationship between patterns of modernization and domestic instability in seventy-four countries.[91] These authors attempted to test the assumption that unevenness of development among the institutional sectors of a developing society is apt to exist, and that the degree of imbalance and the pattern which the imbalances assume have consequences for domestic instability. They gave primary concern to political, economic, and educational institutions. Contrary to expectations, their findings revealed "little, if any, relationship between magnitudes of imbalance for the political, economic and educational sectors considered singly and instability." However, when the notion of sectoral imbalance was invoked, relationships between particular patterns of imbalances and instability did emerge. Sofranko and Bealer summarized their findings by saying that "isolated disequilibria in a sector of society apparently need not be highly disruptive to the system. Conversely, widespread imbalances appear to have considerable impact on overall stability."[92]   Although this study does not deal with the question of the extent to which imbalances arise from outside sources, it does seem to confirm that patterns of widespread imbalances of the type alleged by dependency theorists to be imposed from without do exist, and that such extensive sectoral imbalances indeed have a negative impact on overall stability in developing societies.

As already mentioned, dependency theorists differ among themselves in various ways, including their views on what strategies ought to be followed by the leadership in dependent countries to cope with current dependency conditions.   Those interpreting dependency as the outcome of the global spread of capitalism play down any imperialistic tendencies on the part of Communist powers such as the USSR or China, and see the path of revolutionary socialism as the answer. They claim that this alternative can break the chains of external dependency and eliminate internal colonialism, resulting in a redistribution of national income, the elimination of marginality, accelerated economic growth, higher standards of living, and greater participation by the masses of the population in the process of development.

Writers who regard dependency as the product of a new imperialism, shared by the United States and the USSR, which is spreading rather than receding, tend to look upon the options available to the dependent countries as quite restricted, and to advise their leaders to seek an accommodation under the best circumstances available subject to the hegemony of one of the superpowers. They see the process as a continuation and extension of what has been called the "development of underdevelopment," with the typical country likely to pass from satellite to provincial dependency, using Jaguaribe's terms. Their outlook is essentially pessimistic, with the most hopeful prospect being avoidance of a nuclear confrontation between the superpowers and the consolidation of a modern Pax Romana, with its advantages in terms of stability and its price in terms of institutionalized submission on the part of dependent regions of the world.

A third, somewhat less negative, point of view is that possibilities for autonomous development do exist and that they should be taken advantage of to the fullest possible extent. This option stresses a reformist approach under the leadership of local elites, making maximum use of discretion left by operation of the international system. It is probably feasible only if the superpowers show restraint and a willingness to encourage or at least tolerate it. This alternative is usually described by such terms as "autonomous capitalism" or "state capitalism." The assumption is that it will be a mixed system with strong state involvement in planning and execution of plans, and with public enterprises playing a prominent role. Its success requires national leadership capable of bringing about drastic reforms without a revolutionary disruption of the basic social structure. Dominant domestic classes must be persuaded or forced to loosen their control so that the polarization of internal colonialism can be converted into an integrated process of development. Where national entities are small or weak, particularly in Latin America and Africa, groupings of existing nation-states may be a condition for exploring any realistic prospects for autonomous development.

Advocates of autonomy as a feasible option place great emphasis on the importance of local innovation and willingness to experiment. For example, a Malaysian commentator named Inayatullah has recently argued that the lack of an adequate level of development in Asian countries is due in part to overreliance on borrowing from external sources and insufficient creativity in evolving new development models. He considers modernization to be a process that is historically and culturally specific, and doubts the relevance of any foreign model of development evolved in different cultural and historic circumstances. This places, he believes, "the main burden of evolving an appropriate model of development on a society itself, by examining what it can learn and maintain from its own history and culture, by full comprehension of the constraints and opportunities available in its internal and external environments."[93] For instance, he doubts the relevance for Asian societies of the elements of traditional capitalism and liberal democracy from the Western model as compared to the concepts of the nation-state or of an instrumental public bureaucracy.

Another common theme is the extreme importance of timing, of taking advantage of opportunities before they disappear. A number of writers urging autonomy for Latin America are discouraged that such a strategy is not being actively pursued where it has chances for success. They warn that developmental autonomy may be a short-lived option that will be gone before the end of the century. Jaguaribe is a prominent spokesman for this view which combines the conviction that reformist autonomous development presents hypothetical possibilities with a prediction that chances for realizing them are extremely small.

Change

Uneasiness about the general applicability of both the terms modernization and development has been voiced frequently, even by those who have continued to use one or the other, or both. For instance, as noted earlier, Joseph LaPalombara as early as 1963 pointed out pitfalls resulting from concepts of modern, modernity, and modernization. His concerns seemed to be about equally applicable to concepts such as developing and development, yet his essay and the book containing it, which he edited, carried the title bureaucracy and political development. Gabriel Almond and his associates have been primarily concerned with the process of change in political systems but have tended to prefer to talk in terms of political development rather than political change, even though in practice they seem to consider the two phrases to be substitutable one for the other.

John Kautsky, writing in 1972 on *The Political Consequences of Modernization*, confines the concept of modernization in a rather unusual way to the social and economic antecedents and consequences of industrialization, and excludes the political antecedents and consequences. The latter are his main concerns. In dealing with them, he deliberately avoids both the terms political modernization and political development, for the reason that "these concepts suggest development toward a single pattern and in a single direction, often . . . the one generally referred to as Western democracy." He prefers the more neutral concept of political change to either political modernization or political development, in order to "leave the question of which way politics changes under the impact of modernization open for our investigation rather than to foreclose it by the use and the definition of a term."[94] He then proceeds to write about political change under the impact of modernization as defined, with particular attention to modernization of traditional societies from within and from without, and to the politics of modernizing regimes.

In their review of trends in the literature, Huntington and Dominguez point out that in the late 1960s and early 1970s, "political scientists who had been talking about political development began to think in more general terms about theories of political change," and they note that as the tradition–modernity dichotomy becomes less useful for political analysis, which appears to be the case, "it seems likely that the study of political development will become increasingly divorced from the study of modernization and more closely identified with broader study of political change."[95] They expect this to result in more attention to cultural factors than to levels of modernity in comparative studies, and to the identification of "distinctive patterns of political beliefs and behavior for the Latin, Nordic, Hindu, Arab, Chinese, Slav, Japanese, Malay, African, and possibly other major cultural groupings."[96] They also anticipate more of a focus on how changes in particular components of a political system relate to changes in other components.[97]

The extent to which such a shift toward substitution of the concept of change for modernization and development actually takes place in the future remains to be seen, but it does appear to be a desirable trend. It offers the obvious advantage of replacing terms that are subjective and value-laden with a concept that is more neutral and value-free. That in itself should be a sufficient reason for a gradual transition in usage.

Another consideration may become even more persuasive. Aside from its value connotations and identification with particular groupings of nation-states considered to be modernized or developed on the one hand, or traditional or developing on the other, the terminology linked to modernization and development as concepts has a very limited capability for dealing with potential future change that may occur among nation-states in each of these groupings. Current terminology encounters great difficulty, as previously mentioned, in coping with change which moves societies now tabbed as developed toward some future condition in which their characteristics might be substantially different. Modernization and development are static concepts as they relate to what may be in the offing.

A different set of problems crops up with regard to the developing societies. Their future, as built into the adjective itself, is presumably to be movement in the direction already taken by developed societies, and the key questions to be answered are how they follow and at what pace. But what if all or some of these countries are either incapable of, or not desirous of, taking such a path? How do we deal with change in these cases if it is in some other direction than that already taken by societies whose course can be traced historically?

Signs are already on the horizon, or even above it, that indicate something about what is coming. Should these changes materialize, they would soon convert these potential conceptual dilemmas into actual ones. Therefore, we need to have a brief further look at recent forecasts and speculations concerning both the so-called developed and developing countries.

Social forecasting about the future of advanced industrial countries has taken shape in the concept of the postindustrial society,
with the implication that this emerging type of society will be as
distinctly different from industrial society as this form was from
agrarian society. In the United States, Daniel Bell is the best known
expositor of this formulation of what lies ahead.[98]

The transition discussed by Bell and numerous other social
scientists in this country and abroad does not lead clearly to a new
type of society with fully laid out characteristics. The very label that
has gained general acceptance indicates this. The choice of a term
using a prefix meaning "after in time" or "following" is almost an
admission that industrial society is much better understood than
what is expected to succeed it. Bell acknowledges this, in explaining
his preference over alternatives such as the knowledge society, the
information society, the professional society, the programmed
society, the technetronic society,[99] and other possible choices based
on salient aspects of what is deemed to be emerging. He does not
anticipate that the postindustrial society will achieve the degree of
societal unity "which was characteristic of capitalist civilization from
the mid-eighteenth to the mid-twentieth century," and so he thinks
that the prefix post indicates an appropriate sense of "living in inter-
stitial time."[100] He does identify, however, the major source of
structural transformation as "the change in the character of knowledge,"[101] and he discusses several dimensions of the consequent
social structure modifications that he foresees taking place during
the next half-century.

The core of this concept is that technology and theoretical
knowledge will have an increasing role in the functioning of society.
The professional and technical class will be pre-eminent. Levels of
education and affluence will rise. The university will be the primary
institution of the postindustrial society. Conflict will be generated
between populism and elitism by the meritocracy principle which is
central to the allocation of position in such a society.

Ramifications will include a change in the economic sector from
a goods-producing to a service economy, with white-collar workers,
particularly professionals and scientists, becoming predominant in
the labor force. Cultural norms will be profoundly affected, with the
primacy of theoretical knowledge promoting confidence in technological assessment and control, expanding the scope of political
decision-making, and fostering a pervasive cultural orientation toward
the future.

An aspect of this line of thinking of special import to us is that
the forecast of postindustrialism is not confined to the United States

and Western Europe. In Bell's view, the same basic social pattern is
in prospect also for Japan, a non-Western capitalist society, and for
the Soviet Union, a noncapitalist Western or semi-Western society.
Geographic location is not a crucial consideration. Neither is the distinction between capitalism and socialism. "Today both systems,
Western capitalist and Soviet socialist, face the consequences of the
scientific and technological changes which are revolutionizing social
structure."[102] Communist theorists have tended with a few exceptions to avoid substituting this kind of analysis for more orthodox
Marxist views as to the role of the working class as the agent of
change and as to expectations for achieving a classless society. However, European social scientists with a neo-Marxist orientation, such
as Alain Touraine,[103] have taken a different approach to the post-
industrial theme. Recognizing the decisive role of science and
technology and the emergence of scientific and technical personnel
in all industrial societies, they are inclined to reinterpret the usual
Marxist view as to the role of the working class, or to enlarge the
definition to include the increasingly important technically trained
personnel. Touraine asks whether the working-class movement is
still at the center of conflicts in society, and answers that "in the
programmed society, the working class is no longer a privileged
historic agent . . . simply because the exercise of power within a
capitalist firm no longer places one at the center of the economic
system and its social conflicts." Neither firms nor unions are today's
chief actors in the struggle over social power. Their conflicts "do
not come to grips with real social power—in the United States, the
Western social democracies, or in the Soviet bloc." The most highly
organized sectors of the working class have not provided the leadership in support of new themes of social conflict; it has appeared
instead "in the economically advanced groups, the research agencies,
the technicians with skills but no authority, and, of course, in the
university community. . . . Tomorrow's struggle will not be a repeti-
tion or even a modernization of yesterday's."[104]

What these prognostications as to the postindustrial society
have in common, despite their variations in detail, is that a transition
is already well underway which is taking modernized, developed,
industrial societies into a period as traumatic and disruptive as they
faced earlier themselves, or as is faced by the present-day modernizing, developing, industrializing societies, and with the outcome
equally indeterminate. If accurate, such forecasts will require as a
by-product more adequate social science terminology concerning
change in the general social system and in the political subsystem.

We have already considered the dependency theories which focus on the obstacles confronting the developing nations as a group as they seek to develop further toward the industrialized model. The emphasis is on incapacity for development and the explanatory reasons, with slight attention being given to the question of whether development in the usually understood sense is a desirable goal.

This exact fundamental issue is currently being raised by some social scientists. Their position is that the contemporary advanced industrial societies are rapidly losing their appeal as models for underdeveloped countries. Instead, these leader societies, as they have previously been regarded, are being reduced to antireference groups in the context of global society. In brief, the argument is that the newer nation-states of the world no longer are aiming toward development of the kind considered attractive in recent decades, but are in actuality searching for and experimenting with alternative models as they shape their futures. They are groping for paths of societal change different from the road taken by present-day industrialized societies. The direction chosen may therefore be one not previously tried by countries ordinarily considered developed. Moreover, it may be a direction now foreclosed to these societies because of choices and commitments made in the past. If so, the historical experience of these countries becomes relevant less as a guide than as a warning. The developing countries as a group still share common characteristics and face similar problems which justify treating them as a major societal category, but standard development theory and practice are unresponsive to their requirements.

This cluster of views obviously has not yet jelled into any stabilized form, but the phrase most used to describe them is social systems delimitation.[105] This concept is intended as an alternative to conventional approaches to the allocation of resources and manpower in social systems, which are claimed to be predicated upon the requirements of the market and its utilitarian ethos. Criteria for assessing development are essentially concerned with "the activities constituting the dynamics of the market," and "the process of expansion of the market by which it becomes all inclusive in a country is, in general, an indication of development."[106] A country with a "dual economy," having populations not included in the market, is by definition underdeveloped or backward. Indicators of development are such measures as the size of the gross national product, the percentage of people living in urban areas, and the percentage of the labor force employed in the service sector. The individual in society is considered primarily as a jobholder and an insatiable consumer, and the socialization process is geared toward improving individual capacity to succeed in employment and in consumption. Organizational and institutional effectiveness, in turn, is assessed "from the standpoint of their direct or indirect contribution to the maximization of society's economic activities,"[107] leading to unidimensional types of organizational theory and practice, and undesirable policy science models of public choice.

Social systems delimitation offers a counterapproach. The key assumption is that the market "should be politically regulated, dimensioned and delimited as an enclave among other enclaves constituting the global social fabric."[108] The quality of national social life depends on productive activities which enhance the sense of community of citizens. Since these activities are not necessarily to be assessed from the standpoint inherent in the market, strategies of allocation of resources and manpower at the national level should reflect an optimal combination of one-way transfers resulting from public policy decisions as well as two-way market-type transfers. This calls for expertise congenial to social systems delimitation for economic planning and budgeting in an expanded role for public policy-makers.

Along with this delimitation of the market sector goes a de-emphasis on the individual as a jobholder and consumer. Indeed, consumption and the time required for it are viewed as inversely proportional to individual actualization. "Moreover, insofar as unlimited consumption is essentially depletive of natural resources, it is ultimately to be considered as unethical."[109] Socialization through the educational system should be refocused away from job-holding and consumption, making them secondary considerations for individual growth. In addition, the effectiveness of organizations and institutions should be assessed on the basis of their contributions to a sense of community among individuals, leading to "a multidimensional type of political and organizational theory and practice qualified to optimize both the citizen's productive activities and . . . sense of meaningful personal and social actualization."[110]

Proponents of social systems delimitation are convinced not only that this is a preferable theoretical base, but also that it is already in the process of acceptance by public opinion in developing societies, resulting in rejection of the example provided by advanced industrial societies, both capitalist and socialist, which have achieved high levels of material welfare through the development and application of technology. What Dunn calls the "demystification" of development is due to a combination of factors. One is growing awareness of the internal crises of the advanced industrial societies themselves, demonstrated in such spiraling problems as unemployment, energy depletion, and environmental pollution. Another is moral revulsion over the values and life-styles of "modern" persons. In Dunn's words, "consumptive North Americans and Europeans, together with elites in most of the Third World, continue to find it conscionable to ignore massive unemployment and sickening standards of living in their own countries and those that surround them." Most directly relevant, the promises of development have proven to be elusive or empty. "Despite remarkable technological advances and the radical expansion of global productive capacity, development activities have generated negative unanticipated consequences everywhere in the world."[111] Income and wage distribution has become more skewed, per capita income in Third World countries has increased very slowly, and chronic misery, hunger, and malnutrition are the fate of one-third of the world's population. On top of this is the feeling that "Western theories of development, Marxist and non-Marxist, rest on the assumption that underdeveloped societies do not possess the capacity for indigenously generated change."[112] Such considerations have, in Dunn's judgment, led so-called "follower" countries to reject the example supposedly set by "leader" societies and even to regard them as antireference groups. Along with this goes skepticism about extrapolating from the historical experience of European countries and the United States to predict or plan the course of Third World countries.

Behind the demystification of development is a more deep-seated challenge to reason as understood in the West, and what appears to be a breakdown in technical rationality, "partly reflected in an incapacity of advanced industrial societies to resolve problems of technological dehumanization, ecological destruction and an increasingly stratified international society," which is exercising a profound influence in the Third World. According to Dunn's interpretation of the doctrine of social systems delimitation, the solution is not to renounce but to reorient technical rationality. In centrally planned and market societies sociocultural, political-administrative, and economic activities are dominated by technical rationality. Instead technical rationality should be subsidiary or accessory to the sociocultural order. "The task is . . . to make and execute policy in such a way as to resubmerge and pacify technical rationality within the sociocultural and political order."[113] This Dunn calls the paratechnical paradigm, and he considers it to be a fundamentally different approach to development.

An underlying assumption of this point of view is that modern
societies show, as an essential characteristic, a tendency for the
market "to expand continuously into other enclaves and spheres and
replace sociocultural, political and personal values with a uniform set
of utilitarian values."[114] The proposed solution under a theory of
social systems delimitation is essentially to create by deliberate
planned action a series of enclaves and spheres of action within the
overall social fabric that lie outside the operation of the market and
are not dominated by utilitarian economic values. Dunn elaborates
in some detail hypothetically how such a delimitation of enclaves
might be planned, the variety of organizational settings to which the
theory of delimitation might be applied, and subtypes of work
organizations that are small, socially owned, and self-governing.

The published writings to date on social systems delimitation
are rather vague and unspecific as to actual or potential application
of these theories in particular countries. The only cited instances of
national efforts along these lines seem to be China, Yugoslavia, and
Tanzania, without elaboration as to just how delimitation techniques
have been applied. Both Ramos and Dunn seem to be in agreement
that a model of development based on social systems delimitation
would depend on a large measure of national self-reliance and
inventiveness within the society. It would not be modernization by
imitation of advanced industrial societies, and it would certainly
reject any notion of unilinear evolution in the process of change.

As this review of concepts of modernization, development, and
change has shown, development continues to be the most commonly
used of these terms, but the degree of consensus on what development means and of satisfaction as to its adequacy is markedly less
now than it was ten or fifteen years ago. This is especially evident
in the work of the dependency, postindustrial, and social systems
delimitation theorists. Therefore, the question can legitimately be
asked whether the term development and related words should be
abandoned altogether, and whether a distinction should continue to
be made between a group of nation-states which are considered
developed and another group considered to be underdeveloped or
developing. Recognizing the handicaps involved, the position taken
here is that in the contemporary world a distinct difference does
exist and will continue to exist for at least the next few decades
between these two sets of nation-states, and that the nation-state will
continue to be the dominant system for societal organization. During
our time, the so-called Western nations, plus the Soviet Union and
Japan, do in fact have characteristics in common that justify grouping

them together for purposes of analysis of their systems of public administration. The other present-day nation-states, although more numerous and displaying a dazzling and complex variety, also share characteristics making it worthwhile to consider them as a second major grouping, with identifiable subgroups. Perhaps some substitute set of terms will eventually be proposed and generally accepted, but that has not yet happened. The phrase Third World has come into common use with reference to the developing nations, but the first and second worlds in this triad are the United States and other Westernized democracies on the one hand, and the USSR and the East European Soviet bloc on the other. For our purposes, this usage is no improvement. I do not propose to attempt the introduction of a novel alternative. Hence, we will use these categories of developed and developing nation-states as we proceed, even though for purposes of analytical progress in future comparative studies, I agree that there are advantages in starting to shift discussions of basic societal transitions from development, as the most prevalent term used, to the more generic and neutral concept of change, as has been suggested by a number of the scholars whose ideas have been examined.

Notes

1. Daniel Lerner et al., *The Passing of Traditional Society* (New York: Free Press of Glencoe, Inc., 1958), p. 401.
2. Alex Inkeles and David H. Smith, *Becoming Modern* (Cambridge: Harvard University Press, 1974), p. 15.
3. *Ibid.*, pp. 15, 16.
4. Monte Palmer, *The Dilemmas of Political Development* (Itaska, Ill.: F. E. Peacock Publishers, Inc., 1973), pp. 3, 4.
5. Alfred Diamant, "Political Development: Approaches to Theory and Strategy," in John D. Montgomery and William J. Siffin, eds., *Approaches to Development: Politics, Administration and Change* (New York: McGraw-Hill Book Company, 1966), p. 25.
6. Edward Shils, *Political Development in the New States* (The Hague: Mouton and Company, 1962), p. 10.
7. S. N. Eisenstadt, "Bureaucracy and Political Development," in Joseph LaPalombara, *Bureaucracy and Political Development* (Princeton, N.J.: Princeton University Press, 1963), p. 98.
8. Reinhard Bendix, *Nation-Building and Citizenship* (New York: John Wiley & Sons, Inc., 1964), p. 300.
9. "Industrialization can be initiated only once; after that its techniques are borrowed; no other country that has since embarked on the process can

start where England started in the eighteenth century. England is the exception rather than the model." *Ibid.*, p. 71.

10. In William J. Siffin, ed., *Toward the Comparative Study of Public Administration* (Bloomington, Ind.: Department of Government, Indiana University), pp. 23-116.

11. *Ibid.*, p. 28.

12. These considerations led in part to the reformulation by Fred W. Riggs of "fused" and "diffracted" for the polar types, with intermediate systems as "prismatic," as he explains in the Preface to *Administration in Developing Countries: The Theory of Prismatic Society* (Boston: Houghton Mifflin Company, 1964).

13. Joseph LaPalombara, ed., *Bureaucracy and Political Development* (Princeton, N.J.: Princeton University Press, 1963), pp. 35-39.

14. Norman T. Uphof and Warren F. Ilchman, eds., *The Political Economy of Development: Theoretical and Empirical Contributions* (Berkeley, Calif.: University of California Press, 1972), p. ix.

15. Ralph Braibanti and Joseph J. Spengler, eds., *Tradition, Values and Socio-Economic Development* (Durham, N.C.: Duke University Press, 1961), p. 8.

16. *Ibid.*, p. 9.

17. W. W. Rostow, *The Stages of Economic Growth* (Cambridge: Cambridge University Press, 1960).

18. For one publication in English which is representative and which refers to others holding similar views, see Andre Gunder Frank, *Latin-America: Underdevelopment or Revolution* (New York: Monthly Review Press, 1970).

19. Several summarization efforts have been made of the literature on political development. An early influential summary and analysis was by Lucian W. Pye in *Aspects of Political Development* (Boston: Little, Brown and Company, 1966). More recent comprehensive reviews are Helio Jaguaribe, *Political Development: A General Theory and a Latin American Case Study* (New York: Harper & Row, 1973), Chapter 8, "Review of the Literature," pp. 195-206; and Samuel P. Huntington and Jorge I. Dominguez, Chapter 1, "Political Development," pp. 1-114, in Fred I. Greenstein and Nelson W. Polsby, eds., *Handbook of Political Science*, Volume 3, *Macropolitical Theory* (Reading, Mass.: Addison-Wesley Publishing Company, 1975).

20. Huntington and Dominguez, "Political Development," pp. 3-5.

21. *Ibid.*, p. 5.

22. Gabriel A. Almond and G. Bingham Powell, Jr., *Comparative Politics: A Developmental Approach* (Boston: Little, Brown and Company, 1966).

23. *Ibid.*, p. 34.

24. *Ibid.*, p. 37.

25. *Ibid.*, pp. 299-300.

26. *Ibid.*, pp. 323-24.

27. *Crises and Sequences in Political Development*, Leonard Binder et al. #7

Series Studies in Political Development (copyright © 1971 by Princeton University Press; Princeton Paperback, 1974) published for Social Science Research Council. Excerpts reprinted by permission of Princeton University Press.

28. See particularly Chapter 2, "The Development Syndrome: Differentiation–Equality–Capacity," pp. 73-100, by James S. Coleman.
29. *Ibid.*, p. 75.
30. *Ibid.*
31. *Ibid.*, pp. 78-79.
32. *Ibid.*, p. 80.
33. *Ibid.*, p. 82.
34. Binder, Chapter 1, "The Crises of Political Development," p. 53.
35. *Ibid.*, p. 56.
36. *Ibid.*, p. 58.
37. *Ibid.*, pp. 52-64, for summary explanation of these categories.
38. Sidney Verba, Chapter 8, "Sequences and Development," pp. 283-316.
39. Binder, Chapter 1, "The Crises of Political Development," pp. 64-65.
40. Harry Eckstein, *The Evaluation of Political Performance: Problems and Dimensions* (Beverly Hills, Calif.: Sage Publications, 1971). A related work based on a comparative analysis of twelve countries, using Eckstein's conceptual groundwork, is Ted Robert Gross and Muriel McClelland, *Political Performance: A Twelve-Nation Study* (Beverly Hills, Calif.: Sage Publications, 1971).
41. Decisional efficacy "denotes the extent to which polities make and carry out prompt and relevant decisions in response to political challenges. The greater the efficacy, the higher is performance." Eckstein, *The Evaluation of Political Performance*, p. 65.
42. Roger W. Benjamin, *Patterns of Political Development* (New York: McKay, 1972), p. 11.
43. Palmer, *The Dilemmas of Political Development*, p. 3.
44. John B. Powelson, *Institution of Economic Growth: A Theory of Conflict Management in Developing Countries* (Princeton, N.J.: Princeton University Press, 1972), p. ix.
45. Martin C. Needler, *Political Development in Latin America: Instability, Violence and Evolutionary Change* (New York: Random House, 1968), p. 5.
46. Helio Jaguaribe, *Political Development: A General Theory and a Latin American Case Study* (New York: Harper and Row, 1973). © 1973 by Helio Jaguaribe. Excerpts by permission of Harper and Row, Publishers, Inc.
47. *Ibid.*, pp. 197-98.
48. Karl W. Deutsch, "Social Mobilization and Political Development," *American Political Science Review* 55 (September 1961): 493-514.
49. Samuel P. Huntington, "Political Development and Political Decay," *World Politics* 17, No. 3 (April 1965): 386-430, at p. 393. See also his book, *Political Order in Changing Societies* (New Haven, Conn.: Yale University Press, 1968).

50. Pye, *Aspects of Political Development.*

51. David Apter, *The Politics of Modernization* (Chicago: University of Chicago Press, 1965).

52. Myron Weiner, "Political Integration and Political Development," *Annals* 358 (March 1965): 52-64.

53. Irving Horowitz, with Josué de Castro and John Gerassi, eds., *Latin American Radicalism* (New York: Vintage Books, 1969).

54. Jaguaribe, *Political Development,* Chapter 9, "A Comprehensive Theory of Political Development," pp. 207-218.

55. *Ibid.,* pp. 210-211.

56. *Ibid.,* pp. 212-213.

57. *Ibid.,* pp. 213-217.

58. Almond's original formulation of the kinds of capabilities required for development is in "Political Systems and Political Change," *American Behavioral Scientist* 6, No. 10 (June 1963): 3-10. A later version is in "A Developmental Approach to Political Systems," *World Politics* 17, No. 2 (January 1965): 183-214.

59. Eisenstadt, "Bureaucracy and Political Development," p. 104.

60. Alfred Diamant, *Bureaucracy in Developmental Movement Regimes: A Bureaucratic Model for Developing Societies* (Bloomington, Ind.: CAG Occasional Papers, 1964), pp. 4-15. See also his *Political Development: Approaches to Theory and Strategy,* prepared for the Comparative Administration Group, Summer Seminar, Indiana University, 1963, pp. 19-25.

61. Diamant, *Bureaucracy in Developmental Movement Regimes,* p. 14.

62. Whether events connected with the ouster of Emperor Haile Selassie and the overthrow of the ancient dynasty he represented call for a reclassification of Ethiopia is a question without a clear answer yet in this frame of reference.

63. Samuel P. Huntington, "Political Development and Political Decay," *World Politics* 17 (1965): 386-430; *idem, Political Order in Changing Societies* (New Haven, Conn.: Yale University Press, 1968).

64. Huntington, *Political Order in Changing Societies,* p. 3.

65. *Ibid.,* pp. 33-4.

66. *Ibid.,* pp. 53-4.

67. *Ibid.,* pp. 78-80.

68. *Ibid.,* p. 86.

69. *Ibid.,* pp. 86-92.

70. *Ibid.,* p. 1.

71. *Ibid.,* pp. 7-8.

72. Gerald A. Heeger, *The Politics of Underdevelopment* (New York: St. Martin's Press, 1974).

73. *Ibid.,* p. 1.

74. *Ibid.,* p. 10.

75. *Ibid.,* p. 99.

76. *Ibid.,* p. 127.

77. John Kautsky, *The Political Consequences of Modernization* (New York: John Wiley & Sons, Inc., 1972).

78. *Ibid.*, p. 227.

79. Among numerous publications in several languages presenting these views, some of the most accessible are James Petras and Maurice Zeitlin, eds., *Latin America: Reform or Revolution?* (New York: Fawcett, 1968); Suzanne J. Bodenheimer, *The Ideology of Developmentalism: The American Paradigm—Surrogate for Latin American Studies* (Beverly Hills, Calif.: Sage Publications, 1971); Andre Gunder Frank, *Latin America: Underdevelopment or Revolution* (New York: Monthly Review Press, 1970); Helio Jaguaribe, *Political Development*, particularly Chapter 18, pp. 353-387; James Petras, ed., *Latin America: From Dependence to Revolution* (New York: John Wiley & Sons, Inc., 1973); and Ronald H. Chilcote and Joel C. Edelstein, eds., *Latin America: The Struggle with Dependency and Beyond* (Cambridge: Schenkman Publishing Co., Inc., 1974), pp. 26-46. Other social scientists identified with dependency points of view include Horacio Flores de la Pena, Raul Prebisch, Alberto Guerreiro Ramos, Octavio Fanni, Candido Mendes, Claudio Veliz, Sergio de la Pena, Rodolfo Stavenhagen, and George Liska.

80. Bodenheimer, *The Ideology of Developmentalism*, p. 36.

81. *Ibid.*, p. 39.

82. Christian Bay, "Politics and Pseudopolitics: A Critical Evaluation of Some Behavioral Literature," *American Political Science Review* 59, No. 1 (March 1965): 39-51, at pp. 45-46.

83. Jaguaribe, *Political Development*, pp. 381-82.

84. *Ibid.*, p. 382.

85. *Ibid.*, p. 378.

86. *Ibid.*, pp. 383-85.

87. Rodolfo Stavenhagen, "Siete tesis equivocadas sobre America Latina," in *Sociologia y Subdesarrollo*, 3rd ed. (Mexico: Editorial Nuestro Tiempo, 1975), pp. 15-38. This article was published originally in the newspaper *El Dia*, June 25 and 26, 1965.

88. In addition to treatment in Stavenhagen's book, see, for example, Andre Gunder Frank, *Desarrollo del Subdesarrollo*, 2nd ed. (Mexico: Escuela Nacional de Antropologia e Historia, Comité de Lucha, 1970).

89. Jaguaribe, *Political Development*, p. 409.

90. *Ibid.*, pp. 410-25.

91. Andrew J. Sofranko and Robert C. Bealer, *Unbalanced Modernization and Domestic Instability: A Comparative Analysis* (Beverly Hills, Calif.: Sage Publications, 1972).

92. *Ibid.*, p. 51.

93. Inayatullah, *Transfer of Western Development Model to Asia and Its Impact* (Kuala Lumpur, Malaysia: Asian Centre for Development Administration, 1975), pp. 45-46.

94. Kautsky, *The Political Consequences of Modernization*, pp. 21-22.

95. Huntington and Dominguez, "Political Development," p. 96.

96. *Ibid.*

97. An effort at computer modeling of complex change involving demographic, economic, and political variables, applied to the political experience of Turkey and the Philippines during the 1950s, is made in Ronald D. Brunner and Garry D. Brewer, *Organized Complexity: Empirical Theories of Political Development* (New York: The Free Press, 1971).

98. Daniel Bell's thesis is set forth most fully in *The Coming of Post-Industrial Society: A Venture in Social Forecasting* (New York: Basic Books, 1973).

99. Zbigniew Brzezinski, *Between Two Ages: America's Role in the Technetronic Era* (New York: Viking Press, 1970). He describes the technetronic society, at p. 9, as one that is "shaped culturally, psychologically, socially, and economically by the impact of technology and electronics— particularly in the area of computers and communications."

100. Bell, *The Coming of Post-Industrial Society*, p. 37.

101. *Ibid.*, p. 44.

102. *Ibid.*, p. 41.

103. Alain Touraine, *The Post-Industrial Society: Classes, Conflicts and Culture in the Programmed Society*, transl. Leonard F. X. Mayhew, 1st American ed. (New York: Random House, 1971).

104. *Ibid.*, pp. 17-18.

105. Alberto Guerreiro Ramos of the University of Southern California is a leading spokesman for the social systems delimitation approach. His views are summarized in a "Brief Note on Social Systems Delimitation," 6 pp. mimeographed, prepared for the 1976 National Conference of the American Society for Public Administration, and in "Theory of Social Systems Delimitaton: A Preliminary Statement," *Administration and Society* 8, No. 2 (1976): 249-72; they will be amplified in a forthcoming book entitled *The End of Human Behavior, A Substantive Approach to Social Systems Delimitation*. Another presentation is by W. N. Dunn of the University of Pittsburgh in a paper also prepared for the 1976 National Conference of the American Society for Public Administration, with the title "The Future Which Began: Notes on Development Policy and Social Systems Delimitation," 63 pp. mimeographed.

106. Ramos, "Brief Note on Social Systems Delimitation," p. 1.

107. *Ibid.*, p. 2.

108. *Ibid.*

109. *Ibid.*, p. 3.

110. *Ibid.*,

111. Dunn, "The Future Which Began," p. 2.

112. *Ibid.*, p. 4.

113. *Ibid.*, pp. 12, 20.

114. *Ibid.*, p. 33.

4

HISTORICAL ANTECEDENTS OF NATIONAL ADMINISTRATIVE SYSTEMS

Each of today's nation-states has an administrative heritage combining in various proportions historical antecedents from the geographic region in which the contemporary nation-state is located, and from external sources through either imposition or importation of administrative concepts and institutions.

The need for an awareness of historical antecedents is self-evident, but providing historical background adequate to understanding is a difficult task. Sorting out and weighting the complex elements of any nation's administrative inheritance must be on a judgmental rather than a scientific basis. Such an effort is also handicapped by the relatively slight attention given to administrative history either by professional historians or by students of public administration.[1] In any case, only a brief, cursory, and highly selective treatment is possible here, focusing primarily on the political and administrative evolution of Western European countries because of their own importance and their global influence. Some attention is given to historical systems only remotely linked to this Western cultural tradition, but we will be more concerned with ancient and medieval civilizations which have contributed directly to evolution of the nation-state as the dominant model for ordering society, and bureaucracy as the most common form of large-scale organization.

Organizing Concepts for Historical Interpretation

Given the tremendous time span of human history and the enormous
variety of human experience to be taken into account, any effort at
summarization and explanation must be based on some interpretive
theme or themes. Leading students of administrative history have
advanced various concepts intended to serve this purpose, and we
will review several that are particularly suggestive.

The best known generalized attempt at interpretation summarizes the process as one of demystification, rationalization, and
bureaucratization. Associated primarily with the historical studies of
Max Weber, this view is that mankind has endeavored more or less
continuously to move from myth to reason as a way of understanding phenomena, and that rational methods of operation have led
gradually to more complex forms of organized effort, culminating in
fully developed bureaucracies which approximate the characteristics
of Weber's "ideal type." This explanation is closely echoed in
Jacoby's recent book, *The Bureaucratization of the World.*[2] "Bureaucratic systems developed," he says, "in all instances where large
groups of men existed in large areas creating the need for a central
agency to deal with problems."[3] Modern all-encompassing bureaucratic organizations are the culmination of a long process of centralization and accumulation of power. Weber spoke with concern of
the "overtowering" power of fully developed bureaucracy. Jacoby
amplifies this concern, stating that the basic problem of our times is
the concept of bureaucracy and what it entails by way of regulation,
manipulation, and control. Mankind simultaneously demands,
depends on, and deplores the apparatus of bureaucracy. Our age is
characterized, according to Jacoby, by "the forceful transformation
of rational administration into the irrational exercise of power, the
lack of clearly defined limits to coercion, and the increasing competence of a state which arrogates independence to itself."[4] This interpretation centers on the paradox that bureaucracy is necessary and
indeed inevitable on the one hand, but dangerous and potentially
usurpative on the other. The seeds for this predicament were sown
early, when historical civilizations found it necessary to create and
then rely on the prototypes of present-day bureaucracies.

Nash has suggested a less disturbing theme in his monograph,
Perspectives on Administration: The Vistas of History.[5] He is
primarily concerned with the historical relationship between civilization and administration, using the term civilization to refer to the
"achievement levels" of a society and administration to refer to its

"organizational structures and techniques." His thesis is that
"civilizations have flourished and maintained themselves only as they
were able to effect a satisfactory balance between cultural achievement and the development of an organizational framework for
society."[6] Closely related from the dawn of history, civilization and
administration have helped determine the rise and fall of societies by
the balance or lack of balance between them at various periods of
time. Nash cites numerous examples of success by societies in
making progress toward higher levels of culture because of supporting achievements in administration, and corresponding instances of
societal decline when administrative systems have not been adequate
to sustain existing civilizations at previously attained levels of complexity. He illustrates from the history of ancient Egypt and China,
Greek city-states, Imperial Rome, Byzantium, Europe during the
Middle Ages, mercantilist regimes of post-Renaissance absolutist
monarchies, and nation-states of the last two centuries, among
others.

In summary, Nash argues that past and present experience

. . . underscores the nexus between cultural progress and the attainment of
administrative rationality. For better or worse, civilization and organization
have been mutually dependent . . . some form of balance between cultural
accomplishments and administrative organization is desirable. Undue emphasis
on one may undermine the very existence of a society. For example, the
Athenians were preoccupied with intellectual accomplishments and neglected
administration; in the case of Sparta, there was undue concentration on administrative rationality at the expense of creative cultural endeavors. A subtle blending of the two components, such as Rome achieved during the period of her
greatness, as the Catholic Church maintained in the Middle Ages, and as the
Atlantic civilization seems to have developed during the last 150 years, may
promise the most enduring progress.[7]

Karl A. Wittfogel's main historical interest has been to explore
the combination of circumstances in the past leading to the growth
of complex bureaucratic systems as aspects of despotic patterns in
society and government. His *Oriental Despotism: A Comparative
Study of Total Power*[8] is the product of a lengthy and wide-ranging
study which led him to the conclusion that such systems evolved in
what he terms "hydraulic" societies. These were Oriental river valley
civilizations which took advantage of opportunities to cultivate large
areas of potentially fertile soil by supplying water not provided
directly by nature. He distinguishes between small-scale irrigation
farming when on-the-spot rainfall was not available, which he calls

hydroagriculture, and hydraulic agriculture, requiring extensive construction of facilities to provide enough but not too much water.
Realization of the possibility of hydraulic society depended not only
on a natural setting combining an ample supply of water and sufficient fertile soil, but also cooperative human action on a large scale.
The necessary degree of highly organized effort to construct the
required irrigation and flood-control works could only be obtained
through governmental institutions capable of planning and executing
such projects. The long-range consequence of the growth of these
early hydraulic societies at various locations in the ancient world was
"Oriental despotism" involving the claim to and exercise of "total
power" by the rulers of such societies.

Wittfogel explores in great detail many aspects of this type of
society, including the natural setting, the economy, the state and its
despotic system of power, property patterns, and the class structure.
Of special interest to us is his treatment of the reliance of the rulers
of hydraulic societies on bureaucratic officialdom. The monopoly of
societal leadership exercised by the masters of hydraulic society was
dependent on their control of a complex governmental machinery.
Hydraulic rulers permitted "no conspicuous and bureaucratically
organized rivals," and exerted "exclusive leadership by ruthlessly and
continually operating as a genuine monopoly bureaucracy."[9]

In Wittfogel's view, hydraulic society has two major subdivi-
sions. "The masters and beneficiaries of this state, the rulers, constitute a class different from, and superior to, the mass of the commoners—those who, although personally free, do not share the privileges
of power. The men of the apparatus state are a ruling class in the
most unequivocal sense of the term; and the rest of the population
constitutes the second major class, the ruled."[10] The ruling class in
turn is divided into several subgroups. Atop the vertical structure is
the sovereign ruler with his court, including the members of his personal entourage and perhaps a vizier or other official who shares
authority operationally with the sovereign. Next are the ranking
officials, both civil and military, who serve the ruler by exercising the
limited decision-making power entrusted to them and who enjoy the
status conferred by their stations. Below them in the bureaucratic
hierarchy are large numbers of scribes and menial aides who carry on
the routine work of administration. Horizontally, the ruling network
of officials often covered a wide territorial area, but with central
dynastic authority firmly maintained except in periods of disruption
or dynastic decline, when greater local autonomy could be asserted.
Despite obvious and significant differences among members of the

ruling class, Wittfogel asserts that "there can be little doubt that the masters of hydraulic society, who enjoyed extraordinary privileges of power, revenue and status, formed one of the most class-conscious groups in the history of mankind." In all hydraulic societies "the potential and the actual rulers are deeply aware of their superiority to, and difference from, the mass of the ruled—the commoners, the 'people.' "[11]

Naturally, in such a society there were many social antagonisms—between the masses of the ruled and the rulers, among subgroups of the ruling class, and to some extent among different groups of commoners, but the monopolistic claims of societal leadership in the "total apparatus state" succeeded in hydraulic society in keeping the level of antagonisms under control while such a society persisted.

Wittfogel sheds much light on the historical origins of large-scale bureaucratic organizations in these early river valley civilizations with many shared characteristics, which evolved not only in Asia and the Middle East, but elsewhere under similar circumstances, such as in the Inca civilization of South America. His monumental study also attempts, much more controversially, to extend the concepts of "Oriental despotism" and the "Asiatic mode of production" to the USSR as the present-day heir of hydraulic society, but we do not need to describe or evaluate this aspect of his work here.

Our last and most significant example of a thesis for historical interpretation is presented by S. N. Eisenstadt in *The Political Systems of Empires*.[12] His interest is centered on a particular type of political system, which he considers of great importance for comparative purposes because these polities stand between "traditional" and "modern" political regimes, combining features of both and having had to contend with problems similar to those being faced by "new states."

Eisenstadt calls these examples "centralized historical bureaucratic empires" or "historical bureaucratic societies." This major type of political system is only one of seven which he suggests as a basis for classifying the most common forms of political systems in human history. Others include primitive political systems, nomad or conquest empires, city-states, and feudal systems. Modern societies, whether democratic, autocratic, or totalitarian, are grouped together as a type.

Polities with this label show great variety in their historical and cultural settings, but are claimed to share some fundamental characteristics which distinguish them from patrimonial and feudal societies on the one hand, and from modern political systems on the other.

They achieved a limited differentiation of political activities, organizations, and goals, but not to the extent common in modern contemporary societies. "Thus," states Eisenstadt, "in these political systems—*within the framework of the same political institution*—traditional, undifferentiated types of political activities and organizations coexisted with more differentiated and autonomous ones, all closely interwoven in the major aspects of political activity."[13] Among these institutions were "distinct and separate organs devoted specifically to fulfilling various administrative and governmental functions,"[14] with such attributes as recruitment based mainly on criteria such as skill, wealth, achievement, or political loyalty rather than membership in a kinship or local-territorial group; internal organizational autonomy tending toward task centralization and specialization, hierarchical authority, and abstract rules for regulating work; and growing staff professionalization indicated sometimes by salaried personnel and usually by an ideology stressing service to the polity as represented by the ruler rather than personal service to the ruler. In other words, these were centralized *bureaucratic* empires.

A tremendous range of examples is offered by Eisenstadt as meeting these requirements. Ancient Egyptian, Chinese, Hindu, and Persian empires are included, and possibly those of the Incas and Aztecs as well. The later Roman, Byzantine, and Ottoman empires also qualify. Perhaps more surprising is that the absolutist empires of Europe after the fall of feudalism are also put in this category, as are the colonial empires of European countries established in other parts of the world by conquest. Admittedly, these polities differ tremendously in geography, history, and culture, but Eisenstadt argues that they share political attributes which justify grouping them together.

The place of the bureaucracy in the political process is fully explored,[15] with special emphasis on two paradoxical features. Bureaucracies were crucial for success to the rulers of such empires. Only through the development of bureaucratic institutions could the necessary degree of societal control and regulation be achieved following the growth of differentiation and the increase of "free-floating" resources. Also bureaucratic institutionalization helped provide stabilization of relations among groups in the society. The result was a considerable degree of dependency on the bureaucratic apparatus for the survival of these political systems. At the same time, the bureaucracy was in a position to achieve substantial autonomy because of its crucial role in perpetuation of the regime, and this presented possibilities for the bureaucracy to stray from the desired service orientation to the rulers and other major social groups. The resulting tendency was often for the bureaucracy to become self-oriented and displace service goals with goals of bureaucratic aggrandizement, and to escape from effective political control. This was a potential danger that would not always materialize because, as Eisenstadt says, "the conditions that gave rise to the extension of the bureaucracy's technical and service activities were not necessarily compatible with those which made its usurpation of political control and its displacement of service-goals possible."[16]

Thus Eisenstadt's analysis of the political systems of historical bureaucratic empires reaches the conclusion that in these polities can be found partial and ambivalent manifestations of two tendencies which continue to offer alternatives for modern political systems— either toward the growth of "latent despotic and totalitarian power" or toward realization of "the potentialities for the fuller free participation of different social groups in the political process."[17]

With these interpretive themes as points of reference, we will embark on a survey of the historical background for the contemporary nation-state political system and its administrative subsystem.

Ancient World Origins

Long before the time of any written historical records, mankind had laid the groundwork for the civilizations of recorded history. Administration in its basic sense of cooperative human endeavor aimed at achieving identified objectives obviously began very early. During Paleolithic and Neolithic times (extending roughly to 5000 B.C.), the discovery of fire and the development of a variety of stone weapons and tools paved the way for later technological advances. Belief in magic and the rise of primitive religious beliefs probably led to one of the earliest instances of specialization or professionalization in the *shaman* or religious practitioner. The antecedents of writing appeared in painting, sculpture, carving, engraving, and other artistic accomplishments. Even nomadic civilizations were dependent on considerable cooperation, the use of hunting weapons produced by skilled craftsmen, and other rudimentary forms of division of labor, specialization, and hierarchy.

More settled societies were made possible by the domestication of animals and the cultivation of crops, permitting transition from a food-gathering to a food-producing economy and the growth of communities with permanent sites and sizable populations.

Beginning around 5000 B.C., in several parts of the world where conditions were favorable, river valley civilizations developed independently of one another, but sharing the attributes of "hydraulic society" as described by Wittfogel. The earliest of these civilizations is now generally conceded to be that of the Sumerians in the valleys of the Tigris and Euphrates rivers leading into the Persian Gulf, settled by emigrants from central Asian plateaus between 5000 and 4000 B.C., who gradually formed urbanized communities surrounded by agricultural lands made fruitful by irrigation and protected from flooding by large-scale public works, all of which was accomplished only because of Sumerian contributions in agriculture, engineering, mathematics, government, and other areas.

Rather than trace chronologically similar developments elsewhere, it will serve our purposes better to mention briefly the chief examples of such river valley civilizations, widely separated geographically, which had little or no impact on the more interconnected chain of civilizations contributing directly to the Judaic–Greco–Roman cultural tradition of Western Europe, and then turn to the historical antecedents of that tradition.

In the Eastern Hemisphere, these autonomous examples are the ancient empires of China and India, and in the Western Hemisphere, the pre-Columbian civilizations located in present-day Mexico, Central America, and the northern parts of South America.

Chinese civilization has been marked by continuity and autonomy from very early times to the recent past, with Imperial China extending into the twentieth century. Although no doubt having considerably earlier origins, Chinese culture can be traced only to about 1500 B.C., when the Shang dynastic system was already established in the Yellow and Yangtze river valleys, with what appears to have been a strong centralized government organized into ministries and staffed by powerful officials. Shortly before 1000 B.C., the Shang people were conquered by the Chou, ushering in the classical period of Chinese history under the Chou dynasty, which lasted until 247 B.C. Under the monarch, known as the Son of Heaven, a hierarchy of officials extended from a chief minister to functional ministers in areas such as agriculture, public works, and military affairs, and then to officials with territorial jurisdiction in areas ruled directly. A much wider control was exercised through feudal lords owing allegiance to the emperor but because of distance and other factors able to maintain considerable autonomy in handling local affairs. Literature and culture flourished during the Chou period, which produced the great philosophers Confucius, Mencius, and Lao Tsu. A system of education emerged which provided lengthy programs of study for those preparing for official careers and opened government officialdom to individuals chosen by ability rather than by birth.

Despite the length of the Chou dynasty, there were ups and downs in political stability and in the extent and degree of territorial hegemony, with numerous semi-independent states contending with one another during its later centuries. Out of this struggle came the brief Ch'in (256-207 B.C.) and longer Han (206 B.C.-A.D. 220) dynasties, which created what is usually considered China's golden age. Ch'in ruler Shih Huang Ti was known as the Great Unifier. He replaced feudal institutions with a system of prefectures whose administrators were frequently transferred, and in other ways undertook to standardize and centralize administration. He strengthened military defenses, and improved agricultural production. Chinese society became more highly stratified into five main classes, i.e., scholars, farmers, artisans, merchants, and soldiers.

After a brief interlude of resistance to centralism following the death of Shih Huang Ti, the Han dynasty built upon and extended his empire, organizing it eventually into a three-tiered system of provinces, prefectures, and districts. The Han rulers, following Confucian philosophy, undertook to shape an officialdom capable of governing such a large and complex empire. They perfected a method of selection based on competitive examinations, and revamped the educational system to prepare candidates according to their abilities rather than birth. These reforms, building on earlier similar efforts, succeeded in producing a stable and competent civil service which set the pattern for many centuries. Along with its good points, this strongly hierarchical system also carried the seeds of subsequent internecine struggles and a tendency toward overemphasis on stereotyped literary preparation for official careers.

Over three centuries of division into several separate states followed the weakening of the Han regime soon after A.D. 200, before the Sui dynasty restored order and undertook massive public works, including canals, palaces, and extension of the Great Wall in the north. These large-scale projects were accompanied by an overhaul of the administrative system, including improvements in the examination scheme and its supporting library facilities, and creation of a corps of traveling inspectors to check on the performance and loyalty of officials. Sui rule was brief, with the T'ang dynasty taking over in A.D. 618 for a period of almost 300 years to A.D. 907. This dynasty made no drastic break with the past, but gave special attention to agricultural production and grain storage, and to improvement of the system of schooling and examinations. Printing was introduced during this period, marking an advance with widespread ramifications on administration in China and elsewhere later on.

Following the downfall of the T'ang dynasty early in the tenth century, China was split for most of the following three centuries into the Liao empire in the north, founded by nomad invaders, and the Sung empire in the south. Liao ruling practices were a peculiar combination of nomadic conquering power and Chinese administrative institutions adapted to the regime's purposes, with the empire divided into two regions, one more nomadic and the other more settled, each with its own set of governmental offices and officials.

The contemporary Sung dynasty in the south reached what Gladden calls China's "pinnacle of culture and science."[18] The governmental system was based on earlier Han and T'ang models adapted to new circumstances but not fundamentally changed. In external affairs, the concern was mainly with centers of power to the north—the Liao regime until it was overthrown in 1125, and then the Chin empire until 1234. A greater threat arose from the rapid expansion out of central Asia of the Mongols, who by 1280 had conquered all of China and had founded the Yuan dynasty, which in turn after less than a century was replaced by a Chinese regime, the Ming, which concentrated on restoration and consolidation of traditional Chinese civilization, succeeding at the task until the quality of its rulers fell and opened the way for yet another barbarian invasion by the Manchus in 1644. The Ch'ing dynasty of the Manchus lasted until the Chinese revolution of 1910 brought an end to this remarkable Imperial Chinese legacy.

The Chinese civil service, which evolved in ancient times and retained its basic characteristics through two millenia, is notable in two respects. As Gladden points out, the Chinese bureaucracy as an institution was "the one steadying factor that contributed more than anything else to the remarkable staying power of the Chinese civilization."[19] By carrying over to modern times, it eventually exercised great influence on the development of modern civil service systems in the West.

The Indian subcontinent, in contrast, neither produced as much continuity in its civilizations nor had as much impact on the West. Wittfogel's hydraulic society thesis does seem to be applicable, however. Between 2500 and 1500 B.C., the river valleys of the Indus and the Ganges had produced flourishing civilizations, before there

occurred stagnation and decline probably due to neglect of irrigation systems and denuding of the forests. This process was reversed
for a relatively brief period under the Mauryan dynasty, which
lasted from 322 to 184 B.C. Founded by Chandragupta, a military
leader who ousted the occupation garrisons left a few years earlier by
Alexander the Great, this kingdom included much of what is now
Afghanistan and northern India. Essentially despotic and military,
the regime nevertheless was highly organized, with a departmental
structure staffed by officials hierarchically arranged and responsible
for a pervasive network of state enterprises and monopolies as well
as extensive health and welfare facilities. In the administration of
this realm, Chandragupta was assisted by his vizier, Kautilya, reputed
to be the author of a surviving Sanskrit treatise on statecraft, the
Arthasastra.

Aside from this brief interlude, the history of India has revealed
no ancient regimes comparable in extent or degree of complexity to
those of China. Not until the rise of the Mughal empire in the
sixteenth century did India produce a rival to the Mauryan regime of
a millenium and a half earlier.

The civilizations of early America were in their origins contem-
poraneous with but of course completely autonomous from the
ancient civilizations of the Old World. The cultures of the Mayas,
the Incas, and the Aztecs, which are of most interest to us because of
their impact on contemporary Latin American countries, trace their
beginnings at least as far back as the second millenium B.C., although
they peaked much later. We will comment on each briefly, discussing them roughly in the chronological order in which they reached
their apex, and in ascending order as to their influence on currently
existing nations.

The territory inhabited by the Mayas consisted of the Yucatan
Peninsula and adjacent areas, including present-day Guatemala,
Belize, and parts of Mexico, Honduras, and El Salvador. The Mayan
culture, dating back to at least 2000 B.C., was at its height during the
period 500 B.C. to A.D. 900, and was in decline for several centuries
before arrival of the Spaniards soon after 1500. Mayan society consisted of a widely scattered group of autonomous cities. Societal ties
were not primarily political, since during most of Mayan history
there was no capital city and no centralized empire. The cities were
bound together not only by common language, and religious and
cultural ties, but also were linked by an efficient road network which
permitted extensive trade. Soil and climate combined to provide
amply for the population, which was able to attain a high standard of

living. Massive construction projects were undertaken, including temples and other public buildings, warehouses, and reservoirs and canals for water conservation. This was all accomplished despite the absence of work animals, the wheel, and metal tools.

This city-state system had a two-class society of nobles and farmers. Governance was headed by an official who combined civil and religious functions. Ordinarily, this office was filled by descent from father to son but another blood relative might be chosen. A council of members of the ruling family made this decision, as well as authenticating the exercise of power by the head of state. Elaborate ritual controlled appearance, adornment, dress, and performance, with religious significance pervasive.

The Mayas are famous for their accomplishments in astronomy and mathematics, linked no doubt to their emphasis on religion and their support of a priestly class who acted as official astrologers. The only written record was in documents with pictorial glyphs, most of them destroyed by the Spanish. Little is known about their administrative structures and processes, but presumably these were relatively simple and confined mostly to each city-state. Only late in Mayan history, after 1200, is there evidence of a league among the city-states in northern Yucatan, with Mayapan as the capital, and this unusual experiment ended in 1441, before arrival of the Spanish.

Although descendants of the Mayas survive in large numbers today, the Mayan impact on colonial and contemporary society has been relatively slight, owing to such factors as less interest on the part of the conquering Spanish and a slower rate of conquest, the remoteness and scattered nature of the Mayan cities, and the fact that Mayan culture was on the decline after A.D. 1000 with earlier accomplishments still being discovered.

The Incas of South America dominated an area stretching along the Pacific coast from modern Ecuador through Peru and into Chile. Pre-Inca cultures in the area can be traced to 1200 B.C., but these were later absorbed by the Incas, who suppressed information about them in order to build up the oral Inca tradition. Inca dominance came rather late, around A.D. 1250, resulting from successful expansion from the Cuzco Valley into surrounding areas. The organizational skill of the Incas seems to be largely responsible for their prominence. Life in Inca society was highly controlled. The basic social unit was the *ayllu*, a group of families varying in size from inhabitants of a small area to a large city. Land was owned by the *ayllu* and loaned out to members. A council of elders and an elected leader controlled the *ayllu*. These units were then combined into districts and other higher levels in a hierarchical system culminating in the *Sapu*, or Lord Inca, as a combination of supreme ruler and god. This position was hereditary, with the Lord Inca choosing his successor from among his sons. A sun-worshiping religion was closely linked to the state under a state-supported priesthood.

The organizational skills of the Incas were reflected in their management of public services. Power was centralized over a large geographic area through a hierarchy based on a span of control of ten for each level of supervision, leading from the individual worker to the Lord Inca at the apex of the hierarchy. Despite the lack of a system of writing, methods of communication, reporting, and recording were impressive, relying to a large extent on the *quipu*, which was a cord of threads of different colors which could be knotted so as to record statistical information. In addition, a road network, including bridges, provided an empire-wide means of communication and trade. There were no wheeled vehicles, but the llama was used as a beast of burden. Irrigation systems were built and extensive terracing aided in stimulating agricultural production and the cultivation of numerous foods now known worldwide, including the potato. The whole economic system was under state direction and control. Gladden sums up this way: "Authority and religious acceptance were at the root of the Inca system of government, but without the superb sense of organization which permeated their administrative arrangements and procedures their empire could not have functioned so efficiently as it did."[20]

When Cortez arrived in Mexico in 1519, he found a situation in which the Aztecs, from their base in the city of Tenochtitlan, where Mexico City now stands, had established a tributary system which enabled them to control most of the central plateau and the coastal area on the Gulf of Mexico. Aztec dominance was relatively recent, having been achieved only in the twelfth and thirteenth centuries. The Aztecs were preceded by and built upon the cultures of the Olmecs on the coast who dated back to 800 B.C., the Zapotecs inland to the south who centered at Monte Alban from 500 B.C., and the Toltecs on the central plateau who, beginning about 200 B.C., built the ceremonial city of Teotihuacan northeast of Mexico City. Arriving in the area of the Toltec civilization 500 years after it had mysteriously gone into decline, the warlike Aztecs combined a theocratic political system with an efficient military machine to conquer and then maintain control over a large number of tribes through indirect rule based on exaction of tribute.

Although the Aztecs inherited the cultural achievements of

their predecessors rather than being innovators themselves, they did improve on what they found and contributed a talent for efficiency in both warfare and civil administration. The Aztec social system was based on clans, each with an elected leader, and an interclan council, which chose the Aztec ruler from among the brothers or nephews of the previous ruler. This overlord combined state, religious, and warfare leadership roles, all conducted according to elaborate customary ritual.

Aztec power was based on military prowess. Aztec administration was effective without being highly centralized, since subject tribes were allowed considerable local autonomy provided they remained submissive and met their tribute obligations. This decentralized system was feasible because of well-maintained roads that allowed rapid movement of warriors and messengers.

The nature of the Aztec empire also made it vulnerable, helping to explain its rapid overthrow by the Spanish, who were able to gain allies from subject tribes to combine with their advantages in weaponry and ruthlessness, with the result that Aztec civilization was systematically destroyed, not to be extolled again until recently following the 1910 revolution, as a manifestation of Mexican nationalism.

Although all these historical societies have had some influence on contemporary Western systems, either through peripheral contacts during their heyday or because of more recent borrowings from their experience, the mainstream of Western development resulted from the convergence in the Roman Empire of three cultural currents—those from Fertile Crescent, Egyptian, and Mediterranean city-state civilizations.

The Sumerian civilization was only the first of a series of great empires that rose and fell in the Fertile Crescent area over a time span of 3000 years. The successor Babylonian, Assyrian, Chaldean, and Persian empires flourished for varying periods of time from different geographical bases, with overlaps, borrowings, and adaptations by the later from the earlier cultures. From this Middle East region came some of the most noteworthy contributions to technology and statecraft. These included, just to mention a few examples, the first use of the wheel; the first instances of urbanization on a large scale; the coming of the written record, produced initially on sunbaked brick, later on clay tablets, and leading from pictographs to cuneiform signs and eventually to the development of a written alphabet; and the promulgation of comprehensive law codes, the most famous being the Laws of Hammurabi of about

1000 B.C. in Babylon. This era provides some of the most impressive cases both of Wittfogel's "hydraulic society Oriental despotisms" and Eisenstadt's "centralized historical bureaucratic empires." Governments were generally despotic with minimum popular participation, but they recorded remarkable accomplishments in material undertakings made possible by administrative systems which could harness and direct the immense manpower resources available for exploitation.

Ancient Egypt, although now thought to have been antedated by Sumer as the birthplace of civilization, reached a similar level at nearly the same time, and thereafter sustained a distinctive and homogeneous culture for at least 3000 years to 332 B.C. The Nile provided the setting for a river valley civilization without parallel. Long and narrow, with desert on each side, the Nile offered the ideal combination of fertile land which could be dependably and amply irrigated, and natural defenses against external invasion. Village settlements sprang up first in the delta of the lower Nile during the fourth millennium B.C., with communities spreading up the valley as time passed, leading initially to separate political institutions in the lower and upper halves. Integration of northern and southern Egypt is credited to Menes, the first Pharaoh, in about 3200 B.C.

Subsequent Egyptian rulers are grouped into thirty-one dynasties, with Egyptian political history divided into four major epochs: the Old Kingdom (to 2180 B.C.), the Middle Kingdom (2080–1640 B.C.), the New Kingdom (1570–1075 B.C.), and the Late Period (1075–332 B.C.). Before the end of the Old Kingdom, several developments closely identified with Egypt had already taken place, including the use of papyrus as a writing material and the construction of tomb pyramids and other monumental edifices. Following a century of division, the country was again united, power was centralized, new construction projects were completed, and expansion by conquest and trade was accomplished during the Middle Kingdom.

The Middle and New Kingdoms are separated by a seventy-year period of rule by the Hyksos people from the southern uplands, before a liberation war ushered in a 500-year golden age of glory and territorial expansion which reached as far as Palestine and Syria. Then began a long era of gradual decay, economic decline, social unrest, and retraction of boundaries, with invasions once by the Assyrians in 670 B.C. and twice by the Persians in 525 and 341 B.C., during the so-called Late Period.

Despite vicissitudes, the hallmarks of ancient Egyptian history are stability and continuity. Rule by the Pharaohs, firmly sanctioned by religious beliefs, was an absolutism generally touched by benevolence. The idea of life after death was a powerful motivator, accounting for lavish use of resources in preparation for the afterlife, and incidentally responsible for the preservation of so much information about Egyptian life-styles.

Clearly one of the reasons for Egyptian institutional longevity was the high level of administrative services achieved, ranking the Egyptians with the Chinese as creators of the most impressive bureaucracies in the ancient world. The pattern was set under the Old Kingdom, which was extensive enough to call for delegation and specialization. The practice of appointing a deputy to the Pharaoh in the position of vizier was adopted early, as was a system of functional central officers including a treasurer, a chief architect, a superintendent of public works, and a chief justice. Territorial jurisdiction for local government purposes was through units called *nomes*, each under a *nomarch* appointed by the Pharaoh. The *nomarch* was an all-purpose official, whose responsibilities included irrigation and agricultural production, care of temples and other public structures, tax collection, control of the local militia, and local administration of justice. Royal deputies posted as aids to the *nomarch* were in fact inspectors acting in behalf of the central authorities.

Egyptian officialdom was a mixture of members of the royal family, priests, holders of sinecures, scribes, architects, engineers, and craftsmen of various kinds. There was no single public service organized along standardized lines. Offices had a tendency to become hereditary and sometimes were subject to purchase. For important posts, knowledge of hieroglyphics was needed, requiring lengthy training to master reading, writing, and arithmetic, and leading to a degree of professionalization and shared interests among those with such skills.

Along with what must have been competent performance by many officials, evidence of abuse and inefficiency also exists. Overstandardization, bribery, duplication of offices, excessive red tape, extortion, and laziness were all complained against. The ebb and flow of administrative performance no doubt helps explain the peaks and valleys in Egyptian political history. Gerald Nash uses the Egyptian experience as a prime example of his thesis that cultural achievement and organizational framework must be balanced. Attributing the long gradual decline during the Late Period in large measure to the administrative system's decreasing efficiency, he summarizes: "The decrease in the effectiveness of royal administration led to the decline of agricultural innovation and development. The inability of the central government to protect the nation from foreign invaders hastened decay. Similarly, the preoccupation of royal administrators with religious formalism led to the gradual deterioration of the communications systems and of engineering projects in which the Egyptians had once pioneered. The belief in magic retarded scientific and artistic work and helped to slow cultural advance. Thus, the level of Egyptian civilization was closely related to its organizational framework."[21]

The ancient societies which most influenced later developments in Western Europe were situated in the land areas surrounding the Mediterranean basin. Various of the Fertile Crescent empires extended their domains to the eastern fringes of the Mediterranean, and of course Egypt, from its very beginnings in the Nile Delta, was a Mediterranean society.

Geography also helps to explain the impact of the Hebrew people of the Old Testament, whose promised land was found at the eastern end of the Mediterranean after their exile in Egypt. Relatively insignificant in contrast to the great ancient empires in terms of territorial power, as shown by the Babylonian captivity and other historical evidence, the Hebrew kingdom was nevertheless the source of the Judaic–Christian religious tradition which became so central to Western development after the Christianization of the Roman Empire.

None of these societies, however, provided the distinctive political contribution of the Mediterranean borderlands. The Mediterranean city-state which evolved here was a dramatically different political entity from the ancient Oriental despotisms and bureaucratic empires. The city-state apparently took shape independently, or by colonization, in various locations in the Mediterranean basin, in response to conditions which facilitated emigration, communication, and trade by sea among widely scattered Mediterranean communities.

Earliest among these city-state societies were the Phoenicians of the eastern coast, the Mycenaeans and Minoans of mainland Greece and the island of Crete, and the Etruscans of the Italian peninsula. Their colonizing efforts, particularly those of the Phoenicians, reached throughout the circumference of the Mediterranean over a long period extending back into the second millenium B.C. The principal successors to these earlier city-state civilizations were Carthage in North Africa (originally a Phoenician colony), the city-states of classical Greece (notably Athens and Sparta), and Rome as a city-state and republic prior to establishment of the empire by Augustus in 27 B.C.

These city-states characteristically had a central metropolis surrounded by a rural hinterland, with the whole area relatively small as compared to either earlier ancient empires or modern nation-states. Usually they were located on or near the sea, and dependent on water routes for communication and trade. City-state autonomy was highly valued, with confederations among even friendly neighboring communities shifting and usually short-lived. Although several such city-states (including Carthage, Athens, and Rome) eventually developed into extensive empires, they tended to retain their basic political configuration, with only Rome eventually deliberately abandoning the old forms and turning to an imperial regime.

The city-state did not have a standardized set of political institutions, but a common tendency was to move from early kingships linked to a class system of nobles and lesser groups toward a governmental pattern which provided for political control by the free male citizens of the city-state through mechanisms which emphasized, in various degrees of combination, seniority and rotation in office. Sparta and Athens offered contrasting examples. Sparta retained more elements from the monarchic era, had a more rigidly stratified social structure, and was much more highly organized. A dual kingship survived representing the two royal houses from which the city-state had emerged. The two kings and twenty-eight nobles who had to be at least sixty years old formed a Council of Elders, with their selection being formally approved by an assembly of Spartan citizens over thirty years of age. Over time the principal governmental authority became centered in the ephorate, consisting of five citizens originally chosen by lot for one-year terms, but who later became eligible for reelection and began to serve for extended periods of time. Service to the state was the paramount value of the Spartan citizenry, but participation was barred to a large proportion of the population, the Helots, who were held in a condition of serfdom.

In Athens a more flexible and participative system evolved, but it also was predicated on a social system which reduced half the population to a status of subservience. By 500 B.C., under reforms sponsored by Cleisthenes, a Council of Five Hundred had been established, representing Athenian freemen, as the chief governing authority, under the Ecclesia or general assembly. Selection of council members was done annually by lot, on the basis that this method represented the impartial judgment of the gods, thus theoretically providing equal access to all Athenian citizens. To facilitate the conduct of state business under such an unwieldy council, the practice evolved of dividing the membership into ten committees, each with fifty members functioning on behalf of the council for a tenth of the year.

Rome also was under a king originally, with political leadership in the hands of aristocratic families who formed the patrician class, with tribal units serving as the basis for governmental operations. Joint meetings of tribal groups constituted the first popular assembly, which gave formal ratification to the choice of new kings, but had no actual authority. A council of elders, or Senate, made up of members of patrician families, served in an advisory capacity, but had the crucial responsibility of selecting a new king in case of a vacancy, since the office was not hereditary.

Gradually the kingship gave way to a system in which two consuls held office jointly for a year, with the Senate continuing as an advisory body but really the source of power because of its responsibility to choose the consuls annually. This republican system evolved slowly, with the most important development being the organization of the plebeian class and creation of a new set of institutions with an assembly, and officers called tribunes to represent the plebeians with the Senate and consuls. Numerous other offices emerged in connection with this involved dual system, which permitted patrician dominance but protected strongly held plebeian interests in a complex, flexible, and slowly shifting set of institutions. This highly traditional system survived long after Rome had expanded from its city-state base to control first the Italian peninsula and by the last century B.C. an empire which included nearly all the territory surrounding the Mediterranean Sea.

Public administration in the Mediterranean city-state was neither clearly differentiated nor amply staffed. Public officials held office for short intervals and were amateurs rather than professionals. Being generally wealthy, with high social status, they were expected to and were able to contribute to the state from their personal resources and to rely for help on family members and household slaves. Nothing comparable to a permanent civil service was created. Only minor posts with routine functions such as policing, record-keeping, providing messenger services, and performing other minor administrative tasks were held on a semipermanent basis, often by either public or private slaves. Administrative functions, initially simple and manageable using this approach, gradually outgrew the capability of the available administrative machinery, with grave consequences for survival of the city-state as a political entity. The decline of the classical Greek city-states is frequently linked to this deficiency in coping with political and administrative demands. Nash observes, for example, that "the relatively brief span of Greek supremacy may in part be attributed to the failure of the Greeks, despite their great cultural contributions, to develop an administrative system within which their culture could flourish."[22]

The Roman response was slow and deliberate, but it was sufficient. J. H. Hofmeyr mentions three reasons to explain the long delay in adjusting the governmental system to the fact of empire.[23] Foremost was the power of tradition and the inherently conservative nature of the Roman people, who preferred to adapt old institutions rather than create new ones. Next was the circumstance that most of the territory conquered by the Romans up to the end of the republic contained settled communities organized usually on a city-state basis, so that the government in place could continue to be used. Finally, Rome did not deliberately set out to become an imperial power, and hence did not plan ahead for an administrative system suited to empire.

As military successes multiplied and boundaries expanded, Rome began to experience increasing difficulties at the center, with unrest and inaction leading to repeated seizures of power from early in the second century B.C., by leaders such as the Gracchi brothers, Marius, and Sulla, none of whom succeeded in maintaining power or bringing about lasting reforms. By 70 B.C., Pompey had established himself as the most prominent leader, only to be challenged by Julius Caesar, who eventually forced the Senate to recognize him as a constitutional dictator. Caesar's efforts at overhaul were cut short by his assassination in 44 B.C., leading to the triumvirate of Lepidus, Mark Antony, and Octavian (who was Julius Caesar's adoptive son). In the ensuing struggle for supremacy, Octavian won out. He returned to Rome in 29 B.C. firmly in control, and in 27 B.C. the Senate conferred upon him the title Augustus, paving the way for him to undertake the conversion of Rome from a republic to an imperial empire.

Imperial Rome and Byzantium

The Roman Empire persisted from 27 B.C. to A.D. 476 in the West, centered in Rome, and for a much longer period, to A.D. 1453, in the East, with the capital in Byzantium (renamed Constantinople). The heritage of the Roman Empire, in combination with the Catholic church, clearly provides the dominant historical influence on development of Western European political and administrative institutions. We can mention only a few of the most important features from a system which changed over centuries of time, and took distinctly different shapes in the western and eastern segments after breakup of the unified empire.

As the principal architect of the imperial structure which replaced the republic of the Roman city-state, Augustus proceeded in a slow step-by-step manner which suited both his own personality and the temper of the Roman people. As Hofmyer puts it, he succeeded because he made the Romans believe that he was not really founding anything at all. Originally, he rejected the title Emperor, preferring Princeps or first citizen. The arrangement he arrived at with the Senate was to create a diarchy under which he and that body ruled as two concurrent authorities, dividing legislative powers, supervision of executive agencies, and governance of provinces of the empire between them. His obvious intent, however, was for the diarchy to move toward monarchy. That is in fact what happened, to a major degree under Augustus himself, and by stages under his successors, until imperial rule was eventually legally sanctioned after it had been established in practice. By the time of Diocletian, who ruled from A.D. 284 to 305, the last traces of republican institutions disappeared, and the emperor became an absolute monarch. Nevertheless, as Brian Chapman points out, Roman law continued to embody two legal principles which have a direct bearing on the modern state. The first was that the head of state received his powers from the people, even though the ruler might be invested with all-embracing authority. "Even the virtually all-powerful Roman Emperors," Chapman says, "remained the representatives of the state, and held and exercised their powers in the name and interests of the state."[24] The second was that a distinction must be made between the private and public personalities of the head of state, meaning in practical terms a differentiation between the resources of the state itself, and the personal resources of the head of state. Acknowledged by Augustus and many of his successors, these principles later became eroded and sometimes even rejected, but remained as Roman legal concepts to be revived as precedents long after the Roman Empire had itself dissolved.

Among the reforms initiated by Augustus, improvement of the administrative system was most important. Gradually the transition was made from unpaid amateur short-term officials drawn from the privileged classes to a paid professionalized civil service with more open access and offering the prospect of lifetime careers. Faced with the necessity of broadening recruitment of officials beyond the nobility as represented by the Senate, Augustus drew upon two elements of the population. Members of the Equestrian order became the source for filling many important posts below the highest levels, which continued to be reserved for representatives of the Senate. The Equites were originally the cavalry arm of the Roman army, made up of citizens wealthy enough to provide horses when they entered military service. Later these military connotations disappeared, but the Equestrian class remained as an upper middle class in Roman society, barred from the privileged circle of the Sena-torial order, but distinguished by their wealth from the bulk of the population. Augustus reserved most of the posts in his sphere of administration for members of the Equestrian class, and used them effectively as a counterweight to the Senate, with the result that over time they provided the core of the imperial bureaucracy. The other element was the extensive slave segment of the population, including many highly educated and cultured slaves from the eastern portions of the empire, as well as skilled artisans and other specialists who could provide a variety of much needed services, at minimal cost. The use of household slaves by public officials in carrying out their duties was a long-standing practice which could be followed by reliance upon imperial household slaves, with the distinction between private and public status becoming blurred gradually, so that the slave ranks eventually produced the bulk of the civil service. Slavery in this context did not necessarily mean abject servitude in menial tasks. Often slaves were freed in recognition of their services, and many slaves or ex-slaves came to occupy influential posts.

To bring order to this expanding bureaucracy, steps were taken to clarify hierarchical relationships and to set up grades for purposes of establishing salary levels for both the Senatorial and Equestrian career categories (with six and four stages, respectively). Less elaborate organizational arrangements were worked out for the lower services.[25]

Augustus also undertook a rationalization of the administrative structure to provide more adequate machinery for centralized control and to engage directly in activities which had formerly been contracted out. For example, the practice of collecting taxes through tax-farming arrangements was largely replaced by the use of new revenue-collecting agencies. Provincial officials generally were subjected to much closer scrutiny and were made more accountable. Great emphasis was placed on the development and codification of legal rights and duties applicable to inhabitants throughout the empire.

Along with these efforts to improve capabilities for direction from the center, the administrative system of the early Roman Empire continued to rely heavily on the pre-existing city-states which had been brought within the sphere of Roman rule. A high degree of devolution of administrative functions not requiring uniformity had the twin advantages of reducing unrest among the subject population and lessening the demands on the imperial bureaucracy.

Later developments both improved upon and detracted from the accomplishments initiated by Augustus. His successors continued with the process of expanding, organizing, and professionalizing the imperial civil service. This process peaked in the reign of Hadrian (A.D. 117–138). By that time, the administrative system was at its most effective level, as evidenced by the generally prosperous condition of the empire and the impressive accomplishments in road-building, aqueduct and drainage works, monument construction, provision of hospitals and libraries, and many other state-sponsored activities. Later on, in the view of most historians, the bureaucracy became too large, overcentralized, inflexible, and oppressive, contributing significantly to the eventual decline. How much blame should be placed on bureaucratic excesses and how much on intractable problems such as threat of invasion, civil disorder, pestilence, and economic stagnation is of course hard to unscramble. At any rate, it seems clear that by A.D. 300, during the reign of Diocletian, the bureaucracy was most highly organized on hierarchical lines patterned after the military but was also beyond its prime as an effective instrument for preserving the empire.

In A.D. 330, Emperor Constantine moved the capital of the empire to Byzantium, which became the center first for a weakened unified empire and then for an eastern realm which lasted for 1000 years. The division of the empire took place in A.D. 395, at the death of Theodosius the Great. After a losing struggle against barbarian invasions and internal decay, the western empire succumbed late in the fourth century. After one final unsuccessful attempt to regain the west by Justinian the Great in the middle of the fifth century, the Byzantium Empire became the inheritor of the Roman tradition, modified in two basic aspects. From the time of Constantine, Christianity became the official religion. Culturally,

Byzantium was highly influenced by Oriental civilizations. The resulting mix was a complicated and intricate amalgamation of political institutions similar to those of Rome during the later empire, overlaid by a state religion with a worldly quality, and borrowing many features from nearby cultures in the East. Resiliency and adaptability were prime characteristics, permitting an accordion-like expansion and contraction of boundaries as the fortunes of the regime rose and fell, until its final overthrow by the Ottoman Turks in 1453.

The keystone to governmental power was the absolutism of the emperor. The incumbent chose his successor whose coronation was by church officials. The prerogatives of office were dramatized by elaborate Oriental court ceremonial. The pattern was set under Justinian in the sixth century. The Justinian Code restated and revised Roman law for the needs of Byzantium. The royal court in Constantinople included high officials who functioned as a central executive, heading the various administrative offices. Military and civil hierarchies were kept separate, in order to strengthen imperial control. The civil administration was organized under a tight hierarchical system of provinces and several lower administrative levels, all closely accountable to the central administration. The approach to government was comprehensive and paternalistic, with the state regulating the economy closely, operating a variety of industrial enterprises directly, supporting an elaborate educational system, and providing at least rudimentary social services.

The extensive bureaucracy required to carry out these multiple functions seems to have been generally competent, chosen with merit considerations foremost and trained for specialized roles. A ranking system and corresponding titles conferred by the emperor provided an orderly framework for management of bureaucratic careers and identified officials as servants of the emperor. The longevity of the Eastern Roman Empire is at least in part accounted for by the performance record of the Byzantine administrative machinery.

Byzantium certainly had widespread influence, not only in political and administrative matters, but in art, architecture, religion, and other fields. The impact on Western Europe was somewhat muted and indirect as compared to the Byzantine inheritance of imperial Russia and other countries of Eastern Europe, as channeled not only through their political institutions but through the Eastern Orthodox church.

For our purposes, the main reason for interest in administration in the Roman Empire, as manifested in both West and East, is its

attraction centuries afterward to the builders of postfeudal governmental institutions in Europe. Chapman puts it this way: "The
long-lasting success and the logical clarity of the administrative
structure could not fail to impress the statesmen and jurists of later
generations when once again the achievements of the Roman Empire
came to be known." He also points out that in the Roman administrative system, four of the five "main pillars of administration" can
already be identified in the administrative pattern: military affairs,
finance, justice, and police. Modern systems follow this basic model,
with the "police" function broken into its component parts, and
with the fifth "pillar," foreign affairs, becoming more institutionalized than it was under the Roman Empire as the direct responsibility of the head of state or his personal representatives.[26]

To summarize, the main legacies of Roman law and administration are (1) the principle that the head of the state receives his
powers from the people, (2) a distinction between the private and
public personalities of the head of state, (3) the hierarchical nature
of the administrative structure, and (4) the division of government
into major constituent parts which are still recognized for purposes
of administration.

European Feudalism

The breakdown of the Roman Empire, and the centuries of
feudalism that followed, drastically disrupted the Roman concepts
of government administration and reduced public services to a
rudimentary level. The result, as Bendix points out, is that "the
overall similarity of the Western European experience" arose "from
the common legacies of European feudalism," rather than from the
influences of an earlier time.[27] The dominant authority relationship
in feudalism was between lord and vassal, with reciprocal ties providing an element of stability. In Western Europe these relations
between ruler and vassals were "consecrated through the affirmation
of rights and duties under oath and before God."[28] Legal rights were
personal rather than territorial; each man belonged to a jurisdictional
group, which determined his rights and duties for him.
"Accordingly," says Bendix, "medieval political life consists in
struggles for power among more or less autonomous jurisdictions,
whose members share immunities and obligations that are based on
an established social hierarchy and on a fealty relation with the

secular ruler whose authority has been consecrated by a universal church."[29]

These characteristics of feudalism emerged very slowly as Western Europe adjusted its social system to the circumstances of the dissolution of Roman authority. Weakened Roman institutions crumbled gradually, not all at once, as their support from the center faded and their effectiveness dropped. Roman ways of life had been absorbed by inhabitants of the empire, and were assimilated by the infiltrating barbarians and mixed with their tribal customs and patterns of authority. Withdrawal of Roman legions therefore did not mean an immediate transition to feudalism. Indeed, the initial successor regimes were extensive kingdoms, such as those of the Visigoths in the Iberian peninsula and the Merovingian Franks in Gaul and Germany. These kingdoms soon had to develop governmental capabilities beyond the reach of tribal institutions. Political control was highly personalized in the king, who offered protection in return for obedience. The king, as described by Gladden, "exercised paternal rights over his subjects and could issue orders and interdicts as any Germanic leader, but he also exercised certain powers rooted in Roman practice, such as the right to create currency and levy taxes. The shadow of the Empire manifested itself in the adoption of the doctrine of *lese-majeste* as a protection of the royal person but the ruler's despotic sway was greatly diminished by the restricted nature of the governmental means at his disposal. The *Palatium*, or Royal Household, was a mere shadow of its imperial prototype: it consisted of councillors, officers and bodyguards, but there were no offices, or bureaux to form a central administration. It was just the ruler's mobile household."[30]

By the end of the seventh century Merovingian rule had declined, to be revived by Charles Martel, who repelled the Arabs at Tours in A.D. 732, and especially by his grandson Charlemagne, who was able to extend his control south of the Pyrenees, to Rome and beyond in Italy, and north to the Elbe and the Danube. In A.D. 800, Charlemagne was crowned by the pope in Rome, and the Holy Roman Empire was born, claiming to be the legitimate successor to the Roman Empire, with the duty of protecting the universal church. It combined the Merovingian pattern between ruler and subjects with a close relationship with the church and an attempt to identify with the imperial tradition of Rome. As an idea, the Holy Roman Empire continued to receive lip service for centuries, but as a political reality it was short-lived. Charlemagne's realm declined rapidly under his successors into a number of power centers, which in turn gave way to the network of contractual relationships which became known as the feudal system, under which comprehensive political jurisdiction essentially disappeared. The only ordered hierarchical entity which continued to function throughout what had been the Western Roman Empire came to be the Church of Rome. It established temporal power in the Papal State based in Rome and surrounding areas, and elsewhere it not only provided spiritual bonds but also acquired extensive property holdings and became the provider of administrative services that in other times would have been the responsibility of civil authorities.

With the fall of the Carolingian empire, responsiblity had to be localized for such measures as could be marshalled for defense purposes and protection of public order. As Chapman says, "Communal self-help rather than organized administration was the key to early feudal society. . . Men were forced back on one of the most primitive forms of association, the search for a chief who would protect them at the price of personal homage and fealty. . . The very concept of the state disappeared together with the concept of the public service."[31]

The feudal system was able to accomplish the minimum that was necessary, which was to allow the basically agrarian society to survive. Feudal lords, in return for vassalic fealty, undertook to offer protection, dispense justice, and provide rudimentary services. Governing power was fragmented among numerous small entities constantly in conflict with one another and requiring increasing resources for defensive and offensive purposes. The long-range consequence during the period up to roughly the eleventh century was declining population, diminished agricultural production, and generally a reduction in the level of social interaction.

Feudal society also contained, however, the seeds for its eventual transformation. The key was gradual development of a money economy to replace the barter economy of the middle feudal period, which led to wealth not based solely on landed property and broke the economic monopoly of the feudal nobility. A self-sufficient agricultural economy began to give way in connection with what Eisenstadt refers to as "the development of free-floating resources" and "the emerging predominance of non-ascriptive rural and urban groups."[32] The new wealth based on exchange of commodities was centered in medieval towns which were able because of their growing economic power to loosen the hold on them of feudal lords and establish their own spheres of power. Municipal burgesses began to gain experience in the handling of matters of trade, finance, and the provision of minimal administrative services. The guild approach to organization of craftsmen provided a way of mobilizing specialized skills, although in a static and rigid way which limited competition and innovation.

Feudalism fostered continuous efforts by medieval kings and princes to extend their domains and to increase the dependence of the notables of the realm on the ruler and his immediate entourage, with the local notables in turn trying to exact guarantees of rights or extension of privileges for the services demanded of them. This process during the later medieval period produced kingships with greater territorial claims and with a greater power differential over the lesser nobility. Emergence of the autonomous medieval cities with their new middle class populations offered an opportunity for alliance between these aspiring monarchs and urban interests against the old aristocracy. Mutually advantageous to the rising monarchies and the growing cities, this alliance hastened the breakup of feudal patterns of political authority, to be replaced eventually by absolutist monarchical regimes organized on national lines.

Rise of European Absolutist Monarchies

The conversion of medieval political patterns into such national monarchies took place gradually, over a period of centuries, at different rates in different places. After 1200, consolidation of royal power was achieved at intervals in England, France, Spain, and Central Europe. This occurred earlier in England than on the Continent, partly as a consequence of the Norman conquest. On the other hand, the prompt growth of countervailing power in England resulted in a balance that was not achieved in the Continental countries, where either the absolutist regimes brought a greater ascendancy of royal power, as in France, or many principalities arose at the expense of overall unity, as in Germany.

During the 400 years required for transformation of feudal monarchies into the absolutist monarchies of the sixteenth to eighteenth centuries, the most important changes of interest to us were (1) vesting sovereignty in the monarch, (2) securing resources for support of the monarchy, (3) adopting mercantilism as state policy for controlling social and economic activity, and (4) expanding and centralizing governmental administration.

In the feudal order, the king was the first among peers rather than standing apart from other feudal nobility. Royal decrees were issued on the authority of the king and his royal council, made up of barons of the realm, who in turn bore major responsibility for their execution. This basically contractual conception of kingship came to be replaced by claims of royal prerogatives referring back to the Roman imperial tradition.

The lead in this reorientation was taken by *legistes* in the royal service who cited Roman law precedents for their arguments on behalf of kingly power. As early as the thirteenth century, a claim could be made such as the following: "The King is sovereign over all the nobility; only he can issue edicts, he is in overall charge of the churches, and all worldly justice is in his hands."[33]   Monarchical claims to political power were bolstered by a succession of jurists who reinterpreted concepts of Roman law by transferring the Roman imperium to the monarch and identifying the imperium of the monarch with the individual's private property. "The 'right' of sovereignty, they argued, was vested in the monarch. The state then was 'owned' by the monarch, and sovereignty belonged to him personally; he alone could legally exercise it, transmit it to his heirs, or otherwise dispose of it. . . Sovereignty was the right to command, and those commanded had a duty to obey. Laws were the tangible expression of the will of the monarch, and there was no higher authority to which further appeal could be made."[34]   The king shared his powers only with the oligarchic estates, and such political struggle as took place was between king and estates, with the former establishing greater and greater ascendancy.

The material resources available to the monarchy had to be increased in order to fulfill the claims to sovereignty. This was a long and arduous process, in which royal efforts to raise revenue were strenuously resisted, both by the feudal lords and by the towns. In the feudal order, each fiefdom stood on its own financially. Feudal kings could obtain revenues for unusual expenses, including even defensive warfare, only by convoking an assembly of the general estates to give consent. Feudal lords demanded a share of any taxes imposed, and the towns, where most of the readily available wealth was concentrated, tried to protect what they had, with the wealthiest towns also being able to maintain the most autonomy.

A centralized system of government required a centralized system of taxation. Aspiring monarchs realized this, and strove to establish their taxing authority as a major step in breaking down feudal society. In France, for example, a royal decree of 1439 forbade collection of taxes by feudal lords without the king's permission. In the absence of an administrative mechanism for collecting royal revenues, the levying of taxes was initially leased out to the highest bidder, but before the end of the sixteenth century financial officials had been stationed around the realm acting directly on behalf of the crown. Revenues raised from these newly exploited tax sources soon far surpassed income from the king's own holdings. Success in establishing the taxing prerogative of the crown had the twin advantage of providing the material resources necessary for carrying out royal policies and at the same time further weakening the autonomy of the nobility and the towns.

As monarchical power grew, so did the monarchical policy of increasingly extensive control of economic and social activities. The initial thrust was to seek the security of the realm and foster conditions conducive to trade and economic expansion. These common objectives were the basis for the alliances between crown and town common toward the end of the feudal period. The eventual outcome was the mercantile system of the later absolutist regimes in the sixteenth and seventeenth centuries. Jacoby describes how under centralized monarchy the state "made it its business to protect the wealth of the middle class. Systems of coinage and measurement were developed. The exportation of raw material and the importation of finished goods were forbidden. Subsidies were given to certain enterprises and trade monopolies were distributed. Guild regulations, forbidding the expansion of businesses, were discontinued. Roads and canals were built, improved and maintained. Mercantilism was born."[35]

Mercantilism as an economic concept considered wealth as the basis of state power. State policy was aimed at economic arrangements which were designed to achieve an excess of exports over imports in foreign trade. A favorable balance of trade would be reflected in payments enabling the state to build up its wealth by acquiring the precious metals, gold and silver. Encouragement of domestic manufactures required both subsidies and detailed controls. High tariff barriers reduced reliance on imported goods. Overseas colonies, as they were acquired, became a source of additional revenue for the benefit of the colonizing power.

The policy objectives of mercantilism in its various national manifestations could only be realized by installing an intricate network of laws and regulations, which in turn called for specialized administrative officials capable of harnessing available sources of strength for the maximum buildup of the mercantilist state's potential wealth.

These developments—in the legitimacy base, the resources, and the economic and social policies of European monarchies—were therefore all accompanied, and indeed made possible, by far-reaching revamping of the simple governmental apparatus available as the feudal period drew to a close.

An early significant move toward this end was the gradual conversion of the feudal *curia regis*, or royal council, into the king's privy council. This process began by admitting royal officials, in addition to the nobility. Dependent on the monarch, and more regular in their participation than the aristocratic members, who had to journey from their parts of the realm to attend, these officials provided the king with a source of support to counterbalance the nobility and enhance royal authority. As the councils became more controllable and more secret in their operations, responsibility for administration on behalf of the crown became the responsibility of privy council committees. Spain, France, Prussia, England, and other countries evolved their own versions of such privy council committee systems for supervising administration as the absolutist monarchies consolidated their authority.

Meanwhile, the scope of public services and the number of public functionaries grew dramatically. Defense and justice had been the primary concerns of the king during the Middle Ages. In addition, the crown now assumed responsibilities for a range of activities which had been left to local regulation since the breakup of the Roman Empire.[36] The administrative apparatus which made this expansion and centralization possible was achieved by a conversion, put in simplest terms, of the royal household into the royal service. In Weberian terminology, the change was from patrimonial to bureaucratic administration.

The medieval king, engaged in a constant struggle to maintain and extend his domain, protect his prerogatives against competing claims of the nobility and the church, manage his own extensive estates, preserve a minimum of order in the realm, and free himself from administrative minutiae, depended on his own corps of officials. Servants of the crown, with training and duties entitling them to be thought of as professional administrators, go far back in medieval European history. H. F. Tout has traced the growth of centralized administration in England in fascinating detail. He points out that these early public administrators, "like all early public officials, were simply members of a king's household. The king's clerks, accountants, and administrators belonged to the same category as the king's cooks, scullions, grooms, and valets. The public service of the state then was hopelessly confused with the domestic service of the court. . . The time was still far distant when the modern distinction was made between the king in his private and public capacities, between the royal officers who ruled the king's household, and those who carried on the government of the country."[37]

Max Weber used the concept of patrimonialism to characterize this pattern of authority relationships. In the patrimonial structure of authority, the royal household and the royal domains are managed by the king's personal servants. In principle, grants of power to these officials are arbitrary decisions made by the ruler which can be altered by the ruler as he sees fit. Of course, under patrimonialism, even the ruler is subject to the dictates of tradition.

Turning claims of absolutist supremacy into reality depended on success in professionalizing, directing, and controlling a royal service which could be identified mainly with the monarchy as an institution rather than with the reigning monarch as an individual. This required thoroughgoing reform efforts which fitted differing circumstances but had similar overall results. As Leonard D. White puts it in citing notable examples, "Richelieu in France, Henry VIII and Elizabeth in England, and the Great Elector (Father of Frederick William I of Prussia) are among the chief architects who reconstructed the concept of the State, of office, of civil life, and of permanent officials out of the debris of the feudal system."[38]

Experience in France and Prussia is especially relevant because of the influence of these absolutist administrative systems on subsequent nation-state bureaucracies and on later bureaucratic theory as formulated by Weber and others.

Although France eventually produced the most centralized European monarchy, under Louis XIV in the seventeenth century, this came only after a long period of struggle to assert the supremacy of the crown against centrifugal forces. As early as the thirteenth century, a hierarchical administrative system designed to enforce the king's authority had begun to operate through officials in each province specializing in military, legal, and financial matters. Difficulties of communications and control also led to efforts before 1300 by King Philippe le Bel to send out royal emissaries to tighten supervision, investigate complaints, and try to reduce the growing number of officials. As the territorial boundaries of France expanded by conquest, marriage, and treaty, subsequent rulers made similar attempts to strengthen the powers and curb the excesses of officialdom.

It remained for Richelieu, as principal minister under Louis XIII from 1624 to 1642, to consolidate the system through the office of intendant, which he converted from its earlier function as an intermittent agent of the king. He made the intendant a continuing provincial representative of royal authority, concentrating in his hands "very considerable powers covering taxes, tutelage, war supplies, recruitment, public works, and so on."[39] During the reign of Louis XIV later in the seventeenth century, Colbert improved the effectiveness of the intendant system and brought the French monarchy to its point of greatest strength.

Nevertheless, these royal reforms were only partially successful. Part of the problem was continuing resistance from local sources, but the main deficiency was the failure to create a body of competent officials adequate to cope with the burdens placed upon it. The intendants themselves had legal training which was not particularly suited to administrative tasks, but the principal fault was that generally posts in the royal service were obtained through influence and intrigue rather than merit, and could then be transferred by sale or inheritance. The result was a centralized administrative apparatus firmly under royal direction but staffed by officials of uncertain and unequal quality with their own vested interests in officeholding regarded almost as private property. Favoritism and venality rather than competence became the touchstones for obtaining positions in the French royal service.

Meanwhile, a different approach toward recruitment for administrative careers was being taken beginning during the seventeenth century in Prussia. Previously one of the poorest and most backward of the German states, Prussia at the end of the Thirty Years War in 1648 entered a period of reconstruction and rapid progress, under a succession of four kings who ruled from 1640 through 1786 and who devoted much of their attention to creation and maintenance of a professionalized state service. Frederick William of Brandenburg (the Great Elector) began the process by undertaking to centralize and militarize the country. He worked through his Privy Council, which he converted from an advisory to an executive body supervising specialized administrative departments. The king appointed officials assigned to local provinces with duties in economic, fiscal, and social matters on behalf of the central authority.

Recognizing the importance of a professionally trained corps of royal servants to staff the centralized state he was creating, Frederick William began to expand and improve the civil service. Reforms which he started gradually became more formalized, particularly under Frederick William I (1713–1740), who created chairs in cameralism, or administrative science, at German universities, and made a university diploma the usual prerequisite for office. Examinations were then given for ranking candidates who had good academic records and had completed a period of practical field training. "Certainly Prussia has the distinction," says Gladden, "of being the first modern state to introduce and develop a system of entrance examinations for the public service in which both the central administration and the individual departments were involved, and which comprised both written and oral tests, in subjects of a practical as well as an academic nature."[40]

Similar measures were taken to regularize and control the conduct of public business. According to Herman Finer, "Various instructions settled exactly the hours of work, procedure, and official secrecy. Employment outside the official service was prohibited, the acceptance of presents was prohibited, excise officials were forbidden to buy confiscated goods, and from those who handled money a guarantee was required. The officials who came into direct contact with the public were ordered to be polite. . . Residence in the neighborhood of the work was exacted, and the conditions of leave were rigidly regulated. For breaches of the regulations there was a series of heavy fines, which were imposed. A Spartan quality was introduced into the service."[41]   Finer goes on to summarize the significance of these reforms as follows: "The administration of the state had been professionalized: that is to say, it now depended upon a body of men permanently employed upon special work, their activities being uniquely at the service of the state and being purposively regulated and disciplined to accomplish its specific ends."[42]

The Prussian civil service reached its peak during the reign of Frederick the Great (1740–1786), declining after that from excessive militarization in an increasingly militarized state, and from overdependence on personal leadership from the king, which was no longer provided by his successors. By the end of the eighteenth century, the positive features of the elite administrative corps created by Prussian monarchs had been overshadowed by tendencies toward caste status, aloofness, exclusiveness, and inflexibility. Although extensive reforms were carried out by Baron vom Stein in 1808 following the collapse of Prussia under attacks from Napoleon's armies, the Prussian bureaucracy never again attained its earlier level of performance, which had made it the most notable example of absolutist monarchical administration.

Emergence of the Nation-State

The French Revolution and the advent of Napoleon brought about vast changes in the nature of the state and in the conduct of public administration. Out of this period of drastic transformation at the beginning of the nineteenth century emerged the nation-state as the dominant form of political system and the modern public bureaucracy as the vehicle for conducting the nation's business.

The concept of the state was depersonalized by the French Revolution. "The French theorists took over one version of the patrimonial state and replaced the king by the nation. The country was no longer the patrimony of the king but the patrimony of the nation, and the state was the machinery which the nation set up for its own government and to organize its public services."[43] Under Napoleon, the state did not cease to be authoritarian and centralized, but the allegiance of the public official shifted from the monarch to the nation. "The status of the public official changed at once. He was no longer the servant of the Crown or the prince, he was the servant of the state, and indirectly of the nation. He became an instrument of public power, not the agent of a person. He acted according to the law, and not according to the wishes of the individual, and his allegiance was to the law because the law was the expression of the will of the nation."[44]

Thus the royal service was converted into the public service. The change was primarily in allegiance and purpose rather than being a transformation from amateurism to professionalism, since the tradition that a career as a public official was one of the most honorable professions had already been established in France before the Revolution, and did not result from the administrative reforms of Napoleon.

The Napoleonic approach to administration stressed order, hierarchy, specialization, and accountability. As emperor, he incorporated many military-like features into a tightly knit command structure which assigned duties clearly and demanded personal responsibility for performance. He created the Conseil d'Etat to act in a general staff capacity, revamping the former king's council for this purpose. Having only advisory functions to the emperor, the Conseil d'Etat nevertheless exerted considerable influence by making studies and recommending policies, and it gradually developed into a control agency exercising general supervision over the work of administrative agencies.

The administrative structure of the central government consisted of five basic ministries (finance, foreign affairs, war, justice, and interior) closely resembling the much earlier Roman model, with other units being added later by breaking out functions from the comprehensive Interior Ministry. Each ministry was subdivided into divisions and bureaus for purposes of specialization, some with field offices outside Paris. The hierarchy of territorial governmental units was revised into a three-tiered system under the Minister of Interior. The department became the major jurisdictional subdivision, headed in each case by a prefect who was the principal representative of central authority and the conduit for representing local interests at the center. Each department was divided into arrondissements under subprefects, and at the base were communes with mayors as chief executive officers. Although representative councils existed at each level, they did not participate in the conduct of administrative affairs, which were handled under a pattern of authority firmly managed from above.

Among Napoleonic administrative reforms, none surpassed his insistence on competence in the selection of higher public service personnel. His own capacity for work was prodigious, and he expected devotion to duty and productive results from his subordinates. He apparently participated directly in the selection of many officials, and later personally judged their records of performance. The stress was on talent wherever it could be found, with particular emphasis on training in science, mathematics, and engineering. He had available specialists from the former royal regime with civil engineering experience in the public works field. He created a new specialist corps in mining and explosives. To provide a continuing source of competent officials, the Ecole Polytechnique was established. Since its graduates possessed "a prestige of quite a different kind from that conferred by caste or social class," and it promised prospects of the highest posts in the state, "it attracted not only the brightest of the middle class but also those members of the upper class who happened to be both ambitious and able." As a result, from its graduates came, according to Chapman, "many of the most prominent administrators, scientists, scholars and generals in the nineteenth century."[45]

As Gladden observes, "Napoleon's object of shaping a highly authoritarian system and of furnishing it with an efficient administration was a remarkable achievement considering the magnitude of the task and the short time he had at his disposal. By a judicious selection of ancient institutions, modified to the purposes of the world he was moulding right across Europe, he brought order out of chaos and achieved a level of administrative efficiency far above that of the preceding era. . . But it had the defects of all systems that depend ultimately upon the selective favouritism of the leader and upon decisions from above that cannot be modified except through the initiative of the leader himself."[46]

With both its virtues and its faults, it is the system of governmental administration in the type of modern Western nation-state which appeared first in France that Weber characterized as bureaucratic in contrast to the earlier patrimonial pattern of administration in Western Europe. He shows point by point the way in which the two types vary. According to Weber's definition, as given in abbreviated form by Bendix, a bureaucracy tends to be characterized by (1) defined rights and duties, which are prescribed in written regulations; (2) authority relations between positions, which are ordered systematically; (3) appointment and promotion, which are regulated and are based on contractual agreement; (4) technical training (or experience) as a formal condition of employment; (5) fixed monetary salaries; (6) a strict separation of office and incumbent in the sense that the employee does not own the "means of administration" and cannot appropriate the position; and (7) administrative work as a full-time occupation.

This combination of characteristics is generally regarded as common to the public service systems of the nation-states of Western Europe. "Each of these characteristics," says Bendix, "stands for a condition of employment in modern government administration. The process of bureaucratization may be interpreted as the manifold, cumulative, and more or less successful imposition of these employment conditions since the nineteenth century."[47]

Notes

1. The first comprehensive historical account of public administration has been published only within the last decade: E. N. Gladden, *A History of Public Administration* (London: Frank Cass, 1972), Volume I, *From Earliest Times to the Eleventh Century*, and Volume II, *From the Eleventh Century to the Present Day*.

2. Henry Jacoby, *The Bureaucratization of the World* (Berkeley, Calif.: University of California Press, 1973). This is a translation of the original, published in Germany in 1969.

3. *Ibid.*, p. 9.

4. *Ibid.*, p. 2.

5. Gerald D. Nash, *Perspectives on Administration: The Vistas of History* (Berkeley, Calif.: Institute of Governmental Studies, University of California, 1969).

6. *Ibid.*, p. 4.

7. *Ibid.*, p. 23.

8. Karl A. Wittfogel, *Oriental Despotism: A Comparative Study of Total Power* (New Haven, Conn.: Yale University Press, 1957).

9. *Ibid.*, p. 368.

10. *Ibid.*, p. 303.

11. *Ibid.*, p. 320-21.

12. S. N. Eisenstadt, *The Political Systems of Empires* (New York: Free Press of Glencoe, Inc., 1963).

13. *Ibid.*, p. 23.

14. *Ibid.*, p. 21.

15. *Ibid.*, Chapter 10, pp. 273-99.

16. *Ibid.*, p. 299.

17. *Ibid.*, p. 371.

18. Gladden, *A History of Public Administration*, Vol. I, p. 172.

19. *Ibid.*, Vol. II, p. 227.

20. *Ibid.*, Vol. II, p. 119.

21. Nash, *Perspectives on Administration: The Vistas of History*, pp. 8-9.

22. *Ibid.*, p. 10.

23. J. H. Hofmeyr, "Civil Service in Ancient Times: The Story of Its Evolution," *Public Administration* 5, No. 1 (1927): 76-93. Reprinted in Nimrod Raphaeli, ed., *Readings in Comparative Public Administration* (Boston: Allyn and Bacon, Inc., 1967), pp. 69-91.

24. Brian Chapman, *The Profession of Government*, (London: George Allen and Unwin Ltd., 1959) pp. 9-10.

25. Gladden, *A History of Public Administration*, Vol. I, pp. 121-3.

26. Chapman, *The Profession of Government*, p. 12.

27. Reinhard Bendix, *Nation-Building and Citizenship* (New York: John Wiley & Sons, Inc., 1964), p. 101.

28. *Ibid.*, p. 37.

29. *Ibid.*, p. 39.

30. Gladden, *A History of Public Administration*, Vol. I, p. 202.

31. Chapman, *The Profession of Government*, pp. 13-14.

32. Eisenstadt, *Bureaucracy and Political Development*, p. 106.

33. Philippe de Remi, sire de Beaumanoir, in 1283. Quoted by Jacoby, *The Bureaucratization of the World*, pp. 14-15.

34. Chapman, *The Profession of Government*, pp. 15-16.

35. Jacoby, *The Bureaucratization of the World*, p. 18.

36. "For the first time since the Romans, finance, justice, foreign affairs, internal affairs and defense were clearly distinguished from each other with specialized administrative services." *Ibid.*, pp. 16-17.

37. H. F. Tout, "The Emergence of a Bureaucracy," in Robert K. Merton, *Reader in Bureaucracy* (Glencoe, Ill.: The Free Press, 1952), p. 69.

38. Leonard D. White, *The Civil Service in the Modern State* (Chicago: University of Chicago Press, 1930), p. xi.
39. Chapman, *The Profession of Government*, p. 21.
40. Gladden, *A History of Public Administration*, Vol. II, p. 163.
41. Herman Finer, *The Theory and Practice of Modern Government*, rev. ed. (New York: Holt, Rinehart & Winston, Inc., 1949), p. 731.
42. *Ibid.*, p. 733.
43. Chapman, *The Profession of Government*, p. 25.
44. *Ibid.*, p. 26.
45. *Ibid.*, p. 29.
46. Gladden, *A History of Public Administration*, Vol. II, p. 297.
47. Bendix, *Nation-Building and Citizenship*, p. 109.

5

ADMINISTRATION IN THE DEVELOPED NATIONS
General Characteristics and "Classic" Administrative Systems

Given the historical background of the dominant lines of evolution in the process of political and administrative modernization, as this process is identified with the Western European experience, we need to consider more closely the current leading characteristics of these particular "modernized" polities and of others like them. Also, we should try to identify some of the attributes of the bureaucracies in these polities which may be shared despite substantial individual divergences, and which may distinguish them as a group from those countries that are less developed generally and less modernized politically. Then we can proceed to examine in more detail some of the more important representative individual countries. Public administration in the countries we have called developed does not suffer from lack of attention. Much is known and much has been written about these administrative systems. Our task is briefly to characterize administration in a few of these countries, to show differences among them, and to distinguish them as a group, with respect to public administration, from the developing countries. This does not permit the qualifications and amplifications a fuller treatment would demand.

Shared Political and Administrative Characteristics

The characteristics shared by the modernized polities of Western Europe and elsewhere have been described with substantial agreement by a number of students of comparative politics.[1]

1. The system of governmental organization is highly differentiated and functionally specific, and the allocation of political roles is by achievement rather than ascription, reflecting general characteristics of the society. Among other things, this means a bureaucracy with a high degree of internal specialization and with competence or merit as a standard for bureaucratic recruitment.

2. Procedures for making political decisions are largely rational and secular. The power position of traditional elites has been eroded and the appeal of traditional values greatly weakened. A predominantly secular and impersonal system of law reflects this orientation.

3. The volume and range of political and administrative activity are extensive, permeating all major spheres of life in the society, and the tendency is toward further extension.

4. There is a high correlation between political power and legitimacy, resting on a sense of popular identification with the nation-state which is widespread and effective. Such a system makes a prolonged discrepancy between power and legitimacy less likely, and is more efficient "in the sense that power relationships are more often translated into legitimizations and less frequently left outside the political sphere."[2]

5. Popular interest and involvement in the political system are widespread, but this does not necessarily mean active participation by the citizenry in general in political decision-making. The concept of modernization is not linked with any particular regime or ideology; it does not imply, for example, democracy and representative government. Nevertheless, one of the characteristics shared by modernizing societies is that commonly "modernization begins under autocracy or oligarchy and proceeds toward some form of mass society—democratic or authoritarian."[3] In the mass society, the range of effective popular participation in the process of political decision-making may be extensive or it may be drastically curtailed by the dominance of a relatively small elite group.

Counterpart characteristics may be anticipated in the bureaucracies of these polities, despite substantial variations in the pattern of the bureaucracy from one country to another.

1. The public service of a modernized political system will be large scale, complex, and instrumental in the sense that its mission is understood to be that of carrying out the policies of the political decision-makers. In other words, it will tend to have the attributes Weber specified for his "ideal type" bureaucracy, including both the structural prerequisites and the behavioral tendencies mentioned by him.

2. The bureaucracy will be highly specialized and will require in its ranks most of the occupational and professional categories represented in the society. This is a reflection both of the range of governmental activities in a modernized polity and of the technical requirements for success in carrying out governmental programs.

3. The bureaucracy will exhibit to a marked degree a sense of professionalization, both in the sense of identification with the public service as a profession and in the sense of belonging to a narrower field of professional or technical specialization within the service, such as law, nuclear engineering, or social work. This professional outlook springs from a combination of such factors as the standards of competence applied in recruitment and the common background in education and training that this implies for various specialties, pride in the work being done and in the manner of its performance, and career orientation to the public service as against private sector careers. The positive values for the public service associated with professionalization are apt to be accompanied by tendencies toward bureaucratic self-protection. Such behavior has been variously referred to as dysfunctional, latent, expedient, self-defeating, and pathological. It is the opposite side of the coin of professionalism in bureaucracy.

4. Because the political system as a whole is relatively stable and mature, and the bureaucracy is more fully developed, the role of the bureaucracy in the political process is fairly clear. The desirability of a line of demarcation between the bureaucracy and other political institutions is generally accepted, although the line may be somewhat blurred. Some indicators point toward a double transfer of power in recent years—from the legislature to the executive, and from the executive to the top civil service—which has resulted in a partial merger of political power and administrative action in the careers of higher ranking bureaucrats who have been dubbed "the Western mandarins,"[4] but this has not meant the replacement of politicians by bureaucrats. In functional terms, the bureaucracy continues to be primarily involved in the output function of rule application, to a lesser extent in the output function of rule-making, and to a quite limited degree in input functions such as interest aggregation.

5. The bureaucracy in a modernized polity will be subject to effective policy control by other functionally specific political institutions. This is partly due to the specialized orientation of bureaucrats. Morstein Marx has advanced the general proposition that "present-day Western bureaucracies have grown more multiminded than they were before. In turn, they are less capable of

staging their own campaigns over general issues of public policy. Activation is likely to be broader only when policy ends impinge on the immediate occupational interests of the career service as a whole."[5] Even more important is the fact that the bureaucracy and its competitor institutions in the political system have developed more or less simultaneously over a considerable period of time. Political growth is more likely to have been balanced. If there is imbalance, it is not probable that the bureaucracy is the political institution that has the upper hand in a modernized polity; such a situation is much more likely in a developing country. Fred Riggs has placed unusual emphasis on this matter of imposing effective policy control over the bureaucracy, making it a necessary condition for positive political development. In his earlier formulation, he stated that such development occurs "only if these functionally specific institutions actually succeed in imposing policy control over the bureaucracy—if their effective control matches their formal authority. Otherwise, we have negative political development."[6] More recently, he has applied the term "constitutive system" to these institutions of control, but he continues to stress their importance.[7] It should be noted, in line with the earlier rejection of the idea of identifying political modernization with either democracy or totalitarianism, that effective policy control over the bureaucracy need not come from the sources considered proper in a Western political democracy. It may be exercised in a totalitarian system by the dominant single party or its elitist leadership. The mark of bureaucratic control in a modern political system is not the source from which the control comes but the fact that it exists.

"Classic" Administrative Systems—France and Germany

The writings of Max Weber have sometimes been referred to as "classic" bureaucratic theory. It is in the sense that the bureaucracies of France and Germany conform most closely to Weber's description of bureaucracy that they are called here "classic" administrative systems.

The political cultures of Germany and France are similar in two basic respects. One is that during the preceding two centuries each country has been the victim of continuing political instability; successive regimes have often had drastically different political orientations, and political change has been abrupt, drastic, and frequent. In France it meant the violent overthrow of the monarchy brought about by the French Revolution, followed by the era of

Napoleon, experiments with constitutional monarchy alternating with republican government to 1870, and a succession of crises during the Third and Fourth Republics, culminating in the Fifth Republic of De Gaulle in 1958. Since 1789 France has been a constitutional monarchy three times, an empire twice, a semi-dictatorship once, and a republic five times, with most of the transitions taking place as the result of violence. Germany has gone through even more extreme and disruptive changes. The rise of Prussia eventually led to the establishment of a unified Reich under Bismarck in 1871, the German Empire to 1918, the Weimar Republic after World War I, Nazi dictatorship, and the post-World War II division between West and East Germany. The German political heritage is one of disunity, frustration, and the absence of any well-established political culture.

In contrast to discontinuity in politics, both France and Germany have had remarkable administrative and bureaucratic continuity. Prussian administration, acknowledged to be the forerunner of modern bureaucracy, became the core of government in a unified Germany, and this pattern of administration remains essentially unchanged. In France, the administrative apparatus that had been created to serve the *ancien régime* transferred and maintained its allegiance to the nation, after the brief interruption of the Revolution, whether its government took the form of empire or republic. Stability in administrative affairs has been a phenomenon as marked in these two countries as political instability.

What have been the consequences in France and Germany for bureaucratic operating characteristics, for the scope of bureaucratic activity, and for the maintenance of controls over the bureaucracy?[8]

France under the Fifth Republic is evolving a governmental system which combines old and new features in a pattern which is still fluid. The state remains unitary and highly centralized, with the prefect as the principal representative of the central government in each of the ninety-six *departments*, units of local government since the Napoleonic era. At the center, however, a major transition has occurred, with a mixed presidential–parliamentary system controlled since 1958 by Gaullist parties replacing the multiparty parliamentary system with frequently changing coalition cabinets of the Third and Fourth Republics. The President, directly elected since a constitutional amendment in 1962, is an extremely powerful chief executive, able to dominate the Premier and Council of Ministers in the mixed system. In various ways, the powers of the National Assembly have been curtailed to shift the balance of authority from the legislature to the executive and to separate the two branches, including a prohibition against cabinet ministers holding parliamentary seats. Structurally, the central government is divided into fifteen ministries, each in turn subdivided into *directions* as the principal operating units, plus a ministerial cabinet with staff assisting the minister, and various consultative and control organs. The field services of these ministries are extensive, with 95 percent of the total work force located outside of the central offices in Paris.

The French higher level bureaucrats, who provide direction for this "centralized State administration that is wholly or partly responsible for conducting almost every activity in the nation,"[9] are the direct successors of the "corporate body that does not die" which Napoleon wanted to create, and which was in turn linked to the royal service of the *ancien régime*. The most notable characteristic of members of the French administrative elite is that they are considered members of a corps or cadre representing and closely identified with the state. The bureaucrat views himself and is viewed as a public official rather than as a public servant. Speaking for the state and acting on its behalf, he tends to consider himself as possessing a bit of sovereignty which entitles him to respectful attention, and this view is as least partly shared by the citizenry.

The civil service is a career service, ordinarily chosen early in life and pursued to retirement, with slight movement of individuals into and out of the administrative corps in mid-career. Entrance to the bureaucracy, particularly to the higher levels, is difficult and through prescribed channels. The recruitment system is closely geared to the educational system, so that access to the higher civil service is effectively restricted to those who also have access to higher education.

A unique feature of the French bureaucracy is the existence of an administrative superelite, made up of members of groupings known as the *grands corps*, tracing their origins in most cases to the Napoleonic period. Included are major technical corps (such as Corps des Mines and Corps des Ponts et Chaussees) and nontechnical corps (such as Conseil d'Etat, Cours des Comptes, and Inspection des Finances). The number of members in each corps is quite small: for instance, in 1970 it was only 229 in the Conseil d'Etat and 364 in the Inspection des Finances. "Each corps has its own jurisdictions, and has a particular sphere of activity. For example, that of the Inspection des Finances consists of the verification of the State's finances and expenditures; that of the Conseil d'Etat consists of its dual role as advisor to the government and as an administrative court;

and that of the Cour des Comptes in its role as a court that verifies all public accounts. In performing these tasks the corps are fiercely independent institutions: they have their own statutes, by which all members are bound, and they are subject to little interference by the State. They have thus come to be regarded as being at once an integral part of the State apparatus and the State's means of checking its own excesses."[10] Members of the prestigious corps are not confined to assignments in these specialized spheres of activity, however. They are frequently placed on detached duty in other influential positions throughout the administrative system. As many as one-third of the members of a corps such as the Conseil d'Etat may be on such assignments at a given time. In the case of the Inspection des Finances, members often take other assignments after an initial tour of regular duty and may never return to the specialized work of the corps. The Corps des Mines retains its prestige among technical corps despite the decline of mining engineering as a field of activity, with membership serving as a springboard to important administrative posts not requiring this particular specialization. Such practices mean that these corps in effect serve as means to confer status and prestige on those individuals fortunate enough to be chosen for membership at the time of entrance into bureaucratic careers.

Prior to World War II, recruitment into the higher civil service was on a fragmented basis, with each of the *grands corps* making its own selections, and individual ministries doing their own separate screening of other civil administrators. Extensive reforms undertaken in 1945 were aimed at broadening the recruitment base and bringing more uniformity into the selection process. Because of the direct tie-in with the system of higher education, this in turn meant educational reforms. For nontechnical administrators, the first steps were to nationalize the private political science school in Paris where most future officials had for decades received their formal higher education, and then in addition to create a series of similar institutions at locations spread across the country. The most significant innovation was to establish a National School of Administration (ENA) as a common training center for future higher administrators, with entry through a common examination open to university graduates. The intent was to open up the service to a broader spectrum of applicants, screen them through a single examination device, train them through an intensive three-year postselection curriculum, and then parcel them out to the *grands corps* and the ministries on the basis of matching the most promising young administrators with the most desirable career opportunities. Coupled with these moves, for the first time a central civil service directorate was established and a uniform code dealing with rights and responsibilities of civil servants was enacted.

The consensus is that these reform efforts have accomplished much less than was anticipated. Democratization of the civil service has not occurred, mainly because access to higher education continues to be primarily confined to students from upper social class origins, with a heavy concentration of graduates from metropolitan Paris rather than from the provinces. About 40 percent of the entrants into the *grands corps* continue to come from family backgrounds in the civil service, mostly in the higher ranks. A provision designed to permit entry into the National School of Administration of a limited number of civil servants with prior executive experience has not in fact opened up many such opportunities. ENA graduates have access to the *grands corps* and the ministries according to a well-established pecking order of desirability. All aspire to membership in a prestigious corps, but only about the top 20 percent of the graduates can qualify for one of the *grands corps,* which "retain their existence, their prestige, and the loyalty of their members, who are still the mandarins of the French bureaucracy."[11] The others enter the corps of particular ministries, with finance and interior being the most attractive, and others such as agriculture, labor, and justice having much less drawing power. The result is an uneven distribution of talent among program areas of government operation.

Although only partially successful, the postwar reforms nevertheless led to significant changes. The aim of instilling a more common outlook among the administrative elite gained headway through the replacement of separate examinations by a common examination for entry into the ENA, and the sharing by newly selected recruits for the higher administrative service of a three-year training program which combined internship for practical experience, concentrated study in one of four fields of specialization (general administration, economic and financial administration, social administration, and foreign affairs), and placement for a brief period in private industry to provide insight into industrial management. The result has undoubtedly been to reduce separatist tendencies, despite the continued prevalence of the corps tradition within the bureaucracy.

The postwar period has also seen an almost total replacement in the ranks of higher level bureaucrats, due in part to wartime manpower losses and purges at the time of liberation, opening up opportunities for younger products of the administrative reform movement. Moreover, the Fifth Republic political leadership has stressed national renewal to be gained by technological expertise provided by technicians in the bureaucracy, which has brought many higher civil servants into prominent positions as ministerial advisors and frequently as ministers themselves. Opportunities for the meaningful use of administrative skills have never been better. As summarized by Ridley and Blondel, the civil service "is still the reservoir of talented and enterprising men, the best training ground for many careers outside the public service, and the source of much power. Its economic, social, and even cultural influence has probably increased over the years. It has been one of the main driving forces, if not *the* driving force, in French life—and it is likely to remain so."[12]

Recent years have also brought about a clearer definition of the relationship between the state and civil servants. In theory, the French civil servant has always been subject to employment conditions determined unilaterally by the state, as distinguished from the contractual relationship between private employees and employers. This basic concept has been unaffected by the shift from monarchy to nation, or by variations in political regimes. In practice, this meant during the nineteenth century that although civil servants were given advantages such as security of tenure and generous salaries and fringe benefits, they were also denied rights extended to private employees in such matters as union recognition, collective bargaining, and resort to strikes.

The civil service statute of 1946, although reaffirming the concept that conditions of public employment are to be set by the state and can be unilaterally changed by state action, in fact retained prior privileges while recognizing rights previously denied. Consequently, the French civil servant continues to enjoy security of tenure on a lifetime basis, subject only to the unlikely loss of job on the basis of redundancy (in which case compensation must be provided), or dismissal as a disciplinary sanction available only in accordance with detailed procedures by special disciplinary tribunals on which officials are represented. Salaries are intended to maintain status and recognize the public obligations of the official rather than to pay for actual work performed, and the remuneration is adequate although not lavish. Comprehensive fringe benefits include family allowances, various social security programs, and generous retirement pensions. Promotions and other changes in status are controlled in large measure by the civil service itself.

The 1946 law gave formal recognition of the right of civil servants to organize trade unions, following decades of uncertainty as to legality. Strikes by civil servants had been ruled as illegal earlier, and the 1946 reforms did not clearly define whether a right to strike exists. In the absence either of a prohibition or a positive authorization, decisions of the Conseil d'Etat have held that disciplinary action cannot be taken against civil servants solely because they have gone on strike, but with reservations that essential services must be maintained and that higher civil servants cannot strike. The civil service union movement has grown markedly in the postwar period, and strikes by civil servants have in fact become commonplace.

Participation in political activities has also been clarified. Most civil servants are free to join political parties and take part in party activities. Those in positions of responsibility are not barred but are not supposed to disclose their civil service status or make use of information acquired because of their official assignments. Civil servants may become candidates for elective office, and may serve in most local offices without giving up active duty, but if they run and are elected to the national legislature they must go on inactive status during the term of service, with a right to return later.

Within this legal framework, French bureaucratic behavioral traits as related to more general French cultural characteristics have been analyzed thoroughly and perceptively by various scholars, most notably by Michel Crozier and Ezra N. Suleiman. Crozier views the bureaucratic pattern of decision-making as well fitted to basic French cultural traits in stressing the qualities of rationality, impersonality, and absoluteness. "Frenchmen do not dislike change; they dislike disorder, conflict, everything that may bring uncontrolled relationships; they cannot move in ambiguous, potentially disruptive situations. . . What they fear is not change itself, but the risks they may encounter if the stalemate that protects them (and restricts them at the same time) were to disappear."[13]

Crozier's view of France as essentially a "stalemate society" reflects his conclusion as to the consequences of two deep-seated yet contradictory attitudes—an urge to avoid as much as possible direct face-to-face authority relationships, and a prevailing view of authority in terms of universalism and absolutism. The

bureaucratic system provides a means of reconciling these contradictory attitudes through impersonal rules and centralization, which
combine an absolutist conception of authority with the elimination
of most direct dependence relationships. "In other words," says
Crozier, "the French bureaucratic system of organization is the
perfect solution to the basic dilemma of Frenchmen about authority.
They cannot bear the omnipotent authority which they feel is
indispensable if any kind of co-operative activity is to succeed."[14]

Although suited to the basic requirements of a stalemate
society, the French administrative subsystem suffers, according to
Crozier, from inherent dysfunctions. One is that decisions are
inadequate because those making decisions are too far removed from
those affected by the decisions. A second is that coordination is
difficult. Fears of conflict and face-to-face relationships lead to
organizational self-restraint to avoid overlapping, about which
French higher civil servants have "a sort of panicky fear." This is
caused, Crozier suggests, "by their conception of authority as an
absolute that cannot be shared, discussed, or compromised. If they
prefer restraint to imperialism, this is not for co-operative purposes,
but for the preservation of the integrity of the organization's power;
this attitude tends, therefore, to result mostly in caution and conservatism, and reinforce the pattern of over-all centralization which
curtails the possibilities of initiative and autonomous development
of each organization."[15]

The final "overall and recurrent" problem is that of adjusting
to change. Crozier believes that the usual response of a bureaucratic
organization to change shows a pattern of routine and crisis, with
long periods of routine alternating with short periods of crisis—a
pattern especially pronounced in France. "The difference between
France and other Western countries concerns much more the way
change is achieved than the actual degree of change. To obtain a
limited reform in France, one is always obliged to attack the whole
'system,' which is thus constantly called into question. This explains
why the rules of the game can never be completely accepted.
Reform can be brought about only by sweeping revolution. . . On the
other hand, revolutionary utterances tend to have only a symbolic
value, and they suffer a constant erosion."[16] In Crozier's judgment,
the *grands corps* offer the most promise as agents of change, being
remote from pressure and capable of cushioning at least minor crises.
However, such intervention has only limited possibilities. The
direction of reform is usually toward more centralization, because
this has resolved earlier crises. Citizen participation is minimal or

nonexistent. "Peace, order, and harmony" are the objectives, rather than "experimentation and innovation." Hence the *grands corps* "cannot really play the role of prime mover," and major issues of change must be referred by the bureaucracy to higher level policy-makers.[17]

Suleiman's more recent study of the French administrative elite supports Crozier on most basic matters, offers some different interpretations, and deals with additional questions. He concurs as to the rigid centralizing tendencies in French administration and the urgency of far-reaching administrative reforms. He also confirms the pivotal role of the *grands corps* in the apparatus of administration, essentially undisturbed by postwar reform efforts. However, he challenges Crozier's suggestion that these corps function as agents of change within the bureaucracy. Rather than mediating between the bureaucracy and the environment in times of crisis, he interprets the available evidence as indicating that these corps are an integral part of a system that is resistant to change. "These corps and their members are part and parcel of the administrative system. And since the members of the Grands Corps occupy posts throughout the administration, they come to be at the same time members of a corps *and* officials within institutions that have little or no relation to the corps. As the latter they enter into the administration proper, engaging in the defense of their institution, its conflicts and rivalries. They call on the network of their corps to help them achieve their institutional goals." Suleiman concludes that "the existence of numerous corps is indissolubly linked with a centralized State."[18] He cites a case study of the Corps des Mines showing how members of this corps have succeeded in stationing themselves in a variety of key administrative positions despite the declining importance of the mining sector. Such corps networks, Suleiman argues, set the standards by which the desirability and pace of change are judged. Moreover, since numerous networks exist and often work at cross-purposes, policy formulation is "reduced to the lowest common denominator between the rival corps."[19] As a result, internecine rivalry takes precedence over public policy issues, tending to dampen change. Suleiman does hypothesize that although the corps as organized entities do not serve as change agents, an individual corps member can initiate change when occupying an important agency post outside the corps, and may use the corps network to which he belongs to support the innovative policy, provided the interests of the corps itself are not threatened. In summary, Suleiman seems to be even less optimistic than Crozier about the prospects for change to be initiated from within the bureaucracy, except in special circumstances.

An interesting question explored by Suleiman is whether the social class origins of members of the administrative elite affect their attitudes and behavior as bureaucrats. After confirming that the higher civil servants continue to come predominantly from the middle and upper-middle classes, he compiles and analyzes available data as to the degree of correlation between socioeconomic background and bureaucratic performance.[20] His tentative conclusion is that the attitudes and behavior of the higher civil servants included in his study were not determined by their social origins, in view of the lack of evidence of division on issues and attitudes along class lines. Without claiming proof, he does state that the data presented strongly suggest that "administrative behavior is not determined by the socioeconomic status of the officials. Greater weight must be ascribed to the training of higher civil servants, the administrative structure itself (for example, the existence of tight units known as corps), and the work environment." Acknowledging the force of the argument against undemocratic recruitment of French bureaucrats, Suleiman nevertheless cautions that "one must avoid the temptation of concluding that the structure of French society, as well as the functioning of the administrative machine itself, would be radically transformed by a proportional representation of the society's classes in its administrative elite."[21]

From what has already been said about the role of the state in French society and about the role of higher civil servants as agents of the state, it is apparent that members of the French administrative elite are involved in a wide range of activities extending well beyond the function of rule application. Two principal features of the French bureaucracy account for this: the permanence of bureaucratic structures and the ubiquity of bureaucratic personnel. Administrative continuity, particularly through the *grands corps*, has already been examined. We need also to review the extent to which members of the bureaucratic elite occupy positions of power and influence both inside and outside the administrative agencies of government.

Within the ministerial structure itself, career civil servants are found at all levels, including an increasing proportion of the ministerial appointments at the apex of the hierarchy. As would normally be expected, members of one of the *grands corps* or a ministry corps almost invariably serve as directors of the *directions*, or operating divisions, of each ministry, although this is not a legal requirement.

For practical purposes, the minister's choice is not only limited to the civil service, but in some instances to members of a particular corps which has "colonized" that sector of the administration. These factors, plus others, greatly circumscribe the actual range of choice and firmly retain these pivotal positions in the hands of the civil service, making the transitory minister greatly dependent on the key professional administrators heading up the *directions*.[22]

Service in the uniquely French institution of the ministerial cabinet offers another channel for input from civil servants. The cabinet is the product of custom rather than statute (except for a partially unsuccessful effort to place a limit of ten on the number of members), consisting of staff associates of the minister chosen by him and serving at his discretion. Its role has shifted over time and may vary from ministry to ministry, but the cabinet is usually viewed as a buffer or intermediary between the minister and external political figures on the one hand, and the permanent internal administrative apparatus on the other. The cabinet has its own hierarchy despite its small size, with a cabinet director who is the key official in the ministry after the minister himself, several members who act as links to particular *directions*, and a lesser number who deal with external matters or have a close personal working relationship with the minister.

Assessments as to the value of these ministerial cabinets vary, some commentators viewing the cabinet as a positive creation making administration more effective, and others looking on it as a device designed to cope with inadequacies in the ministerial system although in practice aggravating them; there seems to be agreement, however, that the cabinet's role is crucial, that it has been growing, and that it engenders conflict. The author of one recent report says that ministerial cabinets "are simultaneously the product and reflection of the French administrative system as a whole," and that cabinet members "occupy a choice position in the French government because of the advice they lavish, the decisions they prepare, and the implementation they supervise."[23]

If such a view is accurate, the fact that civil servants predominate in these assignments is important evidence as to the sphere of activity of higher administrators. Currently under the Fifth Republic 90 percent of the members of ministerial cabinets are civil servants, as compared to 60 percent during the Third Republic. The average length of service in a ministerial cabinet is about three years. At least one such tour is becoming part of the normal career pattern of an aspiring bureaucrat, with approximately half of the members of several of the *grands corps* having had such experience, usually in relatively early stages in their careers.

Suleiman has analyzed carefully the conflict and tension between members of ministerial cabinets and directors of *directions* within ministries, which exists despite the similarities in background and training of individuals in the two groups. He found a marked hostility on the part of the directors toward the cabinet and a reciprocal lack of confidence in the directors by cabinet members, reflecting greatly divergent views between the two groups as to what their degree of authority should be, and as to the relationship between politics and administration. The power of cabinet members tends to be exercised in the name of the minister and with due regard for general governmental policies. The sphere of authority of the directors is more narrowly defined and is little concerned with overall policy questions. The directors regard politics and administration as "distinct domains that only infrequently come into contact with one another, and which, in any case, ought always to remain strictly separate." Cabinet members believe that "the two domains cannot be separated at the highest levels of the administrative system, where decisions are prepared for and alternatives submitted to the minister."[24]

Although Suleiman considers that this conflict reflects two diametrically opposed role perceptions, he also stresses that the occupants who assume these seemingly incompatible roles at different stages in their careers nearly always come from the civil service. "They are the same people; they merely alternate positions and, hence, roles." He concludes that it is dangerous to speak of an administrative "mind" or "mentality" when such diversity of role perceptions exists even among higher civil servants who have "shared a common socialization experience." Loyalties can shift with relative ease. Cabinet members who become directors "adopt a view totally at odds with the view they held while in the cabinet. . . . Evidently a civil servant's interests change with the position he occupies in the politico-administrative hierarchy, and his perception of his role changes too."[25]

Not only do civil servants have a virtual monopoly on the important positions in the *directions* and in the ministerial cabinets, but they also in recent years, particularly since the beginning of the Fifth Republic, have been appointed in increasing numbers to key ministerial posts, with over one-third of the ministers in some recent governments being drawn from the ranks of the civil servants. The Fifth Republic has been referred to as "*La Republique des fonctionnaires,*" and Mattei Dogan says that its hallways have become "the paradise of modern mandarins."[26]

Finally, it should be noted that French civil servants, particularly those who have achieved membership in one of the *grands corps*, hold numerous influential posts beyond the governmental ministries. Included among major political offices are the current president of the republic, Valery Giscard d'Estaing, several postwar premiers, and numerous members of the national parliament. Leadership in most of the nationalized industries is in the hands of civil servants.[27] Frequently higher civil servants have moved at mid-career into private sector positions. This diffusion, greatest under the Fifth Republic, justifies Suleiman's reference to "the ubiquity of civil servants in all the crucial institutions in France."[28]

In view of the prevalence of French bureaucrats, the question must be addressed as to what this means in terms of the long-run "political" role of the bureaucracy and the effectiveness of controls over the bureaucracy. Various interpretations are offered by different authorities. The most common generalization, one that plainly has much to support it historically, is that the bureaucracy has been able to compensate by its own competence and continuity for the fragile and shifting political leadership, and has taken measures to keep its own house in order. As Alfred Diamant has put it, "The Republic passes but the administration remains."[29] Certainly prior to the Fifth Republic, executive control of the bureaucracy was weak, and legislative control was sporadic and fragmented, often directed toward obtaining favors or blocking programs rather than guiding bureaucratic efforts. In the absence of effective external controls, mechanisms of internal control were developed as an "inner check" on the bureaucracy. The Conseil d'Etat has gradually become the most important such agency, by taking on the judicial function of evaluating administrative acts for the protection of citizens' rights, by advising on bill drafting and executive decrees, and by consulting with ministries on administrative problems and suggesting remedial measures.

This hypothesis of political instability offset by administrative stability has come under increasing attack. Crozier objects to a simplified contrast between "permanent and efficient administrative bureaucracy" and "unstable governments unable to choose and carry out consistent policy." He regards this situation not as a paradox but as a reflection at the organizational level of basic French traits of rationality, impersonality, and absoluteness which are present in the decisions produced by a decision-making pattern in which the administrative system is dominant. He finds this situation to have been well suited to the problems of the stalemate society of the late nineteenth century, because it introduced "the exact amount of change that was tolerable," but he believes that "the more the political system has become bureaucratic, the less has it been able to bring to the administrative system the renewal needed." He maintains that as long as the predominance of the administrative system persists, the whole political system will remain unbalanced.[30]

Suleiman's study of the French administrative elite, being more recent, is able to devote fuller attention to the evolution of political control over the bureaucracy during the Fifth Republic. He sharply criticizes the theme that under the Third and Fourth Republics power was shifted from the politicians to the civil servants because of ministerial instability, and raises doubts about assertions that long-range policies were largely the work of permanent officials rather than politicians, maintaining instead that they were usually the product of shifting alliances between the two groups. He does argue that the Fifth Republic has brought significant changes in political control over the bureaucracy. The impact of parliamentary supervision has definitely weakened, a by-product of the relative impotence of the legislative branch under the mixed presidential-parliamentary system. Executive control has been considerably strengthened, particularly since the 1962 constitutional changes which enhanced the powers of the presidency. Ministerial direction has been assisted by the somewhat longer average term in office of ministers.

The really crucial development in Suleiman's view, however, is the rise of a dominant political party. Since 1962 the Gaullist party, under various names and with shifting combinations of party factions, has brought about a basic alteration of the traditional multi-party system. President Giscard d'Estaing was elected in 1974 with support from a Gaullist coalition called the Union of Progressive Republicans, which despite internal splits and subsequent losses to left-of-center opposition parties has maintained control of the central government. The political system in France in recent years, as characterized by Suleiman, "has combined the chief elements of the British parliamentary system and the American presidential system. The presidency and the legislature have been in the hands of a single political party, which has been able to govern on its own. . . . ministers are now able to exert greater influence in the administrative and political spheres—not because of the diminished role of parliament or the ministers' relatively long stay in office, but because they have had the support of a dominant political party."[31] With its strong hold over state institutions, including the bureaucracy, the dominant party has been able to hold a tighter rein over the higher civil service and identify it with the Gaullist political movement. The result is a higher degree of control from the political sector, but it is "not a neutral control; it is control by and subordination to a particular political force."[32] Consequently, Suleiman and others have speculated that should political power shift to a leftist party or party coalition in the future, a purge of the upper echelons of the bureaucracy would likely follow. The prospect in any case seems to be that the French administrative elite, despite its impressive capabilities for self-protection, faces a greater challenge to its autonomy than it has been accustomed to in the past.

The political institutions of Germany differ in some basic respects from those of France. Since the unification of the Reich under Bismarck, Germany has had a federal system of government, except for the period of Nazi rule. With the division of the country at the end of World War II, West Germany (the German Federal Republic) reverted to the federal system, whereas East Germany (the German Democratic Republic) retained under its Communist totalitarian regime a unitary centralized structure much like the Nazi pattern. In the West German federal system, the constituent units are the ten *Laender* plus West Berlin as an associated entity. Each *Land* has extensive administrative and adjudicative responsibilities delegated to it, but the national or Reich government dominates in the legislative arena. Essentially the division of functions in this federal system is that most important legislative decisions on policy are made by the central government, but the *Laender* are relied on primarily as the vehicles for administration of the programs legislated. As a consequence, only 10 percent of the bureaucracy is attached to the national government, with the bulk of the bureaucrats being in the administrative services of the *Laender*.

The Bonn constitution of 1949 also provided for a parliamentary government, with a bicameral legislature, a chancellor as the chief executive officer, and a president functioning essentially as an elected constitutional monarch with very limited powers, chosen for a term of office of five years. The chancellor was designed to be a strong executive. Elected by the Bundestag, or lower house of the legislature, every four years at the beginning of a new Bundestag, the chancellor can be removed only by a motion of no confidence coupled with election of a successor by an absolute majority of the Bundestag members. Moreover, the chancellor can ask for a vote of confidence any time he chooses, and if he is defeated, he can request the president to dissolve the Bundestag and hold new elections. The chancellor appoints cabinet ministers to serve at his discretion.

The executive structure under the chancellor includes the chancellor's office and a variable number of ministries as determined by him. The chancellery now consists of about 100 higher civil servants, with a supporting staff three times as large, and is headed by a director whose powers are second only to those of the chancellor. Under Adenauer, tight control was exercised over the ministries by the chancellor's office, which set program priorities, prepared cabinet agendas, and served as a communication channel between the executive and the legislature. Under later coalition governments, control from the chancellor and his office has been somewhat diluted.

The number of ministries has varied in the past from a high of nineteen to a low of twelve, and now stands at fifteen. The typical German ministry is quite small as compared to those in most other countries, with a range of from about 1800 down to only about 300 employees, due to reliance in most instances on *Laender* officials to provide the necessary administrative infrastructure. As Mayntz and Scharpf point out, "most federal ministries should be regarded primarily as fairly large policy-making staffs rather than as administrative line organizations."[33]

The typical ministerial structure is organized along lines that emphasize hierarchical authority but also allow for considerable decentralization in operation. Staff capability around the minister at the top is relatively limited, but this small staff is selected by the minister and usually leaves office when he does, so that personal loyalty to the minister is its hallmark. The staff consists of a personal assistant and a press or public relations assistant, a bureau to perform routine clerical and administrative tasks, and one or two state secretaries. The latter, usually picked from among the permanent civil servants in the ministry, provide the strongest element of continuity and may continue in office from one minister to another, although they have no claim to do so. In recent years, an additional role of parliamentary secretary has been created, designed to deal with parliamentary relations for the ministry, and filled by a member of parliament who usually is a close political associate of the minister.

Below the level of the minister and state secretaries, the typical structural breakdown is into divisions, which in turn are subdivided into sections as the basic working units. The divisions and sections are ordinarily set up on the basis of programs provided or clienteles served. An exception is a division in each ministry where management or housekeeping functions are centralized, such as budgeting, personnel administration, and provision of legal services. Most of the operating sections are quite small, but the working capacity of the ministry, as Mayntz and Scharpf point out,[34] is almost entirely concentrated at this lowest hierarchical level. Policy-making is decentralized, with limited capacity for policy direction from the top.

The bureaucrats of the German Federal Republic are the modern-day offspring of the Prussian officialdom of earlier centuries, which has been accurately described as "a social elite recruited on the basis of competitive examination and dedication both to efficiency and to the principle of autocracy."[35] This bureaucracy, consisting of university-trained professionals, held a dominant position in the industrialization of Germany during the nineteenth century. Nominally responsible during the Second Reich to the prime minister and the monarchy, the federal bureaucracy in practice made most domestic policy decisions, relying for their administration on the bureaucracies of the *Laender*, which were in turn patterned on the same model. This bureaucratic system became famous for its competence and integrity and earned high prestige, although it also must bear some of the responsibility for the slow development of institutions of popular self-governance in Germany.

The harmony between the bureaucratic elite and the dominant political leadership was disrupted during the Weimar Republic and the Nazi Third Reich. Many higher level bureaucrats were unsympathetic to the republic and were not trusted by its political leaders. Later, under the Nazis, the bureaucrats were made subservient to the party leaders, who were suspicious of them at the same time they were dependent on them.

After World War II, the occupying powers made efforts to reform the German public service, with very little lasting impact in West Germany, where the tendency has been to revert to many of the bureaucratic patterns which had been altered temporarily by the political turmoil earlier in the century. Hence the lines of continuity are strong with the Prussian bureaucracy, despite the fact that most of the area that was Prussia is no longer in the German Federal Republic, and even though a successful transition to a parliamentary political regime has been made since World War II.

The public service sector in West Germany is extensive, amounting to about 12 percent of the gainfully employed in the country. Less than 10 percent of these public servants are in the federal bureaucracy, however, because of reliance on the *Laender* for program administration, and the rate of growth is lower for the federal bureaucracy than for areas such as health and education at the

Laender level. Public employees are divided into three principal
categories: permanent members of the civil service (*Beamten*),
salaried employees (*Angestellten*) who do not have the same tenure
and pension privileges, and wage-earning manual laborers (*Arbeiter*)
employed on short-term contracts. The *Beamten* have higher status
and theoretically are assigned to the more responsible positions.
They account for about 45 percent of the total number of public
servants, and their ranks include judges, teachers, and managerial
personnel in the railroad and postal systems as well as most of the
occupants of higher level positions in other ministries. Although the
status and prestige of the *Beamten* still set them apart, the differences between this group and the salaried employees have been
diminishing in recent years, both as to responsibilities assigned and
employment conditions. Identical functions are now often performed by members of the two groups, and job security and retirement
provisions are not markedly different in actual practice, although
handled under separate systems. The remaining significant differences have more to do with career training, recruitment, and patterns
of advancement. Proposals for unification into a single uniform
public service of all persons employed full time have been made
recently, but do not seem likely to be adopted soon.

Vertically, the civil service is divided into four classes—lower,
medium, intermediate, and higher. Each class is in turn broken into
numerous functional categories, such as general administration,
finance, teaching, health, and other technical fields. Each functional
category within a class normally consists of five ranks constituting a
career ladder, with entrance of new recruits at the bottom rank of
the category for which they qualify, only rare horizontal movement
later between functional categories, and very slight opportunity for
advancement upward into the next higher class. As evaluated by
Mayntz and Scharpf, this system has advantages in ease of comprehension, easy comparability of positions, and equality of promotion
chances, but "has obviously not been designed to increase efficiency
by permitting personnel allocation to follow functional requirements.
The boundary lines between classes and categories often do not
correspond to any clear breaks in the difficulty of tasks or in the
qualifications actually necessary to fulfill them. Potentially meaningful careers where the experience gained in performing a lower
function serves as preparation for the next higher one often cut
across the boundary between two classes. Conversely there are often
no significant real differences in the job requirements of positions
assigned to different ranks within a class, which means that the

five-step pattern produces artificial differentiations. These are serious handicaps for a flexible system of personnel management."[36]

The *Beamten* in the higher civil service continue to characterize the German bureaucracy. Expected to have a special loyalty to the state, they are restricted as to political activity and denied the right to strike. In return, they receive deference in various ways, including lavish use of titles extended not only to the civil servants but to their wives as well, and which confer status not only within the service but in society generally. Recruited on a career basis, they are expected to be prepared for assignment to positions covering a wide variety of duties, particularly in the functional category of general administration.

Access to these policy-making positions in the higher civil service is along a well-defined path open ordinarily only to members of the upper and upper-middle classes, much as in France. A university degree is essential. Traditionally, a legal education has been preferred, and 60 percent of the higher civil servants today have had legal training, but more diversification is occurring gradually, particularly in fields of technical specialization. Even so, top positions in the federal bureaucracy are still filled mostly by individuals with legal training.

University graduates who are selected on the basis of general examinations enter a three-year period of further training within the service, combining academic and on-the-job instruction. Those who are successful in a second examination at the end of this period then enter the higher civil service on a career basis. Owing to the extended preparatory steps, entrance is rarely possible earlier than age twenty-five. In addition to screening through university curricula and examinations, a self-selective tendency is indicated in recent studies pointing toward attraction to the civil service of students who emphasize occupational values such as job and old-age security, tasks that are clearly structured, and well-circumscribed demands on abilities and time, rather than values such as work that is interesting and autonomous, or that leads to more than average success in terms of income and position. Dogmatism, rigidity, and intolerance of ambiguity are among the personality traits of the typical recruit, who is at the same time performance-motivated to a high degree. "The higher civil service still seems to attract those who are by disposition a typically bureaucratic version of organization man," with a self-selective tendency which "appears dysfunctional from the viewpoint of personal characteristics favorable to the needs of active policy-making."[37]

Advancement within the system after entry seems to depend on a combination of two sets of criteria. Most important are the traditional civil service considerations such as seniority, professional competence, loyalty, and good working relationships with colleagues. There are indications that other criteria of a more political nature are now being given more weight as well, including "partisan affiliation, political skills, the political support someone can muster or enjoys, and a record of good relations to one or more important client groups."[38] Officially criteria in the first category continue to be the ones recognized, and periodic evaluations are intended to be the instruments for measuring them, but such criteria are difficult to operationalize, and the subjective judgment of superiors is clearly an influential factor, so that it is not easy to measure the actual mix of these competing sets of criteria.

For the individual higher civil servant, promotion is crucial if he is to gain the benefits of higher salary, old-age pension, and social benefits which are tied in with the rank system. In addition to these material benefits, promotion also opens up opportunities for moving into more influential and responsible positions with corresponding autonomy, prestige, and authority. However, this kind of incentive is somewhat muted by the lack of strict correlation between the hierarchy of formal ranks and the hierarchy of positions, with advancement in rank and in position not necessarily coinciding. The result is a tendency for the civil servant in his own material self-interest to emphasize primarily promotion in rank. Since seniority and experience are more important here and present fewer risks than the exercise of initiative, some commentators think that the consequence is a tendency by federal bureaucrats to take a passive rather than an active stance in policy-making.

Normally, the higher civil service continues to be a career pursued to retirement by those who succeed in getting in during early maturity, but as in France instances of departure at mid-career to accept lucrative opportunities in the professions or in the private sector have been on the increase, causing concern as to the long-range impact on the quality of the higher civil service.

Based on the historical background of the German bureaucracy, its structural features, and the pre-entry experiences and views of those who enter it, one might naturally expect that German senior civil servants would hold attitudinal values conforming closely to those of "the classical Weberian bureaucrat: legalistic in his orientation, a-political in his views, impartial in his judgment, an obedient instrument in the hands of his masters and a strict, impersonal

superior to his subordinates."[39]   Until recently, this has been the
accepted view, and undoubtedly it continues to be accurate for large
numbers of German bureaucrats. However, empirical studies during
the last few years indicate that a growing number of German bureaucrats do not fit this classical image. Robert D. Putnam, reporting on
results of a cross-national research project on the political attitudes
of senior civil servants,[40] concluded that German federal bureaucratic
respondents did not, as had been anticipated, cluster heavily toward
the "classical bureaucrat" type in a continuum postulating this and
the "political bureaucrat" as polar syndromes. The distinction between these types has to do with attitudes toward politics and
political actors, with the classical bureaucrat believing that public
issues can be resolved in terms of impartial and objective standards,
and distrusting political institutions such as parliaments, political
parties, and pressure groups. The political bureaucrat, on the other
hand, has a more pluralistic concept of the public interest, recognizes
the need to bargain and compromise, and is more willing to accept
the legitimacy of political influences on policy-making.

Contrary to expectations, the German respondents proved to be
as "political" in orientation and to hold the associated attitudes at
least as much as their colleagues in Great Britain, and to a much
greater extent than the Italian respondents. "By all the measures
now available, they are hardly less egalitarian, hardly less liberal,
hardly less politically responsive or programmatic in outlook" than
their counterparts in countries such as Britain or Sweden who have
been viewed as conforming more to the "political bureaucrat"
image.[41]

These findings, supported by related research, point toward significant ongoing attitudinal shifts among German bureaucrats.
Although part of the explanation may be interview bias and the turnover in top positions which took place in 1969 when the Social
Democratic party came to power, the age structure of the respondents offers what Putnam calls the "essential clue" to interpretation
of his data. A rapid generational change seems to have been taking
place during the 1960s. Because of decimation of the male population during World War II, as male civil servants have retired at 65 in
recent years, they have been replaced by considerably younger men
of 55 or even 50. Rapid changes in age structure have resulted as the
prewar generation of civil servants began to retire. A secondary explanation is that the Social Democratic "purge" was more a generational
purge than a partisan one, bringing in replacements who were usually
younger than their predecessors. Since age turns out to be the best

predictor of political attitudes, this transition from older to younger bureaucrats has meant an overall shift away from "classical" bureaucratic attitudes in the bureaucracy as a whole. This interpretation is bolstered by the fact that German respondents showed a much greater diversity of attitudes than did their British counterparts, reflecting an ambivalence that is associated with the wider age spread in the German group. Of course, it is possible that the correlation between attitude and age is due, as Putnam puts it, to "the temporary effects of being a particular age," rather than "the permanent effects of being in a given historical generation," but he argues that the generational change more likely accounts for the correlation, and observes that "as Germany has finally come to terms with the age of democracy, her bureaucracy seems likely to continue to move toward greater responsiveness, at least insofar as this is a function of the norms and values of senior bureaucrats."[42] Mayntz and Scharpf concur that the evidence indicates that "federal bureaucrats involved in policy-making are by and large characterized by attitudes favorable to the fulfillment of their function." The authors add that this is so, however, "not because of, but rather in spite of the current civil service system with its typical patterns of training, recruitment, and promotion."[43]

Given the historical precedent of bureaucratic initiative, augmented by current inclinations to work cooperatively with the political leadership, the implication would be that the current German bureaucracy is actively and extensively engaged in policy-making functions, and this is corroborated by available evidence. In their analysis of the process of policy-making, Mayntz and Scharpf absolve the bureaucracy from any deliberate intent to usurp political control, saying that "the federal bureaucracy does not attempt actively to circumvent executive control and to impose upon the political executive a course of action developed to its own preferences."[44] However, they conclude that much policy is initiated on a decentralized basis and that the executive does not direct the policy-making process systematically by formulating explicit policy goals and closely controlling new program development. This in turn reflects unusual difficulty in obtaining political consensus among divergent interests. Acknowledging that this is a problem "characteristic of all ideologically heterogeneous, socio-economically pluralistic, and politically differentiated Western democracies," they nevertheless argue that "institutional conditions in the Federal Republic increase these difficulties beyond the level that is characteristic of either the classical parliamentary systems or the American presidential system."[45] Elections do not usually reduce interest complexity requiring consideration, governments tend to be coalition governments, West Germany's "peculiar type of federalism adds to the range of interests that must be taken into account," and the federal government itself "consists of a plurality of semi-independent actors" with the chancellorship lacking unifying potential. The resulting decision-making deadlocks often mean that policy issues are left unresolved or are dealt with in the bureaucracy by default.

Despite political turbulence and the variety of political regimes in German national history, the record is one of effective external political controls over the bureaucracy. During the Second Reich, direct controls were few but, as Herbert Jacob comments, "the confluence of interests and values among all participants in the political process almost automatically produced responsiveness," with dissenters from the conservative consensus simply being excluded from the political arena. The Weimar Republic resorted to more stringent hierarchical controls, and the Nazi Third Reich placed even more emphasis on direct hierarchical controls plus exerting various other external pressures to keep the bureaucracy in line. The German Federal Republic uses a mixture of hierarchical and political controls. "In retrospect," Jacob summarizes, "each German regime commanded a loyal enough administration so that not once in the last century did a breakdown of the administrative process lead to the collapse of a regime. . . . To an amazing extent the civil service identified with whatever regime possessed power and served it ably."[46]

A closer look at the mix of controls existing in the period since World War II underlines the strong element of continuity with the past. The German civil service is to a considerable extent self-regulating out of necessity, because of political regime instability. Certainly the comment that governments come and go but the bureaucracy remains is at least as applicable to Germany as to France. With its elite composition, shared professional perspective, and public prestige, the German bureaucracy has acknowledged an obligation and has had the means to police itself in many respects.

Hierarchical controls within the ministries, strong in the past, tended to be weaker during the early years of the German Federal Republic, according to Mayntz and Scharpf, because of inadequate executive attention, which was in turn accounted for by "the limited capacity at the top and the confluence of a multitude of diverse and pressing demands,"[47] leading to later reform efforts which have been only partially successful.

Parliamentary control through the chancellor and the ministers conforms basically to standard practice in a parliamentary system, although there are obstacles to effective clear-cut directives from these political sources, as has already been mentioned. A point to remember is that traditionally in Germany civil servants have been permitted to serve in parliament, taking leave from their civil service duties temporarily and resuming their bureaucratic careers later if they wish. Even during the postwar period, public employees have made up about 20 percent of the members of the Bundestag. This overlapping of membership in parliament and the bureaucracy probably eases relationships between the two institutions.

The federal structure of German government also affects bureaucratic control. The Bundesrat, which is the upper chamber of the legislature, represents the interests of the *Laender* and has constitutional powers designed to protect the integrity of the federal system. Membership of the Bundesrat consists of representatives of the *Laender*, chosen by the *Land* governments, with the number varying from five to three depending on *Land* population. All constitutional amendments require Bundesrat approval, as does all legislation affecting *Land* administrative, tax, and territorial interests— amounting to more than 50 percent of all laws passed. Even "ordinary" legislation outside of these categories is subject to a limited veto power by the Bundesrat, which can be overruled only by an equivalent majority in the Bundestag, or lower house. If a two-thirds majority rejects a proposal in the Bundesrat, for example, it must be passed by a two-thirds majority of the Bundestag to become law. The threat of a Bundesrat veto is a consideration which must be taken into account by federal government officials, including both politicians and bureaucrats.

Finally, Germany has a well-articulated system of administrative courts which have jurisdiction over acts of administrators at both the federal and *Land* levels. Decisions of the supreme administrative courts of the *Laender* are subject to appeal to the federal administrative court, which also has exclusive jurisdiction over cases that arise at the federal level. Rulings of the administrative courts provide uniform interpretations for policies mandating administrative action and in other ways ensure responsive administration.

As we have seen, the bureaucracies of both France and Germany have been quite actively involved in the conduct of governmental affairs, including intimate participation in policy-making and program-planning. This has been an inevitable result of the cohesion and professionalization of the bureaucracy, the necessity of new political regimes to rely on bureaucratic skills to keep the government machinery functioning, and the value placed in the society on the claims of expert knowledge in the conduct of public affairs. It has been facilitated by the relative lack of restrictions on engaging in political activities by civil servants in these countries, which has permitted leading bureaucrats to shift to active political life with the option of returning later to their service careers. Both political appointment to ministerial posts and service in national legislatures has thus been possible for individuals who have established themselves as administrators. Indeed, at crucial times, such as in Bismarck's Germany or recently in De Gaulle's France, many of the most important governmental posts have been held by officials from the bureaucracy.

Granted that there has been a long-standing centrality of the bureaucracy in sustaining government functions in both France and Germany, it would be a mistake to conclude that these bureaucracies have taken the initiative in political change, or that they have effectively resisted the policies of new political regimes. Instead, the record shows that they have obediently and even subserviently responded to whatever political leaders have gained power. Even the Nazis encountered little difficulty in converting the civil service of the Weimar Republic to their own ends. These bureaucracies have a tradition of professional identity, of service status and prerogative, and of maintaining continuity in the management of governmental affairs, but the tradition is also one of service to the state, whatever masters the state may have. The bureaucratic elite does not lay claim to becoming the political elite as well.

Notes

1. These include Robert E. Ward and Dankwart A. Rustow, eds., *Political Modernization in Japan and Turkey* (Princeton, N.J.: Princeton University Press, 1964), pp. 3-7; Joseph LaPalombara and S. N. Eisenstadt, in *Bureaucracy and Political Development* (Princeton, N.J.: Princeton University Press, 1963), pp. 39-48 and 98-100; Leonard Binder, *Iran: Political Development in a Changing Society* (Berkeley, Calif.: University of California Press, 1962), pp. 46-48; Finer, *The Theory and Practice of Modern Government*, rev. ed. (New York: Henry Holt and Co., 1949), Chapter 27, "The Civil Service in the Modern State," pp. 709-723; and Stanley Rothman, Howard Scarrow, and Martin Schain, *European Society and Politics* (St. Paul: West Publishing Co., 1976), Chapter 16, "Bureaucracy and the Political System," pp. 322-25.
2. Binder, *Iran*, p. 47.
3. Ward and Rustow, *Political Modernization*, pp. 4-5.

4. "The top civil servant who plays an important political role has a hybrid personality: half-political, half-administrative. Like Janus the Roman god, he has two faces. He is a kin to the mandarins of old Imperial China." Mattei Dogan, "The Political Power of the Western Mandarins: Introduction," in M. Dogan, ed., *The Mandarins of Western Europe* (New York: John Wiley & Sons, 1975), pp. 3-24, at p. 4.

5. Fritz Morstein Marx, *Bureaucracy and Political Development* (Princeton, N.J.: Princeton University Press, © 1963), pp. 73-74.

6. Fred W. Riggs, *Administration in Developing Countries—The Theory of Prismatic Society* (Boston: Houghton Mifflin Company, 1964), p. 422.

7. Fred W. Riggs, *Prismatic Society Revisited* (Morristown, N.J.: General Learning Press, 1973), pp. 28-29.

8. Major sources on French bureaucracy include Finer, *The Theory and Practice of Modern Government*, Chapters 29 and 32; Rothman, Scarrow, and Schain, *European Society and Politics*, Chapter 16, pp. 332-42; Alfred Diamant, "The French Administrative System: The Republic Passes but the Administration Remains," in William J. Siffin, ed., *Toward the Comparative Study of Public Administration* (Bloomington, Ind.: Department of Government, Indiana University, 1957), pp. 182-218; Jerzy S. Langrod, "General Problems of the French Civil Service," in Raphaeli, *Readings*, pp. 106-18; F. Ridley and J. Blondel, *Public Administration in France* (London: Routledge & Kegan Paul, 1964); Michel Crozier, *The Bureaucratic Phenomenon* (Chicago, Ill.: University of Chicago Press, 1964), and Ezra N. Suleiman, *Politics, Power, and Bureaucracy in France: The Administrative Elite* (Princeton, N.J.: Princeton University Press, 1974). For information on German bureaucracy, refer to Finer, *The Theory and Practice of Modern Government*, Chapters 28 and 31; Rothman, Scarrow, and Schain, *European Society and Politics*, Chapter 16, pp. 343-47; Herbert Jacob, *German Administration Since Bismarck* (New Haven, Conn.: Yale University Press, 1963); and Renate Mayntz and Fritz W. Scharpf, *Policy-Making in the German Federal Bureaucracy* (Amsterdam: Elsevier, 1975).

9. Excerpt from Ezra N. Suleiman, *Politics, Power, and Bureaucracy in France: The Administrative Elite* (copyright 1974 by Princeton University Press), p. 19. Reprinted by permission of Princeton University Press.

10. *Ibid.*, p. 241.

11. Rothman, Scarrow, and Schain, *European Society and Politics*, p. 337.

12. Ridley and Blondel, *Public Administration in France*, p. 54.

13. Crozier, *The Bureaucratic Phenomenon*, p. 226.

14. *Ibid.*, p. 222.

15. *Ibid.*, p. 253.

16. *Ibid.*, p. 287.

17. *Ibid.*, p. 255.

18. Suleiman, *Politics, Power, and Bureaucracy*, p. 271.

19. *Ibid.*, p. 274.

20. *Ibid.*, Chapter IV, "Social Class and Administrative Behavior," pp. 100-12.

21. *Ibid.*, p. 109.

22. Suleiman asserts that under a parliamentary regime such as that of the Fourth Republic, the real power of civil servants lay in obstruction, and he quotes the observation of one director that "when a minister wanted something unfeasible done, we only had to say 'fine,' and chances were that we would hear no more of it." *Ibid.*, p. 167.

23. Jeanne Siwek-Pouydesseau, "French Ministerial Staffs," in Mattei Dogan, ed., *The Mandarins of Western Europe* (New York: Halsted Press, 1975), pp. 208-9.

24. Suleiman, *Politics, Power, and Bureaucracy*, p. 222.

25. *Ibid.*, Chapter IX, "The Cabinet and the Administration: Political and Administrative Roles in the Higher Civil Service," pp. 201-38, particularly pp. 202, 233, and 234.

26. Dogan, *The Mandarins of Western Europe*, p. 11.

27. Daniel Derivry, "The Managers of Public Enterprises in France," in *The Mandarins of Western Europe*, pp. 210-25.

28. Suleiman, *Politics, Power, and Bureaucracy*, p. 374.

29. Diamant, "The French Administrative System," pp. 182-218.

30. Crozier, *The Bureaucratic Phenomenon*, pp. 251-63.

31. Suleiman, *Politics, Power, and Bureaucracy*, p. 358.

32. *Ibid.*, p. 371.

33. Mayntz and Scharpf, *Policy-Making in the German Federal Bureaucracy*, p. 46.

34. *Ibid.*, p. 64.

35. Rothman, Scarrow, and Schain, *European Society and Politics*, p. 342.

36. Mayntz and Scharpf, *Policy-Making in the German Federal Bureaucracy*, p. 52.

37. *Ibid.*, pp. 53-54.

38. *Ibid.*, p. 55.

39. *Ibid.*, p. 58.

40. Robert D. Putnam, "The Political Attitudes of Senior Civil Servants in Britain, Germany, and Italy," in *The Mandarins of Western Europe*, pp. 87-127. (Reprinted from *British Journal of Political Science* 3 (1973): 257-90.) This and other recent studies are summarized by Mayntz and Scharpf in *Policy-Making in the German Federal Bureaucracy*, pp. 57-62.

41. This excerpt is reprinted from Robert D. Putnam, "The Political Attitudes of Senior Civil Servants in Britain, Germany, and Italy," in *The Mandarins of Western Europe: The Political Role of Top Civil Servants*, Mattei Dogan, Editor © 1975 p. 113, by permission of the Publisher, Sage Publications, Inc. (Beverly Hills/London).

42. *Ibid.*, p. 116.

43. Mayntz and Scharpf, *Policy-Making in the German Federal Bureaucracy*, p. 62.

44. *Ibid.*, p. 95.

45. *Ibid.*, p. 171.

46. Jacob, *German Administration Since Bismarck*, pp. 198, 202.

47. Mayntz and Scharpf, *Policy-Making in the German Federal Bureaucracy*, p. 90.

6

ADMINISTRATION IN THE DEVELOPED NATIONS
Some Variations in Administrative Systems

Although developed nations as a group constitute only a small proportion of the total number of existing nation-states, there are too many of them to permit individualized treatment. A choice must be made designed to illustrate significant variations among them, even though this means omission of important countries and scanty attention to innovative features such as the use in Scandinavian countries of collegial administration in ministries and the Ombudsman as a device for administrative control.

In addition to France and Germany, we have selected four other administrative systems for discussion—those of Great Britain, the United States, Japan, and the Union of Soviet Socialist Republics. The first two countries share a common political heritage, exhibit many similarities in their systems of administration, and have been unusually influential as models for developing nations. Japan is the outstanding and possibly the only non-Western nation which clearly has achieved recognition as developed, whatever scale for measuring development might be used. The USSR, as one of the world's superpowers and the primary model for developing nations in the Communist bloc, offers a dramatic contrast in its totalitarian party-dominated politico-administrative system.

Administration in "The Civic Culture"—
Great Britain and the United States

Despite the differences between them, and the close relationship that each (particularly Great Britain) has to the political systems of continental Europe, we have chosen to group Great Britain and the United States together. In contrast to Germany and France, the history of their political development is one of relative stability. Circumstances permitted them for the most part to take an incremental approach to the problems of political change, and to develop their political institutions without violent discontinuities and abrupt changes of direction. Great Britain achieved political integration by the early seventeenth century, and the political heritage of the United States is largely British. Both countries have been able to establish stable democratic political systems and to maintain them over considerable periods of time.

The political characteristics which to a large extent are shared by Great Britain and the United States have been called "the civic culture" by Almond and Verba. They describe it as a political culture that is participant and pluralistic, "based on communication and persuasion, a culture of consensus and diversity, a culture that permitted change but moderated it."[1] Since the political culture and political structure are congruent, the political system is relatively stable and its legitimacy well established. The Almond and Verba study attempts to test certain hypotheses concerning the diffusion of democratic culture, through country studies in five operating democratic systems, including Germany, Italy, and Mexico, as well as the United States and Great Britain. They find that the latter two countries have the civic culture to the greatest degree, with basically similar patterns in each but with somewhat different dimensions, reflecting differences in national histories and social structures. They summarize these differences by labeling Great Britain a "deferential" and the United States a "participant" civic culture.

This gradualist pattern of political development led to decidedly contrasting basic characteristics, with Great Britain retaining a figurehead monarchy linked with a unitary and parliamentary system, and the United States opting for a federal system with an elected president as chief executive. The greatest consequence of gradualism on public administration was that the administrative system also was able to take shape feature by feature in a way that reflected the political changes and was consonant with them. Political and administrative adaptations were concurrent and fairly well balanced, but the political theme was dominant. At no time has the administrative apparatus been called upon to assume the whole burden of government because of a breakdown of the political machinery.

This background has had profound effects on the composition, behavioral characteristics, and political role of the British and American bureaucracies, accounting both for their similarities and for the differences between them.[2] Compared to France and Germany the civil service in Great Britain and the United States was markedly slow in becoming professionalized and in acquiring other important characteristics of Weberian-style bureaucracy. It was not until the middle of the nineteenth century that the British reformed their civil service by putting recruitment on a merit basis. Earlier, most appointments were filled on patronage considerations, and many posts were sinecures requiring very little work, although some use was made of qualifying examinations before appointment. Reform of the defects of the civil service came about as the result of the famous Northcote-Trevelyn Report of 1854, which in turn was strongly influenced by personnel practices which had been adopted by the Indian Civil Service during the previous two decades. The principal recommendations which were put into effect included the abolition of patronage and the substitution of appointment on a career basis at an early age through a system of competitive examinations to a unified service which drew a clear distinction between intellectual and routine work, with subsequent promotion also to be based on merit rather than nepotism, connections, or political considerations. These British reform measures provided the model—with important adaptations—for a civil service reform movement in the United States, where the spoils system had been carried to excess during the middle part of the nineteenth century, eventually leading to enactment of the Pendleton Act by Congress in 1883. Although substantial, this reform measure was limited in its impact, applying only partially to the federal civil service and not at all to state and local levels of government service. However, it did start a process, still not completed throughout the American public service, of putting selection and advancement on a merit rather than a patronage basis.

A bureaucracy of competence, it should be noted, did not appear in either country until representative political organs decided that it was needed and provided for it. This has basically influenced the conception the bureaucracy has had of itself and of its relationship to political leaders and to the public at large. In political cultures such as these, where the participative role is highly developed, the citizenry regards the bureaucracy as performing in a service capacity and being properly subjected to firm political control, however expert the bureaucrat may be, and however intimately he may be involved in the consideration of policy alternatives. Partial myth though it is, the bureaucracy is viewed as the neutral agent of the political decision-makers.

Within this framework, the British service seems to have a clear advantage over the American in terms of prestige and status. This reflects general patterns of deference toward governmental and other forms of authority in the society, as well as more specific historical factors such as timing of conversion from a spoils to a merit service, the tradition in the United States of political party reliance on public service patronage, and the relative standing of governmental as against business careers. Some evidence indicates that the gap is narrowing, as simultaneously the British service loses and the American gains prestige, but the difference is still there.

The structural setting in which these two civil service systems function presents contrasts reflected in bureaucratic operations. In Britain, ministries are the basic administrative units, supplemented by nationalized industries and public corporations outside the ministerial framework. Decisions as to executive organization are considered a prerogative of the crown, meaning that they can be made by the government of the day. Changes in the lineup of ministries are relatively frequent. The standard arrangement is for each ministry to be headed by a minister who is responsible before Parliament for all ministry affairs, and who heads the ministerial hierarchy. Directly under the minister is the uniquely British office of permanent secretary, held by a senior civil servant with the obligation to serve any minister and any government with equal skill and devotion. One or more deputy secretaries assist the permanent secretary, each in charge of several sections. Undersecretaries and assistant secretaries head up lower echelon divisions, with principals and assistant principals in turn heading up smaller units within these divisions. The pattern is orderly and symmetrical, with the prime minister and cabinet able to make adjustments which the government considers timely.

In the United States, on the other hand, the executive departments are the major entities, but included in the executive branch are a plethora of regulatory commissions, government corporations, and other units. Decisions as to executive reorganization are basically matters of legislative action. Congress has retained control over the creation or abolition of executive departments (currently there are twelve), but has usually been willing to delegate limited discretion to the president to make less major organizational changes, subject to congressional review and potential disapproval. Issues of executive reorganization are recurring agenda items for Congress and the president. Departmental internal structure follows a less standard pattern than in the British ministry. The department secretary at the head is a political appointee of the president (subject to Senate confirmation) and serves at his pleasure. Usually a department has an undersecretary and several assistant secretaries. No equivalent to the British permanent secretary exists, although most departments now have an assistant secretary for administration with much more limited functions of a housekeeping nature. The successive program units by level are most commonly called bureaus, divisions, and sections, but the terminology is not uniform. Beginning at the bureau level, career civil servants are likely to be in charge, but this is not necessarily so and the incumbent has no tenure claim on the office.

Traditionally the British Treasury, along with its many other important functions, has had responsibility for supervising the civil service, including recruitment, training, promotion, and compensation. Only within the last few years has responsibility for personnel management been shifted from the Treasury to a Civil Service Department directly under the control of the prime minister. In the United States, the central personnel agency for the federal government from 1883 through 1978 was the Civil Service Commission, a three-member board with statutory powers designed to guarantee the integrity of the merit system. Its functions have now been divided between a new Office of Personnel Management and a new Merit Systems Protection Board, as one feature of civil service reforms initiated by President Jimmy Carter.

In composition and operation, the two systems have shown in the past and still at present show substantial contrasts, some of which are decreasing as the consequence of recent reforms in both countries.[3] Generally, the British have shown a preference for career-staffing and candidates with general capacity, the Americans, for program-staffing and candidates with specialized capacity. These priorities are reflected in a variety of ways.

During most of its history, the British civil service was divided into three major classes—clerical, executive, and administrative—in an ascending order of responsibilities and qualifications. The elite of the service were in the administrative class, comprised of fewer than 3000 members in 1968, or less than 0.5 percent of the total civil service. This select group had responsibility for policy initiation and implementation and dealt directly with political officials. In 1971, as recommended earlier by the Fulton Committee, these three classes were merged in a new administrative group as part of a system of occupational groupings, but it appears that a small select cadre continues to bear similar responsibilities, although no longer identified as members of a distinct administrative class.[4]

From the beginning, the American approach has been to emphasize the position held and the requirements for satisfactory performance of the duties connected with it, rather than assessment of individual potential for placement in an appropriate rank category. As a result, there has been no clear-cut grouping equivalent to the British administrative class. In the American system of grades reflecting levels of responsibility in the system, the top three "supergrades" have been generally considered to constitute the elite of the civil service. In contrast to the "professional amateurs" of the British administrative elite, the occupants of these posts are experts in a professional specialty. Frederick C. Mosher has suggested "the professional state" as an appropriate way to designate this clustering of professional elites.[5] Just as recent modifications in the British system have moved toward American concepts, the idea of a "senior civil service" with similarities to the British administrative class was recommended in several versions beginning with that of the Second Hoover Commission in the 1950s, but was not adopted until 1978, when a Senior Executive Service (SES) was authorized to become operational in 1979. It remains to be seen whether the SES will produce a servicewide category of administrative generalists with more clear-cut lines for promotion to positions of high level administrative responsibility.

In recruitment, competition for the British higher service until the end of World War II took the form of competitive examinations on a variety of subjects paralleling the courses of study offered in the universities and open only to recent university graduates. Some common test subjects were required, such as ability in written expression and knowledge of contemporary affairs, but most stress was placed on performance in subjects chosen from a wide range of possibilities not necessarily having anything directly to do with later work assignments.[6] An alternative approach, called Method II, was provided at the end of World War II, primarily for the benefit of returning war veterans, with emphasis placed mainly on a series of individual and group interviews, in addition to performance on the usual required examinations. The 1971 reforms have involved a shift to a system of selection of administrative trainees for careers in the new administrative group. Candidates are put through a series of examinations and interviews along Method II lines. Most of the successful candidates continue to come from honors graduates of the universities, but an increasing number are being chosen from persons already in the service with a minimum of two years of experience. Those chosen enter a probationary period of at least two years during which they serve as trainees, followed by a sixteen-week course at a newly founded Civil Service College. During the succeeding four years further assessment and training leads to "streaming" into ability groupings of those considered promising for high level posts in their later careers and those deemed more suitable for middle management positions, thus resulting apparently in career patterns corresponding roughly to the old administrative and executive classes.

The American tradition has been to offer more specialized and practical examinations on an open competitive basis to those meeting prescribed minimum qualifications. However, beginning in the late 1930s, entry level general subject matter examinations have been offered to university graduates designed to bring promising young people into the government service. Increasingly, students preparing for administrative careers in the public service pursue undergraduate or graduate curricula in public administration or public affairs in preparation for these examinations. The result has been the recruitment of large numbers of potential higher level administrators, but the channels for their career advancement are much less planned and more haphazard than in the British system, with its clearer demarcation of those civil servants who occupy, or are in training to occupy, the posts of higher managerial responsibility.

The social background of higher civil servants has in the past been much less diversified in Britain than in the United States. The administrative class before World War II came almost exclusively from upper class graduates of Oxford or Cambridge, who earlier had attended public schools such as Eton and Harrow. During the last thirty years, however, three factors have helped broaden the social and educational base from which higher civil servants are being drawn. Scholarship assistance to talented students from lower class backgrounds has diversified the student composition at "Oxbridge" universities. The less prestigious "Redbrick" universities have gained in stature and now provide more graduates who succeed in the competition for entry into the civil service. Opportunities for promotion into the former administrative class were broadened for individuals with experience in the executive class. Further diversification of background can be anticipated from the recruitment and training modifications of the 1970s. In the United States, because of a more open society with less pronounced class distinctions, and because of the methods used for appointment and advancement in the civil service, the upper echelons of the bureaucracy have been considerably more representative, with less of a caste or elite quality. Although public executives have been better educated than the general population and have tended to come from families with business and professional backgrounds, a study made in the 1960s indicated that nearly one-fourth of them had fathers who were blue-collar workers. The distortion has been on the basis of sex and ethnic background, with disproportionate numbers of white males, particularly in the higher brackets, leading to extensive programs of "affirmative action" which have made some slight progress in improving the representation of women and men from black and other minority ethnic groups. Compared to most national public services, the American record is certainly better than average, despite these group deficiencies in representation.

Career-staffing in Great Britain, with entry ordinarily barred except at an early age, has meant a minimum interchange of personnel between governmental and nongovernmental careers. Even today, as Christoph reports,

> ... the higher civil service does not serve as an instrument for systematically recruiting talent into other elites, whether they be members of parliament, political executives, local government officials, or managers in the private sector. However attractive their skills may appear at the middle or ends of their careers, few civil servants trade their places in Whitehall for ones elsewhere. . . . Bureaucrats have not been coopted into ministerial posts as in Fifth Republic France, or gone into parliamentary politics as in the Bonn Republic. . . . Indeed, those who would reform the civil service have been more concerned with stimulating greater mobility in and out of its ranks than with either the threat of losing top talent or unseemly connections with other elites, public or private.[7]

Again by way of contrast, in the United States such movement back and forth at various levels has been and continues to be quite feasible and even encouraged under existing personnel practices in both the public and private sectors, leading to proposals to move toward a more closed civil service system for greater expertise, continuity, and stability.

Guarantees of civil service status, although substantial in these two countries, do not take the form of comprehensive codification. In Great Britain, the civil service is an establishment of the crown, and its affairs are almost exclusively controlled by orders-in-council or other executive action. In the United States, the executive and legislative branches share in regulating the bureaucracy, so that it has a partial statutory base, but there is no constitutional protection for the national civil service. The merit bureaucracy depends more on a protective tradition than on elaborate legal provisions.

Both in Britain and the United States, high ranking bureaucrats play substantial roles in governmental decision-making, but the rules of the game differ decidedly. The British operate under a convention that imposes upon the official and the minister clearly understood mutual obligations based on the principles of impartiality and anonymity. The civil servant is expected to offer his advice to the minister, who has political responsibility, but he is obligated to carry out loyally whatever decision is reached. The principle of anonymity means that the career man is to be protected by the political leadership from disclosure of the advice he gave, and he is not to be brought into the limelight of the political arena.

This system is supposed to and does keep out of the public eye the extent and nature of the involvement of civil servants in policy-making, but it certainly permits the higher ranking career officials to initiate and choose among policy proposals, subject to ministerial discretion. Apparently, there are considerable variations in the powers actually exercised by civil servants, depending on the characteristics of individual ministers. Both Brian Chapman and James B. Christoph have pointed out how the attention of British civil servants is highly concentrated on the minister as the key political referent in their lives as officials. In some respects, ministers are much alike. For example, they must be members of Parliament, and they usually are experienced members, with the average length of service in recent governments being fifteen years, which means that their skills are associated mainly with parliamentary success. More than likely, the minister will not have expertise that is relevant to the work of the ministry. Tenure is often brief; the average in recent governments has been only 26 months. Individuals are frequently shifted from one cabinet post to another with widely differing functions. All are extremely busy, putting in work weeks of sixty hours or more, and are limited in the time they can devote to ministerial policy-making.

Within this common frame of reference, ministers do differ in the ways in which they approach their tasks, including relations with top civil servants. Christoph and others have contrasted "strong" and "weak" ministers. A strong minister views the role of civil servants as "largely one of informing the minister fully, analyzing his choices in terms of their technical feasibility, freeing him from trivial paper work, and ensuring that his policies are put into effect swiftly and positively. Because they are left in no doubt over what their minister wants, civil servants act as handmaidens rather than brakes."[8] Weak ministers lack focus as to mission, show little strength in dealing with cabinet colleagues and permanent officials, are passive on policy issues, and become preoccupied with routines and trivia, thus enhancing opportunities for civil servants to engage in independent policy-making.

Bruce W. Headey has carried such analysis further by suggesting a fivefold typology of ministers, based on interview data from both current and former ministers and civil servants. His five types are policy initiators, policy selectors, executive ministers, ambassador ministers, and minimalists. The policy initiators emphasize that their role is to state objectives and priorities. They initiate the search for appropriate policy programs, with the role of the civil servant being essentially responsive. They tend to think that only ministers can make major changes, and that proposals generated by civil servants are apt to be unimaginative and avoid risks. In practice, this type of ministerial practice rarely occurs and is the most difficult role to carry out effectively, for various reasons, including ministerial inadequacies, resistance on the part of civil servants, and situational constraints which prevent implementation of policy changes desired by the minister. The policy selectors as a group have a quite different view of the minister-civil servant relationship. "Ministers who see themselves as policy selectors accept the objectives of the department as they find them. Their main emphasis is on the necessity of choice. The minister must take decisions and dispatch the business, not delay or vacillate."[9] This seems to be a more commonly accepted role, and is understandably viewed favorably by most civil servants. The danger for the minister is that he may be presented with a "united view" and not have all the possible options fully laid out for consideration. Headey notes that the possibility of foreclosed policy options is present because "in almost no other Western country is there a top official with as much potential influence as the British permanent secretary."[10] Presumably, ministers of the policy selector type consider the risk minimal, or at least acceptable.

Executive ministers have "a management textbook view of their job. They believe it is a mistake to divorce questions of policy from questions concerning costing and resource control, organizational structure and personnel management."[11] They are few in number and usually have a background of business experience. Their role conception is an ambitious one, involving large time commitments, and infringing on what has been generally considered the management function of the permanent secretary.

Ambassador ministers "give high priority to their role as departmental representative or ambassador in dealing with interest groups, local government, professional associations, and other organized publics who constitute the department's clientele."[12] Although civil servants tend to have policy matters devolve on them under such a minister, they do not regard this ministerial role favorably, because it often causes delays in decisions which need to be taken at the minister's level. Ministers who are minimalists, as the term suggests, do no more than is necessary, such as formal acceptance of responsibility for departmental decisions, putting up a respectable effort to win support for departmental measures, and avoiding parliamentary trouble. Civil servants express disapproval of minimalists on two grounds: a poor standing by a minimalist minister reflects unfavorably on the whole department; and officials are forced to formulate policy objectives as well as advise on alternatives. "Officials prefer a minister who makes some contribution to policy if only because, as one of them put it, 'that is the way the constitution is supposed to work.' "[13]

Headey summarizes by stating that constitutional theory regarding the minister-civil servant relationship "is highly misleading. Civil servants are not always restricted to advisory and administrative roles in relation to policies laid down by ministers. . . . A realistic picture of relations between ministers and their officials needs to recognize that ministers have markedly different role conceptions and that time constraints mean that giving high priority to one role is likely to mean that other roles are downgraded and, implicitly, delegated to civil servants."[14] Although recognizing that different types of ministers are needed, depending on time and circumstances, he concludes that only the political initiator and policy selector types actually exert much influence over policy, and expresses concern about the undesirable consequences of failure by ministers to define policy objectives and priorities, since proposals generated by civil servants are apt to be status quo-oriented rather than innovative.

Christoph offers a useful summary of the political roles now commonly played by higher civil servants in Great Britain, cautioning that the exact mix will depend on the functions of the ministry and the orientation and skills of its minister. The traditional and still pre-eminent role is substantive policy implementation, which involves a wide range of discretion because of the general terms of much legislation and the volume of delegated legislative powers. The offering of political advice to the minister as a basis for policy decisions is a second crucial and exacting role, requiring sensitization to the political implications of actions recommended. Third is a symbiotic relationship with the minister of providing mutual political protection, through which civil servants, "in return for their protection and enhancement of their minister's reputation, . . . are shielded by him from direct political interference from parliament, the press, and the public."[15] Advancement of clientele claims in various arenas, and efforts to reconcile pressure group claims, are the final two related roles in this analysis. Christoph also mentions several "non-roles," activities engaged in only marginally, if at all, as clues to understanding the system. British civil servants do not have to try to substitute for ineffectual party or electoral machinery, as has been the case historically in Germany and France, for example. They do not usually deal directly with the public by providing goods and services; generally, "the power and impact of the central government is buffered rather than direct."[16] Direct control of the populace or of subordinate governmental units is likewise untypical. Finally, higher civil servants do not leave their careers for service in other elites in the society, or actively participate in partisan politics. Taking these "do's and don'ts" into account, Christoph says that "the higher bureaucracy in Britain will continue to be called on to carry a substantial share of political decision-making. . . . It is still a share, though, not a monopoly. By temperament, socialization, situation, and resources, top civil servants are well placed to strongly influence the outcome of policy, but not to transform it into a sole proprietorship."[17]

In the American setting, there is probably no dramatic contrast in the overall impact on policy-making of higher ranking civil servants, but the rules of the game are quite different. Bureaucratic policy-makers in the United States must operate much more in the public eye, which gives greater leeway but also involves greater risks. The relationship between the top career man and his political superior is more ambiguous. The civil servant has an obligation either to render loyal service or to resign or transfer, but he is likely to be linked with his policy preference in any event, and he may very well be called on to defend the agency's policy position in a congressional hearing, whatever his own position. The system is less closed and more competitive. Contesting elements must seek allies not only elsewhere in the government but outside it as well. Many of these characteristics result from the lack of a definite or inviolable demarcation between bureaucratic and political officialdom. Lewis C. Mainzer sums up the American situation this way: "no clear line between career and political executives exists in law, regulations, policy, or tradition. . . . The mixture of career administrators and outsiders in high executive posts which are not sharply differentiated as to their political or administrative character has been our pragmatic solution to the management of political bureaucracy."[18]

Instead of behind-the-scenes activity protected by a carefully preserved veil of secrecy, as in the British practice, the American expectation is that bureaucratic participation in policy-making will be much more in the public view, with the inevitable reactions that follow, whether favorable or unfavorable, to the individual concerned. Moreover, movement across the vague line between career and political activity is easy and frequent. Indeed, as Sayre remarks, "The American civil servant who earns high and lasting prestige in his society is usually one who most completely breaks the mask of anonymity and becomes a public figure."[19]

External controls over bureaucracy are extensive and adequate in both Great Britain and the United States, although concern has often been expressed in recent years about the growing complexities of maintaining accountability in view of increasing grants of discretionary authority to administrators and the burdens of legislative surveillance over a constantly widening range of governmental programs.

Responsiveness to political authority is not only given lip service but is genuinely accepted as appropriate by career officials, reflecting the historical fact that representative institutions antedated a modern civil service in each country and have established the legitimacy of their authority. Putnam's recent report on the political attitudes of senior civil servants in Britain confirms that they continue to tend toward the "political" rather than the "classical" model of bureaucrat in acceptance of responsiveness to political institutions. The data indicated that this was less characteristic of specialist and technical officials in the sample than of generalists in what was then the administrative class, indicating that a bureaucracy led by such men might be less responsive than has been the case up to now. On the other hand, British "high-fliers" (younger officials considered likely to be assigned major responsibilities later) were "the most politically conscious, the most programmatically committed, the most egalitarian, and the most tolerant toward politicians and pluralism" of any of the groups interviewed.[20] Although this comparative study did not include data from American officials, other indicators, such as some of the tenets of the "new public administration" movement in the United States, would point toward younger bureaucrats as being nearer than older ones to the "political bureaucrat" model.

Legislative oversight over administration relies in Great Britain on the doctrine of ministerial responsibility and makes slight use of specialized parliamentary committees. In the United States, the approach to legislative control is through specialized legislative committees acting in a fragmentary fashion. Each system has weak points which have been the subject of reform proposals, although neither system appears to be ineffectual.

Ministerial responsibility, as it took shape during the nineteenth century, was intended as a parliamentary check on the powers of ministers and civil servants. "The doctrine required," as explained by Christoph, "that all actions of civil servants be taken in the name of the minister, who would be held accountable by the Commons for such actions and, in cases where evidence of malfeasance in the performance of duties came to light, censured or made to resign."[21] Christoph and others now contend that as British government has evolved, the doctrine of ministerial responsibility has been warped so that it no longer serves the intended purpose, but instead makes it difficult for Parliament to deal with bureaucratic operations. The argument is that two developments in British politics in this century have brought about this result. Governmental activities have expanded to the point that ministers no longer can reasonably be expected to have full awareness or give active approval to every action taken by civil servants in their ministries, and this has led to a weakened application of the doctrine when civil service abuses or blunders have been revealed. The other change is the growth of party and cabinet power over Parliament, which overlays the earlier precept of ministerial responsibility with "the politics of collective responsibility," making it hard for opposition members of Parliament or even government party "backbenchers" to penalize a minister if he is supported by the prime minister and his colleagues in the cabinet. As a consequence, the doctrine is alleged to strengthen the hand of the executive rather than the legislature, by making it impossible for Parliament to summon civil servants because only the minister is supposedly accountable, by throwing a cloud of secrecy over minister-civil servant relationships as well as over negotiations with outside groups, and by reinforcing "the centralized and hierarchical nature of British administration by channeling control from above."[22] Attempts to abandon the doctrine of ministerial responsibility and to increase the number and strengthen the expertise of specialized parliamentary committees have made little headway, however, up to now. A partial response is found in the office of the British Parliamentary Commissioner, created in 1967 as a modified version of the Scandinavian Ombudsman to deal with citizen grievances against administrators. However, this official can act only if a complaint is received through a member of Parliament, and can only investigate and report back to Parliament as to defects of procedure in administration. Christoph correctly judges that this mild reform "does not impinge greatly on the behavior of higher civil servants and must be considered at best a minor influence on their overall political role."[23]

In the United States, legislative committees undoubtedly exert potent controls over many aspects of the operations of the agencies which fall under their respective jurisdictions. Reform suggestions have usually taken the form of recommendations to weaken the direct control powers of particular committees over particular agencies, in favor of a more centralized and coordinated program of legislative oversight focused on large rather than small issues. "The gravest reservations about congressional procedures of control of administration center on the fragmentation of power within Congress and the consequent use of influence for personal, constituency, and interest group purposes," according to Mainzer.[24] Congress has shown little inclination, however, to alter the pattern. Proposals for an Ombudsman, for example, have been considered but never adopted, apparently because of apprehension that such an office would interfere with the rapport between legislators and their constituents.

A separate system of administrative courts to review allegations by citizens of administrative excesses, along continental European lines, has not been appealing either in Great Britain or the United States. "The common-law courts, plus the efficacy of external political controls, were seen as sufficient bulwarks against the misuse of public authority."[25] Aside from departing somewhat from the traditional doctrine that the state cannot be sued and is not liable for the actions of its officials, and the creation of specialized administrative tribunals in fields such as workmen's compensation cases, there have been few departures from common-law patterns which rely on the regular courts for judicial redress.

Bureaucracy in the civic culture as represented by the British and American cases shows the effects of societal forces where the participant role of the citizenry is highly developed. The civil service has gradually become more competent in its composition and more professional in its outlook, in response to the demands placed upon government for performance, but the service orientation remains and responsiveness to the political organs of government is universally accepted in theory and largely recognized in practice. The bureaucracy enjoys the benefit of a widespread although somewhat skeptical acceptance of the job it is doing, but it must be prepared to fit into its proper niche in the political system. Major political innovation or transformation is not likely to have a bureaucratic source.

Their similarities should not be allowed to obscure the distinctive ways in which British and American bureaucracies vary. One important difference pointed out by Crozier is that in Britain administrative organizations "maintain their effectiveness by relying on the old patterns of deference that binds inferiors and superiors within the limits of the necessary cohesion." In the United States, on the other hand, organizations "must use many more impersonal rules in order to achieve the same results."[26] The differences are also reflected in the choices the two countries have made in arranging for staffing and operating the bureaucracy. As Sayre summarizes it, the British responses have produced "a more orderly and symmetrical, a more prudent, a more articulate, a more cohesive and more powerful bureaucracy." The American choices have produced "a more internally competitive, a more experimental, a noisier and less coherent, a less powerful bureaucracy within its own governmental system, but a more dynamic one."[27]

Modernizing Administration—Japan

In only slightly more than a century since the Meiji restoration of 1867-1868, Japan has undertaken a mammoth program of modernization which has converted an Asian kingdom with its own type of feudalism, long isolated by its own choice from outside contacts, into the only Asian society that ranks as highly modernized and developed. In this transformation the bureaucracy, both civil and military, has played a leading part, one which makes the Japanese experience unique in important respects.[28]

The so-called "centralized feudalism" of the Tokugawa shogunate, which began in 1603, developed a civil bureaucracy which had basic patrimonial characteristics. Bureaucrats were recruited from specified feudal family ranks, and great emphasis was placed on status distinctions among classes in the hierarchy. "Appointments to office, promotions and dismissals were made at the discretion of superiors. The powers and responsibilities of offices were poorly defined, and there was a great deal of room for inefficiency, imbalance, and the personal interpretation of official duties."[29]

Edwin Dowdy's recent study examines historical evidence, particularly during the Tokugawa period, concerning elements within this outwardly patrimonial Japanese bureaucracy before the Meiji restoration which facilitated modernizing processes. He concludes that in Japanese society "there were long in existence some of the prerequisites for the development of a modernized country: a central if somewhat patchy administration operating within mass obedience, elaborate and rational local administrations, large-scale commercial networks, industrial undertakings in both urban and rural areas, and a high standard of literacy, to mention only some of the enabling factors."[30] Moreover, the samurai class provided a source for modernizing bureaucrats. Traditionally warriors, during the long period of peace after 1600 the samurai had to substitute a bureaucratic function for a military one in order to preserve a useful role. Among them developed "a kind of professional bureaucratic ethic" which included dedication to duty, self-reliance and resoluteness, along with attitudes concerning merit, mobility, duty rotation, and various aspects of rationality which facilitated the transition to a modernized bureaucracy. With characteristics such as these extending far back into Japanese history, Dowdy argues that "Japanese modernization continued organically from traditional sources, certainly with increased tempo but without any serious break."[31] Much imitation of other societies certainly occurred over a considerable period of time, "but that imitation was selectively adapted to home conditions. Spontaneous growth was more important than any policy of quick imitation. The Meiji bureaucracy was not a break with the past but rather a modified continuation of it. Its legitimacy depended largely on popular compliance to centralized authority and to the continuance of accustomed patterns of interaction. The bureaucracy was an organic growth, not something mechanically added from outside."[32].

The arrival of Commodore Perry in 1853 precipitated a crisis for the Tokugawa shogunate which triggered the vast changes leading within a few years to the Meiji restoration. One of the immediate results was modification of the ascriptive pattern for appointment of officials. Talented individuals, including many of relatively low social status, were appointed to staff new offices that were created in response to the crisis situation. They became part of an intellectual aristocracy of talented individuals who were exposed to and had respect for Western learning in the years prior to the restoration, and who took part in the overthrow of the shogunate under the guise of restoring the emperor to his rightful place. "The spiritual motive force of modern Japan," says Inoki, was the set of beliefs that members of this new intellectual aristocracy held in common, combining "national loyalty, symbolized by loyalty to the emperor, and respect for achievement."[33]

The wielders of political power who brought about the restoration and directed the governmental experimentation leading to the Meiji constitution of 1889 were a modernizing oligarchy. The system they devised provided for a sharing of political power among several competing groups during a period of several decades until the authoritarian resurgence of the 1930s. One of these groups consisted of the higher ranking civil bureaucrats, along with holders of the top civilian governmental positions, the professionalized military bureaucracy, leaders of the important conservative political parties that developed, representatives of big business, and the hereditary peerage. This oligarchy was a modernizing one, but it was not designed to encourage the establishment of a democratic political system. Its principal foreign model was imperial Germany, with which it shared a preference for monarchical institutions and a tradition of aristocratic control. It successfully curbed for a significant period of time tendencies toward popular participation in government and it kept political order while the country was advancing economically at a rapid rate.

The bureaucratic establishment was well suited to take a leading part in this type of modernization. The social background of the Meiji bureaucrats was predominantly lower samurai, since this group had been dislocated by the transition from feudalism and its members had skills that could be utilized in the bureaucracy. As bureaucratic growth and reform took place, recruitment by examination was introduced in the 1880s, and graduates were drawn from the rapidly expanding educational institutions, particularly Tokyo Imperial University. The higher civil bureaucracy thus created was "relatively small, cohesive, and professionally trained."[34] It was not indoctrinated in a tradition in which the bureaucrat was viewed as a public servant. Instead, the bureaucrat was "officially viewed as a chosen servant of the Emperor, a politically and socially superior being who derived status and privileges from his Imperial connection."[35] The bureaucrat's attitude toward the public continued to be well expressed by an old Tokugawa adage: "officials honored, the people despised." The legal framework for the bureaucracy reflected this orientation. All regulation of the civil bureaucracy prior to the end of World War II was by means of imperial ordinance and beyond the reach of parliamentary controls.

Japan's defeat and surrender at the end of World War II, followed by the Allied Occupation from 1945 to 1952, led to new patterns in Japanese politics and administration, embodied in a new constitution which became effective in 1947. The monarchy was preserved, but the emperor was stripped of any claim of divine right, and the institution was transformed into a constitutional monarchy. The peerage was abolished. Legislative authority was vested in a bicameral parliament or Diet, designated as "the highest organ of state power," with little resemblance to its prewar counterpart. The House of Representatives is dominant, with the upper chamber, or House of Councillors, having only limited power to delay legislation. Executive power is vested in a prime minister and cabinet collectively responsible to the Diet. At least a majority of the cabinet ministers are required to be members of the Diet. In case of a no-confidence vote in the House of Representatives, the cabinet must resign unless the House is dissolved and a new election held. Control of this parliamentary system has been in the hands of the Liberal Democratic party (which is conservative in its political orientation) since it was founded in 1955 by the merger of two pre-existing parties. Opposition parties, which have never succeeded in reducing the Liberal Democratic representation below a majority in either chamber of the Diet, include the Clean Government party and three leftist parties.

The cabinet consists of the heads of the ministries (currently twelve) plus three to six ministers "without portfolio." Units not given ministerial status are parceled out among this latter group of cabinet members or assigned to the prime minister's office. The ministries have quite similar internal structures. The cabinet minister is assisted by one or two parliamentary vice-ministers, who like the minister are political appointees although the incumbents may be former career civil servants. An administrative vice-minister occupies the highest career position in the ministry. Each ministry has one secretariat and a number of bureaus. The bureaus are usually further subdivided into divisions and sections, headed at each level by senior career officials.

The postwar Japanese civil service blends the prewar bureaucracy with efforts during the occupation period to reform and democratize it. Article 15 of the 1947 constitution declared: "All public officials are servants of the whole community and not of any group thereof." A new civil service law enacted also in 1947 detailed the reform provisions and established a National Personnel Authority with a guaranteed semiautonomous status. Commentators generally agree that these efforts have had an impact but have not fundamentally altered the bureaucratic system.

The Japanese civil service has grown remarkably, with a fivefold increase in the twenty-year period between 1940 and 1960, and a slower rate of change since. As in other countries, the higher civil service is a relatively small group with somewhat indeterminate boundaries. The occupants of the ministerial posts mentioned earlier total slightly over 1000. When others in the higher grades of the administrative service are added, the number reaches between 4000 and 5000, less than 0.5 percent of the civilian employees of the national government.

The present-day government service continues to be a career that attracts Japanese youth. Hence, it has been possible to restrict access to the upper ranks of the bureaucracy to those able to survive a hazardous series of qualifying steps. With an annual replenishment rate of around 200, competition is intense among those who pass the higher civil service examinations. The educational base for successful candidates has been very narrow. "The proportion of higher administrators with a university education is remarkably high, even in comparison with major Western bureaucracies."[36] Graduation with honors from one of the leading universities has been a prerequisite to success in the examinations, and this in turn has restricted access to those who had earlier done superior work in the better elementary and secondary schools. Thus, in practice, only the exceptional sons of families able to afford such educational preparation have ordinarily been able to enter the higher bureaucracy.

In content, the tests have largely been under the control of law school faculties and designed for law school graduates. Although this has meant continued stress on legal technicalities, a fairly broad range of subject matter is covered, reflecting the fact that law faculties generally offer work in political science and economics and to a more limited extent in management skills.[37] The remarkable extent of dominance of this academic specialization is highlighted by the fact that more than two-thirds of postwar higher civil servants are law school graduates.

Even more exceptional is the extent to which one institution, Tokyo Imperial University, has been the source of entrants to the bureaucracy. Kubota found that nearly 80 percent of postwar higher civil servants had attended and in most cases had graduated from this one university. Another 13 percent had come from five other government universities. The four major private universities supplied less than 3 percent. "The extent of this dominance by graduates of a single university is staggering," as Kubota says, "even in comparison with the combined share for Oxford and Cambridge in the British bureaucracy,"[38] which totaled slightly over 47 percent in 1950.

This domination by Tokyo Imperial University graduates, particularly from its faculty of law, has led to widespread charges of favoritism in appointments and promotions based on school cliques, or *gakubatsu*. Kubota examines the evidence as to the pervasiveness of the *gakubatsu* system, with mixed conclusions. With regard to Tokyo University graduates, he states that the fact of their great numbers "made ingroup favoritism not only probable but also less provable, since there were always many Tokyo University graduates who did not rise as fast as others." He believes that school tie favoritism is practiced subtly, but doubts that Japanese higher administrators are apt to choose subordinates "solely on the basis of school background and without regard to competence." He also notes that a common university background does not necessarily mean shared attitudes and values, and that Tokyo University graduates show wide variations in outlook. He points out properly that as the leading and most prestigious university, it attracts and graduates the most able students, who in turn become the most promising future bureaucrats. On the positive side, the existing system has made possible the recruitment of many of the brightest Japanese youth, and has contributed to the stability and success of the bureaucracy. A negative aspect is the group homogeneity that results. "The narrow educational base in the recruitment of postwar higher civil servants resembles in some ways the narrow social base of recruitment in the Tokugawa and early Meiji governments."[39]

Available data as to the social origins of postwar bureaucrats point, however, toward a much more heterogeneous higher civil service than has been the case historically in Japan, despite the relatively narrow educational base for recruitment. All parts of Japan are represented, although with disproportionately large numbers from towns and cities, particularly Tokyo. A majority came from middle class origins. Eminent families were somewhat over-represented also, but Kubota's conclusion from this part of his study was that the data did not show any one social or political group providing a dominant share of higher administrators, or any significant number of families supplying higher civil servants in successive generations. He attributes this current diversity to the cumulative effects of the disappearance of most traditional forms of social stratification, and opportunities for greater social mobility through the modern educational system and the system of examinations for the higher civil service. Noting that the Japanese people are remarkably homogeneous ethnically, linguistically, and religiously, he does point out that the factor of heterogeneous social origins does not have the importance in Japan that would attach to it in other nations with more diversified populations.[40]

Career patterns for those who enter the higher civil service are highly particularized. The successful candidate tries to be accepted where his prospects for promotion, access to power, and postretirement opportunities would seem to be greatest. He is likely to remain with whatever ministry he enters, since lateral movement between ministries is limited. Approximately a third of those who enter a given ministry remain with it throughout their careers; another third begin and end careers in the same ministry, with interim transfers elsewhere. Such low interministerial mobility promotes loyalty to a particular ministry rather than to the public service as a whole, and tends toward compartmentalism rather than coordination among different bureaucratic units. On the other hand, it does permit a buildup through long experience of specialized knowledge about the ministry in which the typical bureaucrat makes his career home.

Promotion within the system is also along a standardized path, and demotion is virtually nonexistent. The principal factors that are taken into account for promotions are university attended, field of academic specialization, and years since graduation—all of course settled matters at the start of a civil servant's career. Educational background and seniority are what count, making the timing and nature of promotions generally well known in advance. An interesting incidental fact, confirming the school clique phenomenon, is that those promoted most rapidly and in closest conformity with seniority have proved to be law graduates of Tokyo Imperial University.

A most unusual feature of the Japanese civil service is the early age of retirement, even in the absence of any compulsory retirement provision. The average retirement age varies somewhat from ministry to ministry, but is in the neighborhood of fifty years, which means that the typical retiree is in the prime of life, can expect to live another twenty years, and is very likely to seek a postbureaucratic career of some kind. Kubota attributes this massive outflow at such a relatively early age to the rapid movement of civil servants from post to post during their careers and the promotion system based mainly on seniority. "Junior bureaucrats usually could not be promoted until their seniors vacated higher positions, and this tended to

create pressures for early retirement. At the same time, the willingness of senior bureaucrats to retire at an early age depended in large
part on the availability of reasonable alternatives to government
service."[41]   Although there seems to be a slow long-term trend
toward a slightly higher average retirement age, there are no indications of a sharp movement away from this aspect of standardization in career patterns.

   In essence, the record shows that continuity and stability are
the chief features of the postwar higher civil service in Japan,
despite the reform measures instituted during the occupation and
the tremendous changes which have taken place generally in Japanese
life during the last three decades. After temporary adjustments
which were unavoidable in the early postwar period, the tendency
has been to follow what has been called the "reverse course" of
returning to earlier practices stressing generalist training, seniority,
ministerial loyalty, and early retirement.

   When we turn our attention to multifunctionalism in Japanese
bureaucratic operations, the most striking observation is that political activism has long been, and continues to be, an accepted part of
the bureaucratic tradition. The Japanese higher bureaucrat is likely
to be deeply absorbed in making political decisions and may become
involved in active political life. This is partly explained by the
blurring in Japan historically of the distinction commonly made in
Western theory between the politician and the bureaucrat. As
Dowdy observes: "In Japan at the higher levels this distinction has
not always been evident, for often both the political and bureaucratic
functions were discharged by the same official."[42]   In more recent
times, this background has helped account for the persistent role of
the bureaucracy as one of the prime sources of policy initiative in a
modernizing society.

   Not only do active career bureaucrats often hold positions and
carry out functions usually reserved for political appointees in other
countries, but perhaps of more importance is the prevalence of
retired bureaucrats in a wide variety of influential positions both inside and outside of government. The elitist status of higher civil
servants is retained after they retire, giving them better prospects for
postretirement placements than are usually available to their counterparts in Great Britain or the United States. With early retirement as
the norm, this means that an individual can make and carry out
career plans that include a second phase after leaving active service
which frequently is even more lucrative, influential, and prestigious.
Kubota's estimate is that about three out of ten retiring higher civil

servants go into semiautonomous public corporations, another three move into business enterprises (often as directors of major private corporations), and the remaining four enter a wide variety of professional and governmental activities. Substantial numbers of them have run successfully for elective political office and often they have served as members of postwar cabinets. For example, in 1959 a total of 165 former career bureaucrats made up 18 percent of the total membership of the lower house and 32 percent of the upper house in the Diet. Former bureaucrats made up 35 percent of the total membership of cabinets during the period between 1954 and 1961.[43] The most impressive statistic demonstrating this phenomenon of bureaucratic political prowess is that half of the postwar Japanese prime ministers have been former career civil servants.

From a long-range perspective, the resilience and adaptability of the Japanese bureaucracy are exceptional. As Kubota comments, "the effectiveness and efficiency of the higher civil service appear to be independent of political ideology. The bureaucracy has functioned with at least relative success under the Meiji oligarchy, under political parties of the prewar type, under militarist and ultranationalist control, under the Allied Occupation, and now under parliamentary democracy based upon the 1947 Constitution."[44] This record has not been built on the basis of bureaucratic neutrality toward the existing political regime, but rather of conformance to changes in the political climate.

In the postwar period, this has meant a close identification between the higher bureaucracy and the ruling Liberal Democratic party. Writing in the early 1960s, Inoki remarked on this tendency toward fusion of high civil servants and Liberal Democratic leaders. He pointed out that more and more retired civil servants were serving as Liberal Democratic members of the Diet, and charged that party leaders were "seeking to gain control of the civil bureaucracy through partisan promotions and demotions of high civil servants."[45] The growing interlinkage between the higher civil service, the ruling Liberal Democratic party, and organized interest groups outside the government has also been commented on by Robert Ward, who asserts that considerable corruption is present because of these relationships, with interest groups seeking to influence critically placed bureaucrats, and trying to reinforce this influence "by promises of sinecure jobs upon retirement, gifts of stock, lavish entertainment, or outright bribes."[46] The prevalence of such problems even at top levels was highlighted by the resignation in 1974 of former Prime

Minister Tanaka under a cloud of financial scandal allegations, and his replacement by Takeo Miki.

The consequences of this partial fusion of the higher civil service and the leadership of the dominant political party are not clear. Inoki argues that it not only undermines civil service neutrality, but that it makes civil service careers less attractive to able university graduates and is contributing to a steady decline in the formerly high prestige of the civil service. Ward and Kubota, on the other hand, seem to regard it as further evidence of the strength and unity of the bureaucracy, which continues to seize its opportunities by moving into any partial power vacuums that exist.

Certainly members of the bureaucratic class still belong to the political elite of Japan, and the bureaucracy continues to be an integral part of the governing power structure. The situation clearly raises questions as to the adequacy of controls over the bureaucracy, at least when viewed in relation to European parliamentary democracies. The Japanese Diet, despite its constitutional status and obvious political centrality as compared to the prewar period, conspicuously lacks the historical record of power and prestige of legislative bodies such as the British House of Commons or the French Chamber of Deputies. Its membership, as already indicated, includes a large segment of recently retired higher civil servants, who are unlikely to disturb the prerogatives of career bureaucrats. For its part, the bureaucracy as a political institution seeks to keep the legislature weak or at least sympathetic to bureaucratic interests.

Political party leadership in the dominant postwar Liberal Democratic party has tended to be multifactional, shifting, semisecretive in its methods, without widespread mass appeal, and decidedly conservative in its orientation. The opposition parties, although differing in political orientation, also have not developed mass membership bases of support and function essentially as parliamentary parties. Because they have had no prospect of overcoming the Liberal Democratic majority in the Diet, their members have frequently resorted to disruptive or obstructive tactics which have further lowered the effectiveness and reputation of the legislative branch.

Factionalism and jockeying for position within Liberal Democratic ranks have also been reflected in the composition and tenure in office of cabinet ministers. Although highly educated, they have tended to be elderly, with the average age close to sixty. Pressures for factional representation and personal recognition have led to frequent cabinet changes, with a resulting high rate of turnover which has detracted from the ability of ministers to gain the knowledge and time needed to exert firm control over their agencies. "Since this merry-go-round of Ministers cannot readily hold the reins of power," Ward comments, "political leadership actually resides with the Prime Minister, the leaders of the several factions in the majority party, and the somewhat more stable members of the higher ranks of the professional bureaucracy."[47] The office of prime minister has provided the only conspicuous focal point for political and administrative leadership, but the powers of the office are meager compared to those of chief executives in the other developed polities we have considered.

Judicial controls over administration in Japan are minimal. The 1947 constitution included sweeping reforms of the legal system and the judiciary, introducing Anglo-American common-law principles and a judicial branch with independent status and powers of judicial review. The earlier legal system had been largely derived from European sources, with the courts being administered by the Ministry of Justice of the national government. The existing court network possesses powers to hold government servants accountable in much the same manner as in the United States. No separate system of administrative courts now exists. The traditional attitude in Japan has been to avoid rather than seek litigation, and there is little indication of resort to the courts for controlling the bureaucracy.

The degree of bureaucratic self-control in Japan is problematical. The constitutional provision converting bureaucrats from "the Emperor's aides" to "servants of the people" is given lip service but whether basic bureaucratic attitudes have altered correspondingly is more questionable. Kubota, as part of his comprehensive recent survey of the postwar bureaucracy, finds that the public is more openly critical of the civil service than it has ever been, indicating citizen skepticism about the conversion. However, his own view is that the bureaucracy, "whether from conviction or from expediency," has responded to the postwar changes "by making a greater effort to create harmonious relations with the general public and to adjust itself to the new political environment."[48] Perhaps the best assessment to make is that Japanese higher bureaucrats are prepared to conduct themselves in a way which will fit them acceptably into the current political scheme of things, without impairing their traditional power position.

The Japanese bureaucratic system owes its unusual strength to certain basic features of Japanese development. Modernization in Japan was internally stimulated and led by the ruling groups themselves, including the bureaucracy. The governing elite enjoyed relative solidarity and its leadership was accepted by the population, so that, as Bendix remarks, here a modernizing autocracy "succeeded for a significant period of time in advancing a country economically while containing her political conflicts within manageable limits."[49] The transition and the role played in it by the bureaucracy reflected in part the pervasiveness of respect for authority in Japanese society generally. This in turn has affected the operating characteristics of the bureaucracy. Crozier comments that in Japan a strong authoritarian pattern of hierarchy "has been internalized, and conflicts are handled more by subservience than by avoidance." The problem of controlling the behavior of subordinates in the Japanese system of organization

. . . is centered on a model of stratification which presents some similarities to the French system. One finds, indeed, in Japanese society the same pattern of strata isolation with the same difficulties of communication across strata and the same egalitarian pressure within each stratum. . . . At the same time, and in contrast to the French patterns, the prevailing pattern of participation is collective and not individual, founded upon the fact of belonging to a class and the predominance of the primary group. . . . Unlike French bureaucracy, whose main function is to maintain law and order in a rebellious society, Japanese bureaucratic power has a decisive role as prime mover. It is the only way out for an over-controlled society that cannot find other sources of initiative.[50]

Looking ahead, Kubota predicts that the bureaucracy's role will continue to be decisive. "For years to come Japanese higher civil servants are likely to exert a degree of influence that is impressive by any comparative standards."[51] Thus in the past, currently, and for at least the near future, the Japanese higher bureaucracy has had conferred upon it a position of central political power outstripping that accorded to the bureaucracies of other developed countries.

Administration under Communism—The USSR

Even an elementary understanding of public administration in the Soviet Union requires a drastic reorientation of expectations based on experience in Western constitutional democracies. The nature of the state bureaucracy and the scope of the demands made upon it reflect the needs of the Soviet system of totalitarianism as developed in Russia since the 1917 revolution.[52] The system aims at monolithic unity under the aegis of the Communist party. "Soviet administration is one-party administration, . . . suffused with political content. Every field of administration, however technical, is regarded as a channel for the propagation of the Party line and the directives of the top leadership."[53] The phraseology of liberal democracy has been borrowed and used by Soviet leaders in matters of administration as well as other aspects of politics, but Fainsod cautions that this "verbal masquerade which Communism adopts . . . should not be permitted to obscure the dictatorial essence of its organizational philosophy."[54] Hazard points out that the Soviet political apparatus "can be understood and contrasted best to that of Jeffersonian democracy when it is described as incorporating Western democratic forms counterweighted with the controls established as fundamental to socialist democracy."[55]

Control of the state apparatus is the primary means through which the Communist party has established and maintained its power. Administration of state affairs is a major concern of the party, so it is intimately involved in administration and ultimately dependent on bureaucratic organization to preserve its political control. Nevertheless, a characteristic feature of the Soviet system is the consistency with which the Communist party and the state apparatus have been maintained as separate instrumentalities. Amalgamation of the two hierarchies has been avoided. Instead, party control is assured through a network of interlocking directorates at each hierarchical level.

The Party has its units in every major organization and establishment in Soviet society. The Party leadership holds its local representatives responsible for the fulfillment of plans in all areas and organizations to which they are assigned. To be sure, day-to-day operating responsibilities are vested in the governmental hierarchy of managers and administrators. But every level of the government hierarchy is both interpenetrated with, and subject to check by, the corresponding level of the Party hierarchy.[56]

Without questioning the general success of Soviet leadership in controlling the state bureaucracy and using it as an instrument for modernization, it would be a mistake to assume that the relationship between the party and the bureaucracy has been in practice exactly what the theory of monolithic unity calls for. Instead, the actual relationship originally reflected factors from Russian history and Communist ideology; it has been modified significantly since the revolution, and promises to be further altered in the future.

Initially, the Communist revolutionaries were confronted with the dilemma of reconciling the expectations of Marxist doctrine concerning "the withering away of the state" with the facts of governing through administrative machinery inherited from imperial Russia. Lenin's original hope was that a professional civil service could be dispensed with. Certainly the Bolsheviks came to power determined to purge the bureaucracy of the old regime.

Hard reality soon brought reassessment. To meet the immediate needs for survival and to assume the burden of forced draft industrial development, it was clear that the existing bureaucracy could not be eliminated wholesale but would have to be reshaped. Bolshevism has been described as "an indigenous, authoritarian response to the environment of Tsarist absolutism which nurtured it."[57] Similarly, the Soviet bureaucracy, like its predecessor, became "a serving bureaucracy, privileged but duty-bound," despite the transformation carried out by the new regime.[58] The reform task was twofold. Although there had been numerous attempts to modernize it along Western European lines going back to the strenuous efforts of Peter the Great two centuries earlier, the administrative apparatus was still slow and backward, and had to be made efficient enough to get results for the Soviet leadership. Even more important, its loyalty had to be assured. The strategy adopted was to utilize the old bureaucrats as long as this could not be avoided, while surrounding them with controls, and to train a new generation of Soviet administrators as soon as possible. Thus, the initial stance of the regime toward the bureaucracy was one of forced reliance coupled with distrust.

The system of administration that developed under Stalin during the late 1920s and 1930s was highly centralized and increasingly staffed with products of the massive Soviet educational program. The new Soviet technical and administrative intelligentsia became more and more important to the party leadership, and large numbers were recruited into the party during the middle and late 1930s, until its social composition was substantially changed. This emergence of a managerial elite was fostered and encouraged by the core party leadership, but at the same time viewed with some apprehension. The importance of support from the technical and administrative intelligentsia was recognized, provided firm controls could be maintained.

This ambivalent attitude toward bureaucracy and bureaucrats is a continuing feature of the Soviet polity. Fleron explains the reason succinctly: "The continued existence of bureaucratic administration and control in the socialist experience represents a contradiction with the basic philosophy, while in the capitalist experience it does not."[59]

Having abandoned at an early stage the objective of eliminating a professionalized bureaucracy, Lenin later expressed worry about the dangers of "bureaucratization"; his famous so-called Testament, written in 1922 shortly before his death, warned about the enormous power that Stalin had concentrated in his hands as general secretary of the party. Trotsky, after his break with and ouster by Stalin, expounded his theory of the "degenerate workers' state." As summarized by Lane, Trotsky maintained that "the Soviet system, having abolished in the October Revolution the class relations of capitalism, had degenerated into a new form of elite rule. The party had betrayed the revolution and, with the bureaucracy ensconced in a privileged position, acted as a privileged stratum or caste."[60]

If such charges of deviation from Marxist principles had a basis during Stalin's era, they would appear to be even more relevant during the post-Stalin period. Ruthlessness and terror have diminished, but not extensive bureaucratization. Indeed, most interpreters of Soviet society have relied primarily on the bureaucratic model to explain the USSR under Khrushchev, and more recently under Brezhnev and Kosygin. Alfred G. Meyer, for example, has stated that the USSR "is best understood as a large, complex bureaucracy comparable in its structure and functioning to giant corporations, armies, government agencies, and similar institutions . . . in the West. It shares with such bureaucracies many principles of organization and patterns of management."[61] Developments at the time Khrushchev was replaced in 1964 were labeled by Zbigniew Brzezinski as a "victory of the clerks," as rule by an "ossified bureaucracy," resulting from a tendency of "bureaucratic politics . . . to elevate nonentities," and meaning that "bureaucratic conservatism is now dominant."[62] Jerry F. Hough sums up the common judgment when he says that "Soviet society quite literally is a 'bureaucracy writ large' with all large-scale organizations ultimately being subordinated to a single political institution."[63] Adam B. Ulam similarly says that "the Soviet state has been, because of the size and complexity of its administrative structure, *the* administrative state of recent times."[64]

One of the reasons for such characterizations, as well as one of the difficulties in applying Western modes of analysis to the Soviet situation, is that lines of distinction commonly used are blurred and indistinct here. Attempts to identify a state bureaucracy comparable to the higher civil service in non-Communist polities inevitably run into problems. Two groups in particular must be dealt with. One consists of the Communist party officialdom staffing the elaborate apparatus maintained by the party. The other group is made up of what might be called the managerial-technical or economic bureaucracy responsible for operation of the whole economic system which is under state control. The party apparatus officials would roughly correspond to the category of politicians or political leaders in other societies we have considered, and the managers of economic entities to private sector bureaucrats; neither group would be included as part of the public bureaucracy. In the Soviet Union, such distinctions between politicians and bureaucrats, and between public and private sector bureaucrats, are inapplicable or misleading unless used with caution.

When the USSR is referred to in terms describing it as the bureaucratic society par excellence, the usual reason is inclusion of a tremendous range of groups of officials sharing bureaucratic traits who are intimately connected with the Soviet polity in action. Among them are not only members of the higher state bureaucracy in the widest Western sense (including military and police professionals as well as civilian officials), but also the two exceedingly important groups just mentioned. Hough points out that although distinctions among such groups "do reflect differences of actual significance in Soviet society, they tend to obscure one basic fact: in almost all meaningful senses of the term, the Party apparatchiki, the military, the heavy or light industry managers, the agronomists or agricultural experts (assuming that one is talking about those in high positions), and the police are bureaucrats just as much as the officials actually given this label by Western scholars. All these persons . . . have worked and risen within a centralized hierarchy, learning to operate successfully within the framework of superiors' rules and instructions, achieving many of their aims through the medium of 'committee politics,' knowing that promotion (particularly to significant administrative posts) depends on the judgments of those above them in the hierarchy." In short, all of these groups "are composed of officials who increasingly have had orderly, 'Weberian' career patterns."[65] Whatever may be their differences with regard to what in other settings would be considered political versus administrative roles, the party officials share with members of these other groups a common bureaucratic socialization experience.

The formal structure within which these Soviet officials work is complex, intricate, and illusory. Constitutionally, the Soviet government is a federal union of Soviet Socialist Republics, with the highest organ of state power being the Supreme Soviet of the USSR, a bicameral legislature made up of the Soviet of the Union and the Soviet of Nationalities. The first chamber consists of deputies directly elected and the second of deputies representing units in the federal system. Exercising formal authority between the two annual sessions of the Supreme Soviet is a thirty-five-member Presidium, consisting of the heads of the fifteen Union Republics and twenty members elected by the Supreme Soviet, including the president of the Presidium who also serves as chief of state. The Supreme Soviet also appoints the chairman and other members of the Council of Ministers, bearing direct responsibility for usual state functions and for running the economy.

Paralleling this fairly standard constitutional structure—with its elections, legislative and executive organs, and administrative machinery—is the much more important informal structure of the Communist party, with its own institutional arrangements. These include the party Congress, which meets at irregular intervals, the Central Committee, the Politburo (currently consisting of fifteen regular and seven candidate members), and the party Secretariat headed by the general secretary (currently Leonid Brezhnev). Theoretically, a process of election operates for the selection of representatives at each successive higher level of the party pyramid, but Lenin's doctrine of "democratic centralism" as a way of reconciling democratic participation with the need for firm leadership means in practice that decisions taken at the higher levels are absolutely binding on lower levels.

In the actual pattern of power relationships in Soviet society, party decisions are what count, and they are made at the top. "The constitutional structure of the Soviet Union has always been an elaborate facade behind which one-party rule and totalitarianism have occupied the political scene. No meeting of the Supreme Soviet has ever even faintly approached in importance a Party congress." Similarly, the Council of Ministers has never rivaled the role of the Central Committee or the Politburo of the party as "the supreme maker of policies." The power of the primary Soviet leader—whether Lenin, Stalin, Khrushchev, or Brezhnev—has never depended on whether the individual held a high state position. "From the top to the bottom of the Soviet structure the Party has played a more important role than the corresponding state organs."[66]

With these fundamental considerations in mind, our attention will be directed at the Council of Ministers, the administrative apparatus of the state which comes under its jurisdiction, and the higher ranking bureaucrats who are in charge of these entities (including those involved in economic management). It should be recognized that all of these officers of the state are also party members, and many of them hold important posts in the party.

In 1976 the Council of Ministers, chaired by Aleksei Kosygin, included representatives of seventy-seven central agencies, plus the chairmen of the councils of ministers of the fifteen Union Republics as ex officio members. Of the seventy-seven agencies, sixty-two were ministries with single heads, and fifteen were state committees represented on the Council of Ministers by their chairmen. The ministries consist of two types: "all-Union" ministries which operate directly throughout the Soviet Union, and "Union Republic" ministries which carry out their operations indirectly through corresponding ministries in each of the fifteen Union Republics. Civil Aviation is an example of the first type of ministry, Agriculture of the second. State committees have been increasing in number and importance, and deal with a wide variety of responsibilities, among them Foreign Economic Relations, Labor and Wages, Planning, and Television and Radio Broadcasting.

A breakdown of these units by major function underlines the predominance of the economic management category. Over two-thirds of them belong there—forty-nine of the ministries (thirty-one responsible for a branch of industry, ten for a branch of construction, four for agriculture, and four for transportation or communications), and six of the state committees. Less than one-third account for the whole range of other state functions, including military and police agencies. This distribution gives some indication of the divergence from the administrative pattern in non-Communist countries.

The Council of Ministers, because of its large size, varied composition, and deficiencies as a decision-making body, does not operate in the same fashion as the cabinet in a parliamentary system. A much smaller group, consisting of the chairman of the council, a first deputy chairman, and several deputy chairmen (currently ten), plus an indefinite number of other leading members of the council, apparently acts routinely on behalf of the whole council and functions as sort of an unofficial cabinet, but little is actually known about its methods of operation. As an instrumentality of the Soviet polity, the Council of Ministers seems to be primarily concerned with the execution rather than the formulation of policy, except as its members participate as policy-makers in their overlapping party capacities.

Supervision over the state bureaucracy is centered in the Central Establishments Administration of the Finance Ministry, which sets standards of employment and ceilings on the size of staffs, establishes job classification systems, makes studies of agency efficiency, and keeps data on personnel operations. It would be mistaken, however, to regard this unit as the equivalent of a centralized civilian personnel agency in a Western democracy. In the Soviet Union, recruitment for top leadership positions is essentially in the hands of the Communist party, which makes use of both party and state organs for this purpose. Recruitment into and advancement within the key bureaucratic elites mentioned earlier are basically a single centrally controlled process.

In view of this approach, and the almost monopolistic nature of state employment,[67] public service of some kind is the career ambition of most Soviet youth.[68] The path toward the higher ranking opportunities is a long and arduous one. About half of those who complete the compulsory eight years of state elementary school go on to either general education or specialized secondary schools. Halfway through secondary school, applicants must file for admission to universities or specialized higher educational institutions, with acceptance based on difficult examinations in mathematics and other subjects depending on the specialty chosen. Under Khrushchev, a mandatory quota of those admitted had to be factory or farm workers, but this approach was abandoned after his ouster. Instead there is now a separate competition for such applicants, with more discretion left to the institution as to which ones have the proficiency for acceptance. In practice, few exceptions of this kind occur. According to Hazard, "the separation of those who will eventually be favored as the technicians, the managers, and the intellectuals generally, from those who must remain throughout their lives at the level of the manual laborer, occurs at an early age"—about fifteen or sixteen.[69] After reviewing available evidence, he concludes that "the opportunity for choice of a profession at the age of decision in the U.S.S.R. is about what it is elsewhere" among industrialized societies.[70]

Successful graduates of a university or professional school, having been trained at state expense, are required by law to accept a three-year assignment as determined by the ministry or agency which appoints them. Recruitment is ministry by ministry, based on academic performance and not on a system of entrance examinations. Although personal considerations (such as health factors and not separating husbands and wives) may be taken into account by officials making assignments, initial jobs are usually in remote locations. Following completion of this three-year stint, individual preference is given more consideration; occupational mobility seems to have increased markedly in recent years. Personnel trained in technical specialties, particularly in engineering and science fields, enter the state administration in greatest numbers and have the most opportunities, as might be expected from the functional requirements of many of the agencies.

Although standardized civil service entry examinations are not used, personnel regulations after appointment are highly uniform and similar in many respects to those in civil service systems in other developed countries. Nationwide uniformity is provided in descriptions of job functions, with a specific wage scale attached to each job, incorporating variations to recognize such factors as academic qualifications, years of service, and work locations that are remote or dangerous. A grievance procedure provides for hearings before boards made up equally of members from the labor union to which the worker belongs and the management of the unit where he works. If a grievance is not settled at the grievance board level, it may be taken to a trade union committee (which is really a part of the state apparatus), and eventually to the courts. Hazard cites instances of successful appeal by employees for judicial settlement. Dismissals are legally prohibited except for specified reasons similar to those in other systems for civil servants who have achieved tenure rights. All in all, the usual requisites for a career service seem to be satisfied.

Traits of behavior among state bureaucrats which have been observed and reported on as characteristic reflect the dilemma of officials who are in positions of responsibility and hence of vulnerability in the Soviet political system. On the positive side, members of the administrative cadre share a Communist credo which they in part helped to form, and they can take satisfaction in being among the select governing group in the Soviet system, with attendant benefits and privileges, including high material rewards and perquisites and strong managerial prerogatives. Countervailing negative tendencies stem from the inexorable pressures for performance under conditions of demanding goals, limited resources, and continual surveillance. Fainsod comments, "The typical Soviet administrator functions in an environment in which every major decision is subject to the possibility of check, recheck, and countercheck. . . . The whole range of his activity, as well as that of the control organs, is always under careful surveillance by representatives of the Party. It is not too far-fetched to describe this complex network of controls as a system of power founded on the institutionalization of mutual suspicion."[71]

Undoubtedly, since the Stalinist period ended there has been a lessening of unpredictable terrorism, more restraint in actions of the secret police, somewhat more tolerance of criticism and suggestions, and more opportunity for exercising initiative and decisiveness. Nevertheless, operation under pressure-packed conditions is still the norm.

The Soviet official, especially in a crucial economic sphere, is still expected to perform at a feverish pace. The analogy of an Oriental potentate may no longer be suitable, but insofar as his security and peace of mind are concerned, he may not unfairly be compared to an American baseball manager or football coach. Failure to produce may not always be excused by references to the poor material available or to the hard schedule. He may find himself accused of an improper attitude or the inability to work with people, and no civil service regulations will protect him from a curt dismissal. And the element of terror has not of course been entirely eliminated.[72]

Under the threat of reassignment or drastic punishment for failure of performance or loss of confidence, the highly dependent Soviet administrator does what he can to minimize the danger. Knowing that as an individual he is expendable and replaceable, he strives to protect himself by having goals assigned that are achievable, by increasing the allocation of resources at his disposal, and by mustering as much political support as he can. He maneuvers within the latitude available to him in a struggle that is in essence political. Without a doubt widespread corruption, collusion, influence peddling, black market operations, and other deviations from officially approved conduct have persisted, as evidenced by repeated campaigns to denounce and eliminate such practices. "Precisely because the screws are so tight, Soviet administration has become preoccupied with ways and means of gaining relief. Deals have to be worked out up and down the line to win some slack, by getting at an early date the wherewithal essential to one's own predetermined performance, by being granted exceptions, by having timetables of planned action modified. To this end, one must know the right man—and one must have something to offer in return."[73] Despite efforts to reduce these "economic crimes," using at different times both centralized and decentralized approaches, the party leadership has not been able to break a cycle in which abuses bring about control measures, which in turn, because of their rigidity, contribute to further evasive tactics.

Knowledge as to how to cope with survival requirements in such circumstances must be acquired by the bureaucrat with staying power. As summarized by Fainsod, "The essence of bureaucratic

politics in the Soviet system consists in a search for a viable equilibrium between the pressures from above for maximal output and the
inescapable limitations which factors of scarcity and human frailty
impose. The successful Soviet administrator must be more than loyal
and efficient. He must learn to manipulate the environment around
him to meet the demands which are made on him."[74]

From the perspective of the party leadership, multiple control
devices must be maintained to ensure dependency on the part of the
state bureaucracy. The monopolistic nature of state employment is
in itself a powerful incentive toward conformity. The more obvious
personnel controls in a well-organized bureaucratic system are used
to good advantage. Party membership and adherence to party
doctrine by the higher ranking bureaucrats means a built-in tendency
toward meeting party expectations.

An impressive array of official state control devices has been
put into place for the specific purpose of keeping bureaucrats in line.
Hierarchical authority is of course exercised vigorously on an agency-
by-agency basis. The Ministry of Finance, in addition to the
personnel management functions already mentioned, also has several
fiscal control responsibilities, including budget enforcement, inspection of financial records, and auditing. State banks which extend
credits to industrial plants have access to details as to financial operations. The secret police presumably still keep tabs on plants engaged
in crucial operations or where misconduct is suspected, although this
kind of surveillance is probably much less now than under Stalin.

The procurator general of the USSR is the official with the
clearest mandate to impose legal restraints on administrative behavior.
Appointed for a seven-year term by the Supreme Soviet, the procurator general and his subordinates are responsible for assuring that
laws are interpreted correctly and applied consistently, and have
authority to investigate complaints alleging law violations by administrative officials. Indications are that the primary concern is that
administrators adhere to policy directives, and that investigation of
citizen complaints is secondary.

The USSR does not have an administrative court system. The
civil courts operate under a four-tiered arrangement, beginning with
people's courts consisting of one elected judge and two lay assessors,
and extending through regional and Union Republic courts to the
Supreme Court of the USSR, with judges at these three higher levels
being appointed by the corresponding soviets at each level. Most
judges are party members, and the courts are operated within the
framework of party policy. These civil courts do not provide much

of a vehicle for consideration of citizen complaints against administrative action.

The closest equivalent to legislative control comes through the interlocking network of governmental and party structures at each level in the Soviet system. The formal government structure includes popularly elected deputies in soviets constituted at each level. These soviets have impressive constitutional powers but limited actual powers. The popular election process amounts in practice to ratification of candidates chosen by the party. Nevertheless, these soviets are significant as "agencies of socialization and legitimation. They offer opportunities to millions of people for limited participation in political life that generates support for the state. The fact that a party apparatus dominates the political process is hidden behind a facade of mass representation."[75] One of Khrushchev's reforms was to activate the largely moribund soviets at the local level, involving them more directly in providing for community needs such as housing, roads, libraries, and theaters. Fainsod reports that although they "provide for more widespread popular participation in the governmental process and furnish an outlet for criticism of local officialdom, such criticism usually gives evidence of having been carefully organized in advance by Party authorities. . . . If the Soviets do little more now than provide the trappings and symbolism of 'socialist democracy,' they do represent an embryonic instrument of mass control which may conceivably become more significant under different auspices and circumstances."[76]

This formal structure of soviets is paralleled by the party apparatus at each level. With a total membership approaching fifteen million, plus over twice as many in its youth auxiliary, the Komsomol, the Communist party permeates every community and every sector of Soviet society. Party executives at each level exercise the most important controls over the state bureaucracy, whatever the official interrelationships. To achieve the firm control over the bureaucracy required by the party, the tendency is to "centralize authority at the top while shoving responsibility for results downward." As a technique for getting results, the regime "implements an unremitting drive for achieving the possible by continually demanding the impossible. Conflicting demands are 'on the books' and thus legitimate every demand the highest Party authorities decide to make."[77] Important though he is to the success of the system, the bureaucrat remains a "favorite whipping boy . . . being ridiculed, harangued, and often savagely assailed."[78]

Assessment of the present and potential role of the state administrative bureaucracy in the Soviet political system is a hazardous undertaking, due among other factors to the scarcity of data, the blurring of jurisdictional boundaries, and the shifting pattern of relationships in the system. The usual interpretation has been that the USSR is a "totalitarian directed society," with the state bureaucracy basically subservient to the Communist party, as are all other institutions that intervene between the party and the people. As Bendix points out, Soviet totalitarianism has taken the plebiscitarianism principle which was part of the political tradition of Western Europe, with its insistence that nothing should intervene between the nation and its citizens, and has applied it to destroy all intermediate autonomous centers of action by identifying the party as "the single, exclusive representative body of the people as a whole, while all unorganizable sections of the population are identified as the criminal elements of the society."[79] The Soviet system of domination thus institutionalizes the principle of plebiscitarianism, using a doctrine stressing the equal status of citizens to justify elitist rule by permitting no representative body to intervene between the individual and the supreme authority of the party.

The most widely accepted image of Soviet bureaucracy, consistent with such a "directed society" model for the whole system, characterizes it as subject to unavoidable outside controls which lead to the adoption of protective measures that result in formalism and inefficiency. Crozier, for example, views the Russian system as one with "a whole set of checking and counter-checking relationships" made necessary by "the acceptance of the most arbitrary discretion" and founded on "the dilemma of trust and suspicion." He continues,

Its central problem, of course, arises from the resistance of the subordinates. Subordinates have had to internalize the autocratic rule to the point where they accept favor and arbitrariness as givens one does not discuss. But they cannot help protecting themselves. They do so in two ways: on the one hand, they remain passive, slow, apathetic . . . on the other hand, they constantly build informal groups that traditionally have served as protective networks. . . . Only because, at the middle and lower levels, people trust each other and are ready to enter into all the necessary deals and semi-legal or illegal arrangements can the most glaring discrepancies between the announced objectives and the means provided to achieve them be glossed over and the orders of the sacrosanct 'Plan' respected. . . . At the same time, the rulers are unable to trust anyone, since there is no way to achieve the goals they set except by flouting their orders. The rulers must, therefore, resort to checks and counter-checks. This endless chain of suspicion tends to reinforce the need for the protection of the informal primary group . . ., finally calling for more checks.[80]

Jerry F. Hough has suggested an alternative way of analyzing how the Soviet system, including the bureaucracy, operates. Drawing upon research of his own and by others, he finds increasing evidence of pluralistic tendencies within the system. He points out that currently Soviet administrative hierarchies, even more than in the West, contain specialties covering a vast spectrum, with the professional orientations that go with these specializations. This in turn implies that organizational goals are multiple and diversified rather than monolithic and universal. He argues that the Soviet Union should be viewed "as a total bureaucratic system in which the leaders themselves rose through the bureaucracy and are part of it rather than a parliamentary system in which a cabinet of generalist political leaders gives direction to a pliable bureaucracy."[81]

In a broader context, Hough proposes that the "directed society" paradigm might be replaced by one which takes greater account of characteristics of the Soviet political system which have evolved in recent years bearing a close resemblance to "classic pluralism" as understood in the West. Such features might include "official recognition of the legitimacy of group interests and conflict"; a political culture and political leadership based on acceptance of accommodation, bargaining, and brokerage; and an expectation that political change will normally be incremental in response to the demands of relatively small groups, rather than drastic and abrupt. Hough goes on to recognize that a pluralist model for the USSR would have to exclude "several key features of pluralism in the West: the opportunity for citizens to choose between the programs of competing elites in elections, to form new organizations (that is, pressure groups or parties) to advance their political interests, and to criticize the fundamentals of society while advocating nonincremental change."[82]

The label given by Hough to his suggested model is "institutional pluralism," emphasizing that those who want to bring about political change must expect to work within the official institutional framework. Otherwise they can anticipate severe repression, particularly if they call for more than modest incremental changes. The assumption of this conceptualization is that the political institutions in the Soviet Union (most importantly the Communist party) are now "at least somewhat responsive to broader societal forces."[83]

Without trying to evaluate here the merits of "institutional pluralism" as a means of explaining the Soviet polity, we should note that if Hough is correct a rethinking of the political role of the state bureaucracy would be in order. He emphasizes that the leading political participants in such a system will almost always be "establishment" figures, including civil servants. Under institutional pluralism as an operating system, the state bureaucracy would, without question, be an influential political group.

The record shows that in spite of its traditional basic subservience to the party, the Soviet state bureaucracy has been able to strengthen and consolidate its position, and to extend its privileges. The civil administrative bureaucracy is one of the key competing groups, along with the police and the army, in challenging the party functionaries for power and influence. As Ulam reminds us, industrialization and growth as a world power would have been impossible for the USSR without creating its

... enormous and intricate administrative machinery. For all its shortcomings, for all the tenseness and insecurity in which the Soviet administrator has worked, this machinery has performed the day-to-day tasks of administration and planning. It has served the state well, and the Soviet administrator may soon feel and demand that his rewards should go beyond the enhanced social status and relative physical security accorded to him by the post-Stalin regime. His technical ability and his vital function in the system give him a base of power from which to press such a demand.[84]

The bureaucratic role is likely to grow rather than diminish in significance.

Notes

1. Gabriel A. Almond and Sidney Verba, *The Civic Culture* (Princeton, N.J.: Princeton University Press, 1963), p. 8.
2. For an excellent brief analysis, see Wallace S. Sayre, "Bureaucracies: Some Contrasts in Systems," *Indian Journal of Public Administration*, 10, No. 2 (1964), 219-29. (Reprinted in Nimrod Raphaeli, ed., *Readings in Comparative Public Administration* (Boston: Allyn and Bacon, 1967), pp. 341-54.) Selected sources on the British civil service include: Herman Finer, *The Theory and Practice of Modern Government*, rev. ed. (New York: Henry Holt and Company, 1949), Chapter 30; H. R. G. Greaves, *The Civil Service in the Changing State* (London: Harrap and Co., 1947);

Stanley Rothman, Howard Scarrow, and Martin Schain, *European Society and Politics* (St. Paul, Minn.: West Publishing Company, 1976), pp. 325-32; R. A. Chapman, *The Higher Civil Service in Britain* (London: Constable & Co., 1970); and James B. Christoph, "High Civil Servants and the Politics of Consensualism in Great Britain," pp. 25-62, Bruce W. Headey, "A Typology of Ministers: Implications for Minister-Civil Servant Relationships in Britain," pp. 63-86, and Robert D. Putnam, "The Political Attitudes of Senior Civil Servants in Britain, Germany, and Italy," pp. 87-126—all in Mattei Dogan, ed., *The Mandarins of Western Europe* (New York: John Wiley and Sons, 1975). Selected sources on the U.S. civil service include Paul P. Van Riper, *History of the United States Civil Service* (Evanston, Ill.: Row, Peterson and Company, 1958); Finer, *The Theory and Practice of Modern Government*, rev. ed., Chapter 33; David T. Stanley, *The Higher Civil Service* (Washington, D.C.: The Brookings Institution, 1964); Frederick C. Mosher, *Democracy and the Public Service* (New York: Oxford University Press, 1968); Lewis C. Mainzer, *Political Bureaucracy* (Glenview, Ill.: Scott, Foresman, 1973); Samuel Krislov, *Representative Bureaucracy* (Englewood Cliffs, N.J.: Prentice-Hall, Inc., 1974); James A. Medeiros and David E. Schmitt, *Public Bureaucracy: Values and Perspectives* (North Scituate, Mass.: Duxbury Press, 1977); and O. Glenn Stahl, *Public Personnel Administration*, 7th ed. (New York: Harper & Row, 1977).

3. The most influential recommendations have come from reports of the Second Hoover Commission of 1955 in the United States, and the Fulton Committee of 1968 in Great Britain.

4. "The selection, training, and streaming of the administrative trainees is still designed to produce a class of senior civil servants that can serve ministers by synthesizing the contributions of specialists, placing these in the context of political realities, and by formulating policy alternatives. If the new administrator turns out not quite to fit the old model of the 'talented amateur,' it is even less likely that he will fit the model of the narrow specialist." Rothman, Scarrow, and Schain, *European Society and Politics*, p. 331.

5. Mosher, *Democracy and the Public Service*, Chapter 4, pp. 99-133.

6. "From the British point of view," as a distinguished Nigerian put it, "a first-class brain, particularly if produced by Oxford or Cambridge, can, without any special training, govern anybody and anything in the world." S. O. Adebo, "Public Administration in Newly Independent Countries," in Burton A. Baker, ed., *Public Administration: A Key to Development* (Washington, D.C.: Graduate School, U.S. Department of Agriculture, 1964), p. 22.

7. This excerpt is reprinted from "High Civil Servants and the Politics of Consensualism in Great Britain," by James B. Christoph in *The Mandarins of Western Europe: The Political Role of Top Civil Servants*, ed. Mattei Dogan, © 1975, p. 50, by permission of the Publisher, Sage Publications, Inc. (Beverly Hills/London).

8. *Ibid.*, p. 40.

9. This excerpt is reprinted from "A Typology of Ministers: Implications for Minister-Civil Servant Relationships in Britain," by Bruce W. Headey, in *The Mandarins of Western Europe: The Political Role of Top Civil Servants*, Mattei Dogan, Editor, © 1975, p. 74, by permission of the Publisher, Sage Publications, Inc. (Beverly Hills/London).

10. *Ibid.*, p. 76.

11. *Ibid.*, pp. 77-78.

12. *Ibid.*, p. 79.

13. *Ibid.*, p. 82.

14. *Ibid.*, p. 82.

15. Christoph, "High Civil Servants," p. 47.

16. *Ibid.*, p. 49.

17. *Ibid.*, p. 59.

18. Mainzer, *Political Bureaucracy*, pp. 107, 112.

19. Sayre, "Bureaucracies: Some Contrasts in Systems," p. 228.

20. Putnam, "The Political Attitudes of Senior Civil Servants," p. 117.

21. Christoph, "High Civil Servants," p. 33.

22. *Ibid.*, p. 35.

23. *Ibid.*, p. 56.

24. Mainzer, *Political Bureaucracy*, p. 84.

25. Rothman, Scarrow, and Schain, *European Society and Politics*, p. 331.

26. Michel Crozier, *The Bureaucratic Phenomenon* (Chicago: University of Chicago Press, 1964), p. 233.

27. Sayre, "Bureaucracies: Some Contrasts in Systems," p. 223.

28. This summary relies heavily on the following sources: Robert E. Ward, "Japan," in Robert E. Ward and Roy C. Macridis, eds., *Modern Political Systems: Asia* (Englewood Cliffs, N.J.: Prentice-Hall, Inc., 1963), pp. 17-114; Masamichi Inoki, "The Civil Bureaucracy," in Robert E. Ward and Dankwart A. Rustow, eds., *Political Modernization in Japan and Turkey* (Princeton, N.J.: Princeton University Press, 1964), Chapter 7, pp. 283-300; Kiyoaki Tsuji, "The Cabinet, Administrative Organization, and the Bureaucracy," *Annals of the American Academy of Political and Social Science* 308 (1956): 10-17; Reinhard Bendix, "Preconditions of Development: A Comparison of Japan and Germany," *Nation-Building and Citizenship* (New York: John Wiley & Sons, Inc., 1964), Chapter 6, pp. 177-213; Akira Kubota, *Higher Civil Servants in Postwar Japan* (Princeton, N.J.: Princeton University Press, 1969); and Edwin Dowdy, *Japanese Bureaucracy: Its Development and Modernization* (Melbourne: Cheshire, 1973).

29. Inoki, "The Civil Bureaucracy," p. 286.

30. Dowdy, *Japanese Bureaucracy*, p. xii.

31. *Ibid.*, p. 156.

32. *Ibid.*, pp. 181-82.

33. Inoki, "The Civil Bureaucracy," p. 288.

34. Ward, "Japan," p. 28.

35. *Ibid.*, p. 99.
36. *Higher Civil Servants in Post-War Japan: Their Social Origins, Educational Backgrounds, and Career Patterns*, by Akira Kubota (copyright © 1969 by Princeton University Press), p. 58. Reprinted by permission of Princeton University Press.
37. "In terms of objectives . . . a Japanese faculty of law more nearly resembled a combination of a political science department and a business administration school in an American university than it did a law school." *Ibid.*, p. 78.
38. *Ibid.*, pp. 70, 162.
39. *Ibid.*, pp. 85-91, 165-68.
40. *Ibid.*, pp. 27-57, 160-61.
41. *Ibid.*, p. 140.
42. Dowdy, *Japanese Bureaucracy*, p. xiv.
43. Ward, "Japan," p. 102.
44. Kubota, *Higher Civil Servants in Postwar Japan*, p. 173.
45. Inoki, "The Civil Bureaucracy," pp. 299-300.
46. Ward, "Japan," pp. 101-2.
47. *Ibid.*, p. 85.
48. Kubota, *Higher Civil Servants in Postwar Japan*, p. 174.
49. Bendix, *Nation-Building and Citizenship*, p. 200.
50. Crozier, *The Bureaucratic Phenomenon*, p. 231 n.
51. Kubota, *Higher Civil Servants in Postwar Japan*, p. 176.
52. Sources include Merle Fainsod, *How Russia Is Ruled*, rev. ed. (Cambridge: Harvard University Press, 1964), especially Chapter 12, "The Control of the Bureaucracy—Public Administration in the Soviet Union"; Fainsod, "Bureaucracy and Modernization: The Russian and Soviet Case," pp. 233-67, in Joseph LaPalombara, ed., *Bureaucracy and Political Development* (Princeton, N.J.: Princeton University Press, 1963); Bendix, *Nation-Building and Citizenship*, Chapter 12, "Private and Public Authority in Western Europe and Russia"; Alfred G. Meyer, *The Soviet Political System* (New York: Random House, 1965); John N. Hazard, *The Soviet System of Government*, 4th ed. rev. (Chicago: University of Chicago Press, 1968); David Lane, *Politics and Society in the USSR* (New York: Random House, 1971); Adam B. Ulam, *The Russian Political System* (New York: Random House, © 1974); Jerry F. Hough, "The Bureaucratic Model and the Nature of the Soviet System," *Journal of Comparative Administration* 5, No. 2 (August 1973): 134-67; and Frederick C. Barghoorn, "Politics in the U.S.S.R.," Chapter 10, pp. 255-308, in Gabriel A. Almond, gen. ed., *Comparative Politics Today: A World View* (Boston: Little, Brown and Company, 1974).
53. Fainsod, *How Russia Is Ruled*, p. 387; copyright 1953, 1963 by the President and Fellows of Harvard College.
54. *Ibid.*, p. 209.

55. Hazard, *The Soviet System of Government*, p. 10, © 1957, 1960, 1964, and 1968 by The University of Chicago.
56. Fainsod, *How Russia Is Ruled*, p. 215.
57. *Ibid.*, p. 3.
58. Fainsod in LaPalombara, *Bureaucracy and Political Development*, p. 240.
59. Frederic J. Fleron, Jr., Introduction to "Bureaucracy and Administration in Socialist States," *Journal of Comparative Administration* 5, No. 2 (1973): 131-33, at p. 132.
60. Lane, *Politics and Society in the USSR*, p. 182.
61. Meyer, *The Soviet Political System*, pp. 477-78.
62. Quoted in Hough, "The Bureaucratic Model," pp. 135-37.
63. This excerpt from "The Bureaucratic Model and the Nature of the Soviet System" by Jerry F. Hough is reprinted from the *Journal of Comparative Administration* Vol. 5, No. 2 (August 1973) p. 135 by permission of the Publisher, Sage Publications, Inc.
64. Ulam, *The Russian Political System*, p. 75.
65. Hough, "The Bureaucratic Model," pp. 138-39.
66. Ulam, *The Russian Political System*, p. 59.
67. Alfred Meyer is essentially correct when he says that "every citizen is a civil servant; and many if not all of them belong to a number of bureaucratic agencies." Quoted in Hough, "The Bureaucratic Model," p. 160.
68. "For the ambitious young man or woman seeking a career in Soviet society as it is today, the only thought will be of state employment. State employment opens the road to power, prestige, a desirable apartment in the multi-dwellings maintained by state agencies, and a steady income followed by a state pension." Hazard, *The Soviet System of Government*, p. 187.
69. *Ibid.*, p. 188.
70. "The children of parents who have the educational background associated with the non-manual categories of workers still have the greatest opportunity to gain admission to the professions. This is not because of any bias in their favor but simply because it is easier to maintain good records in school and to pass entrance examinations if parents are interested in such success and provide the environment in which academic pursuits find encouragement and stimulation." *Ibid.*, p. 190. John A. Armstrong, although reporting that large numbers of the present Soviet administrative elite come from lower strata peasant and worker family backgrounds, concurs that "there is no doubt that Soviet children whose parents are better educated and have more prestigious positions have advantages comparable to those from similar Western families in entering professions." *The European Administrative Elite* (Princeton, N.J.: Princeton University Press, 1973), p. 73.
71. Fainsod, *How Russia Is Ruled*, p. 388.
72. Ulam, *The Russian Political System*, p. 81. Ulam might easily have added

university presidents to his list of American comparisons, based on recent turnover rates.

73. Fritz Morstein Marx, "Control and Responsibility in Administration: Comparative Aspects," in Ferrel Heady and Sybil L. Stokes, eds., *Papers in Comparative Public Administration* (Ann Arbor, Mich.: Institute of Public Administration, The University of Michigan, 1962), p. 156.

74. Fainsod, *How Russia Is Ruled*, p. 419.

75. Barghoorn, "Politics in the U.S.S.R.," p. 295.

76. Fainsod, *How Russia Is Ruled*, p. 403.

77. Bendix, *Nation-Building and Citizenship*, pp. 168, 170-71.

78. Morstein Marx in Heady and Stokes, *Papers*, p. 152.

79. Bendix, *Nation-Building and Citizenship*, pp. 146, 174-75.

80. Crozier, *The Bureaucratic Phenomenon*, pp. 228-31.

81. Hough, "The Bureaucratic Model," p. 161.

82. *Ibid.*, p. 163.

83. *Ibid.*

84. Ulam, *The Russian Political System*, p. 89.

7

ADMINISTRATION IN THE DEVELOPING NATIONS

Potentially the most significant political fact of the twentieth century has been the closing out of the colonial era and the emergence, in most cases as newly independent states, of the nations of Africa, Asia, Latin America, and the Middle East. We have chosen the term "developing" as most appropriate to describe these countries as a group, recognizing that any adjective is inadequate to such a task, and that the one selected has shortcomings as noted in Chapter 3. Alternative descriptive labels, such as "emerging" or "modernizing" in earlier and "Third World" or "the South" in more recent usage, have at least equivalent deficiencies for our purposes. Admittedly no single word or phrase can cope with the diversities of such disparate nations as Afghanistan, Ghana, India, and Mexico, to mention only a few countries that do not represent the extremes of contrast but do suggest the variety that exists in location, resources, population, history, culture, religion, and a multitude of other factors.

Despite their differences, all of these countries can be called developing because of what they do have in common. All are caught up in the process of social change, not just the continuous change that any society undergoes, but change that is critical and disruptive. Put in terms of "models" of societies which have often in the past been used for purposes of analysis, they are moving from the traditional toward the modern type. They are all in transition, no longer traditional and not yet modern, either as they view themselves or as others view them. To the extent that "modernity" itself is losing its attractiveness for some of these countries, the alternatives being considered differ markedly from the "postindustrial" society now being forecast as the future of countries which have been considered developed. In sum, we are concerned here with a large group of nation-states whose current status and future prospects have produced a commonality among them in their own self-perceptions, which also provides a basis for our consideration of their political regimes and administrative systems.

The Ideology of Development

Despite recent misgivings, the developing countries continue to share a generalized consensus of the objectives toward which change should be directed. Since this "ideology of development" is crucial to an understanding of politics and administration in these countries, we need to look at its major elements.

The twin goals of development are nation-building and socioeconomic progress.[1] Agreement on the desirability of these goals is found even among political leaders who show wide variation in political orientation, political strategy, social origin, and opportunity for success in goal attainment. To the extent that they are politically motivated at all, the rank and file of the population in these countries share the belief that these are proper objectives, and will tend to bring pressure on political leaders who may be tempted to give precedence to more immediate and selfishly motivated aims. These paired values seem to explain to a substantial degree the accepted ideological commitment in the developing countries.

Esman has described nation-building as "the deliberate fashioning of an integrated political community within fixed geographic boundaries in which the nation-state is the dominant political institution."[2] Nationhood, says Rustow, "now has become the vocal aspiration of 130 peoples all linked tightly through modern means of communication and transport," whereas earlier it was "the proud achievement of a few people isolated from the rest of humanity. . . . Sometime in the nineteenth century in Europe, modernization was wedded to the nation-state, and in Asia and Africa that alliance is being consummated anew in the present day. . . . For the present, throughout Asia, Africa, and Latin America, nationalism and the drive for modernity are parts of the same dual revolution."[3]

It is somewhat paradoxical that the concept of the nation-state has gained so in appeal to the rest of the world at the same time that the nation as a political unit and nationalism as a doctrine have been increasingly questioned in the West where the nation-state system originated. The urge to seek a national identity is probably in part a reaction to escape from colonialism, expressing a desire to emulate the nationhood of the former colonial power once independence has been gained.

Actual achievement of nationhood in most of the emerging areas is not an easy task. It calls for success in meeting the challenge of political development, requiring the creation, as summarized by Palmer, of "a system of political institutions capable of controlling the state's population, of mobilizing the state's human and material resources toward the ends of economic and social modernization, and of coping with the strain of social, economic, and political change without abdicating its control and mobilization roles."[4]

In the case of Europe, this process was indigenous and slow. Kautsky calls it "the politics of modernization from within." He reviews the gradual transformation of society in Western Europe from beginnings as far back as the eleventh century, pointing out that it was brought about by natives of the society and was in a sense organic to the society, thereby allowing more time for adjustment to different strata of the population and reducing the shock of sudden transformation. The developing countries, on the other hand, face the trauma of "modernization from without," which involves "a rather sudden break with the hitherto traditional past and can be brought to a society either by foreigners or by some of its own natives or by both."[5]   Although this distinction is not, of course, clear-cut, since both internal and external factors will always be present, the matter of preponderance is an important point, and emphasizes the difficulties and hazards of rapid "modernization from without," which is the typical prospect for developing nations.

Also in the case of Europe, the movement toward nationalism was largely one of uniting under one government people already speaking a single language. Most of the developing states are artificial entities in the sense that they are the products of colonial activity rather than of a pre-existing political loyalty. Their boundaries likewise were often drawn by imperial powers without regard to ethnic groupings, excluding people with close cultural ties and including minority groups opposed to assimilation. The situation leads Kautsky to remark that whatever nationalism in underdeveloped countries may be, it commonly lacks this key language element.

Indian nationalism is not an attempt to unite people speaking Indian, Nigerian nationalism is not an attempt to unite people speaking Nigerian, for there are no such languages. . . . Virtually nowhere . . . do so-called nationalists in under-developed countries seek to redraw the boundaries of their countries to unite all people speaking a single language. Consequently, the creation of numerous new states and the occurrence of "nationalist" revolutions in old as well as new ones in the past few decades have resulted in almost no boundary changes, even though the present boundaries of most underdeveloped countries were originally drawn by colonial powers or . . . by earlier conquerors, without any regard to linguistic or cultural divisions among the natives.[6]

Such problems, although prevalent throughout the developing world, are especially acute in Africa. "An old recipe has it that, to make rabbit pie, you must first catch the rabbit. By the same token, to engage in nation-building, you must first find the nation. In the African setting, this is likely to be a more hazardous and uncertain venture than anywhere else."[7]

Still another dilemma has been investigated in detail by Inkeles and Smith in their study of individual change in selected developing countries. Observing that many new states were "actually only hollow shells, lacking the institutional structures which make a nation a viable and effective socio-political and economic enterprise," they emphasized that nation-building is an empty exercise "unless the attitudes and capacities of the people keep pace with other forms of development." Independence does not necessarily bring about such articulation, as mounting evidence indicates. "A modern *nation* needs participating citizens, men and women who take an active interest in public affairs and who exercise their rights and perform their duties as members of a community larger than that of the kin-ship network and the immediate geographical locality."[8] The authors explore the process of movement of individuals from being traditional to becoming modern personalities, using a concept of "modern man" which they formulate as a research tool. Their thesis is that the essence of national development is the diffusion through the population of the qualities of the modern man, and their study, intended as an aid to the process of modernization, is addressed to explaining how men become modern.

Such obstacles to nation-building as have been mentioned under-standably lead to expressions of pessimism about the future. Histor-ian Joseph R. Strayer, for example, has predicted that since building a nation-state is a slow and complicated affair, "most of the polities created in the last fifty years are never going to complete the pro-cess." The new states to which he gives the best chance of success are "those which correspond fairly closely to old political units; those where the experience of living together for many generations within a continuing political framework has given the people some sense of identity; those where the political unit coincides roughly with a distinct cultural area; and those where there are indigenous institutions and habits of political thinking that can be connected to forms borrowed from outside."[9] Whatever their prospects, the new states put a premium on establishing their nationhood, and give this priority in political action.

The related goal of social and economic progress in the ideology of development may be equally hard to achieve, but it is somewhat more tangible and measurable. Esman identifies it as "the sustained and widely diffused improvement in material and social welfare."[10] The desire to triumph over poverty and to distribute the benefits of industrialization generally in the society are powerful motivations to people just becoming aware of what is possible as demonstrated by the developed nations, including both those with democratic and those with totalitarian political orientations.

The ideology of development sets the sights for political and administrative action, but it does not specify the exact form of the machinery for either politics or administration. As Merghani observes, "there is a general inclination toward a strong government, a strong executive, and a high degree of centralization," on the assumption that "without a strong government and a strong leadership the task of national unity and rapid economic and social transformation becomes difficult if not impossible."[11] Beyond this, the mood is one that favors experimentation and adaptation from the successful experience of developed countries, whatever may have been the political paths followed.[12] Shils puts the situation neatly: "The elites of the new states have lying before them, not the image of a future in which no one has as yet lived or of a living and accepted past, but rather an image of their own future profoundly different from their own past, to be lived along the lines of the already existent modern states, which are their contemporaries."[13]

In essence, the distinctive quality of the developmental ideology is the agreement on the desirability of the joint goals of nation-building and material progress combined with a sense of movement toward fulfillment of a long-delayed destiny, underlying which is a nagging uncertainty concerning the prospects for eventual success.[14] The combination is a volatile one, mirrored in the political systems of most of these countries.

The Politics of Development

Knowledge of the political process in the developing world is understandably still fragmentary and tentative. It is nevertheless possible on the basis of recent studies of the political experience of developing nations,[15] supplemented by more speculative formulations of political activity in such societies,[16] to identify some of the more obvious and common features of the politics of development. The principal ones appear to be these: (1) a widely shared developmental ideology (discussed earlier) as the source of basic political goals; (2) a high degree of reliance on the political sector for achieving results in the society; (3) widespread incipient or actual political instability; (4) modernizing elitist leadership, accompanied by a wide "political gap" between the rulers and the ruled; and (5) an imbalance in the growth of political institutions, with the bureaucracy among those in the more mature category.

Developmental aims and the urgency with which they are sought inevitably mean that state action is the principal vehicle for accomplishment. Neither time nor means is available for gradualness or for primary reliance on private enterprise, as was possible in the Western countries, which developed earlier. The political element almost automatically assumes a central importance in the developing society. Some version of "socialism" tends to be the dominant preference, and a philosophy with a Marxist label, emphasizing industrial expansion and social welfare and denouncing the evils of foreign capitalism, is commonly given lip service, although one comment is that it is "an ideology resembling that of Ataturk more than Marx— an ideology of development and industrialization based on national culture and tradition and related to local conditions."[17] At any rate, the state is seen as the main hope for guiding the society toward modernization.

Paradoxically, such reliance on political responses is coupled with widespread political alienation and antipathy toward politicians. Shils calls this "the oppositional mentality." He traces it to the fact that prior to independence most political activity was directed toward gaining freedom from the colonial power. Politics was agitational and remonstrative rather than constructive and responsible. The oppositional attitude has carried over and is strong not only among the leaders in the movement for independence, but also among the new intellectuals, and among students in the younger generation. The resulting distrust of politicians and low esteem for them, according to Shils, "is a striking feature of the outlook of the people of the new states. Politicians are frequently thought to be timid, compromising, indecisive, dishonest, wasteful, selfish, etc."[18] At the same time that unprecedented demands are being made for political performance, active political participation does not appeal to many in the most promising recruitment groups, and those who do engage in political careers are apt to lose rather than gain in prestige. This probably is a carryover from the colonial period, as well as one expression of the recognition that the task of reconciling expectations with prospects is an exceedingly difficult one, and the outlook for success uncertain.

Political instability is another prominent characteristic. In his survey of approximately 100 countries, von der Mehden found that in almost two-thirds of them there had been either successful coups or serious attempts to overthrow the government. In eleven of the fourteen colonies that achieved independence from 1945 through 1955, the governments had been either overthrown or attacked. By 1969, extraconstitutional governments had been imposed in twenty-six states in the Afro-Asian area alone. He concluded that the maintenance of stable governments is plainly one of the major problems of the emerging nations, and that such figures are "not such as to give the early optimists much comfort."[19]   Gerald Heeger concurs that in recent years "almost every underdeveloped state has experienced political instability in one form or another—military coups and mutinies, insurrections, political assassinations, rioting, chaotic factional conflict among leaders, and so forth."[20]   Current news reports certainly give no hint of improvement in this condition. As compared to the developed polities, the typical situation in developing countries is one of political uncertainty, discontinuity, and extralegal change.

Heeger's explanation for the politics of instability is that consolidation of the political system in a new state is difficult for any regime, regardless of its characteristics, because of the segmental and amorphous nature of these polities. Independence brings "a political center in the form of central government and political institutions," and political conflict focuses on "gaining access to and control of the various strategic roles within the new political center." The search for dominance leads to efforts at coalition among groups not strong enough to capture the machinery of government without allies. Successful coalitions then try to expand and consolidate by using their power resources. Usually the stability sought is not attained, because the available political institutions "lack the capability to deal with the consequences of social and economic change" in these societies, such as the highly unbalanced effects of modernization, the rapid escalation of demands by groups upon which the new political system depends, and the exacerbation of communal divisions because of competition for scarce resources.[21]

Political leadership is concentrated in a minute segment of the population in most developing countries. The governing elite, in the sense of those wielding major decision-making power in the political system, tends not only to be small in numbers but also separated socially and culturally, as well as politically, from the bulk of the citizenry. The elitist group is not the same everywhere, although there are some common characteristics. During the past half-century, according to von der Mehden, the new nations have experienced four types of political leadership: colonial, traditional, nationalist, and economic. The common pattern has been for the colonial elite, who often worked during the colonial period indirectly through traditional and economic elite groups, to give way after independence to a nationalist elite which holds almost complete power for a time, and is then generally replaced by "a reinfusion of traditional elements into the leadership as memories of the independence struggle wane and recognition of long-term local power relationships increases."[22] In former colonies, the old colonial elite and the economic elite, which frequently consists of resident foreigners, have now been largely excluded from positions of power. In the few independent states that never experienced colonialization, traditional elites have generally been able to retain power longer, although increasingly challenged by modernizing elements pushing for recognition. In Thailand, for example, traditional elements remain strong, as they were in Ethiopia until a few years ago.

Traditional and nationalist elites rise to power from contrasting backgrounds. Traditional political leadership springs from long-established cultural patterns in the society; "its power is based upon tradition, family, land, and religion."[23] Religious elites range from the witch doctors of primitive communities to members of the Roman Catholic hierarchy who have frequently been influential in Latin America, the Muslim religious leaders involved politically in Iran and other Islamic countries, and Buddhist monks who have been active in politics quite recently in Burma, Sri Lanka, and Vietnam. Other elements of traditional society with political power are the nobility and the landed aristocracy, but in both cases their influence has diminished. The institution of monarchy is on the decline, and the lesser nobility has suffered in many countries because of past association with the colonial power. Land ownership as a basis for political influence must contend with reform efforts to break up large estates and the growing strength of the urban middle class.

Members of the nationalist elite, on the other hand, are relatively young, urbanized, Westernized, often Marxist, and reform-minded. They share broad beliefs in nationalism and national unity, anti-colonialism, Marxism in forms "adapted to the local mores and the peculiar characteristics of the respective countries,"[24] and economic and social progress carried out at the most rapid rate possible. They tend to be the intellectuals of their countries, many of whom "were trained in the West and came to admire it and yet turned against the West in their policies. They do so exactly because they admire it and at the same time see the West as denying them, through colonialism, the opportunity to make their own country more like the West."[25]

Notwithstanding their contrasting backgrounds and intellectual orientations, the new and traditional elites may and often do agree in their commitment to the elemental developmental goals of nation-building and industrialization. Moreover, as von der Mehden points out, as time passes following independence, these two elite groups develop closer bonds. "Each sees in the other something worthwhile. The traditionalists realize that the Western techniques of the modern elite may be valuable tools for maintaining their own power and that they must change lest they be overthrown by the newly educated masses. The modern elite sees the necessity of fitting its schemes and desires into the local culture if the hoped-for goals are to be attained. Thus there is developing a steady synthesis of values and techniques in the new nations."[26]

Whatever the elitist combination in a particular country, the political elite is almost certain to be out of close touch with the masses of the population. The gap "is not a gap of inherited traditional status, but one of modern achievement."[27] The peasant majority in most of the new states has been little disturbed from the traditional ways, and still holds the old attitude that the best way to deal with government is by avoidance and noncommitment. Even the desire of political participation is rare, and its practice is rarer. Apathy and withdrawal are common, and efforts to bring about modernizing change may be actively opposed or, just as effectively, resisted. Except in those nations in which a sizable middle class with basic education has emerged, the task of the elite in establishing adequate political communication is immense. The single mass party, a common phenomenon in developing countries, is justified in part as offering the best hope of bridging the gap between the elite and the masses. Even where strenuous efforts are made to involve the people in the villages, they remain, as Shils pointed out, "the 'objects' of modernization and the political activities which seek to bring it about, rather than initiators in the process. Their preferences and responses are of much concern to the political elite, but they do not participate in the dialogue of rulers and ruled."[28]

The isolated position of elitist leadership is emphasized by increasing evidence that in the developing countries, in contrast to the situation in late eighteenth and early nineteenth century Europe, pressures of nonelite groups to be admitted to the elite are often not great, even when the modernizing elite may be open for recruitment and trying to recruit.[29] A permeable elite may not be permeated because eligible candidates cling to traditional values and acquired status in preference to the hazards of political leadership during transition.

Imbalance in political development is another characteristic consequence of past events in the developing countries. Traditional cultural patterns, colonialism, and the telescoping of change have produced political systems that are askew as judged by experience in the more developed polities, particularly those with a representative democratic institutional framework. Means for interest articulation and aggregation, through such instrumentalities as an informed electorate, organized associational groups, competing political parties, and representative legislative bodies, are either weak or absent except in the most rudimentary form. On the other hand, the executive agencies of government are dominant, under the control of an elitist leadership. This leadership may take various forms, among them the continued rule of an absolutist monarchy, such as in several Arabic countries and in Ethiopia until a few years ago, the emergence of a highly nationalistic mass-mobilization regime, such as that of Egypt or Guinea, and the takeover of power by one or a group of "strongmen," usually after a military coup, as in Uganda or Chile. The stability of the regime is likely to be highly dependent on the loyalty and competence of the civil and military bureaucracies, giving these groups with a professional orientation toward government a uniformly influential role, and often making them dominant.

Given our primary concern with the civil bureaucracy, two tendencies toward imbalance have special relevance—the movement away from competitive party systems, and the trend toward military intervention and control of the governmental machinery.

Movement from Competitive Party Systems

One element of the Western political heritage that gained almost universal acceptance in the developing countries was the institution of the political party. If party is defined in the broad way suggested by von der Mehden as "an organized group which seeks the control of the personnel and policies of government—a group that pays at least lip service to a principle or set of principles, including the electoral process,"[30] then the formal structure of party government was introduced in most of the new states. Von der Mehden's 1969 survey revealed, however, the extent to which party competition had either disappeared or never actually developed. Of the ninety-eight states classified, he found that only twenty-four, or one-quarter of them, had a party system in which there existed "a reasonable chance for a peaceful change of office." No effective party government was found at all in two-fifths of them, or thirty-eight countries. In five there were Communist one-party systems, in sixteen other forms of one-party governments, and in sixteen, one-party dominant systems.[31] Von der Mehden concluded that with the passage of time political competition had lessened rather than increased, and that the emphasis on unity and cohesion would continue to foster noncompetitive political systems.[32] Later events have confirmed this prediction.

Some of the reasons are clear enough. The colonial system contained "the intellectual germs of the one-party state,"[33] with the claim of the dominant-party bureaucracy to represent all segments and interests of the population being directly descended from the claims of colonial bureaucratic rule. In addition, the natural inclination of those who led the battle for independence is to think of themselves as "identical with the nation and, after their accession to power, with the state. Those who disagree with them are thus viewed not merely as political opponents but as enemies of the state and nation."[34] A demand for a one-party state may be motivated not only by an urge to safeguard power but also as the only feasible way to push ahead on economic and social fronts and to conserve national unity after the threat of a common external enemy has disappeared.[35] The political doctrine apt to be developed in the new nations is one favoring monopolistic claims to authority in the society by government—what Apter calls a "political religion."[36] When such a doctrine becomes a key feature of the polity, the outcome is likely to be some kind of mobilization system "profoundly concerned with transforming the social and spiritual life of a people by rapid and organized methods."[37] Such a "new theocracy" will be inclined to operate through a party as its chosen instrument.

Naturally any mass-mobilization regime, in connection with its drive to monopolize political power and the means of physical coercion, will seek to keep the civil bureaucracy, as well as the army and the police, firmly in check. This is not a milieu in which bureaucratic officials can safely compete for political power, although Apter suggests that civil servants may be excused from some of the pressures for conformity placed on other significant groups. He believes, in some instances at least, that "a kind of 'positive neutralism' within the state may surround the bureaucratic role, with the effect of exempting them from ritualized practices and religious observances."[38] The higher bureaucracy can anticipate being within the governing elite, provided it does not aspire to senior partnership.

Military Intervention and Control

The phenomenon of military intervention is so marked in developing polities that it has been the subject of much analysis and speculation.[39] The statistics show an increasing tendency toward military regimes. In 1969 von der Mehden reported that approximately 40 of the 100 nations he surveyed had experienced a military takeover since the end of World War II, and that in half of these there had been more than one successful coup. Among fifty-six states which had gained independence following World War II, one-third had been overthrown by the military since independence.[40] Finer states that during the twelve-year period from 1962 through 1974 a total of 101 military coups occurred, bringing the number of countries "governed by men who came to power as a result of military intervention" to thirty-eight. "They represent 25 per cent of the world's 150 independent states and comprise some 55 per cent of the population of Latin America, nearly two-thirds of the population of the Arab states of North Africa and the Middle East, and a like proportion of the population of sub-Saharan Africa. And this is to count only 'hard core' cases: it excludes regimes which exist only by courtesy of their military forces . . . and those where the military, though temporarily disengaged from active politics, continue to dominate political life."[41]

Recent instances of military takeover or interference have added to these numbers. According to Welch, more than a third of the member states of the United Nations are currently ruled by governments installed by military intervention.[42] Certainly Kennedy is correct when he asserts that "military government is the most common form of government in the Third World."[43]

Political action by the military since World War II has usually been related to the tensions that go with major social change, rather than thought of as a simple bid for power by an ambitious military leader or clique. Existing political structures, whether indigenous or imposed by a former colonial power, have succumbed to the pressures resulting from unsuccessful efforts to cope with expectations as to political stability and attainment of developmental goals. Military regimes have replaced other political systems of various types. Most frequently they have supplanted short-lived parliamentary competitive systems installed by a colonial power in a newly independent nation, as in Nigeria or Burma. Occasionally they have ousted traditional monarchies, as in Afghanistan and Ethiopia. In recent years, the most pronounced tendency has been for military regimes to supersede mass party dominance in the polities of numerous Afro-Asian countries. The largest Communist party outside of the Communist world existed in Indonesia until it was decimated by a military takeover. In Ghana the Convention People's Party and in Mali the Sudanese Union were examples of dominant mobilization parties which gave way to the military. For whatever reasons, no alternative political regime type except perhaps Communist totalitarianism seems to have been immune from this movement toward enhanced political involvement by the military in developing countries.

Military involvement is, of course, a relative matter; it occurs in every political system. At a minimum, military activities are "limited to the mark of sovereignty," to use Janowitz' term.[44] When military participation becomes intervention, it may occur in a variety of forms. Von der Mehden suggests a three-way classification of the intensified roles characteristically played by the military.[45] Direct action may be taken by the military as "constitutional caretaker," seizing power because it deems "marked crisis, confusion, or corruption to be paralyzing political institutions," with its avowed purpose being "to establish the conditions under which political authority may eventually be returned to a civilian government through constitutional procedures." Examples are the 1958 government of General Ne Win in Burma (which did result later in temporary restoration of civilian control only to be followed by the return of Ne Win in 1962, continuing up to the present); the intermittent and temporary army interventions which have taken place in Turkey; the caretaker government in Venezuela following collapse of the Perez Jimenez dictatorship in 1958 (which led to subsequent election and installation of a civilian president); the control in Brazil by the military since 1964 but with frequent reiterations of an intent to restore greater political freedom; and the ouster of Isabel Peron by the military recently in Argentina. A second type is direct action where the military, as the spearhead of basic reform or revolution, regards its role as one of creating "new political institutions that, in the long run, will provide for effective civilian government."[46] Notable illustrations are the regime which developed from the 1952 coup in Egypt, and the "basic democracies" system of the Ayub Khan government in Pakistan from 1959 to 1969. Finally, there are numerous instances of "tacit coercion," where the military "does not directly assume power but remains as a major factor in the political environment, setting the conditions for the performance of civilian government."[47] In various degrees and at various times, this has been the situation in recent years in many countries, including Indonesia, Brazil, Iran, Ecuador, Jordan, the Dominican Republic, and several African nations.

Janowitz and Finer have offered similar suggestions for classifying military regimes. Two basic types are identified by Janowitz: civil-military coalitions and military oligarchies. In the former, civilian leadership ordinarily remains in power, but "only because of the military's passive assent or active assistance. . . . Here the military serves as an active political bloc in its support of civilian parties and other bureaucratic power groups. The civilian group is in power because of the assistance of the military." He includes in this category caretaker governments established by the military with the intention of returning power soon to civilian political groups. However, if the military takes the political initiative and "sets itself up as the political ruling group," such a takeover results in a military oligarchy under which "civilian political activity is transformed, constricted, and repressed."[48]

Finer's typology is somewhat more refined. Based on two criteria—"the extent to which the military (or its 'representatives') control the major policies of the society, and the degree of overtness with which they do so"—he generates five major categories of military regimes. Indirect-limited military rule occurs when the military intervenes "only from time to time to secure various limited objectives." Indirect-complete rule refers to instances in which the military is fully in charge, but puppet civilians are in formal leadership positions, as was the case in Cuba during the Batista period from

1933 until Batista himself was elected president in 1940. Dual rule regimes cover alliances in which both military and civilian elements are essential for survival; the period of Peron's dictatorship in Argentina is cited as having been equally dependent on support from the armed forces and from the trade unions and other civilian groups. Finer rounds out his typology by distinguishing between "open" direct military rule and "quasi-civilianized" direct military rule. In each instance, the military is admittedly in control of important decisions, but under "quasi-civilianization" an effort has been made to provide more legitimacy for the arrangement. These five types together represent, according to Finer, "a kind of scale or spectrum" corresponding broadly to "covert intervention, then overt intervention, then the supplantment of the civilian regime, and—in its final manifestation—the intent to perpetuate and institutionalize this supplantment. With quasi-civilianization the regime moves out of the realm of the provisional, and purports to be a regime in its own right." As the military seeks increasing political control or, alternatively, attempts to disengage from politics, "runs" or "sequences" of regimes may occur up or down the scale within particular countries.[49]

Variations in the role of the military among different geographic regions have been quite noticeable, resulting in efforts to analyze and explain. The tradition of military intervention has been long established in Latin America, and is not primarily a post-World War II phenomenon there. It goes back to the period of the wars of independence of the 1820s and 1830s and the postindependence years, when military control was justified on the basis that qualified civilian leadership was not yet available. Later the situation deteriorated to the point at which strongman government under a military caudillo became the most characteristic form of political leadership in Latin America during the latter part of the nineteenth and early part of the twentieth centuries. In general, the military was a conservative force allied with the church and the landed aristocracy for preservation of the status quo. Early in the 1950s, twelve of the twenty Latin American republics still were under the rule of military men who had originally come to power by force. Then followed a period of anti-militarism which led by 1961 to the elimination (by deposition, assassination, or election of a civilian successor) of all but one of these—General Alfredo Stroessner of Paraguay. The military appeared to be shifting to a mediating role and to the preservation of order and stability, leading to predictions that Latin America had purged itself of military regimes and was entering a phase when civilian rule would be the norm.[50] This lull in military activity proved to be brief, with seven military coups occurring during the early 1960s, deposing presidents who had been duly elected under constitutional processes. This resurgence of militarism has continued, with well over half of all Latin American countries under military regimes in 1977, including nations such as Chile and Uruguay which had long been considered as having established democratic competitive political systems.

Second only to Latin America, the area with the most extensive historical political involvement of the military has been the Middle East and North Africa. In 1964 Janowitz reported that four of the twelve states with modern professional armies had a military oligarchy. During the 1960s at least half of the nations in this regional group had extended periods of military rule, and currently about one-third have either open military regimes or regimes in which the military is highly influential. As a consequence of the numerous successful military coups in recent years, "by far the most important single factor in Arab politics is the army; by far the most important type of regime is military."[51] The success of military rule here seems also to be linked with the past, with the military groups benefiting from a political tradition of military involvement and sharing some of the attributes of the administrative services of earlier empires. In South and Southeast Asia, six of eighteen countries had regimes in which the military was dominant in 1973.[52] Since then, two of them (Cambodia and South Vietnam) have been taken over by Communist revolutionary regimes. As of mid 1977, three other countries in the region were being governed under martial law (Bangladesh, Pakistan, and the Philippines).

In sub-Saharan Africa, a colonial history of substantial demilitarization, the relative ease with which independence was granted to many countries without resort to widespread violence, and the newness of most of the African states led to predictions in the early 1960s that political roles for the military would continue to be minor,[53] despite some concern about proclivities for governmental intervention.[54] By the mid 1970s, after a decade of coups, one such optimist reluctantly concluded that it was by then "statistically justifiable to regard military rule as a norm rather than a deviant,"[55] in view of more than a score of successful coups from 1963 through 1974. The armed forces of many African states shifted "from political bystanders to political participants."[56] Currently about half of the states in Africa south of the Sahara have heads of state who came into power by coups. Military intervention has taken place in countries which previously had various political systems (competitive parties, mobilization single-parties, authoritarian personal rule), which represent extremes of poverty and relative affluence, and which offer a range of ethnic homogeneity, polarization, and fragmentation.[57] Military coups d'etat seem to have become almost systemic in the region, after being a rarity in the newly independent African states until the early 1960s.

The literature on military intervention addresses numerous controversial issues, only two of which are touched on here: (1) assets and liabilities of the military in governing, and (2) the effects of military rule on social change.

The prevailing view as to the political capability of the military is neatly summed up by Janowitz when he says that "while it is relatively easy for the military to seize power in a new nation, it is much more difficult for it to govern."[58] The basis for this judgment that the seizure of power is usually easy, is that the military is made up of professionals in the art of violence and has control over the instruments of violence, making effective opposition difficult or impossible. Edwin Lieuwen puts the matter bluntly:

In terms of political institutions, there is no civilian political force or combination of forces able to compete with the armed forces. Once that institution makes up its mind on a given issue, nothing can prevent it from having its way. This is largely because the military has arms, a monopoly on the means of violence, and thus the incontrovertible argument of force on its side. But it is also because the military possesses an organizational structure far superior to that of any civilian political party. Its centralized command, its hierarchical structure, and its disciplined membership make it capable of acting with complete unity.[59]

Others would apparently consider this an overstatement and would stress the societal prerequisites for success in military takeover, rather than innate characteristics of the military as an institution. Samuel Huntington asserts that "the most important causes of military intervention in politics are not military but political and reflect not the social and organizational characteristics of the military establishment, but the political and institutional structure of the society." These causes particularly relate to "the absence or weakness of effective political institutions in the society."[60] The opportunity to intervene in domestic politics if the military leadership decides to do so is frequently present in the semichaotic conditions of emerging societies, but can be lessened by extending the scope of political participation and by the growth of vigorous political parties and other political instrumentalities.

Having seized or been presented the opportunity, the military has certain positive traits which suit it for political participation. In many of the developing countries, modernization and exposure to Western techniques came earlier to the officers in the armed forces than to other groups in society. The army often provided one of the most feasible routes to status and power for upwardly mobile individuals from the lower and middle social classes. The indoctrination given to the officer corps furnished a professional ideology that combined a strong sense of nationalism with a "puritanical" outlook, an acceptance of "collectivist" forms of economic enterprise, and hostility toward civilian politicians and political groups.[61] These themes fit very well with the prevalent ideology of development in the new states, make military intervention aimed at national unity and progress more likely, and help a military regime to be accepted. The military offers a professional outlook, dedication, and an action orientation. In a transitional society, the situation may well be, as Brown asserts, that the army is a "more supple instrument of modernization" than the civil service, embodying to a greater degree the qualities of "dynamism, empiricism and 'know-how.' "[62]

The armed forces also face some typical handicaps in governing, which may outweigh these advantages. Military professionals lack training and may lack interest in economic planning and the administration of civilian programs, leading to dependency on the civil bureaucracy and the necessity usually of working out a modus vivendi with the higher civil servants. A more basic obstacle is military distrust of the give-and-take of politics, despite the lip service given to the ultimate goal of extensive political participation, and the limited supply in the military profession of "those leadership skills in bargaining and political communications that are required for sustained political leadership."[63] These attitudes and deficiencies inhibit the formulation of clear ideological doctrines or the launching of systematic efforts to educate the public politically. They create a basic problem of establishing sufficient rapport with the national community to retain support, or at least acquiescence. Building a mass base of popular support is crucial for assured continuity in power, but this calls for a political apparatus. The political skill of military leadership is strained to meet such a requirement, although it seems to have been done in Turkey under Ataturk and more recently in Egypt under Nasser and Sadat.

S. E. Finer has stressed as a flaw of the military in politics that in the rare cases in which it is prepared to disengage, it does not know how to do so. "In most cases," he says, "the military that have intervened in politics are in a dilemma: whether their rule be indirect or whether it be direct, they cannot withdraw from rulership nor can they fully legitimize it. They can neither stay nor go."[64] As a result, they tend to become "transit regimes" which run up and down the scale of intervention. He cites the roles of the military recently in countries such as Argentina, Brazil, and Ghana to illustrate.[65]

The usual overall evaluation, therefore, is that although a military regime can meet a need in bringing political stability and reform to societies in which they cannot be provided under other auspices, this is likely to be only a temporary and transitional pattern in political development, leading sometimes to a viable competitive political system under civilian leadership, but more often to some variant form of military oligarchy or to Communist authoritarianism. Whatever may be their virtues and faults, the incidence of military regimes has clearly been on the upswing.

On the issue of the effects of military rule on social change in developing countries, consensus is far from achieved and available empirical evidence is inconclusive. Three distinctive points of view have been expressed on this matter during the past twenty years, one portraying the military as a positive modernizing force, one regarding military regimes as inhibitors of modernizing social change, and the third hypothesizing that the impact of military governments varies according to the levels of economic development of the countries concerned. These views have enjoyed prominence chronologically in the sequence just given.

During the 1950s and early 1960s, when military regimes were concentrated in the Middle East and North Africa, were in decline in Latin America, and had not yet spread in sub-Saharan Africa, the prevailing judgment was that military rule was reformist and promised to speed up economic growth and other modernization processes. Lucian Pye and Manfred Halpern were leading spokesmen for this interpretation. Pye looked upon the army as a relatively modernized organization in the typical developing society and the good soldier as also to some degree a modernized man. Army leaders, he asserted, had become "extremely sensitive to the extent to which their countries are economically and technologically backward. Called upon to perform roles basic to advanced societies, the more politically conscious officers can hardly avoid being aware of the need for substantial change in their own societies." While recognizing military officials as the only group with the immediate potential for effective public policy-making in many countries, he also stressed that in the long run political development depended on "the growth of responsible and representative politicians."[66] Halpern saw the army as becoming "the principal political actor and instrument of a new middle class," with few ties to traditional elites with declining power, and with the capability of being transformed "from an instrument of repression in its own interests or that of kings into the vanguard of nationalism and social reform." He described the army as having "special virtues" as a political instrument and army leadership as having a "special caliber," enabling the armed forces to convert from "praetorian guard" to "advance guard" in achieving basic reforms. He likewise qualified his enthusiasm for military regimes by saying that the "final touchstone for achievement" of such a regime is "its success in making its continued existence unnecessary," by yielding to a civilian regime or by gradually converting itself into a civilian regime.[67]

This supportive attitude toward military intervention as likely to enhance prospects for modernization was held mainly by regional specialists in the Middle East (including North Africa) and Southeast Asia. Opposing opinions questioning the progressive nature of military regimes came mostly from Latin Americanists, based on analysis of the record into the mid 1960s of military regimes. Martin Needler found that over a thirty-year period, military takeovers had, decade by decade, become less reformist and more anticonstitutional, as well as involving higher degrees of violence.[68] Other revisionists sought to confirm tendencies of the military to be primarily concerned with the preservation and maintenance of order rather than the attainment of social goals, and to be fully occupied by these law and order tasks. The middle class origins of the officer corps were seen as leading to political decisions which would benefit the military and the middle class at the expense of policies that might channel more resources to programs meeting the needs of lower class civilians. Skepticism was voiced both as to the real concern of the military with general social change as against protection of military self-interest, and the capability of military regimes to carry out modernizing policies even if sincerely proclaimed. The conclusion from this perspective was that generally military regimes had compiled a record of reaction or at best inhibited rather than promoted basic social reforms.[69]

Samuel Huntington has been the primary advocate of the thesis that the actual impact of the military in power depends on the level of backwardness or advancement of the particular society. "As society changes," he argues, "so does the role of the military. In the world of oligarchy, the soldier is a radical; in the middle-class world he is a participant and arbiter; as the mass society looms on the horizon he becomes the conservative guardian of the existing order. Thus, paradoxically but understandably, the more backward a society is, the more progressive the role of its military; the more advanced a society becomes, the more conservative and reactionary becomes the role of its military."[70]

Since Latin American polities as a group are older, have a more significant middle class, and are generally more "advanced" and less "backward" socially and economically than their counterparts in other regions of the Third World, Huntington's hypothesis offers the interesting possibility of reconciling the other two opposing views. His concept would confirm the view, mainly held by students of Latin America, that military regimes are apt to be more conservative in those polities, while at the same time backing the expectation that in other regions of the Third World, military governments hold greater promise as societal reformers, as postulated by observers familiar mainly with these societies.

Two major recent efforts have been made to test these divergent views, utilizing empirical data from many developing countries in different geographical regions, with somewhat contradictory results, but with slight support for claims that military regimes have an impressive record as modernizers. Each study analyzed data collected earlier on seventy-four developing non-Communist countries, and the second study added an analysis of a new set of data for seventy-seven Third World countries covering the decade from 1960 to 1970. The earlier analysis, by Eric Nordlinger, essentially confirms Huntington's hypothesis, with the qualification that "only at the very lowest levels of political participation and only in the context of a minuscule middle class" do military officers sponsor modernizing policies.[71] The later study, by Robert W. Jackman, discounts all three of the points of view summarized earlier, including Huntington's. His finding is that "military intervention in the politics of the Third World has no unique effects on social change, regardless of either the level of economic development or geographic region."[72] According to Jackman, observers who have attributed unique political skills to the military are probably mistaken. Also he finds no support for the proposition that military regimes "assume different mantles" as countries move from one level of development to another.

Even if we accept Jackman's conclusion that "blanket statements portraying military governments in the Third World as either progressive or reactionary are without empirical foundation,"[73] this does not mean, of course, that no military regime at a particular time in a particular country will ever have any effect on what happens with regard to social change. Certainly doubt has been cast on any anticipation that military rule guarantees modernization, even in the more backward and traditional countries. However, it is still a matter of interest and importance as to what stance is taken on issues of social change by the leadership of a given military regime.

In closing this summary of military intervention and governance, I want to reiterate a point agreed upon by commentators who differ on other matters—namely, that collaboration at the operating level with civilian bureaucrats is absolutely essential for the maintenance over any substantial period of time of every variety of military regime, whether it rules directly, indirectly, or on a clear-cut dual basis in a partnership arrangement with the civil bureaucracy.[74]

Political Regime Variations

Attempts to identify patterns of political resemblance among developing countries should not be allowed to obscure what differentiates them. Students of the comparative politics of development have turned more and more to the task of compiling and correlating data on a large number of variables for cross-national comparisons,[75] and to suggestions for classifying political systems into regime types.[76]

Regime classifications which have been proposed show great similarity but little uniformity. This reflects mainly the difficult and tentative nature of the enterprise, although it also demonstrates individual differences in perspective and perhaps even a proprietary interest in having a scheme of one's own. The most significant point of agreement is that the groupings should not be made on the basis of geographical propinquity or common colonial background, important though these factors concededly are. Criteria for classification which cut across locational, historical, and cultural lines are used. A regime type may and usually does include polities from several of the major regional segments of the developing world. Particular categories suggested also frequently match up from one scheme to another, even though the overall systems are not identical and the category labels differ.

Since the classification system we will be using draws heavily on some of these earlier proposals, a sampling of them may be useful for background purposes. Coleman's pioneering effort ranked the political systems of developing nations along two dimensions, based on their degree of competitiveness (competitive, semicompetitive, and authoritarian) and their degree of political modernity (modern, mixed, and traditional). In addition to classification, using these dimensions, of political systems from all geographical areas—South and Southeast Asia, the Near East, Africa, and Latin America—Coleman also grouped the Asian-African (but not the Latin American) countries under functional profiles adapted from an earlier political typology employed by Edward Shils. The types in Coleman's sixfold scheme were traditional oligarchy, modernizing oligarchy, colonial or racial oligarchy, terminal colonial democracy, tutelary democracy, and political democracy. He did not include any countries which at that time had Communist regimes.

Diamant also made use of two sorting characteristics—political system style and political system goals. The style dimension refers to "the manner in which power is exercised and the manner in which decisions on public policy are made in the system." The goals dimension refers to "the major purposes the political system is seeking to accomplish without trying to measure. . . . how successful various systems have been in actually achieving these goals."[77] Our interest is in the four political system style types: traditional-autocratic, limited polyarchy, polyarchy, and movement regime. A movement regime is revolutionary, has an ideological core, rests on a mass movement, and is guided by "a militant, centralized elite or vanguard party."[78] Diamant includes in this category both Communist and non-Communist countries.

The primary purpose of Esman's classification scheme is to assess the relative capacities of different countries to perform developmental tasks successfully by utilizing "the criteria of purposeful leadership, a developmentally relevant doctrine, and capacity to create and effectively to deploy a variety of action and communication instruments."[79] He assumes that regimes sharing common structural and behavioral characteristics "will approach the tasks involved in nation building and socioeconomic progress in similar ways."[80] The five political regime types that he designates with this objective in mind are (1) conservative oligarchies, (2) authoritarian military reformers, (3) competitive interest-oriented party systems, (4) dominant mass party systems, and (5) Communist totalitarian systems.

The criterion of classification used by Merle Fainsod is "the relationship of bureaucracies to the flow of political authority," making his breakdown into types of particular interest to us. He also distinguishes five different alternatives: (1) ruler-dominated

bureaucracies, (2) military-dominated bureaucracies, (3) ruling
bureaucracies, (4) representative bureaucracies, and (5) party-state
bureaucracies.[81] Each occurs in the context of a particular political
system.

In a polity in which an autocratic ruler or dictator "exercises an
approximation of absolute power and . . . uses his bureaucratic establishment to project his control and impose his purposes on the
people whom he rules," the ruler-dominated bureaucracy has a subservient institutional role but one that must be capable of carrying
out the ruler's intent. Bureaucratic innovation is unlikely, because
"whatever elements of dynamism the system possesses derive from
the ruler and his surrounding court."[82]

In the next two types, bureaucracies themselves are in control.
In military-dominated regimes the armed forces hold in their hands
the lines of strategic power, whether they have conservative or
modernizing purposes, and whatever form of intervention they
choose to employ. Fainsod points out the paradoxical possibility
mentioned earlier that the transfer of power from a politician-
dominated regime to a military regime may actually result in "reinforcing the influence and the authority of civilian administrators,
even though they remain subject to military direction in the ultimate
sense."[83] A ruling bureaucracy in Fainsod's usage means that the
civilian officials are making the determining political as well as administrative decisions, even though they are unlikely to hold the top
formal positions of authority. He mentions colonial administrators
as having essentially such a role when granted widespread discretion
by the central colonial government. More relevant is the situation in
which a figurehead monarch or some other symbolic political leadership is out front, but the bureaucratic establishment really rules.
Such a bureaucracy is likely to have a lively sense of its own self-
interest and will try to protect its prerogatives.

The last two types exist when political parties are the dominant
instrumentalities of political control. Representative bureaucracies
are characterized by powers and activities which derive ultimately
from "a process of competitive party politics, and . . . the policies
which they espouse are shaped by and adapted to the popular
support which they can muster." The competitive political process
with its underlying political consensus sets the bounds for bureaucratic initiative and exercise of discretion. When a single political
party dominates the political system, the resulting party-state bureaucracy subordinates the state apparatus to the party apparatus, so that
the official state bureaucracy has only a limited degree of autonomy.

Bureaucratic systems of this type are "usually associated with strong charismatic leadership claiming a monopoly of wisdom, intolerant of opposition, and impatient to move ahead with the tasks of nation building, social reconstruction, industrialization, or other forms of modernization which they have set themselves." These are totalitarian regimes, seeking comprehensive control of the whole society, whether the single party is Communist in its orientation or is a militant nationalistic Third World party. The type is synonymous with Diamant's movement regime.

On the assumption that the political system type would be the most crucial standard for distinguishing among the public bureaucracies of developing countries, we adopted in the original version of this study a classification plan that was designed to place special emphasis on the relationship between the basic political characteristics of the regime and the political role of the bureaucracy in the system. Although influenced by other classification proposals, it most closely resembled those of Esman and Fainsod. The following categories were chosen: (1) traditional-autocratic systems, (2) bureaucratic elite systems—civil and military, (3) polyarchal competitive systems, (4) dominant-party semicompetitive systems, (5) dominant-party mobilization systems, and (6) Communist totalitarian systems.

With one major modification which is explained shortly, this approach is still well suited to our needs. No classification system of this variety can claim to be definitive. These categories are not "ideal types" in the Weberian sense. Instead they are modal types which seek to simplify reality for heuristic purposes, serving as guides for better understanding. No attempt need be made to fit every existing developing nation into one of these categories. Such an undertaking would be extremely hazardous. Borderline or mutating cases are difficult to classify,[84] and these are numerous. A few countries may not be well described by the characteristics of any one or a combination of these types. However, for our purposes, complete classification is unnecessary. We will try merely to identify some of the countries in each category used, and offer illustrative cases to examine the impact on bureaucratic characteristics and behavior of the political features of the regime type.

A decision as to the optimal number of types to be used must be a matter of judgment, taking into account S. E. Finer's advice that "the categories must be neither so many as to make comparison impossible nor so few as to make contrasts impossible."[85] Trends during the past decade raise a serious question as to the adequacy at present of a single category for all bureaucratic elite regimes. As we have seen, one of the most dramatic of recent political phenomena has been the spread on almost a global basis of regimes in which the military bureaucracy is dominant, nearly always in close association with the civil bureaucracy. Variations in the characteristics of bureaucratic elite systems have been pronounced in the past and are continuing to increase. At present, too many political systems with too wide a spectrum of distinctive features would have to be located under the bureaucratic elite label. Since the mid 1960s, numerous polities have moved from other categories into this one—especially from the traditional-autocratic, polyarchal competitive, and dominant-party mobilization groupings. Therefore we will introduce one significant alteration in the earlier classification system by replacing the broader bureaucratic elite—civil and military category with a breakdown into substitute types which are more discriminating.

Four factors appear to deserve special emphasis in selection of the most useful categories for subdividing bureaucratic elite regimes. First is the familiar distinction between military regimes which are headed by one powerful and usually senior individual as against collegial regimes where authority is shared more or less equally by a group of individuals who are usually rather junior in age and rank and less well known before access to power. In Latin American politics since the nineteenth century the caudillo has represented the first option and the junta the second. In the states of contemporary Africa, Claude E. Welch, Jr. has suggested a contrast between "personalist" and "corporatist" regimes, with the former centering on "the head-of-state/commander-in-chief," and the latter being collegial rather than hierarchical in nature with the members holding the same or adjacent ranks.[86]

A second important consideration is the nature and degree of civilian participation in operation of the regime. In the terminology used by Janowitz, a military oligarchy exists if the military leaders are clearly in control and civilians have been coopted in plainly indicated subordinate capacities. A civil-military coalition or alliance implies much more equality in actual influence and a mutual inter-dependency of the two elements, whose combined participation in governance is crucial.

In the third place, it may be important to highlight instances in which the bureaucratic elite regime has recently replaced either an indigenous traditional-autocratic system, or a colonial power which had been dominant for an extended period leaving a distinctive imprint on both the military and civil bureaucracies. In each case, the current regime is preoccupied with carryover forces from the earlier era, usually with the intent of eradication in the first situation and with the objective of preservation with adaptations in the second. Neither of these possibilities exists in Latin America, but each of them can be found in Asia and Africa.

Finally, bureaucratic elite regimes differ in the role they attribute to the state as a corporate entity representing functional interest groupings in the society and in the extent of their reliance on technical expertise for the attainment of regime goals. Elites with a pronounced corporate-technocratic orientation are appearing in Latin America and to some degree elsewhere. They show a marked contrast in their makeup and methods of operation to more familiar examples of military governments mainly concerned with gaining political control, imposing order, and preserving the existing social and economic arrangements.

With these factors in mind, the broader bureaucratic elite category will have substituted for it the following five differentiated types: military elite headed by a strongman or caudillo; military elite under collegial or junta leadership; bureaucratic elite replacing a traditional elite; bureaucratic elite successor to a colonial tradition; bureaucratic elite with a corporate-technocratic orientation. These are not mutually exclusive groupings; for example, a military bureaucratic elite replacing a traditional elite may have either personalist or collegial leadership. Also, not all possible combinations are differentiated; for example, a regime with a corporate-technocratic orientation might be under the control of a strictly military elite or a military-civilian coalition. However, the most common possibilities among developing countries now or in the near future are accounted for better than by lumping them all together.

The previous sixfold scheme for dealing with political regime variations is converted by this revision into a classification plan with ten categories, with only the former bureaucratic elite type being affected. These ten regime patterns will provide the basis for exploration later of political-bureaucratic relationships in selected developing countries. Primary emphasis will be given to the shared characteristics within each type. A secondary interest will be how the various types relate to one another.

In this latter context, two broad groupings among the ten types immediately suggest themselves. As Lee Sigelman has pointed out,[87] there is a "fundamental divergence" of the traditional-autocratic and bureaucratic elite systems from the remaining categories. In these regimes types (totaling six in the reformulation), bureaucracies are,

as he says, "squarely at center stage in the play of political power."
In traditional-autocratic regimes the ruling monarchy or aristocracy
is heavily dependent on the bureaucracy as the instrument of political action, and in the various bureaucratic elite regimes political
power is actually in the hands of military or civil bureaucrats, with
the military professionals usually the senior partners. In the other
four regime types, on the other hand, political power is channeled
through the instrumentality of the political party. In polyarchal
competitive systems, power is dispersed among two or more competing parties. One party has a power monopoly in regimes with
dominant or single parties. The bureaucracy is constricted in its
access to political power in either case when vigorous parties are
operating. These two sets can be conveniently labeled as "bureau-
cratic-prominent" and "party-prominent" political regime groupings
and arranged in tandem for discussion.

Common Administrative Patterns

Before turning to differences flowing from political regime variations,
to which the following two chapters are devoted, let us try to identify some of the principal features that may be considered "typical" of
administration in developing countries, in the sense of their prevalence or recurrence rather than their uniform and identical existence
in all of these polities.

The importance of administration is almost universally recognized among commentators on the problems of development.[88]
Usually an effective bureaucracy is coupled with a vigorous modernizing elite as a prerequisite for progress. Nearly as unanimous is the
view that administration has been a neglected factor in development
and that the existing machinery for management of developmental
programs is grossly inadequate. Most of the recurring features found
in these administrative systems bolster the charge of grave administrative deficiencies alleged to be common to development-oriented
nations. Our purpose at this point, however, is to be descriptive
rather than prescriptive. If these administrative tendencies seem to
point toward serious problem areas, it should be remembered that we
are concerned with societies caught in the midst of tremendous social
change, striving to reach social goals of demanding complexity, and
working under great pressure for early accomplishment.

The following five points are indicative of general features of
administration currently found in countries of the developing world:

1. The basic pattern of public administration is imitative rather than indigenous. All countries, including those that escaped Western colonization, have consciously tried to introduce some version of modern Western bureaucratic administration. Usually it is patterned after a particular national administrative model, perhaps with incidental features borrowed from some other system. A country that was formerly a colony almost certainly will resemble the parent administratively, even though independence was forcibly won and political apron strings have been cut. Kingsley has vividly described how "the organization of offices, the demeanor of civil servants, even the general appearance of a *bureau*, strikingly mirror the national characteristics of the bureaucracies of the former colonial powers. The *fonctionnaire* slouched at his desk in Lomé or Cotonou, cigarette pasted to his underlip, has his counterpart in every provincial town in France; and the demeanor of an administrative officer in Accra or Lagos untying the red tape from his files would be recognizable to anyone familiar with Whitehall or, more specifically, with the Colonial Office."[89] Of course some countries have been more fortunate than others, depending on whether the colonial power was distinguished or otherwise for its skills in administration, and whether or not it systematically undertook to tutor its colonials in these skills. An ex-colony of Great Britain, France, or the United States has an advantage over a former possession of Spain, Portugal, Belgium, or the Netherlands. The British record of successful administrative institution-building is probably the best. Britain showed more permissiveness than did France; according to a Frenchman, French administrators could view natives "only as either unsuccessful or promising Frenchmen."[90] The mark of the United States is much more restricted, but shows up well where it exists, as in the Philippines.

The colonial administrative heritage includes one incidental feature that has lasting effects. The colonial version of British, French, or any other system of administration was suited to the requirements of colonial government rather than government at home. It was more elitist, more authoritarian, more aloof, more paternalistic. Remnants of these bureaucratic traits have inevitably carried over to the successor bureaucracies in the new states.

The fact that precedents from outside have largely shaped the developing bureaucracies does not mean that they are less suitable than they would be if fully homegrown, but it does emphasize the importance of making adaptations after independence as conditions change, particularly to enhance the legitimacy of these bureaucracies and to point them toward the accomplishment of developmental goals.

2. The bureaucracies are deficient in skilled manpower necessary for developmental programs. The problem is not a general shortage of employable manpower; actually, the typical developing country has an abundance of labor in relation to other resources—land and capital. Unemployment and underemployment are chronic in the rural economy and in many urban areas among the unskilled labor force. The public services are almost universally conceded to be overstaffed in the lower ranks with attendants, messengers, minor clerks, and other supernumeraries.

The shortage is in trained administrators with management capacity, developmental skills, and technical competence. Although this usually reflects an inadequate educational system, it is not necessarily equivalent to a deficit in holders of university degrees. A number of countries, for example India and Egypt, have sizable pockets of seemingly highly educated unemployed, who either have been educated in the wrong subjects or are the products of marginal institutions.

This gap between supply and demand for responsible administrative posts in newly independent countries is probably unavoidable and can only be remedied by strenuous training efforts which require time. At the critical early stages of nationhood the shortage is accentuated by the urgency with which "nativization" of the bureaucracy is pushed even in the face of continuing availability of trained foreign personnel during the transition and a desperate absence of suitable local replacements. A Nigerian has given the understandable reasons for such a policy. "The decision was taken by our leaders that the British officials should be replaced, not because they hated or distrusted them, but because they felt that political independence was a sham unless you had also a great measure of administrative independence. You just could not be politically independent and remain administratively dependent, over a long period of time, without misunderstanding and tensions arising between the expatriate administrator and his indigenous political master."[91]

Other factors may complicate the task of staffing from local sources. In countries such as Burma and Indonesia administrators who served during colonial days were unwilling to stay or had their effectiveness impaired by charges that they had been "tools of imperialism." Requirements leading to facility in a new national language or the policy of reserving civil service posts for certain minority groups, as in India, have also restricted access to otherwise qualified candidates.

Given the disparity between minimum needs and maximum possibilities for meeting them, there is no short-range solution to the problem of administrative capacity in most new countries. Even if the public bureaucracy succeeds in recruiting most of the available talent, this only diminishes the available supply for political parties, interest groups, and other organizations in both the public and private sectors.

3. A third tendency is for these bureaucracies to emphasize orientations that are other than production-directed. That is, much bureaucratic activity is channeled toward the realization of goals other than the achievement of program objectives. Riggs refers to this as a preference among bureaucrats for personal expediency as against public-principled interests. It may take a variety of forms, most of which are not unique by any means to these bureaucracies, but which may only be more prominent in bureaucratic behavior in a transitional setting.

The most prevalent of these practices are evidence of the carryover of deep-seated values from a more traditional past, which have not been modified or abandoned despite the adoption of nontraditional social structures. The value attached to status based on ascription rather than achievement explains much of this behavior. Studies of the Thai bureaucracy emphasize that status and status relationships are the prime motivating factors in the system, rather than the urge to reach program goals. Hence, one of the important ways to bring about change is to link status with program accomplishment.

Personnel processes may be deeply affected by these considerations, even though the forms of a merit system are outwardly observed. Riggs refers, for example, to "bureaucratic recruitment," where the choice of the official dominates. "Using the pretext of eligibility based on examination, he chooses from the certified those whose personal loyalty he trusts. The same criterion enables him to choose from his family and friends those in whom he has confidence. He helps them gain schooling, certificates, and examination ratings which make them eligible."[92] Similar nonmerit considerations may greatly influence promotions, assignments, dismissals, and other personnel actions within the service, as well as the conduct of business with agency clientele on the outside.

Corruption, on a scale ranging from payments to petty officials for facilitating a minor transaction to bribes of impressive dimensions for equally impressive services, is a phenomenon so prevalent as to be expected almost as a matter of course. Sanctioned by social mores, semi-institutionalized corruption may serve a useful purpose, but it is at best an indirect and undependable way to carry out governmental programs.[93]

Still another common and socially significant practice is that of using the public service as a substitute for a social security program or as a way to relieve the problem of unemployment. Without question, this is one of the reasons for maintaining a surplus of rank and file employees on the public payroll. Paring down the work force cannot be seriously considered until alternative means have been found for handling such threatening social problems as unemployment.

4.   The widespread discrepancy between form and reality is another distinguishing characteristic. Riggs has labeled this phenomenon "formalism."[94]   It seems to follow naturally from features already mentioned, reflecting an urge to make things seem more as they presumably ought to be rather than what they actually are. The gap between expectations and actualities can be partially masked by enacting laws that cannot be enforced, adopting personnel regulations that are quietly bypassed, announcing a program for delegation of administrative discretion while keeping tight control of decision-making at the center, or reporting as actually met production targets which in fact remain only partially fulfilled. These tendencies are not absent in such developed countries as France, the USSR, Japan, and the United States. However, the risk of making judgments about substance from what the formal record shows—hazardous enough in trying to understand any administrative system—is much greater in most transitional situations.

5.   Finally, the bureaucracy in a developing country is apt to have a generous measure of operational autonomy, which can be accounted for by the convergence of several forces usually at work in a recently independent modernizing nation. Colonialism was essentially rule by bureaucracy with policy guidance from remote sources, and this pattern persists even after the bureaucracy has a new master in the nation. The bureaucracy has a near monopoly on technical expertise, and benefits from the prestige that goes to the professional expert in a society aiming toward industrialization and economic growth. Military bureaucrats have access to weaponry for coercion. Groups capable of competing for political influence or of imposing close controls over the bureaucracy are few and far between, so that often it is able to move into a partial power vacuum.

The political role of the bureaucracy varies from country to country and is intimately related to variations in political system types among the developing countries.[95] To these relationships we turn next.

Notes

1. See Paul E. Sigmund, Jr., ed., *The Ideologies of the Developing Nations* (New York: Frederick A. Praeger, Inc., 1963); Karl W. Deutsch and William J. Foltz, eds., *Nation-Building* (New York: Atherton Press, 1963); Milton J. Esman, "The Politics of Development Administration," in John D. Montgomery and William J. Siffin, eds., *Approaches to Development: Politics, Administration and Change* (New York: McGraw-Hill Book Company, 1966), copyright © 1966; Dankwart A. Rustow, *A World of Nations: Problems of Political Modernization* (Washington, D.C.: The Brookings Institution, 1967); John H. Kautsky, *The Political Consequences of Modernization* (New York: John Wiley & Sons, Inc., 1972); Monte Palmer, *Dilemmas of Political Development* (Itasca, Ill.: F. E. Peacock Publishers, Inc., 1973); and Alex Inkeles and David H. Smith, *Becoming Modern: Individual Change in Six Developing Countries* (Cambridge: Harvard University Press, 1974).

2. Esman, "The Politics of Development Administration," p. 59.

3. Rustow, *A World of Nations*, pp. 2, 3, 31.

4. Palmer, *Dilemmas of Political Development*, p. 3.

5. Kautsky, *The Political Consequences of Modernization*, pp. 44-45.

6. *Ibid.*, p. 56.

7. Rupert Emerson, "Nation-Building in Africa," in Deutsch and Foltz, *Nation-Building*, p. 95.

8. Inkeles and Smith, *Becoming Modern*, pp. 3-4.

9. Joseph R. Strayer, "The Historical Experience of Nation-Building in Europe," in Deutsch and Foltz, *Nation-Building*, p. 25.

10. Esman, "The Politics of Development Administration," in Montgomery and Siffin, *Approaches to Development*, p. 60.

11. Hamzah Merghani, "Public Administration in Developing Countries—The Multilateral Approach," in Burton A. Baker, ed., *Public Administration: A Key to Development* (Washington, D.C.: Graduate School, U.S. Department of Agriculture, 1964), p. 28.

12. Hence the Soviet model of industrial development has a strong appeal, although there may be only slight understanding of the price which must be paid in stringent totalitarian controls to follow the Soviet example. Merle Fainsod, "Bureaucracy and Modernization: The Russian and Soviet Case," in Joseph LaPalombara, ed., *Bureaucracy and Political Development* (Princeton, N.J.: Princeton University Press, © 1963), p. 265.

13. Edward A. Shils, *Political Development in the New States* (The Hague: Mouton & Co., 1962), pp. 47-48.

14. Monte Palmer has expressed well the mood of foreboding: "The road from traditionalism to modernity is not an easy one. Such forces of change as colonialism, war, technology, and mass communications have been more than adequate to assure the steady and apparently irreversible erosion of traditional institutions. The erosion of traditional institutions, unfortunately, does not produce modernity. Disintegration and reintegration are diverse processes. Disintegration involves reducing the utility and effectiveness of traditional institutions, beliefs, and behavior patterns. Reintegration involves inducing individuals to accept a new set of institutions, beliefs, and behavior patterns radically different from the old. . . . Indeed there can be no certainty that those states in or entering the development process must inevitably attain their goal of achieving parity with the world's most economically developed states. . . . The prospects for rapid development in the Third World, then, are not particularly bright," *Dilemmas of Political Development*, pp. 4, 199.

15. In addition to works cited in Note 1, leading sources are Gabriel A. Almond and James S. Coleman, eds., *The Politics of the Developing Areas* (Princeton, N.J.: Princeton University Press, 1960); Samuel P. Huntington, *Political Order in Changing Societies* (New Haven, Conn.: Yale University Press, 1968); Shils, *Political Development in the New States;* Fred R. von der Mehden, *Politics of the Developing Nations*, 2nd ed. (Englewood Cliffs, N.J.: Prentice-Hall, Inc., 1969); Andrew J. Sofranko and Robert C. Bealer, *Unbalanced Modernization and Domestic Instability: A Comparative Analysis* (Beverly Hills, Calif.: Sage Publications, 1972); and Gerald A. Heeger, *The Politics of Underdevelopment* (New York: St. Martin's Press, 1974).

16. Notable examples are by Fred W. Riggs, *Administration in Developing Countries—The Theory of Prismatic Society* (Boston: Houghton Mifflin Company, 1964) and *Prismatic Society Revisited* (Morristown, N.J.: General Learning Press, 1973).

17. Sigmund, *The Ideologies of the Developing Nations*, pp. 39-40.

18. Shils, *Political Development in the New States*, pp. 34-35.

19. von der Mehden, *Politics of the Developing Nations*, p. 1.

20. Heeger, *The Politics of Underdevelopment*, p. 75.

21. *Ibid.*, pp. 49-51, 75-78.

22. von der Mehden, *Politics of the Developing Nations*, p. 72.

23. *Ibid.*, p. 73.

24. *Ibid.*, p. 84.

25. John H. Kautsky, ed., *Political Change in Underdeveloped Countries: Nationalism and Communism* (New York: John Wiley & Sons, Inc., 1962), p. 48.

26. von der Mehden, *Politics of the Developing Nations*, pp. 85-86.

27. Emerson in Deutsch and Foltz, *Nation-Building*, p. 118.

28. Shils, *Political Development in the New States*, p. 25.

29. See Alfred Diamant, *Bureaucracy in Developmental Movement Regimes:*

A Bureaucratic Model for Developing Societies (Bloomington: CAG Occasional Papers, 1964), pp. 42-43, and sources cited therein.

30. von der Mehden, *Politics of the Developing Nations*, p. 49.
31. *Ibid.*, p. 60.
32. *Ibid.*, pp. 68-70. This view is shared by others, including Bernard E. Brown, *New Directions in Comparative Politics* (New York: Asia Publishing House, 1962), p. 23.
33. Victor C. Ferkiss, "The Role of the Public Services in Nigeria and Ghana," in Ferrel Heady and Sybil L. Stokes, eds., *Papers in Comparative Public Administration* (Ann Arbor, Mich.: Institute of Public Administration, The University of Michigan, 1962), p. 175.
34. Shils, *Political Development in the New States*, p. 42.
35. Emerson, "Nation-Building in Africa," p. 111.
36. David E. Apter, "Political Religion in the New Nations," in Clifford Geertz, ed., *Old Societies and New States* (New York: Free Press of Glencoe, Inc., 1963), pp. 57-104.
37. *Ibid.*, p. 63.
38. *Ibid.*, p. 100.
39. Selective comprehensive studies, listed in chronological order, include John J. Johnson, ed., *The Role of the Military in Underdeveloped Countries* (Princeton, N.J.: Princeton University Press, 1962); Morris Janowitz, *The Military in the Political Development of New Nations* (Chicago: The University of Chicago Press, 1964); Henry Bienen, ed., *The Military Intervenes: Case Studies in Political Development* (New York: Russell Sage Foundation, 1968); Henry Bienen, ed., *The Military and Modernization* (Chicago: Aldine-Atherton, 1971); Catherine McArdle Kelleher, ed., *Political-Military Systems: Comparative Perspectives* (Beverly Hills, Calif.: Sage Publications, 1974); Gavin Kennedy, *The Military in the Third World* (London: Duckworth, 1974); Claude E. Welch, Jr. and Arthur K. Smith, *Military Role and Rule: Perspectives on Civil-Military Relations* (North Scituate, Mass.: Duxbury Press, 1974); S. E. Finer, *The Man on Horseback: The Role of the Military in Politics* (Peregrine Books, Second, enlarged edition, 1976) © S. E. Finer, 1962, 1975 (Baltimore, Md.: Penguin Books, Inc., 1976); Claude E. Welch, Jr., ed., *Civilian Control of the Military: Theory and Cases from Developing Countries* (Albany: State University of New York Press, 1976); Henry Bienen and David Morell, eds., *Political Participation under Military Regimes* (Beverly Hills, Calif.: Sage Publications, 1976); and Amos Perlmutter, *The Military and Politics in Modern Times* (New Haven, Conn.: Yale University Press, 1977).
40. von der Mehden, *Politics of the Developing Nations*, p. 92.
41. Finer, *The Man on Horseback*, p. 223. Reprinted by permission of Penguin Books Ltd.
42. Welch, *Civilian Control of the Military*, p. 34.
43. Kennedy, *The Military in the Third World*, p. 3.
44. When its activities are "limited to the mark of sovereignty," the officer

corps "is not involved in domestic partisan politics but functions as an institution symbolizing the independent and legitimate sovereignty of the new nation, both at home and abroad. The mark of sovereignty includes the military's contribution to internal law and order and to the policing of the nation's borders." This may be the situation in countries with markedly different forms of internal political control, including an authoritarian-personal pattern, an authoritarian-mass party system, or democratic competitive and semicompetitive systems. Janowitz, *The Military in the Political Development of New Nations*, pp. 5-7.

45. von der Mehden, *Politics of the Developing Nations*, pp. 92-100.
46. *Ibid.*
47. *Ibid.*
48. Janowitz, *The Military in the Political Development of New Nations*, pp. 7-8.
49. Finer, *The Man on Horseback*, pp. 149-67, 245-52.
50. For example, see Edwin Lieuwen, *Arms and Politics in Latin America*, rev. ed. (New York: Frederick A. Praeger, 1961), p. 171.
51. Gabriel Ben-Dor, "Civilianization of Military Regimes in the Arab World," in Bienen and Morell, *Political Participation under Military Regimes*, pp. 39-49.
52. Robert N. Kearney, ed., *Politics and Modernization in South and Southeast Asia* (New York: John Wiley & Sons, 1975), p. 25.
53. For example, W. F. Gutteridge stated that Africa was "different," and incapable of being "Latin-Americanized." *Military Institutions and Power in the New States* (New York: Praeger, 1965). Quoted in Finer, *The Man on Horseback*, p. 223.
54. Janowitz, *The Military in the Political Development of New Nations*, p. 65.
55. W. F. Gutteridge, *Military Regimes in Africa* (London: Methuen & Co., Ltd., 1975), p. 5.
56. Claude E. Welch, Jr., "Personalism and Corporatism in African Armies," in Kelleher, *Political-Military Systems*, p. 141.
57. *Ibid.*, p. 125.
58. Janowitz, *The Military in the Political Development of New Nations*, p. 1.
59. Edwin Lieuwen, *Generals vs. Presidents: Neomilitarism in Latin America* (New York: Frederick A. Praeger, 1964), p. 97.
60. Huntington, *Political Order in Changing Societies*, pp. 194, 196. Welch concurs, writing that the strongest base for civilian control of the military "comes through the legitimacy and effectiveness of government organs." *Civilian Control of the Military*, p. 35.
61. Janowitz, *The Military in the Political Development of New Nations*, pp. 63-67.
62. Brown, *New Directions in Comparative Politics*, pp. 60-61.
63. Janowitz, *The Military in the Political Development of New Nations*, p. 40. Esman perhaps overstates the point when he says that military reformers "usually reject politics with revulsion. They put a moratorium on political expression. Politics to them are wasteful, corrupt, hypocritical, and above

all, inefficient." "The Politics of Development Administration," in Montgomery and Siffin, *Approaches to Development: Politics, Administration, and Change*, p. 95.

64. Finer, *The Man on Horseback*, p. 221.

65. *Ibid.*, p. 252.

66. Lucian Pye, "Armies in the Process of Political Modernization," pp. 69-89, in Johnson, *The Role of the Military*, at pp. 78, 80, 89.

67. Manfred Halpern, "Middle Eastern Armies and the New Middle Class," pp. 277-315, in Johnson, *The Role of the Military*, at pp. 278-79, 281, 285-87, 307.

68. Martin Needler, "Political Development and Military Intervention in Latin America," *American Political Science Review* 60 (September 1966): 616-26.

69. For example, see Henry Bienen, "The Background to Contemporary Study of Militaries and Modernization," pp. 1-33, in Bienen, *The Military and Modernization*; Lieuwen, *Generals vs. Presidents*; Jae Souk Sohn, "Political Dominance and Political Failure: The Role of the Military in the Republic of Korea," pp. 103-21, in Bienen, *The Military Intervenes*.

70. Huntington, *Political Order in Changing Societies*, p. 221.

71. Eric Nordlinger, "Soldiers in Mufti: The Impact of Military Rule upon Economic and Social Change in the Non-Western States," *American Political Science Review* 64 (December 1970): 1131-48, at p. 1143-44.

72. Robert W. Jackman, "Politicians in Uniform: Military Governments and Social Change in the Third World," *American Political Science Review* 70 (December 1976): 1078-97, at p. 1096. According to Jackman, the contradiction between Nordlinger's analysis and his is explainable in methodological terms.

73. *Ibid.*, p. 1097.

74. As Finer points out, this is an essential but not always a sufficient condition to ensure success. ". . . the military are not necessarily competent to govern even moderately complex societies. Their usual practice is to team up with the civil bureaucracy; but for it to succeed, the bureaucracy must be competent—not always the case—and even if competent, its advice must be heeded; and this does not necessarily happen either." *The Man on Horseback*, p. 253. The case studies in *Political Participation under Military Regimes*, edited by Henry Bienen and David Morell, demonstrate that it is an oversimplification to draw a sharp distinction between military and civilian regimes. More accurately, various types of mixed regimes have emerged, with the military generally retaining final authority but developing civilian alliances under which limited political participation is permitted.

75. The pioneering works are Arthur S. Banks and Robert B. Textor, *A Cross-Polity Survey* (Cambridge: M.I.T. Press, 1963), and Bruce M. Russett et. al., *World Handbook of Political and Social Indicators* (New Haven, Conn.: Yale University Press, 1964). For more recent contributions, refer to Banks, *Cross-Polity Time-Series Data* (Cambridge: M.I.T. Press, 1971);

and Charles Lewis Taylor and Michael C. Hudson, *World Handbook of Political and Social Indicators*, 2nd ed. (New Haven, Conn.: Yale University Press, 1972).

76. Leading examples may be found in James S. Coleman, "Conclusion: The Political Systems of the Developing Areas," in Almond and Coleman, *The Politics of the Developing Areas*, pp. 532-76; Fainsod, "Bureaucracy and Modernization," pp. 233-67; Esman, "The Politics of Development Administration," pp. 59-112; Alfred Diamant, "Bureaucracy in Developmental Movement Regimes," in Fred W. Riggs, ed., *Frontiers of Development Administration* (Durham: Duke University Press, 1970), pp. 486-537; Shils, *Political Development in the New States*; and von der Mehden, *Politics of the Developing Nations*.

77. Diamant, "Bureaucracy in Developmental Movement Regimes," p. 490.

78. *Ibid.*, p. 494.

79. Esman, "The Politics of Development Administration," p. 105.

80. *Ibid.*, p. 88.

81. This classificatory scheme is presented in Fainsod, "Bureaucracy and Modernization," pp. 234-37.

82. *Ibid.*

83. *Ibid.*

84. John Rehfuss has understandably criticized such a classification system as being "very weak at the boundaries" and presenting problems of appropriate placement of individual countries. *Public Administration as Political Process* (New York: Scribner, 1973), p. 208.

85. Finer, *The Man on Horseback*, p. 245.

86. Welch, "Personalism and Corporatism in African Armies," in Kelleher, *Political-Military Systems*, pp. 125-45.

87. Lee Sigelman, "Bureaucratic Development and Dominance: A New Test of the Imbalance Thesis," *Western Political Quarterly* 27, No. 2 (June 1974): 308-13, at pp. 310-11.

88. For a comprehensive recent treatment, see the collection of essays in Kenneth J. Rothwell, ed., *Administrative Issues in Developing Economies* (Lexington, Mass.: D. C. Heath and Company, 1972).

89. J. Donald Kingsley, "Bureaucracy and Political Development, with Particular Reference to Nigeria," in LaPalombara, *Bureaucracy and Political Development*, p. 303.

90. Crozier, *The Bureaucratic Phenomenon*, p. 269.

91. S. O. Adebo, "Public Administration in Newly Independent Countries," in Baker, *Public Administration: A Key to Development*, p. 20. The problems of Nigerianization are well treated in Kenneth Younger, *The Public Service in New States* (London: Oxford University Press, 1960), pp. 12-52. For discussion of this process in a broader context, see Fred G. Burke and Peter L. French, "Bureaucracy and Africanization," in Riggs, *Frontiers of Development Administration*, pp. 538-55.

92. Riggs, *Administration in Developing Countries*, pp. 230-31.

93. For an up-to-date review of corruption as a social phenomenon, including references to the problem in developing countries, see Gerald E. Caiden and Naomi J. Caiden, "Administrative Corruption," *Public Administration Review* 37, No. 3 (May/June 1977): 301-9.
94. Riggs, *Administration in Developing Countries*, pp. 15-19.
95. In a paper prepared for the 1978 National Conference of the American Society for Public Administration, Metin Heper and Chong Lim Kim explore the proposition that the political roles of public bureaucracies vary significantly with political regime types and suggest that in the two countries they studied historical bureaucratic traditions appeared to be more helpful than regime type in explaining variance in bureaucratic roles. "The Role of Bureaucracy and Regime Types: A Comparative Study of Turkish and Korean Higher Civil Servants," 50 pp. mimeographed. Similar studies of countries representing a range of regime types and bureaucratic traditions would be helpful in identifying the relative importance of these two factors.

8

BUREAUCRATIC-PROMINENT POLITICAL REGIMES

In several of the political regime types identified earlier, the public bureaucracy wields the preponderance of political power in one form or another. Career government officials—military or civilian, or more often a combination of both—occupy most of the key positions in which important political decisions are made. These are societies in which the traditional elites may in some cases still be influential and a reigning monarch may be actively exercising power, but more likely traditional elitist groups will have been displaced from substantial political influence and monarchy as an institution either eliminated or reduced to a figurehead role. Modernizing goals are proclaimed by leadership groups, although with varying degrees of commitment and considerable divergence as to content. The general populace has not been brought actively into the political arena, and political participation is severely limited. A competitive party system with related instrumentalities for representation and political decision-making either has never developed or has been superseded. On the other hand, no dominant mass party has emerged capable of engaging in a program of mobilizing general support for the regime. The official-dom has often moved in to fill a partial political vacuum, and it is generally motivated by the announced twin objectives of preserving law and order, and of providing guardianship for the presumably unprepared masses during a period of tutelage toward fuller partici-pation in government. A more hidden secondary motive that may grow in importance with time is the desire of the guardian class to consolidate and perpetuate control.

283

Traditional-Autocratic Systems

These regimes are the most traditional in their style of rule. The dominant political elites owe their power position to a long-established social system, which usually emphasizes inherited monarchic or aristocratic social status. As a group, these countries have not proceeded far along the path toward modernization, but they show considerable variation in the extent to which change is permitted or encouraged. The range is from Yemen and Saudi Arabia (which have changed least) to Jordan, Morocco, and Iran (in which major modifications have already taken place).

Countries in this category are shrinking in number. Within the past decade, traditional-autocratic regimes have been replaced in several instances, including Afghanistan, Ethiopia, Libya, Cambodia, and Laos. Successor regimes have been installed either as the result of military coups or Communist takeovers. Clearly the prospects for survival are precarious for such a regime. Those that remain tend to be located in the Near East or North Africa. Most of them are large in area and have a widely scattered population, predominantly rural and often including tribal groupings alienated from the national government.

Although the traditional political elite in such a regime will probably be committed to modernizing goals, these are likely to be limited in scope and designed not to jeopardize the political status quo. The emphasis will instead be on rapid industrialization and provision of public services, particularly if the country is fortunate enough to have extensive oil reserves which can be exploited, as in Iran and Saudi Arabia. These elites, as Esman says, are "seldom political risk takers, but rather cautious reformers."[1] In such a setting, political activity is severely curtailed. Competitive politics is usually not permitted. Political parties and associational interest groups with diverse programs either are not tolerated or are weak. On the other hand, the political elite does not attempt to mobilize the mass of the population in any official political movement, and little interest is shown in articulating a political ideology. A political attitude of acquiescence and conformity in the community suits the dominant elite, and it is not inclined to invite trouble by pushing hard for programs to increase literacy or otherwise stimulate political awareness and activity.

The ruling family or cluster of families in such a regime must rely on the army and the civil bureaucracy both as instrumentalities of change which has been invoked as desirable and as inhibitors of unwanted change. The administrative machinery is the principal vehicle for action, but its ability to operate effectively is hampered by its own traditional characteristics and by the difficulties it faces in penetrating the community. Reforms to remedy these handicaps are undertaken reluctantly and tentatively, if at all.

Saudi Arabia and Iran are prime examples of traditional-autocratic regimes, with Iran being of greatest interest for our purposes. Saudi Arabia is a most exceptional society, combining the extension into the late twentieth century of what has been termed a "patriarchal desert state" with immense wealth in the form of the world's largest known petroleum reserves. Wenner has described Saudi Arabia as retaining "the essential elements of a value system, a set of behavior patterns for both elite and mass alike, and a political system which is in most respects an anachronism in the modern world."[2] The political framework barely qualifies to be labeled a territorial nation-state in the usual sense. The ruling Saudi dynasty has, however, been able to sustain a society with internal solidarity resting on the traditional bases of custom, heredity, and religion. The royal family has sought to retain the pattern of personal patriarchal government to the extent possible while embarking on mammoth economic development projects and social reform measures. Although the governmental machinery now includes a standard roster of ministries, most of them have been created within the last thirty years, and the Council of Ministers did not begin to function in a meaningful way until the mid 1950s. Even today, members of the royal family hold nearly all of the important posts, and members of the traditional upper class occupy most higher echelon positions. However, a "new" middle class of secularly educated Saudis is coming into increasing prominence in "modern" sector ministries such as commerce, health, and communications. Wenner sums up the limited available information about Saudi Arabian bureaucracy by saying that "it is possible to document the rise and increasing influence of what has been called a 'new middle class' among whom are to be found the predominance of rationalist, universalist and secular value systems. On the other hand, one cannot yet point in Saudi Arabia to the beginnings of a political system dominated by mass participation, populist ideologies, much less the prominent role which a modernized and rationalist military structure is often expected to play in the 'drive for modernization.' "[3] The Saudi political system continues to be largely traditional, under aristocratic leadership, without differentiated political institutions, and with only a rudimentary bureaucracy.

Iran presents a more complex modernizing example of a traditional-autocratic regime.[4] Binder asserts that "Iran recapitulates within living memory most of the varied political experience of all the Middle East," and that "the variety of coexisting and competing legitimizing formulae and patterns of political activity" testify to the impermanent nature of the Iranian political system.[5] On the other hand, the present political regime "has demonstrated an astounding capacity for survival and stability. While monarchs and presidents throughout the Middle East and the developing world have been deposed or dismissed and political chaos has been rife, Iran does appear as an island of stability."[6] Among other differences from most of the Middle East, Iran has escaped from ever being a colony of a Western power, directly subject to foreign control, with resulting benefits in national self-esteem and experience in diplomacy as an independent power. Avoidance of colonial status also had its costs, however, as Zonis points out. For instance, Iran never had a colonial bureaucracy which could provide a later model for structuring an indigenous bureaucracy or for the behavior of indigenous bureaucrats. More importantly, "Iran never gained the experience of having a palpable enemy with tangible symbols of that enemy's control. There was never, then, the rallying point for national aspirations that independence or anticolonial struggles provided other nations. Myths of national unification or bases of national identity failed to develop. The Iranians did not develop a sense of the concept of Iranian citizenship. Rather, as is the case today, people were considered 'subjects' of the monarch."[7] The monarchical tradition is the main unifying and legitimizing force, and the state is identified with the institution of monarchy. Consequently, service to the Shah is seen as the primary duty of all Iranian subjects.

In recent years, Iran's rate of economic growth has been impressive, with the gross national product increasing at an average annual rate of over 10 percent, among the highest national growth rates in the world. Dramatically expanded oil revenues are mainly responsible. Close to two-thirds of the government's budget is now provided by oil earnings. This dependency on oil, although hazardous in the long run, offers an opportunity in the near future to build a springboard for continued economic growth after oil revenues start to decline. The Shah's "White Revolution," inaugurated in 1963, has involved massive expenditures intended to create such an infrastructure. Projects have included investment in roads, communications facilities, dams, and education. Limited land reform programs have been undertaken. Currently, however, the emphasis has turned more toward building up of steel production and other heavy industry projects, and to expansion of the size and capability of the armed forces. The pattern of the "White Revolution" has been described by Bill as expressing "the politics of system preservation," rather

than aimed at any fundamental alteration of the existing system.[8]
Marvin Zonis likewise states that the consequences of Iranian politics
can be analyzed "in terms of the colonial analogy. Iran is a society
characterized by the 'trickle effect' whereby cultural innovations,
consumption patterns, standards of proper behavior, political power,
and economic wealth are located in or enter the society through an
expanding but still very small political, economic, and social elite
based in Tehran. These phenomena trickle down the social ladder
with most of the significant changes never reaching the large mass of
the population. As a result, the gap between rich and poor continues
to expand. Iran is a society characterized by far more growth than
development."[9]

The nature of the political regime readily explains these
consequences. All observers agree that political power is highly
centralized in the person of the Shah, and that the total political elite
in Iran consists of a very small group. In Bill's study, he refers to the
political elite as the Shah and only thirty other Iranians who are
closest to him in terms of political influence. Zonis extends the
range somewhat, but the political elite as identified by him includes
only 307 individuals. In fact, Zonis asserts that the Shah is "clearly
the 'pivot' around whom the entire system of power and privilege in
Iran revolves," and that "the Shah himself plays a role equivalent to
the political elite in other societies," so that even this small elite
group can perhaps be best viewed as the "second stratum" of the
ruling class "located structurally between the Shah and the
non-elite."[10]

The members of this political elite or "second stratum" function to put the Shah's policies and decisions into action. Zonis
identifies three "overarching pillars" of the Shah's policy, which
provide the framework for day-to-day decisions. These are "preserving and strengthening his own power and that of his family," assuring
"survival for the institution of the monarchy," and seeking to "build
the power of the Iranian state."[11] Within these guidelines, the Shah
himself makes a phenomenal number of decisions, and he keeps a
close rein on others who act on his behalf. The whole system is
designed to push conflicts toward the very top before they can be
resolved. Members of the political elite who share in the exercise of
power do so subject to the overriding requirement that the ultimate
control of the Shah not be endangered. Access to and retention in
the elite is conditioned on acceptance of the Shah's supremacy, but
for those enjoying the Shah's favor the rewards in prestige and
material benefits are exceptional. In numerous instances, the Shah
has "co-opted his former critics by making available to them rewards

over whose distribution he maintains control."[12] On the other hand, he has been ruthless in excluding from the elite persons who do not measure up to his expectations. The result is a congruence of interests between the elite and the monarch which intensifies the centralizing characteristics of the regime. "The elite wish to minimize their role in decision making for fear of the consequences; the Shah wishes to make the maximal number of decisions so as to maximize his control over the political process."[13]

As Zonis points out, members of the select political elite are also almost invariably members of the official elite. That is, they occupy formal positions within the governmental structure. This structure, however, is fragmented and unwieldy. In addition to a score of ministries, it contains a variety of councils, companies, and other agencies. For example, the all-important National Iranian Oil Company is an institution not represented in the cabinet. Instead of a working cabinet system to provide operational coordination, it must be provided by influential officials with access to the Shah. An apt description of the Iranian system, according to Zonis, "would be that of the sun around which revolve men and organizations mostly in direct contact with the Shah, facilitating his direct control of the administrative apparatus."[14]

The bureaucracy has also been segmented along agency lines rather than uniformly structured. No central personnel agency existed until 1959, and the one created then was not operationally effective. Recruitment procedures have not been centralized but have been set up on an agency-by-agency basis. A basic personnel law enacted in 1922 undertook to set general rules concerning such matters as pay, promotion, retirement, and disciplinary action, but some of its provisions have had unfortunate effects, and others have been largely inoperative. Basic salary scales for the service have been low, leading to a bewildering variety of supplemental payments, and to pressures for special treatment for employees in favored agencies. Aside from initial appointments at a grade considered appropriate for the educational background of the appointee, the pay levels have not been geared to training or level of work performed, but to total length of time in service. Promotions are provided for at regular intervals, based on seniority, so that theoretically an employee can start at the bottom and work his way through all of the regular pay grades if he survives long enough, and it is quite common for a supervisor to have under him employees with greater seniority, and hence higher pay. The retirement program was never put on a sound financial basis, and the disciplinary machinery has been largely unworkable.[15]

Within this unusual political and administrative environment, members of the political elite and of the career bureaucracy exhibit some shared characteristics. One is the gradually broadening social base from which they are recruited. Bill describes the emergence in Iran of what he terms a "new class,"[16] consisting of individuals possessing skills and talents acquired through access to modern educational opportunities in Iran and abroad. Its members form a professional-bureaucratic intelligentsia which is profoundly different from and is rapidly replacing the traditional Iranian middle and upper classes, whose status was based on factors such as property, material wealth, or family ties. They question traditional power relationships, have been exposed to Western ideas and culture, and have a tendency to discard or de-emphasize Islamic religious values, while at the same time possessing the professional and technical training needed for achievement of Iranian national objectives.

Members of this growing group are moving into both the top political elite and the bureaucracy. The Shah has deliberately recruited from this pool of technically educated individuals for major governmental posts in order to improve the level of competence, weaken his dependence on the traditional social elite, and enhance his political position generally. As a consequence, the emerging "skill elite" exhibits an unusually high level of formal education. Similarly, the Iranian civil service reflects in its composition an increasing number and proportion of members with higher education qualifications. Bill reports that between 1956 and 1963, in a sample of twenty-one agencies accounting for about four-fifths of government employment, the percentage of employees with higher education almost tripled from 8 percent to over 21 percent, and the absolute number more than quadrupled from 12,000 to 53,000.[17] Although later statistics are not available for these same agencies, Bill estimates that during the ten years from 1956 to 1966 the "new class" increased in size by over 60 percent, with the proportion of Iranians belonging to it rising from one in seventeen to one in twelve. Undoubtedly such a trend has continued, both within the government service and elsewhere in Iranian society.

Along with their shared technical training, this intelligentsia also is the point of focus for criticism, both voiced and hidden, of the regime. "To the degree that it is a new force concerned with different relationships, its expansion represents all the more deadly a challenge to the old system. As it grows, it can confront the former relationships on increasingly more fronts. At the same time, it will have more forces available for concentrated assaults at vital points in the traditional system."[18] Bill examines the divisions within the "new class" as to degree of alienation from the regime, identifying four groups as "ideal types," and labeling them uprooters, technocrats, maneuverers, and followers. Only the first of these groups consists of open opponents of the existing political system, however. The others, in one way or another, accommodate themselves to the regime for their own self-protection and advancement.

Flowing from this dilemma of having to reconcile dissatisfaction with conformance are widely shared attitudinal characteristics among the political elite and higher ranking bureaucrats which can be summed up as a syndrome of distrust and covert resistance in response to the political environment. From his interviews with members of the elite, Zonis identified and analyzed four prinicipal attitudinal dimensions—"political cynicism, personal distrust, manifest insecurity, and interpersonal exploitation."[19]

At the conclusion of his study of the political elite, Zonis sums up the profound consequences of this situation on the problems of governance in Iran. The hallmark of these problems is inefficiency, explainable by "the general character orientations of the centrally placed political elite. . . . An inability to predict, with surety, the behavior of others; a disbelief in the sincerity and integrity of others (and, in a real sense, of oneself); absence of cooperation and mutual interdependence; a flight from responsibility and decision making; and the pursuit of personalized, systematically nonsubstantive goals characterize the elite and their political sytem. The bureaucracy, principally charged with the task of implementing measures designed to move Iran closer to modernity and the more developed West, does not and cannot function in ways that will contribute in an appreciable degree to these goals."[20]

Iran thus well exemplifies the type of traditional-autocratic regime which deliberately discourages widespread popular participation in political affairs. The Pahlavi monarchy in Iran during the last half-century, says Bill, "has been characterized by traditional patterns in which the Shah promotes passive servitude in all relationships that others maintain toward him and balanced rivalry in all other personal, group, and class interaction. The former pattern is often buttressed by the latter since forces that are constantly checked by others seldom have time to challenge the strongest force in the system."[21] Zonis reaches essentially the same judgment about the reign of the current Shah, characterizing it as a period in which "the civil and military bureaucracies have continually expanded their control over the activities of the population at large," while the Shah "has even more relentlessly expanded his power over the bureaucracies."[22]

The bureaucratic role in Iran, tending as noted by Binder to institutionalize nonrational patterns of administrative behavior, accurately mirrors the political regime it serves.[23] The regime wants change, but not too much, and not change that will get out of hand. This calls for a bureaucracy that is at once loyal, competent, and conservative. The political leadership tries to avoid loss of support from officialdom, particularly those entrusted with maintaining state security.[24] Such leadership depends on bureaucratic initiative for policy recommendations, since there are few alternative sources, but the policy guidelines tend to be fuzzy and obscure, and the responses from bureaucrats are apt to be cautious and guarded, so as to avoid suspicion of advocating policies that might undermine the existing order. Both the political elite and the bureaucracy are caught in the dilemma of trying simultaneously to respond to an urge for change and to protect a social order that is still basically traditional. A capacity to control the populace has been demonstrated, but success has been slight in mobilizing the populace behind the regime's modernization programs. "Political reform from the bottom up has become virtually impossible. But such reform from the top down, now referred to as the White Revolution, has become increasingly unattainable." Existing political relations "have become more intractable as they have become more enduring." These considerations lead Zonis to conclude that the stability of the present regime remains tenuous and its power problematic.[25] Writing late in 1978, Bill concurs that "the Shah of Iran rules from behind bayonets," and predicts that the political future of Iran will involve "either a continuation of some kind of Pahlavi rule or a government led by a radical-progressive military group."[26]*

Strongman Military Systems

Among bureaucratic elite regimes, some are characterized by what is essentially one-man rule by a leader who almost invariably comes from a military background. This military strongman or caudillo type of regime has occurred most commonly in Latin American countries during the nineteenth and early twentieth centuries and in recent years among countries of sub-Saharan Africa.

The Spanish word *caudillo*, meaning leader or chief, was applied during the nineteenth century to what became a characteristic form

---

* In January 1979, a civilian cabinet replaced a military cabinet which had been operating under martial law for several months, and the Shah left Iran, although he did not relinquish his claim to the throne. Whatever the nature of Iran's uncertain political future, the country is unlikely to continue as a traditional-autocratic regime.

of political leadership in Latin America. Caudillos, usually of mestizo or Indian origin, assumed power to fill the void left by the disappearance of colonial governments and the widespread constitutional failures following independence. The resulting geographical fragmentation of political power led to the rise of caudillo-led armies which often consisted of nothing more than an armed band led by a self-designated "general." Gino Germani and Kalman Silvert observe that in this Latin American tradition of caudillismo "the geographical fragmentation took the form of a 'federal' state, the absolute rule of the caudillo that of the 'president' and, at the same time, 'general' of the army."[27]   This alternative frequently seemed preferable to continuing factional rivalries. The most common pattern was for caudillo-style dictatorships to replace intervening periods of political chaos, but occasionally caudillos succeeded in maintaining themselves in power over long stretches of time, notable examples being Rodriquez de Francia, known as "El Supremo," who ruled in Paraguay from 1814 to 1840, and General Porfirio Diaz, who served as Mexican president from 1877 to 1910.

Less typical in Latin America since early in this century, political regimes with caudillo or strongman characteristics have appeared since World War II in numerous recently independent countries in Africa. In his classification of sub-Saharan political regimes with a high degree of military involvement in politics, Claude E. Welch, Jr., contrasts "personalist" and "corporatist" categories, with the former closely corresponding to the strongman or caudillo model. According to Welch, personalist regimes focus on the head of state or commander in chief and exhibit the following five general characteristics:

1. The act of intervention reflects, inter alia, (a) affronts to the institutional prerogatives of the armed forces, (b) personal challenges to the commander-in-chief, or (c) invitations from the head of state to the commander-in-chief to assume control.
2. The act of intervention is initiated by the ranking officer.
3. Given the extensive experience of the ranking officer with the armed forces, he will identify himself closely with their interests.
4. Both officers and civilians are named to cabinet positions; however, rapid and frequent changes in policy by the head of state are paralleled by equally rapid and frequent changes in cabinets.
5. To the extent that a national "ideology" is coined and propagated, it stresses the head of state.[28]

In these personalist regimes, as Welch points out, the head of state becomes "the focus, the prime mover," evoking the image of "the benevolent, modernizing leader" who can promote national unity. With power so centered in the head of state, cabinet instability almost invariably results. The personalist leader ensures that important governmental positions will be distributed to those he considers his most dependable and avid supporters. He "indulges in time-honored exercises: reward the faithful; build support through incorporating as many regions and tendencies as possible; find congenial supporters." The vagaries of the leader are "writ large in national policies," leading to a comment quoted by Welch concerning one ruling general in the Central African Republic that only his cabinets change even more frequently than his policies.[29]

The life span of personalist regimes is unpredictable. With power resting basically on the claims of hierarchy, any breakdown in military discipline and cohesion raises the threat of further intervention. As Welch observes, the ranking officer and his close associates "may rule well or they may rule poorly; they may disengage themselves from extensive contact with their fellow officers or they may retain close identification with the armed forces: yet they cannot avoid reinforcing the idea that political power derives from coercive might."[30] These are continually vulnerable regimes.

It may safely be assumed that in this political regime type there will be a distinctive impact on the characteristics of the administrative system. For example, with the bulk of administrative power centralized in the leader, he is the one who makes most major administrative decisions. Higher ranking bureaucrats are personally scrutinized by him; the bureaucracy resembles a patriarchal community headed by the caudillo. Those bureaucrats who are loyal to the leader and supportive of him are amply rewarded with increased pay, promotion, or other recognition. Those officials who do not display these attributes are promptly punished by demotion, dismissal, or perhaps even death. In general, high ranking administrative officials will be appointed by the caudillo based on his own self-defined criteria, with personal loyalty and adherence to regime ideology usually given primary emphasis. It may also be assumed that merit recruitment criteria such as the possession of technical skills, degree of education, past work experience, or professional competence will be held in low regard, if considered at all.

The strongman, caudillo, or personalist style of rule is currently represented in Latin America by Paraguay (where General Alfredo

Stroessner has been in power since 1954), Nicaragua (ruled by members of the Somoza family since 1937), and Haiti (where Francois Duvalier and his son Jean-Claude have been in power since 1957). Numerous other examples occurred earlier in this century, one of the more notable being in Guatemala prior to 1944. Welch includes the following African countries among those with existing personalist regimes: Algeria, Burundi, Central African Republic, Togo, Uganda, Upper Volta, and Zaire. He also lists Dahomey, Nigeria, and Sudan as having had such regimes sometime during the 1960s.

Reliable information concerning the public bureaucracies and their operational characteristics in such polities is understandably hard to obtain. This is particularly so for contemporary Latin American examples. For this reason, we will illustrate from Latin America with pre-1944 Guatemala, about which more is known. Owing to the special attention it has received in both news media reports and in scholarly publications, the personalist military regime in Uganda under General Amin will serve as an African illustration.

Prior to 1944, Guatemala's political system was highly personalized and centralized. According to Whetten, presidents exercised dictatorial power, "ruling with varying degrees of benevolence, and managing the affairs of government in their own way without permitting much interference either from the written constitution or from political opponents. The army and the national police force were relied upon to enforce the decrees and mandates of the chief executive. The inhabitants were kept pretty well under control; there were few political disturbances; peace and order tended to prevail."[31] Public adherence to regime policies could be attributed to the fact that the caudillo was able to deal with any seditious activity effectively at an early stage. "Critics and potential political rivals could be quietly banished from the country and their properties confiscated; or in extreme cases, their lives could be snuffed out with little or no explanation of the whys and wherefores."[32] Similarly, Weaver characterizes Guatemala until 1944 as being ruled by "a classic Latin American political elite: plantation owners, senior military officers, social and economic notables, and representatives of major foreign commercial interests. Authority was exercised by the traditional strong man, whose rule was paternalistic, arbitrary, and predicated on his ability to hold the confidence (or keep alive the fear) of garrison commanders and other key military officers."[33]

The last of these caudillos was General Jorge Ubico, who ruled from 1930 to 1944. Weaver's study of Guatemalan bureaucracy, although focused on more recent years, sheds considerable light on caudillo-bureaucratic relationships. Ruling the nation with an iron hand, Ubico made full use of a wide array of repressive measures, meanwhile taking extreme precautions to protect his own safety.[34] He insisted on "punctuality, Calvinist comportment, and absolute rectitude. Primitive capitalism, the sanctity of private property, and classic Latin American liberalism were dominant elements of official ideology."[35]

The Guatemalan bureaucracy received special attention from the caudillo. Stressing "strict discipline, formal deportment, and absolute loyalty," Ubico socialized civil servants "in a small bureaucracy which was personally scrutinized by the *caudillo*, which stressed Victorian-like behavior and attire, and in which service was a family tradition to be preserved and passed along. Ubico typically began each day by visiting the offices in the National Palace; bureaucrats who were absent from their seats when the work bell rang were summarily dismissed."[36] Jensen confirms this, stating that Ubico "expected hard work of others, and he would not hesitate to call an employee early in the morning for a report. He dismissed people who did not do their duty fully, and also those who came late to work. He saw to details, and he demanded and got obedience. The magnificent National Palace . . . had an electric board at which each official checked in and out, so that he could keep close tab on them. He removed public officials who displeased him, or simply on whim."[37]

Evidence presented by Weaver strongly suggests that the impact of the regimes under Ubico and his caudillo predecessors is still clearly visible in the Guatemalan bureaucracy, as shown by data gathered in the mid 1960s. For example, in response to a question as to the most important qualities an employee must possess to get ahead, only a relatively small number of his respondents (19 percent) mentioned a specific skill, experience, and training; similarly, only 21 percent suggested general skill, basic education, and seniority. Much more frequently mentioned as criteria for advancement were "honesty, respect, and integrity, often mentioned in combination with *capaz* (competence—knowing one's way around)."[38] When asked about the most important qualities that a good public employee ought to possess, respondents again emphasized character or personality attributes, with nearly half of them stressing loyalty, respect, and honesty. About a quarter of them mentioned *capaz* or competence, and another quarter referred to a high school diploma, some kind of training, or an ambition to serve the public. The responses to these two questions confirm Weaver's observation that supervisors in the Guatemalan bureaucracy "are placed in positions of responsibility because they have demonstrated their reliability—personal and political if not necessarily administrative. Most of them are not highly educated nor are they familiar with modern technical and administrative procedures."[39]

Perhaps even more illuminating was Weaver's investigation of the attitudes of Guatemalan bureaucrats toward their work. He discovered that an overwhelming majority of the respondents submitted uncritical responses, if they responded at all, to the question "If you were to become the chief of this office, what changes would you make around here?" In sum, almost one-half of the respondents refused to suggest that their work situation should be changed in any way. Perhaps this item would not appear as interesting if Weaver had not discerned a slight trend toward greater critical expression with increased seniority, a trend which was firmly reversed, however, by the most senior respondents, those older bureaucrats with more than twenty years of service. Weaver provides a possible explanation for this seemingly unlikely phenomenon. Having already discarded the hypothesis that an increase in age is characterized by more prudence, caution, and, hence, a more conservative response, he points out that "all members of this group joined the bureaucracy prior to the revolution. The most-senior bureaucrats received their early training and prerecruitment socialization during the Ubico regime."[40] Apparently, Ubico's caudillo style of rule, with its emphasis on discipline, proper deportment, and absolute loyalty, still exhibited a discernible impact on the attitudinal and behavioral patterns of Guatemalan bureaucrats even after twenty years.

The most striking example of African strongman personalist regimes is Uganda under General (now Field Marshal) Idi Amin Dada.[41] During the brief fifteen-year period since gaining independence from Great Britain and becoming a member of the Commonwealth in 1962, Uganda has moved from being a federal system with semiautonomous status for several traditional kingdoms within the country, to a centralized republic under a president (Milton Obote) who established a one-party state, to a military regime following a successful coup by the commander in chief of the armed forces (General Amin) who soon installed a personalist regime with himself as president, having assumed full governmental powers and suspended all political parties.[42]

Uganda under Amin is not easily classifiable, being a unique product of historical forces in the area and personality traits of the individual in charge. Mazrui, who was on the faculty of Makerere University in Uganda for ten years, including the beginning years of the Amin regime, refers to developments since the 1971 coup as the making of a "military ethnocracy," combining the warrior tradition in Africa with ethnocracy as a basis for political organization, and as a "military theocracy," likewise having its origins in the historical politicization of religion in Uganda. In essence his themes are that the warrior tradition, which connected physical virility and martial valor, and which had been in decline during the colonial period, is being revived; that ethnocracy, in the sense of a system for distributing political power primarily on the basis of kinship, which has persisted in African society, is now stronger than ever; and that Amin and the military as rulers have succeeded earlier Christian missionaries in claiming a monopoly on the setting of standards of personal conduct and the legitimate use of spiritual sanctions.

Whether or not this approach to interpretation of events is correct, clearly there have been dramatic changes in both the political and administrative systems in Uganda since the military takeover. Originally, General Amin adopted a conciliatory stance following seizure of power, engaged in various well-publicized efforts to consult with representatives of divergent groups, encouraged political participation by civilians, retained a largely civilian cabinet, seemed to rely heavily on the professional bureaucracy, and in other ways indicated an intent to follow a course of moderation once military leadership had been established. According to Mazrui, it appeared at first that Amin was aiming at his own version of a military–intellectual coalition. "Amin seemed to have considerable deference towards the educated in his society. He created the most technocratic and best-educated cabinet in the history of Uganda. The style of leadership provided by his government seemed at first to be primarily bureaucratic—rather than either mobilizational or intimidating. . . . Amin's original cabinet had a range of expertise which included engineering as well as law, zoology as well as economics. The country seemed to be set on a new approach to that old partnership between guns and brains."[43]

This indicated partnership between the military and the intelligentsia soon dissipated, with military dominance becoming more and more evident and being expressed through the personal actions of General Amin. According to Mazrui, "The technocrats in the cabinet and the civil service responded to the moods of the General himself. There were reports of a minister being physically slapped across the face by the General. There were also reports of cabinet ministers being shouted down and silenced on matters that the General did not want to hear about. An important partnership did indeed exist between these technocrats and the new military government, but the military were now clearly and indisputably the senior partner. The tables had been turned on the intelligentsia."[44] One transition that followed was that gradually most of the civilian cabinet members were replaced by military men, who now occupy the critical posts. The Ugandan government currently matches closely with Welch's list of characteristics for a personalist military regime.

The impact of this personalist style of rule on the bureaucracy closely parallels what was reported in Guatemala under Ubico. In the case of Uganda, at the time of independence the country had in place a bureaucratic elite similar to that in other British African colonies, staffed at the top by Britishers but including Ugandans in subordinate and apprenticeship roles. As in other nations gaining independence, rapid Africanization took place soon afterward, displacing most of the non-Ugandans. The criteria for selection to these higher civil service posts placed a major emphasis on command of English and a modern Western education. As a consequence, Ugandan bureaucratic elite members were more highly educated than members of the political elite, particularly after the military take-over occurred, since upward mobility in the armed forces was not nearly as dependent on fluency in English or a high level of general education.

The higher civil service also began with the advantages of tenure status and high social prestige associated with the British colonial pattern. Entry into the civil service became the career ambition of most of the ablest Ugandan university graduates, because of its promise of a secure career as against the risks of either political or entrepreneurial activity.

This privileged position was maintained during the Obote period and the early part of the Amin regime, but has since been almost completely wiped out, placing civil bureaucrats in a role of dependence upon and subservience to the military ruler. This destabilization of the civil service has been accomplished mainly by eliminating guarantees of security of tenure. General Amin announced soon after taking over that inadequate performance would lead to dismissal, and dramatically drove the point home during the second year of his rule by ousting twenty-two senior civil servants, who were "pensioned off," with some receiving retirement benefits subsequently and some not. Soon afterward similar action was taken affecting a group of police officers. The vulnerability of public service careers became increasingly obvious as time passed, with more and more unpredictability as to what whim of General Amin might lead to sudden dismissal, and with dire consequences often following, including exile, imprisonment, or sudden disappearance. Although reliable information is no longer available as to what is happening within Uganda, the deterioration in professional qualifications and performance capabilities of what had been a well-developed civil service is obvious. Uganda under Amin presents a dramatic example of a military bureaucratic elitist regime with power highly concentrated in the hands of a single individual whose access to political control was made possible by his military background.

Collegial Military Systems

The distinctive feature of these regimes is that a group of military officers exercises political leadership. Rule is in the hands of what Morris Janowitz and others refer to as a "military oligarchy." Welch calls them "corporatist" regimes, contrasting them with "personalist" or "strongman" regimes. Generally, the members of a junta which establishes such a regime come from the same or adjacent military ranks. Collegiality rather than hierarchy is stressed as the means of maintaining cohesion, although the leader of a coup which brought the group to power may enjoy a position of pre-eminence in the group, or one individual may later emerge as dominant in the junta.

Welch lists the following characteristics as common in these regimes:

1. The act of intervention reflects varying combinations of societal and organizational tensions. Coups led by junior officers are more likely mounted against personalist regimes than against civilian governments.
2. Intervention is planned and carried out by a coalition of field grade officers, often with academy backgrounds or current academy postings.
3. Maintaining unity within the coalition necessitates rapid distribution of cabinet positions to coup supporters, and removal of potential opponents by means of retirement, exile, and the like.
4. Ideological themes of national unity predominate. The purported unity and goal orientation of the military serve as examplars to the entire political system; "revolution" appears as the catchword.
5. Collegiality cannot be easily maintained. One-man dominance emerges, the results of both military norms of command and heightened fragmentation within the junta resulting from the pressures of governing.[45]

The rationale for military intervention is usually put in terms of protecting the country from some internal or external threat, and the basic thrust as to policy objectives is reduction of disorder and violence and establishment of law and order. The military establishment is viewed as having a special obligation to take action to protect the national interest. As Lieuwen puts it with special reference to the Latin American context, "The armed forces hold that they have a legitimate political mission above that of the government. Their first allegiance is to the nation and to the constitution, as they interpret it, rather than to the ephemeral civilian politician who happens to occupy the presidential chair at a given moment. Thus, the military's custodianship of the national interest . . . makes its political involvement inevitable."[46]

Martin Needler, who has closely examined the internal dynamics of coups that have brought military juntas to power, points out two common phenomena—collaboration with civilian politicians, and the role of the "swing man." He observes that military coups are not made solely by the military. "Almost invariably, the conspirators are in touch with civilian politicians and respond to their advice, counting on their assistance in justifying the coup to public opinion and helping to run the country afterwards. This relationship not infrequently takes the form of a coup only reluctantly staged by the military at the insistence of civilian politicians, who appealed to the officers' patriotism, the historic role of the army in saving the country at its hour of need."[47]

The swing man phenomenon refers to the fact that often the "critical margin of support" before a coup is provided by an individual or group decision to collaborate with the original conspirators. The initiators of the coup plans tend to be in strongest opposition to the current regime, "while other officers of different political orientations and a greater commitment to constitutional procedures have higher thresholds to interventionism."[48] The last adherent or set of adherents is likely to come from this latter group, often providing a swing man who may be extremely important for success of the coup for reasons such as his high rank or critical position in the military command structure, his personal influence within the armed forces, and/or his high prestige with the public. Frequently such a swing man will be selected to head the postcoup military junta or provisional government, even though he may be an individual "who was least committed to the objectives of the coup, whose threshold to intervention was the highest of all the conspirators, and who was a last-minute addition to the conspiracy perhaps out of sympathy with, or not even aware of, the more fundamental aims of the group that hatched the original plan." Perhaps he may not even have agreed with the conspiratorial objectives at all, but joined "at the last minute only to avoid pitting brother officers against each other, possibly precipitating a civil war."[49] The presence of a moderate swing man often leads to a conflict situation later on, if he initiates plans for a return to civilian rule and constitutional normalization, while "the original instigator of the coup and the group around him . . . resist this tendency and instead urge the necessity for the military to keep power for a longer period."[50] The position of the swing man as junta leader may eventually become untenable, leading to an internal reorientation.

If a junta regime retains power very long, some kind of redistribution of political authority is almost certain to occur. It may simply take the form of internal shifts within the coalition, such as replacement of some or all of the original junta members. As time passes, even though political direction by the military is still manifest, the military junta is likely to take steps toward gradual civilianization intended to mask the fact of continued military control. "This shift of emphasis is both symbolic (e.g., wearing civilian clothing) and constitutional. The new constitution is supposed to redefine the separation of functions and power among the military and other executive branches of government. It also should forbid soldiers and officers on active duty to participate in politics. The civilianized military elite itself takes over (with different degrees of success) the leadership of a civilian–political movement."[51] As long as members of the military elite continue to dominate the polity, however, even though they have donned civilian garb, there is no essential shift in the basic regime characteristics. The most difficult problem of possible reclassification is under circumstances in which civilianized military leaders choose to emphasize the instrumentality of a mass-mobilization party as the principal vehicle for governance, while retaining ultimate control options. Egypt presents such an instance, with the choice being to continue considering the regime to be a military oligarchy in disguise, or to classify it as having shifted to the dominant-party mobilization category with former military leaders occupying crucial party posts. South Korea is another such borderline case. Our choice, as detailed later, has been to put Egypt on one side of this line and South Korea on the other.

A third type of power reallocation, of course, is transfer from direct military rule to what is clearly rule by a civilian elite, even though the possibility of future military intervention remains. Such "abdication" or "return to the barracks" occurs when a ruling military junta voluntarily or involuntarily returns power to civilians. According to S. E. Finer, this will happen as the cumulative effect of three conditions: "the disintegration of the original conspiratorial group, the growing divergence of interests between the junta of rulers and those military who remain as active heads of the fighting services, and the political difficulties of the regime."[52]   In this eventuality, there is no doubt about the necessity for a political regime reclassification. Turkey is a clear example of such a transition.

Any military junta is certain to devote attention to a revamping of the civil bureaucracy, but it will at the same time be limited in what can be done by its dependency on the nonmilitary administrative system. Civil bureaucrats are likely to be one of the targets of a newly installed military regime, accused of corrupt practices, wasteful and ineffective performance, and inadequacies as an instrument of social change. Some program of administrative reform is apt to be launched, and it may involve substantial structural changes along with efforts to modify patterns of bureaucratic behavior. However, at most a military regime can hope to effectuate changes in the bureaucratic apparatus; it cannot be supplanted. "The military elite can run a country only with the collaboration of the civil service. Even though it denounces, purges, and transforms it, the elite will inevitably be forced into a coalition with the civil service. The armed forces themselves cannot replace the civil service; they can only supervise it, check it, interfere with it, and, at best, penetrate and dominate it. To do more would be to cease being an army, and no oligarchic military elite in any new state has yet undertaken to do that."[53]

Under a collegial military regime, the strategic position of the civil bureaucracy is intermediate as between the situation under a military strongman and the situation in a civilian–military coalition bureaucratic regime. While a personalist regime lasts, its leader can make bureaucrats subservient and force responsiveness to his whims because of their vulnerability to reprisal for incurring his disfavor. In a coalition regime, equality or near equality in the partnership arrangements offers more leverage to the civil bureaucracy for participation in political decision-making and for protection of group interests. A military junta can subordinate civilian officials but cannot avoid relying on their cooperation to keep the regime intact.

Among numerous current examples of collegial military regimes, notable instances are Argentina since the ouster of Isabel

Peron, post-Allende Chile, Ecuador since 1972, Bolivia since 1969, Indonesia since 1966, and South Korea since 1961. Depending mainly on the length of time since the beginning of military rule, these regimes range from orthodox juntas composed of active duty military officers with one of them perhaps designated as president or head of state (as in Argentina, Chile, and Ecuador), to instances in which the leader of the junta which gained power through a military coup has subsequently had his claim to political leadership ratified by an election process of some kind (as with President Suharto in Indonesia and President Park in South Korea).

Experience under military rule in the Republic of Korea (South Korea) since the early 1960s manifests several of the characteristics commonly found in these regimes.[54] The 1961 military coup ousted a short-lived civilian government which in turn had replaced a year earlier the presidency of Syngman Rhee, who had been in office since the founding of the republic in 1948. Student-led demonstrations against corruption and election frauds had forced the resignation of President Rhee, but the successor government was unable to deal with the problems it inherited. South Korea before the military takeover has been described as a nation in which "economic deterioration, social unrest, and political instability were rampant," with the severity of these conditions directly attributable to the administrations which had been or were in power, which "fostered corruption, favoritism, and factionalism, abusing their positions and public funds."[55] Early that year 28 percent of the urban working force were unemployed, industrial production had declined by 75 percent, and the price index had risen by 30 percent since the student revolt of the previous year. In rural areas, crop failures and exorbitant interest rates on loans had brought millions of farmers to the brink of starvation.[56] Under these circumstances, according to Choy, a coup was inevitable for several reasons: "(1) the armed forces were the only organized power to take over the government; (2) only the armed forces were capable, by training, of reorganizing the administration into one based on efficiency and integrity; and (3) only the armed forces were strong enough to suppress Communist infiltration and subversion."[57]

In May 1961, a young group of officers carefully planned and skillfully executed a bloodless coup, but only after they had secured the cooperation of senior military personnel. The principal architect of the coup and leader of the junior officers was then Colonel Kim Jong-Pil. "Under his direction and coordination, effective neutralization of many potential foes within the officer corps was achieved.

Once the act was committed, the reluctant and indecisive officers were caught up in the whirlwind of the initial thrust. . . . Fully assured of support. . . (he) searched out those who shared his revolutionary penchant. The first one to whom he turned was Major General Park Chung-Hee, who had been long known to represent the dissident elements among the high ranking officers."[58]

Thus General Park became the important "swing man," providing the critical margin of support to ensure the success of the coup conspiracy. "As the highest ranking and oldest officer on active duty, he provided a central unifying element among the coup activists. His reputation as an uncorruptable officer projected a better image for the revolutionary group. Above all, his unflinching determination to push through the highly risky coup at a time of uncertainty made the revolution a success."[59]

The new ruling junta which emerged, called the Supreme Council for National Reconstruction, consisted of a dozen members from all branches of the nation's armed forces, with General Park as chairman. The junta immediately suspended the constitution, dissolved the national legislature, disbanded all political parties, and imposed a series of repressive measures to ensure that no threat in the form of domestic political opposition would materialize. Over 22,000 persons were arrested, assemblies and meetings were forbidden, all publications were censored and many were outlawed. In addition, the junta "fired more than forty-one thousand government employees as corruptionists, draft evaders, concubine keepers, and politically incompetent public officers."[60]

The junta publicly justified the overthrow with the assertion "that they were forced to take over by the failure of civilian government, and that they came to power with the purest of patriotic intentions to save the country from chaos, corruption, and communism," and to replace the prior impotent regime as a modernizing force in South Korea.[61] Park himself also justified the coup as necessary for the prevention of Communist domination and the creation of a true democratic society, describing the coup as analogous to a medical operation needed to cure someone who is ill.[62]

The perspective of the new junta has been described as "revolutionary in tone and strongly nationalistic," as well as "pragmatic and managerial, rather than ideological in its emphasis. There was no deep concern with political or social theories, or particular systems, except for a preference for authoritarian controls."[63] The junta announced a six-point plan that became popularly known as the "Revolutionary Pledges," among which were included the elimination of corruption, opposition to communism, the development of a self-sustaining economy, national unification, and relief for the poor. The final pledge was that "as soldiers, after we have completed our mission, we shall restore the government to honest and conscientious civilians, and return to our proper military duties."[64]

The actual record after sixteen years shows a failure to meet this final pledge. Instead, as Kim states, the regime has manifested "an increasingly centralistic, authoritarian tendency," leading to the conclusion that "if transition from military rule entails political decentralization, a limited resort to coercion, and a peaceful transfer of power, the Park regime has taken a reverse course of development."[65] This does not mean an absence of changes in the formal constitutional arrangements, which have occurred in 1963, in 1969, and again in 1972; however, the power base and ruling methods of the regime have not substantially altered. These shifts in legal formalities reflect a search for a higher degree of legitimacy which would not jeopardize the regime's continuity.

The dilemma was that from the beginning the junta was plagued with a major problem as to political legitimacy. "An assumption of political sovereignty by the military is alien to Korea's deep-seated Confucian political culture. 'Military politics' is regarded with contempt. The coup leaders themselves claimed no superiority and their lowly origins were generally acknowledged. Thus, in pursuit of their goals, they were keenly aware of their limitations and consciously tried to compensate for them."[66] In line with this strategy, a decision was made even as power was being consolidated that an early return should be made to some form of civilian government, rather than indefinite maintenance of direct rule by the military junta, since "only by thus declaring their government's transitory nature could the junta leaders generate support from the country's powerful armed forces and from the general populace."[67]

Several alternatives were explored, including a return to the barracks by the junta leaders, and their retirement from military service conditioned on a guarantee of a privileged advisory status in a new government in the hands of civilians. The option actually chosen was "recivilianization" of the military junta. "This was the assumption of a direct political control by the military revolutionaries. They would take off their military uniforms and fill important governmental positions as either appointed or elected officials."[68] Adoption of this strategy led to promulgation of a new constitution for the Third Republic in 1963, and to creation of a political party— the Democratic-Republican party (DRP)—as a vehicle for assuming political power in the revised structure.

Through this process of "recivilianization," Park and his colleagues in the original military junta have been able to sustain their power position as principal decision-makers. As leader of the DRP, Park was elected president in 1963, and has been successively re-elected several times since, most recently in 1972 for a renewable six-year term. The constitution was amended in 1969 to permit President Park's candidacy for a third term, and in 1972 it was discarded altogether for a new Fourth Republic "Constitution for Revitalizing Reforms," which has been described as a "coup in office" giving broad emergency discretionary powers to the president, permitting re-election for an unlimited number of terms, authorizing presidential appointment of the prime minister and members of the cabinet, and authorizing the president to dissolve the unicameral national legislature or bypass it by calling a national referendum. President Park currently retains his leadership position with no indication that he may relinquish it soon. As one informed observer notes, "The prospects for the future of Korean politics is [sic] not optimistic in terms of the development of democracy. There is no immediate sign of the erosion of the present leadership in Korea. Under the repressive measures of the Park government, there does not seem any prospect for a new interest group whose collective strength would threaten the authoritarian government."[69]

Under the Park regime, the Democratic-Republican party has played a secondary role, serving as an instrument for mobilizing electoral support, but not contributing to policy input. Main reliance has been placed on cabinet ministers, drawn frequently from the ranks of retired military officers but including representatives from a considerable variety of backgrounds as to socioeconomic class, age, and geographic origin. The level of education is high, and many of them are technically trained.

Reform of the bureaucratic apparatus has been a continuing theme since the 1961 coup. The precoup administrative system was notorious for its corruption and self-indulgent practices. During this period, South Korea was characterized as a country "where the 'greased palm' characterizes every transaction and where corruption is deeply embedded in the practices of government, accepted by society, and a traditional perquisite of some of the officials."[70] Chronic inflation and inadequate pay were most often cited as major causes of corruption, but other contributing factors included foreign aid program abuses, the taxation system, government enterprise methods of operation, and the financing of political parties. In the period immediately following the coup, efforts were undertaken to eliminate bureaucratic corruption, including the establishment of an investigatory committee to "wipe out favouritism and weed out corrupt Government employees,"[71] and even issuance of a decree providing that the death penalty could be imposed on dishonest public officials. Despite these and subsequent efforts, evidence suggests that corrupt practices are still present in the Korean bureaucracy.

The Park government apparently has had more success in improving the quality of personnel and in organizational changes to improve productivity. It removed many of the senior officials of the Rhee administration and promoted younger people. "Under the military government . . . many remnants of the old routine-accustomed bureaucracy were cleared away from the upper layers, and many young officials with more positive outlook were promoted to responsible positions."[72] New organizational techniques were employed, labeled by Cole and Lyman as " 'the Fort Leavenworth' style of charts, reports, and military-style briefings all the way down to the local level."[73] The resulting administration has been described as a "mature, complex, efficient, and powerful organization, while other political and social institutions remain in a state of under-development."[74] If this assessment is accurate, it indicates a typical state of imbalance to be expected in such a political regime.

Bureaucratic Elite Systems Replacing a Traditional Elite

In a small number of instances, a current bureaucratic elite regime has directly replaced a traditional regime without a substantial inter-vening period of colonialism, although the country may have been for a time in the status of a protectorate or mandated territory under one of the major powers. These regimes have in common a necessity to adapt to their modernizing objectives the political and administra-tive structures which they inherited, but their approaches to doing this may vary considerably. In most cases, transition to the present regime has taken place since the end of World War II; some of these regimes are quite new and not yet firmly established.

In Afghanistan (1973) and Ethiopia (1974), monarchies with traditional characteristics have recently been overthrown by military coups and replaced by governments with collective military leadership showing little inclination to share power with civilian elements. Particularly in Ethiopia, the military regime has been beset with problems of shifts within the core leadership group, internal disorder, and revolt in the province of Eritrea.

Iraq in 1958, Syria in 1963, and Libya in 1969 likewise have all deposed monarchs, replacing them with military regimes which have espoused revolutionary ideology, advocated Arab unity and opposition to Israel, sponsored official parties which appear to be largely window dressing, and engaged in a moderate sharing of power with nonmilitary officials.

Thailand is an outstanding example of regimes of this type, with some features that are unique.[75]   One of the very few ancient kingdoms managing to survive without being colonized, Thailand has at the same time borrowed heavily from the Western powers. The closest parallel is probably Japan. The resulting amalgam is best described as a bureaucratic polity under "predatory military rule," with a figurehead monarchy which serves a legitimizing role. "Among Third World countries," according to Welch and Smith, "the Thai polity and its participation pattern of civilian–military relations are in many ways highly anomalous." This praetorian political system is one in which "military factions and personal rivalries constitute the crucial factors in governmental change," with political competition limited to a narrowly restricted elite group while the mass of the population remains politically passive.[76]

The Chakkri reformation which took place in what was then Siam during the middle and late nineteenth century was primarily a response to the threat of British and French colonialism. This move- ment of adaptive modernization was led by two remarkable Siamese kings, Mongkut (Rama IV) and Chulalongkorn (Rama V). They sponsored programs of education abroad for young Thais, including commoners as well as members of the nobility. Military personnel were among those receiving foreign training. As a result, by the 1930s "a surplus of able young men, imbued with Western liberal thinking and anxious for a more influential role in government" had materialized. They "had absorbed much of Western liberalism and democracy and had become increasingly discontent with the anachronism of absolute monarchy."[77] Finding upon their return home that members of the royal and princely families continued to hold a monopoly on top posts and to control the decision-making process, these Western-trained civilian and military officials were ripe for bringing about political change.

In 1932 the absolute monarchy was overthrown by a bloodless coup d'etat, a constitutional monarch was substituted, and political power passed from the king and a small number of royal princes to a middle class group of military men and civilians. This new political elite has maintained control for nearly five decades despite a bewildering succession of coups and countercoups as factional strength has shifted. The coup d'etat has become the usual means for transferring political power. Neher suggests several reasons for the coup phenomenon. "Since high political posts are held by only a very few people and since governmental participation is concentrated in the bureaucracy, it is possible to dominate the entire political system merely by controlling the bureaucratic structure. And, since extra bureaucratic institutions have been inconsequential, they are easily bypassed. In addition, the fact that Bangkok is the nation's only major city considerably eases the logistical problems in carrying out a coup. Finally, Thailand has been independent of foreign influence that opposes the means or the results of coups d'etat."[78]

The monarchy continues to serve a legitimizing function, despite being reduced to symbolic rather than active participation. "The continuing importance and inherent power of the monarchy in Thai politics," according to Morell, "place distinct constraints on the military, limiting the degree to which a military leader can exercise national charisma and rendering the armed forces liable to the palace for continuing recognition of their legitimate political role."[79] However, Neher notes that the direct impact of the monarchy on politics has been slight, as evidenced "by the king's inability to prevent coups d'etat and by his silence on issues before the government. His indirect influence is difficult to assess, although the various governments have hesitated to set forth any program that would contravene the values of the king. Thai leaders have not been willing to precipitate a confrontation between themselves and the monarchy, and in that sense the king acts as a moderating influence."[80]

During most of the period since 1932, Thailand has had a constitutional facade of a parliamentary system with occasional elections in which political parties are allowed to compete. Elections in Thailand, however, are not held for the purpose of permitting changes in the government, but "are held when the ruling groups become convinced that elections will enhance their power."[81] Political parties have been generally ineffectual and at times outlawed. Few nongovernmental interest groups exist. "Apart from the commercial and business elites, whose influence in politics is expressed through corrupt linkages to civil service and military bureaucrats, private organizations such as interest groups and political parties have only a minor role.[82]

Except for brief intervals, the longest being from 1973 to 1976, the ruling military-civilian establishment has remained firmly in control, although there have been tentative steps toward experimentation with a less authoritarian style of government. For example, under a new constitution promulgated in 1968 martial law was lifted and limited parliamentary government was permitted, resulting in the election to all the seats in the House of Representatives from major urban centers of candidates of the opposition Democratic Party over candidates of the officially sponsored United Thai People's Party. Because of its electoral strength elsewhere, the existing government under Prime Minister Thanom was able to stay in power, however, and early in 1971 Thanom brought this more open period of political competition to an abrupt end by suspending the constitution, dissolving the legislature, and banning all political parties except for a new government-sponsored party. Morell attributes this action primarily to aggressive parliamentary activity on a number of fronts, which "proved a great annoyance to the military elite and its bureaucratic allies. It was a threat to the elite's continued ability to unilaterally make and implement decisions, a role to which they were not only accustomed, but which they considered their right and private business. . . . For a while, the open political system was able to operate on bureaucratic inertia and military tolerance, while leaders relied on cooptation, corruption, and traditional patron-client relationships to keep parliamentary interference at a manageable level; but by 1971 the pendulum of Thai politics had swung back again."[83]

The most recent attempt to expand popular control over the bureaucratic elite came as the aftermath of student demonstrations late in 1973 which led to the downfall of the Thanom government and the appointment as prime minister of the rector of Thammasat University. These events led to the calling of a constitutional convention and the promulgation of another constitution in 1974, followed by elections in 1975 in which a large number of highly fragmented parties competed. Two short-lived coalition governments followed before another election was held early in 1976, which again failed to reduce the multiplicity of parties represented in the legislature or provide a base for a governing coalition acceptable to the military. After another coup in late 1976, a military-dominated government was installed which in turn was ousted by a coup led by its own defense minister a year later, resulting in the eighth change of government in four years, and apparently further establishing the pattern of power transfer by coup as the means of replacing one clique with another, without moving toward an alternative to elitist military rule.

At least for the near future, political competition in Thailand is likely to follow the pattern described by Welch and Smith, "restricted to a very narrow elite, whose members share a substantial consensus regarding the political structures and values that uphold the status quo," and with cleavages within the elite tending to be based on "struggles between personal cliques for power, wealth, and status, rather than on conflicting political goals or differences in ideology."[84] Dissident political forces will continue to be subject to firm government controls, with those attempting to organize opposition to the government being repressed, "often through bureaucratic harassment or withholding of favors, sometimes more harshly through exile or imprisonment. Potential dissidents generally have preferred to allow themselves to be co-opted into the government bureaucracy, or have entered academic life, or in some cases have accepted exile."[85] Whatever prospects there may be for gradual transition from military rule seem to be dependent on two conditions—the strengthening of civilian institutions to reduce the factionalism and bickering which result in political instability, and arrangements which will allow the military leaders who are accustomed to political roles to continue as participants in policy formulation although in a less dominant capacity. "It seems clear," according to Morell, "that mechanisms of military participation must exist if the transition process is to lead to long-term restructuring of the political process. If the military is excluded from participation in political decision-making, it will almost certainly take advantage of its formidable experience in coercing its opponents and its high level of organization and discipline to reestablish control."[86] Whether or not the military's political authority gradually diminishes, the Thai political leadership is almost sure to maintain a paternalistic attitude toward the public, with few channels of accountablity to the society as a whole.

The pattern of Thai administration within this political environment was determined more by reforms set in motion by King Chulalongkorn in 1892 than by changes following the 1932 revolution. He undertook to transform the traditional system by creating functionally specialized ministries in the European manner and by shifting to a salaried officialdom carefully selected from noble families, trained at home and abroad, and systematically assigned during their service careers. Lines of continuity to the existing administrative structure and the current bureaucracy are remarkably direct.

The executive branch of the Thai government is headed by the prime minister, who wields immense authority as leader of the military as well as the cabinet, and who himself has been a military officer in most instances. Under the prime minister in the cabinet are a dozen ministers heading the major government agencies, the most important of which are the Defense Ministry and the Ministry of Interior (controlling local administration and the police force). Each ministry has an undersecretary, who is the top ranking civil service official. Directors general in turn are in charge of departments within each ministry, which are further subdivided into divisions and sections in a highly rationalized scheme of organization. Nevertheless, observers report that administrative coordination has proved difficult to achieve. The system continues to be plagued by "ministerial and departmental competition, duplication of effort, and lack of cooperation in long-term planning."[87] This is in part due to the operation of the clique phenomenon in Thai politics, which places a premium on solidification of the power position of the dominant clique. Confidants of the clique leader are appointed to the important cabinet posts and then given considerable autonomy in operation. This process of clique solidification "amounts to a 'feudalization' of the government administration, with each important member of the clique being conceded a virtual free rein in directing the affairs of his particular sector of the bureaucracy."[88]

The Thai civil service staffing these ministries consisted in the early 1970s of approximately 260,000 regular officials organized in five hierarchical levels, or classes, with over 80 percent of the civil servants in the lowest of these classes, and only about 5 percent in the top three classes, which include those serving as section chiefs up to the small number who are undersecretaries of ministries or the even smaller handful who succeed in joining the inner core of the government by becoming cabinet ministers. Except for those in the lowest class, these officials are usually college graduates, selected on a competitive basis. The prestige of the service remains high. Advancement depends very much on the approval of an official's superior in the administrative hierarchy. The adequacy of pay rates has been severely depressed by inflation, but fringe benefits are good. Disciplinary action against an official is rare. A civil service career offers status and security, plus the remote chance of breaking into the inner circle of the political elite.

Behavior patterns in the Thai bureaucracy reflect general cultural traits in the society such as deference to authority and stress on proper superior–subordinate relationships. Siffin suggests that the bureaucracy should be viewed as a social system which provides a framework for the behavior of its members. The dominant value orientations of the Thai bureaucrats are not productivity, rationality, and efficiency. He identifies them as hierarchical status; personalism, or "the reliance upon personal relationships and personal concerns as primary bases for behavior within the system"; and security, or "the desire to preserve one's membership in the system."[89] Bureaucratic actions are intended to support these primary values, not the secondary ones of providing goods and services for the general public in an efficient manner. The procurement, allocation, and utilization of resources by the bureaucracy take place in a context which emphasizes the primary rather than the secondary values.

Authority in such a system does not conform closely to impersonal legal-rational patterns; it "remains essentially personal and status-derived."[90] Siffin stresses that authoritativeness in the Thai bureaucracy is hierarchical, that status in the system is expressed by rank, but that these concepts do not necessarily conform to expectations taken from classical models of bureaucracy. "Authority goes with rank, and rank is to a very great degree a personal thing. Thus subordinates are subject to superiors in a range of relationships not limited to 'official business.' They may serve drinks at his parties; they may even help him make money through non-official talents or connections . . . ; certainly they may play mirror to the Narcissism of the boss to a degree uncommon in an egalitarian context."[91] At the same time, the authority of rank is limited in many ways that protect the subordinate against demands not socially acceptable. The total pattern of behavior is more concerned with maintenance of proper personal relationships in the social system than with productive output. Hence, there is "little of the tension between the formal and the informal which is characteristic of output-oriented Western systems."[92] The Thai bureaucracy is not subject to great internal stress; it is well adapted to its environment.

Civil bureaucrats in Thailand have been successfully brought under control by the military. This has been accomplished "by assignment of military officers to crucial positions of authority over civilians and by the continual process of coopting the bureaucrats to work amiably and effectively for the military regime," as well as "through the assignment of supporters or relatives to important subordinate positions, through periodic rotation of potential civilian competitors, and through fragmentation of power and responsibility among various civil agencies."[93] Civilians have normally administered the nation for the military, but they have also shared in the advantages that accrue to the ruling bureaucratic elite in the absence of effective external controls.

In his study of political development in Thailand, Riggs concludes that here is an almost classical case of a "bureaucratic polity." The interests of the bureaucrats themselves shape the organization of government so as to reflect their needs and purposes as its official beneficiaries.[94]   Welch and Smith agree that there is a "distinctly amoral character to the pattern of elite competition in Thailand. The government's civil and military bureaucracies exist essentially to serve their own interests, since no outside social forces are powerful enough to threaten the government with political sanctions and thereby force it to recognize a larger moral purpose for its existence."[95]

Despite the tensions which have built up in recent years, the evidence still backs up the prediction made by Riggs that "the Thai political system will continue without major change as a relatively well-integrated and hence stable bureaucratic polity, a prismatic society in equilibrium, at a low level of industrialization and economic growth and an intermediate level of power distribution between the democratic and authoritarian extremes."[96]   The process of modernization has permitted successful response to the impact of the West, but in the transition the official class has become the ruling class, largely self-recruited from the upper reaches of the military and civilian bureaucracies. This pattern of development has not been balanced; a rapid increase in bureaucratic capabilities has not been accompanied by a compensatory growth of institutions, outside the bureaucracy, able to control it. The resulting polity corresponds closely to Riggs' model of "prismatic" society.

Bureaucratic Elite Systems Successor to a Colonial Tradition

In other regimes with civil–military bureaucratic elites, a pervasive background factor is a prolonged colonial era during which the colonial power was able to implant its political and administrative institutions in the subject territory so firmly as to provide the decisive point of reference for developments following national independence, even though over time significant modifications may have been made in the initial institutional framework. In most of these cases, continuity has proved to be greater in the administrative than in the political sphere, with bureaucratic elites formed during the colonial period gradually taking over political control in what were immediately after independence polyarchal competitive political regimes. Several former British colonies—such as Burma, Pakistan, Ghana, and Nigeria—best fit this description, but it applies also to some former French colonies such as Chad, Mali, Niger, and the Republic of the Congo. For two illustrations from different geographic regions, we will use Pakistan and Ghana.

Pakistan became an independent nation in 1947 when the Indian subcontinent was partitioned upon withdrawal of British sovereignty.[97] Faced from the beginning with tremendous problems stemming from such circumstances as the dislocations of partition and the resulting two-way flow of refugees, the geographic and linguistic division of East and West Pakistan, the lack of a unified leadership, and the low level of capacity of the population for political participation, Pakistan has gone through a series of political crises. The most traumatic episode was, of course, the outbreak of war with India late in 1971 and the concurrent civil war between West and East Pakistan, which led to the emergence of former East Pakistan as the nation of Bangladesh, formally recognized as independent by Pakistan in 1974.

Turbulence in Pakistani internal politics has led to alternating periods of parliamentary or presidential rule and military rule, with the latter being imposed most recently again in 1977. The Muslim League, which had led the campaign for separatism from India, began to disintegrate shortly after independence. It had built up a powerful mass following to support the idea of a Muslim state, but had not constructed an effective organization able to survive the early death of its leader, Mohammed Ali Jinnah. Splits within the league and the rise of new political factions soon produced semichaotic conditions in the government. A constitution was not adopted until 1956, and the parliamentary system it set up was short-lived. In 1958, the army took control of the country with General Ayub Khan designated first as prime minister and later as president. The military regime proclaimed martial law, outlawed political parties, and abrogated the 1956 constitution. As spokesman for the army, General Khan announced that it had taken over reluctantly to prevent political collapse, and that the ultimate aim was "to restore democracy but of the type that our people can understand and work." Subsequently, this took the form of a system of "basic democracies," with direct election at the lowest level of councils representing about 10,000 persons, and indirect election of provincial and national assemblies. A new constitution was promulgated in

1962, setting up a presidential form of government and providing for
indirect election of the president, with the first election scheduled
for 1965. The ban on political activity was partially lifted. The
1965 election left Ayub Khan in control of the government, heading
a regime that was in power for a total of eleven years. His downfall
in 1969 led to an assumption of power by the commander in chief of
the army, who declared martial law, suspended the constitution, and
dissolved the national and provincial assemblies.

     This military government did establish a timetable for a gradual
return to civilian rule under a parliamentary system, reserving the
right to "authenticate" a new constitution before it could take
effect. General elections held in 1970 resulted in capture of most of
the seats in the National Assembly from West Pakistan by the
Pakistan People's Party and in East Pakistan by the Aswami League.
The election results heightened rather than decreased the tensions
between civilian and military–bureaucratic leaders, and between the
civilian leaders in East and West Pakistan, leading the following year
to partition of Pakistan and the formation of Bangladesh as a new
nation. Out of this turmoil came the adoption eventually in 1973 of
a constitution which returned to a parliamentary form of government. Civilian rule in what had been West Pakistan was restored
under Prime Minister Zulfikar Ali Bhutto as leader of the Pakistan
People's Party. Bhutto, who had served previously during 1971 to
1973 as president and chief martial law administrator, survived as
head of a constitutional civilian government until he was toppled in
mid 1977 by a coup in which the army seized power following a
disputed election earlier in the year which was won by Bhutto's
Pakistan People's Party but which opposition parties claimed had
been rigged. The coup came after a breakdown in talks between
Bhutto and opposition leaders about the holding of another election.
Again martial law was imposed, legislative assemblies were dissolved,
and a four-man military council took over, with the army chief of
staff as martial law administrator. After an initial announcement
that national elections would be held later in 1977, the military
government subsequently postponed them indefinitely, and banned
all political activity. Whether and when Pakistan may again restore
a nonmilitary government remains uncertain.

     Perhaps the alternation between military and civilian regimes is
of relatively minor importance in Pakistani politics. According to
Robert LaPorte, political instability has been marked in Pakistan in
"a formal, constitutional sense," but in "a nonlegal, nonconstitution-
al sense," the history of the country "reveals a steady, constant

evolution of military-bureaucratic decision-making (resource allocation for the political system as a whole)" which began shortly after
partition of Pakistan from India.[98] A military-bureaucratic coalition
elite emerged immediately after independence in 1947, replacing the
British colonial rulers, and has maintained its power position ever
since without substantial interruption. "In Pakistan, political power
has been concentrated on the bureaucratic-military elite who were
the successors of the British raj. . . . The main beneficiaries of independence have been (a) the bureaucracy and military themselves who
have enjoyed lavish perquisites and have grown in number, (b) the
new class of industrial capitalists, (c) professional people whose
numbers have grown rapidly and (d) landlords in West Pakistan."[99]

Even though the institutional bases of power may have broadened somewhat in recent years, the military and civilian bureaucracies in combination have remained dominant, but with variations in
their relationships in the coalition. The top level military officials
and higher civil servants trained under British sponsorship had a
definite advantage over their political colleagues following independence. As Sayeed points out, "it is seldom realized that the bureaucratic and army machines that (the British) left behind . . . had been
far better trained than the political leaders, who had had only a
smattering of, and often interrupted, political experience."[100] This,
combined with political apathy and lack of opportunity for participation by the bulk of the population, has given bureaucrats the
upper hand. Furthermore, military officials have increasingly been
able to assert themselves over their civilian counterparts.

The higher civil service of Pakistan, despite its somewhat
diminished role, has had a remarkable part to play under all of the
postindependence regimes. It is generally credited with having made
government operation possible at the start. "The bureaucracy stood
when other segments of society faltered and collapsed. It conducted
the business of government. It helped forge a new state."[101] During
the years prior to 1958, the career bureaucrats were largely responsible for keeping things going. They continued to carry the main
burden of administration under Ayub Khan. While Bhutto was in
office, he deliberately attempted to reduce their influence, and was
partially successful. With the reimposition of martial law, presumably civilian bureaucrats will re-emerge as junior partners to the
current military leaders.

The core of this civil bureaucracy has been a small compact
group of officers composing the Civil Service of Pakistan (CSP). The
CSP is the successor in Pakistan of the Indian Civil Service which had

been the main instrument of British rule in preindependence India. It has retained much closer ties with the British tradition than has been the case in India since 1947. More British expatriate officials were retained to serve the new government. Until 1960, CSP probationers were still being sent to England for further training after a year at the Pakistan Civil Service Academy in Lahore. Entry continued to be by competitive examination for men twenty-one to twenty-four years of age on a highly selective basis designed to preserve the elitist character of the service, despite the acute shortage of managerial personnel. In 1963, the CSP consisted of 410 persons out of a total government civilian employment of about two-thirds of a million and a national population approaching 100 million. Prior to the 1971 war, the number came close to 500. Later the total was reduced to about 300, due mainly to the elimination of those who came from or were suspected of loyalty to East Pakistan.

Control over the CSP has been centered in the Federal Public Service Commission and the Establishment Division of the Cabinet Secretariat, mostly staffed with senior CSP officers, so that the CSP has been in effect self-governed, handling most decisions on selection, training, assignment, and discipline of its members. The pay and privileges that go with CSP status are exceedingly generous, carried over mostly intact from British times, but with an even higher relative social status. Ahmad alleges that "far from being a privileged and secluded community as in the British period, the Civil Service in Pakistan tended to become a part of the wealthy class, leading a life of splendour and luxury completely out of tune with the general standards of living in the country."[102] With promotion based primarily on seniority, and disciplinary action rare, a CSP career has generally been secure as well as prestigious. For reasons such as these, Goodnow concluded that many of the institutional characteristics of the CSP are inherited and that its "performance, strategy, and tactics . . . can be viewed generally as acts of imitation."[103]

The suitability of these arrangements for the needs of independent Pakistan has come under frequent question by both outside and inside observers who doubt that a system devised for control by an alien power, successful though it was for that purpose, also fits current needs. The partial detachment of the higher bureaucracy from the society, its security in insecure surroundings, enabled it to move ahead when preservation of order was the prime requirement, but provoked hostility and resentment from leaders of the embryonic political parties. For their part, the CSP members have taken a dim view of politicians. Because of this antagonism, the CSP has fared less well during periods when Pakistan has not been under martial law rule. Even under Ayub, minor steps were taken to curb the CSP, including dismissal of about a dozen CSP officers, and appointment of a commission to study organization and pay issues in the civil service, but the protective constitutional gurantees provided for the CSP were continued. After Ayub's departure, the interim military government replaced CSP officers with military officers in many instances, so that when Bhutto became president in 1971 the CSP was in a vulnerable position. The electoral victory which Bhutto's Pakistan People's Party had won in 1970 gave him a base of political power not dependent on the military and civilian bureaucrats or others in the more traditional political elite. "He could fashion his regime without the constraints of the previous regimes. This permitted him great flexibility, allowing the removal of military leaders who helped bring him to power and the refashioning of the bureaucracy for his own political ends."[104]

During his six years in power, Bhutto undertook to reform the civil service and to establish political control over both the military and civilian bureaucracies. Early in his tenure, he is reported to have dismissed 1300 civil servants, including CSP members. He restricted the role of higher civil servants in national decision-making, using them as information sources and presenters of alternative options, but reserving final decisions for political leaders. The constitution adopted in 1973 eliminated the earlier constitutional guarantees afforded the civil service. Most important, he set up an administrative reforms commission which recommended that the CSP be merged into a broader "unified service" which would dilute its elitist nature and eliminate its monopoly on the most prestigious positions. This "disestablishment" of the CSP was approved, but its long range impact is uncertain because of the downfall of the Bhutto regime. It is too early to tell what the policy of the new military government will be. Without doubt, during the Bhutto era the CSP suffered in prestige and status. LaPorte found indications that morale in the CSP dropped noticeably, that junior officers began thinking of other options, and that the "cream" of Pakistani youth was no longer as much attracted to civil service careers.[105] All of these trends may be halted or reversed with the return to military rule.

Higher Pakistani civil servants have probably felt more comfortable under military than civilian governments, because their vital role is recognized and there is less of what they might see as petty political interference. As long as they are responsive on a few key matters of importance to the military leaders, and acknowledge their secondary place, their hold on most of the policy-making positions in the governmental structure is not likely to be threatened. As Goodnow anticipated prior to 1958, extended periods of military rule have made the higher civil service and higher military ranks almost indistinguishable. The two groups confront jointly a dilemma he compares to that which the British faced in India. Success in carrying out a program of national development calls for strengthening political and related institutions, the very institutions that may later challenge the existing monopoly of political and administrative power.[106] Whether that kind of self-denial is possible is the crucial issue in such a bureaucratic elitist regime.

The political history of Ghana has many similarities to that of Pakistan, with the additional feature in Ghana of a period during which there was a single dominant-party regime; in both Ghana and Pakistan the military and civilian bureaucracies have occupied crucial roles in the postindependence era.[107] The first West African country to gain independence, Ghana started in 1957 with a parliamentary political system on the British model. Kwame Nkrumah, who had led the struggle for national autonomy, became prime minister under a cabinet system of government, with opposition parties well represented in parliament. Within five years, a "cult of personality" had emerged which bestowed the title of Osagyefo the President upon Nkrumah under a republican constitution. A one-party system was in operation, with Nkrumah announcing that "The Convention People's Party is a powerful force, more powerful, indeed, than anything that has yet appeared in the history of Ghana. It is a uniting force that guides and pilots the nation. . . . Its supremacy cannot be challenged. The Convention People's Party is Ghana, and Ghana is the Convention People's Party."[108] Every aspect of social life became politicized in support of what the party program called "The Socialist Revolution," which had for its main objectives "work and happiness for all the people." Apter viewed the effort as a uniquely Ghanaian blend, consisting of a national form of traditionalism in the name of socialism. "The nation replaced the ethnic community. The Presidential-monarch replaced the chief. . . . Ideology became a political religion increasingly intolerant of all other religions, monopolistic, expressed through the militant elect of the party."[109]

Gradually Nkrumah lost his charisma and the party fell apart. "By 1965," according to Apter, "the party consisted of vast networks of committees which did not meet, organizations which failed to function, and personal manipulations which aroused mutual suspicion, mistrust, and recrimination."[110]   Despite the fact that Nkrumah was made party chairman for life, held a national referendum that made Ghana officially a one-party state, and in various ways attempted to increase his authority, political opposition grew and the economic situation worsened.   The outcome was a skillfully planned and well-executed bloodless coup staged by army and police leaders in 1966 when Nkrumah was out of the country.   An eight-man National Liberation Council was set up, headed at first by Major General Ankrah and later by Brigadier Afrifa.   The ouster of Nkrumah was justified on the basis of his regime's contribution to national "maladministration, mismanagement, the loss of individual freedom, and economic chaos."[111]

The military regime discredited Nkrumah, purged his followers, launched an austerity economic program, sponsored the drafting of a new constitution, and promised a prompt return to civilian rule. This was done following elections in 1969, which resulted in the designation of Kofi A. Busia, a civilian, as prime minister—first under a three-man presidential commission of NLC members and later under another civilian as head of state.   The Busia government lasted only two-and-a-half years, however, before it was ousted following another seizure of control by the military early in 1972.   The leader of this coup was then Colonel (later General) I. K. Acheampong, who served as head of state and chairman of the Supreme Military Council.   This military regime dissolved the National Assembly, formally banned all political parties, and suspended the constitution. Acheampong in turn was forced to resign in mid 1978.   His replacement, Lieutenant General Fred W. Akuffo, pledged on behalf of the ruling supreme military council that power would be handed over to a popularly elected government on July 1, 1979.   Apter may be correct in stating that "Ghana is the one African country with a genuine parliamentary experience,"[112] but bureaucratic elite rule now seems to be firmly established, despite continued lip service to the tenet that the military and political spheres should be separate, and an actual return to parliamentary government appears to be problematic at best.

In all of these Ghanaian civilian and military regimes, the civil bureaucracy in place when British colonialism ended has maintained a stance of indispensability but not dominance.   The British civil service model still formally characterizes public administration in Ghana, referred to by Price as an exceptional instance of "institutional

emulation."[113]   Many of the present senior bureaucrats in Ghana
began their careers in the British colonial civil service, and were
trained under Britishers. Even after independence, many British
expatriots continued to man the upper echelons of the civil service,
which was not fully "Africanized" until the mid 1960s.

The civil service has been able to retain much of its inherited
status and prestige, despite efforts to curb it when civilian politicians
have controlled the government. A split between the political and
bureaucratic elites began in Ghana before independence was finally
won and continued into the period of single-party dominance,
when one observer wrote that "The people who staff the bureaucracy
are not representative of those who control or support the party that
controls the government."[114]   The bureaucrats came from higher
social status groups, were more Westernized, and were less reform-
minded than the leaders of the Convention People's Party. Accordingly, the CPP leadership viewed the higher civil service, along with
the university community, as a possible source of disaffection, and
took precautionary steps. A British-modeled public service commission was replaced by a civil service commission with largely advisory
powers. The 1960 constitution vested full control of the civil service
in the president, including "appointment, promotion, transfer,
termination of appointment, dismissal, and disciplinary control."
The CPP program called for a complete revamping of the civil service
to release it from colonial restraints and mentality and relate its
methods to Ghanaian needs and conditions, but there was more
rhetoric than accomplishment. The actual steps taken were not
drastic. A new school for civil servants was set up, partly to instill
new attitudes, but also in recognition of the mounting need for
managerial personnel. Membership in the government-sponsored
trade union organization was made mandatory for all but the higher
civil servants, but they were denied the right to strike and the government was not bound by an agreement made with their unions.

The basic fact seems to have been that the party and the civil
service needed one another, and Nkrumah needed them both. "What
kept the system going," as Apter comments, "was the quiet alliance
between two often hostile forces, the party bureaucracy and the
civil service. If they had mutual contempt for one another, both
recognized that they were essential for the running of day-to-day
affairs."[115]   During the time Nkrumah maintained firm control of
the state and party apparatus, the career officials remained politically
passive and obeyed their political masters, but they retained essential
governmental powers.

During its brief time in power, the Busia government ousted several hundred public servants for what appeared to be political and ethnic considerations rather than faults in administrative conduct. The military regimes, including the current one, although sporadically displaying their power to humiliate or discipline civil servants incurring the displeasure of military officials, have not undertaken to disturb civil service prerogatives, which seem to be firmly established. Indeed, Price believes that it is "doubtful whether the contemporary political leadership in Ghana . . . would have sufficient political support to engage in a drastic restructuring of the existing 'scheme of service' in public bureaucracy, even if it were so inclined."[116]

Ghana, like other new states in Africa, is still operating basically with inherited colonial administrative institutions.[117] The civil service, as the most significant of these institutions, has retained the aura of the colonial service without conforming to reasonable expectations as to performance in the new national setting. In his study of Ghanaian bureaucracy, Price concludes that "administrative performance suffers . . . because of institutional malintegration, the existence of structurally differentiated organizations in an unsupportive sociocultural environment."[118] He argues that "status" institutionalization has taken place much more thoroughly than "role" institutionalization, with the result that "organizationally dependable role behavior" by Ghanaian civil servants is unlikely because of the social pressure placed on them. Behavior that leads to the accomplishment of organizational goals is not apt to bring social approval in the environment of a traditional African society.

The recurring issue of corruption, for example, may be explainable by social expectations based on the "exalted status" inherited by contemporary Ghanaian senior bureaucrats from their British predecessors, which implies "great expectations" as well. A senior civil service post "brings with it greatly increased influence, obligation, and responsibility within one's extended family. The obligations and responsibilities carry a heavy material burden. Not only will the African civil servant be expected to provide financial assistance to his family . . . but . . . he is also likely to be expected to maintain the material aspects of a European 'life-style' [e.g., a Mercedes-Benz, a Western-style house, imported European clothing]." These socially appropriate symbols of status and family financial obligations "will entail great expense and will tend to outdistance what is financially available to the civil servant through his salary," leading to widespread administrative corruption.[119]

In summary, regimes with bureaucratic elites successor to a colonial tradition have a historical legacy and a reference point for behavior, but these are not sufficient to ensure either balanced political development or goal-oriented administrative performance.

Bureaucratic Elite Systems with Corporate-Technocratic Orientation

Some nations with bureaucratic elite regimes, particularly in Latin America, reveal distinctive characteristics which have been labeled as "corporate-technocratic," calling for special attention because of their historical origin in Iberic-Latin tradition and their consequences for the conduct of present-day governance.[120]

This corporate-technocratic orientation is composed of two complementary elements: "corporatism" and "technocracy." Corporatism refers to a particular pattern of relationships between the state and civil society which is the product of a long-standing traditional view that the state should play the central role in mediating among competing groups and interests in society.[121] The result is "a system of interest and/or attitude representation, a particular model or ideal-typical institutional arrangement for linking the associationally organized interests of civil society with the decisional structures of the state."[122] More specifically, corporatism provides a framework for interest representation in which "the constituent units are organized into a limited number of singular, compulsory, noncompetitive, hierarchically ordered and functionally differentiated categories, recognized or licensed (if not created) by the state and granted a deliberate representational monopoly within their respective categories in exchange for observing certain controls on their selection of leaders and articulation of demands and supports."[123] Robert R. Kaufman describes these corporatist systems as "vertically segmented societies, encapsulating individuals within a network of legally-defined guilds and corporations which derive their legitimacy from and in turn are integrated by a dominant bureaucratic center."[124]

The element of technocracy consists of recognition of "the need to cope with the larger questions of development, conflict, and change from a technical and/or scientific perspective," with the technocratic argument becoming "the very source of legitimation for political control and domination in the name of expertise and science."[125]

The all-inclusive corporate-technocratic state which has emerged with this combined orientation generates, according to Tapia-Videla, "a dramatic and profound transformation of traditional political structures, institutions, and the processes and mechanisms for interest articulation and representation." Such a regime is determined to extend the power of the state over major societal forces. To ensure its preponderance, the state must redefine "the basic social alliance supporting its operations on the basis of a consensus on a dependent neo-capitalist model of development" which in turn requires a state that is "basically authoritarian, whose major focus for legitimization derives from its ability to facilitate this new social alliance and the notion that political, social, and economic problems should (and can) be handled by technical considerations."[126]

The consequence of corporatism and technocracy as a composite ideological rationale is acceptance of the goal that the polity should be depoliticized. The "death of politics" occurs in these polities because the corporatist tradition, "when blended with the technocratic ideology, tends to produce a vision in which the state becomes an organic whole with the society. The new regimes, representing by their own assertion the general interests of the nation, through the careful scientific and technical assessment of the available alternatives become *the* only political actors to arrive at *the* adequate solution. It is contended that the dominant group alone is able to organize and foster balanced economic development."[127]

The dominant ruling elite in such a corporate-technocratic state is ordinarily a combination of military and civilian officials, with the former usually but not necessarily having the upper hand. Whatever the mix, strong ties must exist between the military and civilian bureaucracies to provide the regime with the necessary mastery of scientific and technical knowledge and with the means to maintain power required for institutionalizing the state's expanded scope of control.

The higher level civil bureaucracy, particularly in areas of technocratic expertise, occupies a strategic position. The technocrat becomes the center of attention, being relied on by the regime not only for success in the pursuit of developmental goals but also as a valuable source of legitimacy. Technocrats as a type generally are ready to accept the political ascendancy of a military–civilian coalition with an authoritarian style of rule, in view of the wide range of responsibilities placed on their shoulders and the commensurate rewards made available to them because of their important role.

Corporate-technocratic regime leadership must undertake major adjustments in previous practices as to functioning of the public bureaucracy. In earlier "populist-oriented" regimes, usual functions of Latin American bureaucracies included furnishing a source of patronage for political groups in power, offering support for the regime, providing a major employment outlet for the relief of unemployment and underemployment problems in the society, and acting as a channel for the articulation and representation of interests. Under these circumstances, "while the bureaucracy provides the ruling groups with patronage and support for the regime and the middle-groups with employment, the national community receives in turn only a minimum level of essential services, as compared with its size and cost."[128]   This pattern must be modified enough to produce the technical capabilities in the bureaucracy essential for carrying out the expanded oversight and regulatory activities assumed by the corporate-technocratic state.

Hence emphasis must be placed on "the critical role of expertise, depersonalized leadership, and the development of a new bureaucratic ethos: one stressing the corporate ideology that aims at achieving a balanced interdependence between competing policy and issue areas."[129]   Among other reforms, this calls for a technocratic redefinition of the role of universities, converting them into "knowledge factories," concentrating on the training of a "profession stratum technocratically oriented by the criteria of apolitization, specialization and efficiency," and expected to "produce scientific and technical know-how determined by the necessities of the dominant style of development."[130]

Although political demobilization and increased reliance on an overhauled bureaucracy are prime objectives, they can be only partially realized. Political competition continues to take place, but it occurs in a segmented, subdued fashion within the parameters allowed by the soldiers and technocrats who are in control. The bureaucracy is only partially capable of responding to the new demands put upon it. Therefore, these corporate-technocratic regimes have only limited success in their efforts to form "strong and relatively autonomous governmental structures that seek to impose on the society a system of interest representation based on enforced limited pluralism," and in their attempts to "eliminate spontaneous interest articulation and establish a limited number of authoritatively recognized groups that interact with the government in defined and regularized ways."[131]   Because of their authoritarian style of rule, these regimes tend to resort to repressive measures when thwarted in getting conformity to their expectations as to permissible group interactions in the system. A common resulting pattern is alternation of permissiveness and tightened restraints, depending on assessment by the bureaucratic elite as to how much progress is being made as measured by the key twin criteria of corporatism and technocracy.

Undoubtedly many countries in Latin America and elsewhere exhibit corporate and/or technocratic tendencies in their contemporary political regimes. Malloy, Tapia-Videla, and other recent commentators are inclined to analyze numerous Latin American and some non-Latin American countries in these terms. For our purposes, only a few of the most clear-cut examples need to be identified. Obvious candidates would appear to be Brazil since 1964, Peru since 1968, and the Philippines since 1972. Of these, Brazil is the most typical, with the Philippines varying from the norm in some interesting respects.

What is unusual in the Filipino case is that the bureaucratic elite regime now in power followed a period of almost three decades of political competition after independence in 1946, and that the leadership is civilian rather than military, headed by a president originally elected and then re-elected who imposed martial law as a means of moving toward what are claimed to be national objectives which stress corporate-technocratic considerations.[132]

During the years of polyarchal political competition prior to 1972, the contending Filipino political parties were personality-oriented and shifting in their leadership, but political changeover following electoral victory was a reality, with incumbent presidents usually being defeated in bids for re-election. The Philippine president during this period exerted strong leadership, but the national congress was a legitimate legislative body—not a facade—and interest groups as well as political parties were active and well organized. The civil service, although presumably protected by a comprehensive constitutional merit provision, was in fact operating under a modified patronage system. Higher civil servants were not members of a separate administrative class with cohesive traditions, common indoctrination, or a sense of corporate identity. The bureaucratic contribution to policy formulation was relatively minor, and came more from expertise in a program field of specialization, such as agriculture or public health, than from membership in an elitist bureaucratic in-group. Bureaucratic allegiances were primarily to particular subject-matter specialties or government agencies, or to political sponsors or patrons, rather than to a centralized core political leadership.

The martial law regime proclaimed late in 1972 by President Ferdinand Marcos has brought drastic alterations. Although promising that the modified parliamentary system provided for in a new constitution promulgated in 1973 will eventually be operative, Marcos has extended his term in office indefinitely, political parties are quiescent, the national legislature was suspended until the election of an interim national assembly in April 1978, major opposition leaders have been imprisoned or exiled, and the news media are under strict government control.

The Marcos regime has concentrated its efforts on the imposition of political order, coping with Moslem rebels on the southern island of Mindanao, reform of the administrative system, and attainment of economic development objectives. Unlike most elitist regimes which have replaced competitive systems, leadership is firmly in civilian hands, with the Philippine military continuing to play a secondary but essential supportive role. Corporatism of a somewhat different type than the Latin American variety has been a factor in the operating methods of the Marcos government, and great stress has been placed on the importance of technocratic and professional skills in implementing regime goals.[133]

This technocratic orientation is reflected in measures designed to strengthen bureaucratic capabilities. The civil service system has been revamped to make it more inclusive and more responsive to presidential direction. Summary disciplinary action, including dismissal, was taken early in the martial law period against numerous officials charged with corruption, incompetence, or disloyalty to the regime. Special attention has been directed at higher level civil servants, intended to enhance their professionalism and make them more "development-oriented." A Career Executive Service, patterned after the British administrative class, was created to provide a pool of career administrators available for governmentwide service, with a common training program required through a newly established Development Academy.

These indications of attachment to technocratic values, coupled with reliance on forceful maintenance of control and a record of vacillation between severe and mild measures of doing so, match the current regime in the Philippines with the basic pattern of corporate-technocratic elite systems found elsewhere, despite some unique features.

Brazil since 1964 has been governed by a military elite in collaboration with civilian bureaucrats, motivated by typical corporate-technocratic values.[134] The political history of Brazil after independence from Portugal in 1815 has included a lengthy period of monarchy during most of the nineteenth century, followed by a federal constitutional republic under which elected presidents have alternated with presidents who have been installed as the result of military intervention. In 1930 Getulio Vargas began a fifteen-year authoritarian presidency after a coup d'etat, giving way in 1945 to a period of almost two decades during which elected presidents again held office. The last of these civilian presidents was Joao Goulart, who had been elected as vice-president and took over as president in 1961 when President Janio Quadros resigned. The Goulart administration came under increasing attack for pervasive governmental corruption, pro-Communist sympathies, and inflationary economic policies. The Brazilian military overthrew it in 1964 in a nearly bloodless coup d'etat, ushering in what has now turned into a prolonged era of elitist rule of indefinite duration.

Although the military in Brazil has long been recognized as a moderating force in Brazilian society and has frequently intervened politically, military retention of political power for such a lengthy and indeterminate time span does not conform to the military's traditional role as a "moderator" among competing political factions. Backed by language in several Brazilian constitutions designating the military as a "permanent national institution specifically charged with the tasks of maintaining law and order in the country and of guaranteeing the normal functioning" of the executive, legislative, and judicial branches, it was generally conceded, according to Einaudi and Stepan, that the military "had sanction to overthrow the elected President, but not to assume political power."[135] Drury concurs that the military as an institution had considered itself "the final authority in political conflicts, charged specifically with preventing the imposition of radical solutions to political problems."[136]

Political intervention of such a limited nature, with control being passed back to civilians after military imposition of an effective compromise, is no longer considered sufficient by the post-1964 regime, which has acted on the belief that "the crisis which confronted the political system could be resolved only by an extended period of military rule during which the system would be rebuilt."[137] Even after almost fifteen years in power, the regime has made only minor and temporary concessions toward a partial restoration of normal constitutional government. The president is subject to indirect election for a five-year term by an electoral college firmly under control by the political elite. Political parties, dissolved by decree in 1965, have been allowed to reorganize, but restricted to a single government party and a single "opposition" party. When the latter party won a substantial number of national legislative seats in elections held in 1974, executive officials issued a warning that their emergency powers were still in full force. No early "return to democracy" is in sight.

The objectives of this military-backed regime have centered on political stability and economic development. The record shows that these goals have been attained, but at the price of severely restricted political competition and without a widespread sharing of economic gains among the nation's people.[138] The approach taken has been to adopt corporatist strategies for controlling the political process and to rely on *tecnicos* for progress on the economic front. Corporatism has concentrated on the dampening of lower class protest possibilities by setting up a government-manipulated system of labor organizations, or *sindicatos*, to channel labor interest-group representation. "Under the corporatist labor system," says Mericle, "labor leaders, labor organizations, and rank-and-file workers are highly susceptible to state control. Any government with the will and power to utilize fully the control apparatus has a tremendous capability to suppress, channel, and preempt labor protest. . . . Since 1964, authoritarian Brazilian governments have been virtually unrestrained in their application of the labor controls."[139] The aim of the elite for more rationalized policy-making has led to an increase in numbers and authority of technically trained administrators or *technicos* in decision-making posts where they are expected to act on technical criteria.[140] "The presence of civilian technocrats in the government since 1964 constitutes one of the principal political innovations by the military rulers. The regime's strong commitment and high priority for economic development have facilitated the entrance of this group into the ruling elite. Complete loyalty to the ideology of the regime is required as a condition to admission of all civilian technocrats, as indeed it is of all others holding high posts in the government."[141]

The Brazilian ruling elite as it now exists is described by Daland as "an essentially technocratic alliance of convenience between the old civil bureaucracy and the military bureaucracy. The two have proved compatible since they share the same basic attitudes toward the business of government."[142] Ronning and Keith add a third group—civilian politicians—to the military officers and civilian technocrats.[143] In suggesting this ruling triumvirate, however, they make clear that they consider the military contingent dominant and that the civilian politicians are the least important as wielders of power. They note that the Brazilian presidency has been held exclusively by high ranking military officers since 1964, and that the armed forces maintain a watchdog unit in each civilian ministry. The chief executive, because of the low level of allowable political activity, is able in making appointments to choose individuals "more for loyalty to the regime, competence, and technocratic expertise than from any desire to please this or that pressure group."[144] Civilian politicians are basically distrusted by the military leaders and kept in close check. Even candidates for electrive office on the ticket of ARENA, the government party, are handpicked by the president. Members of MBD (*Movimento Democratico Brasileiro*), the "opposition" party, share still less in the political system. "Excluded from the councils of government, suspected of possible subversion, and relegated to the position of a perpetual minority," their careers offer "little material or political reward, no patronage, and a questionable future."[145]

As in other corporate-technocratic regimes, the civil bureaucracy in Brazil plays an intermediate and mixed role. Civilian technocrats who are trusted by the military leaders and occupy crucial posts are themselves members of the ruling elite, but these constitute a minute fraction of the total. The vast majority of Brazilian bureaucrats certainly are not qualified to be considered technocrats, and the long-range competence of the bureaucracy to measure up to performance needs is questionable. Like its counterparts elsewhere, the Brazilian bureaucratic elite has not yet resolved the dilemma of coping with difficult national problems with inadequate available tools, despite its emphasis on corporate and technocratic approaches as the most promising ones.

Notes

1.   Milton J. Esman. "The Politics of Development Administration," in John D. Montgomery and William J. Siffin, eds., *Approaches to Development: Politics, Administration and Change* (New York: McGraw-Hill Book Company, 1966), p. 88.
2.   Manfred W. Wenner, "Saudi Arabia: Survival of Traditional Elites," pp. 157-91 in Frank Tachau, ed., *Political Elites and Political Development in the Middle East* (Cambridge: Schenkman Publishing Company, Inc., 1975), at p. 167.
3.   *Ibid.*, pp. 177-79.
4.   Helpful sources on Iran include Richard W. Gable, "Culture and Administration in Iran," *Middle East Journal* 13, No. 4 (1959): 407-21; Leonard

Binder, *Iran: Political Development in a Changing Society* (Berkeley, Calif.: University of California Press, 1962), pp. 172-44; George L. Grassmuck, *Polity, Bureaucracy and Interest Groups in the Near East and North Africa* (Bloomington, Ind.: CAG Occasional Papers, 1965); Marvin Zonis, *The Political Elite of Iran* (copyright © by Princeton University Press, Princeton Paperback, 1976); James Alban Bill, *The Politics of Iran: Groups, Classes, and Modernization* (Columbus, Ohio: Charles E. Merrill Publishing Co., 1972); and Marvin Zonis, "The Political Elite of Iran: A Second Stratum?" pp. 193-216 in Tachau, *Political Elites.*

5. Binder, *Iran*, pp. 59-60.
6. Zonis, *The Political Elite of Iran*, p. 338.
7. Zonis, "The Political Elite of Iran," in Frank Tachau, *Political Elites*, p. 203. Reprinted by permission of Princeton University Press.
8. Bill, *The Politics of Iran*, pp. 133-56.
9. Zonis, "The Political Elite of Iran," in Tachau, *Political Elites*, p. 207.
10. *Ibid.*, pp. 195-96.
11. *Ibid.*, p. 195.
12. Zonis, *The Political Elite of Iran*, p. 331.
13. *Ibid.*, p. 334.
14. Zonis, "The Political Elite of Iran," in Tachau, *Political Elites*, p. 198.
15. Ferrel Heady, "Personnel Administration in the Middle East," *Public Personnel Review* 20, No. 1 (1959): 49-55.
16. Bill, *The Politics of Iran*, pp. 53-72.
17. *Ibid.*, p. 65.
18. *Ibid.*, p. 67.
19. Zonis, *The Political Elite of Iran*, pp. 11-14.
20. *Ibid.*, p. 337.
21. Bill, *The Politics of Iran*, p. 133.
22. Zonis, *The Political Elite of Iran*, p. 18.
23. Binder, *Iran*, p. 137.
24. The Shah's 1961 Proclamation on Reform stated: "The most important categories of civil servants must be given priority and these include army, police and gendarmerie employees, schoolteachers and Ministry of Justice officials, all of whom have a specially important standing." Quoted in Grassmuck, *Polity, Bureaucracy and Interest Groups*, p. 34.
25. Zonis, *The Political Elite of Iran*, pp. 340-41.
26. James A. Bill, "Iran and the Crisis of '78," *Foreign Affairs* 57, No. 2 (Winter 1978/79): 323-42, at pp. 335, 341.
27. Gino Germani and Kalman Silvert, "Politics, Social Structure and Military Intervention in Latin America," pp. 227-48, in Wilson C. McWilliams, ed., *Garrisons and Government* (San Francisco: Chandler, 1967), at pp. 230-31.
28. This excerpt is reprinted from "Personalism and Corporatism in African Armies," by Claude E. Welch, Jr. in *Military Systems: Comparative Perspectives*, Sage Research Progress Series on War, Revolution, and Peacekeeping, Volume IV, ed. Catherine McArdle Kelleher, © 1974, p. 131, by permission of the Publishers, Sage Publications, Inc. (Beverly Hills/London).
29. *Ibid.*, pp. 132-33.

30. *Ibid.*, p. 134.
31. Nathan L. Whetten, *Guatemala: The Land and the People* (New Haven, Conn.: Yale University Press, 1961), p. 331.
32. *Ibid.*
33. Jerry L. Weaver, "Bureaucracy during a Period of Social Change: The Case of Guatemala," pp. 314-61, in Clarence E. Thurber and Lawrence S. Graham, eds., *Development Administration in Latin America* (Durham, N.C.: Duke University Press, 1973), at p. 318. Copyright 1973 by Duke University Press.
34. "Every window of his palace was steel-shuttered. There were guards at every corner, and it was surrounded by barracks and protected by anti-aircraft guns. His army was well equipped and well disciplined, and he had an efficient spy system. He trusted no one but himself." Amy E. Jensen, *Guatemala: A Historical Survey* (New York: Exposition Press, 1955), p. 125.
35. Weaver, "Bureaucracy during a Period of Social Change," p. 318.
36. *Ibid.*, pp. 357-58.
37. Jensen, *Guatemala: A Historical Survey*, p. 125.
38. Weaver, "Bureaucracy during a Period of Social Change," p. 348.
39. *Ibid.*, p. 345.
40. *Ibid.*, p. 357.
41. In addition to the military rank, "dada" is an honorific title adopted by Amin, with the meaning of patriarch or father.
42. For information on recent political events in Uganda, with incidental reference to administrative matters, refer to Nelson Kasfir, "Civil Participation under Military Rule in Uganda and Sudan," pp. 66-85, in Henry Bienen and David Morell, eds., *Political Participation under Military Regimes* (Beverly Hills, Calif.: Sage Publications, 1976); Ali A. Mazrui, *Soldiers and Kinsmen in Uganda* (Beverly Hills, Calif.: Sage Publications, 1975); and by the same author, "Piety and Puritanism under a Military Theocracy: Uganda Soldiers as Apostolic Successors," pp. 105-24, in Catherine McArdle Kelleher, ed., *Political-Military Systems* (Beverly Hills, Calif.: Sage Publications, 1974).
43. Mazrui, *Soldiers and Kinsmen in Uganda*, p. 45.
44. *Ibid.*
45. "Personalism and Corporatism in African Armies," in Kelleher, *Political-Military Systems*, p. 135.
46. Edwin Lieuwen, *Generals vs. Presidents* (New York: Frederick A. Praeger, 1964), p. 98.
47. Martin Needler, "Political Development and Military Intervention in Latin America," in Henry Bienen, ed., *The Military and Modernization* (Chicago: Aldine/Atherton, 1971), p. 83.
48. *Ibid.*, p. 87.
49. *Ibid.*, p. 89.
50. *Ibid.*, p. 90.
51. Moshe Lissak, *Military Roles in Modernization: Civil-Military Relations in*

Thailand and Burma (Beverly Hills, Calif.: Sage Publications, 1976), p. 33.

52. S. E. Finer, *The Man on Horseback: The Role of the Military in Politics*, 2nd enlarged ed. (Baltimore, Md.: Penguin Books, Inc., 1976), p. 174.

53. Edward Shils, "The Military in the Political Development of the New States," in John R. Johnson, ed., *The Role of the Military in Underdeveloped Countries* (Princeton, N.J.: Princeton University Press, 1962), p. 57.

54. Sources on South Korea include Bong-youn Choy, *Korea: A History* (Rutland, Vt.: Tuttle, 1971); David C. Cole and Princeton N. Lyman, *Korean Development: The Interplay of Politics and Economics* (Cambridge: Harvard University Press, 1971); C. I. Eugene Kim, "The Military in the Politics of South Korea: Creating Political Order," pp. 361-86, in Morris Janowitz and Jacques Van Doorn, eds., *On Military Intervention* (Rotterdam: Rotterdam University Press, 1971); C. I. Eugene Kim, "Transition from Military Rule: The Case of Korea," pp. 24-38, in Henry Bienen and David Morell, eds., *Political Participation under Military Regimes* (Beverly Hills, Calif.: Sage Publications, 1976); Joungwon Alexander Kim, "Korean Kundaehwa: The Military as Modernizer," *Journal of Comparative Administration* 2, No. 3 (November 1970): 355-71; Hyunjoo P. Kwon, *The Emergence of Military Men in Korean Politics: A Historical Study on the Rise of Military Elites* (Buffalo, N.Y.: Council on International Studies, SUNY at Buffalo, 1974); Chae-Jin Lee and Dong-Suh Bark, "Political Perception of Bureaucratic Elite in Korea," *Korea Journal* 13 (October 1973): 29-41; W. D. Reeve, *The Republic of Korea: A Political and Economic Study* (London: Oxford University Press, 1963); and Jae Souk Sohn, "Political Dominance and Political Failure: The Role of the Military in the Republic of Korea," pp. 103-126, in Henry Bienen, ed., *The Military Intervenes: Case Studies in Political Development* (New York: Russell Sage, 1968).

55. Choy, *Korea*, pp. 325-6.

56. *Ibid.*, p. 325.

57. *Ibid.*, pp. 336-7.

58. Kwon, *The Emergence of Military Men in Korean Politics*, pp. 65-66.

59. *Ibid.*, pp. 66-67.

60. Choy, *Korea*, pp. 331-32.

61. Sohn, "Political Dominance and Political Failure," p. 106.

62. "The military revolution is not the destruction of democracy in Korea. Rather it is a way for saving it; it is a surgical operation intended to exorcise a malignant social, political, and economic tumor. The revolution was staged with the compassion of a benevolent surgeon who sometimes must cause pain in order to preserve life and restore health." Quoted by Kim, "Transition from Military Rule," p. 26.

63. Cole and Lyman, *Korean Development*, p. 37.

64. Kim, "Korean Kundaehwa," p. 356.

65. This excerpt is reprinted from "Transition from Military Rule," by C. I. Eugene Kim in *Political Participation under Military Regimes*, Sage Contemporary Social Science Issues, Volume 26, Henry Bienan and

David Morell, Editors, © 1976, p. 35, by permission of the Publisher, Sage Publications, Inc. (Beverly Hills/London).

66. *Ibid.*, p. 25.
67. *Ibid.*, p. 26.
68. Kim, "The Military in the Politics of South Korea," p. 372.
69. Kwon, *The Emergence of Military Men in Korean Politics*, p. 82.
70. Reeve, *The Republic of Korea*, p. 99.
71. *Ibid.*, p. 155. Several months after the investigation team began operation, all of its members were arrested on charges that they had accepted bribes as compensation for levying only small fines.
72. Kwon, *Military Men*, p. 82.
73. Cole and Lyman, *Korean Development*, p. 43.
74. Lee and Bark, "Political Perception," p. 29.
75. Sources on the political system of Thailand include Henry Bienen and David Morell, "Transition from Military Rule: Thailand's Experience," pp. 3-26, in Kelleher, *Political-Military Systems;* Kenneth P. Landon, *Siam in Transition* (New York: Greenwood Press, 1968); Moshe Lissak, *Military Roles in Modernization: Civil-Military Relations in Thailand and Burma* (Beverly Hills, Calif.: Sage Publications, 1976); Fred R. von der Mehden, "The Military and Development in Thailand," *Journal of Comparative Administration* 2, No. 3 (1970): 323-40; David Morell, "Alternatives to Military Rule in Thailand," pp. 9-23, in Bienen and Morell, *Political Participation under Military Regimes;* Clark D. Neher, "Thailand," pp. 215-52, in Robert N. Kearney, ed., *Politics and Modernization in South and Southeast Asia* (New York: Schenkman, 1975); Claude E. Welch, Jr., and Arthur K. Smith, *Military Role and Rule: Perspectives on Civil-Military Relations* (North Scituate, Mass.: Duxbury Press, 1974), Chapter 4, pp. 81-111; and David A. Wilson, "The Military in Thai Politics," pp. 253-75, in Johnson, *The Role of the Military in Underdeveloped Countries.* The Thai bureaucracy has received an unusual amount of study. The standard works are Fred W. Riggs, *The Modernization of a Bureaucratic Polity* (Honolulu: East-West Center Press, 1966), and William J. Siffin, *The Thai Bureaucracy* (Honolulu: East-West Center Press, 1966). Other helpful sources include James N. Mosel, "Thai Administrative Behavior," pp. 278-331, in William J. Siffin, ed., *Toward the Comparative Study of Public Administration* (Bloomington, Ind.: Department of Government, Indiana University, 1957); Edgar L. Shor, "The Thai Bureaucracy," *Administrative Science Quarterly* 5, No. 1 (1960): 66-86; William J. Siffin, "Personnel Processes of the Thai Bureaucracy," pp. 207-28, in Heady and Stokes, *Papers in Comparative Public Administration;* and Kasem Udyanin and Rufus D. Smith, *The Public Service in Thailand: Organization, Recruitment and Training* (Brussels: International Institute of Administrative Sciences, 1954).
76. Welch and Smith, *Military Role and Rule*, pp. 81, 106.
77. Mosel, "Thai Administrative Behavior," pp. 296-97.
78. Neher, "Thailand," p. 244.

79. This excerpt is reprinted from "Alternatives to Military Rule in Thailand" by David Morell in *Political Participation under Military Regimes*, Sage Contemporary Social Science Issues, Volume 26, Henry Bienen and David Morell, Editors, © 1976, p. 10, by permission of the Publisher, Sage Publications, Inc. (Beverly Hills/London).

80. Neher, "Thailand," p. 239.

81. *Ibid.*, p. 241.

82. Welch and Smith, *Military Role and Rule*, p. 100.

83. Morell, "Alternatives to Military Rule in Thailand," pp. 12-13.

84. Welch and Smith, *Military Role and Rule*, p. 102.

85. *Ibid.*, p. 101.

86. Morell, "Alternatives to Military Rule in Thailand," p. 22.

87. von der Mehden, "The Military and Development in Thailand," pp. 334-35.

88. Welch and Smith, *Military Role and Rule*, p. 103.

89. Siffin, *The Thai Bureaucracy*, pp. 161-62.

90. *Ibid.*, p. 165.

91. Siffin, "Personnel Processes of the Thai Bureaucracy," p. 222.

92. *Ibid.*, p. 220.

93. Bienen and Morell, "Transition from Military Rule, pp. 18-19.

94. Riggs, *Thailand: The Modernization of a Bureaucratic Polity*, p. 348.

95. Welch and Smith, *Military Role and Rule*, p. 104.

96. Riggs, *Thailand: The Modernization of a Bureaucratic Polity*, p. 395.

97. Sources on politics and administration in Pakistan include Mushtaq Ahmad, *Government and Politics in Pakistan* (Karachi: Space Publishers, 1970); Ralph Braibanti, "The Civil Service of Pakistan: A Theoretical Analysis," *South Atlantic Quarterly* 58, No. 2 (1959): 258-304; Braibanti, "Public Bureaucracy and Judiciary in Pakistan," pp. 360-440, in Joseph LaPalombara, ed., *Bureaucracy and Political Development* (Princeton, N.J.: Princeton University Press, 1963); Braibanti, *Research on the Bureaucracy of Pakistan* (Durham, N.C.: Duke University Press, 1966); Guthrie S. Birkhead, ed., *Administrative Problems in Pakistan* (Syracuse, N.Y.: Syracuse University Press, 1966); Muzaffar Ahmed Chandhuri, *The Civil Service in Pakistan* (Dacca: National Institute of Public Administration, 1963); Henry Frank Goodnow, *The Civil Service of Pakistan: Bureaucracy in a New Nation* (New Haven, Conn.: Yale University Press, 1964); Robert LaPorte, Jr., *Power and Privilege: Influence and Decision-Making In Pakistan* (Berkeley, Calif.: University of California Press, 1975); LaPorte, "Pakistan and Bangladesh," pp. 109-52, in Kearney, *Politics and Modernization in South and Southeast Asia*; and Khalid B. Sayeed, *The Political System of Pakistan* (Boston: Houghton Mifflin Company, 1967).

98. LaPorte, *Power and Privilege*, p. 39.

99. Angus Maddison, quoted in LaPorte, "Pakistan and Bangladesh," p. 145.

100. Sayeed, *The Political System of Pakistan*, p. 101.

101. Braibanti, "Public Bureaucracy and Judiciary in Pakistan," p. 409.

102. Ahmad, *Government and Politics in Pakistan*, p. 84.

103. Goodnow, *The Civil Service of Pakistan*, p. 233.

104. LaPorte, *Power and Privilege*, p. 178.

105. *Ibid.*, pp. 118-21.

106. Goodnow, *The Civil Service of Pakistan*, pp. 108, 242-43.

107. Principal sources on Ghana include David E. Apter, *Ghana in Transition*, 2nd rev. ed. (Princeton, N.J.: Princeton University Press, 1972); Dennis Austin, *Ghana Observed* (Manchester: Manchester University Press, 1976); Clyde Chantler, *The Ghana Story* (London: Linden Press, 1971); Victor C. Ferkiss, "The Role of the Public Services in Nigeria and Ghana," pp. 173-206, in Heady and Stokes, *Papers in Comparative Public Administration*; Robert Pinkney, *Ghana under Military Rule 1966-1969* (London: Methuen & Co. Ltd., 1972); and Robert M. Price, *Society and Bureaucracy in Contemporary Ghana* (Berkeley, Calif.: University of California Press, 1975).

108. Quoted by Apter, *Ghana in Transition*, p. 326.

109. *Ibid.*, p. 358.

110. *Ibid.*, p. 377.

111. Ernest W. LeFever, *Spear and Scepter: Army, Police, and Politics in Tropical Africa* (Washington, D.C.: The Brookings Institution, 1970), p. 57.

112. Apter, *Ghana in Transition*, p. xxi.

113. Price, *Society and Bureaucracy in Contemporary Ghana*, p. 150.

114. Ferkiss, "The Role of the Public Services in Nigeria and Ghana," p. 178.

115. Apter, *Ghana in Transition*, p. 360.

116. Price, *Society and Bureaucracy*, p. 216.

117. See Fred G. Burke, "Public Administration in Africa: The Legacy of Inherited Colonial Institutions," *Journal of Comparative Administration* 1, No. 3 (1969): 345-78.

118. Price, *Society and Bureaucracy*, p. 206.

119. *Ibid.*, pp. 150-51.

120. For the best brief presentation of the "corporate-technocratic" state as an emerging type, see Jorge I. Tapia-Videla, "Understanding Organizations and Environments: A Comparative Perspective," *Public Administration Review* 36, No. 6 (1976): 631-36. For a recent comprehensive compilation of essays on the subject, refer to James M. Malloy, ed., *Authoritarianism and Corporatism in Latin America* (Pittsburgh, Pa.: University of Pittsburgh Press, 1977).

121. For an historical account of the corporate tradition, see Howard J. Wiarda, "Corporatism and Development in the Iberic-Latin World: Persistent Strains and New Variations," *The Review of Politics* 36 (January 1974): 12-24.

122. Philippe C. Schmitter, "Still the Century of Corporatism?" *The Review of Politics* 36 (January 1974): 85-131, at p. 86.

123. *Ibid.*, pp. 93-94.
124. Robert R. Kaufman, *Transitions to Stable Authoritarian-Corporate Regimes: The Chilean Case?* (Beverly Hills, Calif.: Sage Publications, 1976), p. 7.
125. Tapia-Videla, "Understanding Organizations and Environments," p. 634.
126. *Ibid.*
127. *Ibid.*
128. *Ibid.*, p. 633.
129. *Ibid.*, pp. 633-34.
130. Jorge Graciarena, "The Social Sciences, Intellectual Criticism and the Technocratic State: An Approach to the Latin American Case." Paper presented at the Seminar on *The Social Bases for a Technocratic Society* (New York: Center for Inter-American Relations, 1975), p. 5.
131. Malloy, *Authoritarianism and Corporatism in Latin America*, p. 4.
132. For sources on the Philippines prior to martial law, refer to Onofre D. Corpuz, *The Bureaucracy in the Philippines* (Manila: Institute of Public Administration, University of the Philippines, 1957); Ferrel Heady, "The Philippine Administrative System—A Fusion of East and West," in Siffin, *Toward the Comparative Study of Public Administration*, pp. 253-77; Edwin O. Stene and Associates, *Public Administration in the Philippines* (Manila: Institute of Public Administration, University of the Philippines, 1955); Raul P. DeGuzman, ed., *Patterns in Decision-Making: Case Studies in Philippine Public Administration* (Manila: Graduate School of Public Administration, University of the Philippines, 1963); Jean Grossholtz, *Politics in the Philippines* (Boston: Little, Brown and Company, 1964); and Thomas C. Nowak, "The Philippines before Martial Law: A Study in Politics and Administration," *American Political Science Review* 71, No. 2 (June 1977): 522-39. The more limited sources for the martial law period include Beth Day, *The Philippines: Shattered Showcase of Democracy in Asia* (New York: M. Evans and Company, 1974); Sherwood D. Goldberg, "The Bases of Civilian Control of the Military in the Philippines," pp. 99-122, in Claude E. Welch, Jr., ed., *Civilian Control of the Military* (Albany: State University of New York Press, 1976); Albina M. Dans, "The Philippine Civil Service: Structure and Policies," 31 pp. mimeographed (Manila: College of Public Administration, University of the Philippines, 1977); and Ledivina V. Carino, "Personnel Policies and Bureaucratic Behavior under Martial Law," 29 pp. mimeographed (Manila: College of Public Administration, University of the Philippines, 1977).
133. "The growing influence of American-trained technocrats and businessmen in the Philippines during the late 1960s signalled the rise of an antipolitical, corporatist ideology. This ideology was opposed both to 'old-style' politics and to the growing nationalism . . . which threatened the continued access by foreign corporations to Philippine raw materials, cheap labor, and markets." Nowak, "The Philippines before Martial

Law," p. 524. Robert B. Stauffer is quoted by Nowak as arguing that the media, key Filipino administrators, and President Marcos "had come to view the political process as inhibiting development: the solution increasingly proffered was a turn to authoritarianism and technocratic rule." *Ibid.*, p. 539.

134. Recent sources on politics and administration in Brazil include Luigi R. Einaudi and Alfred C. Stepan III, *Latin American Institutional Development: Changing Military Perspectives in Peru and Brazil* (Santa Monica: The Rand Corporation, 1971); Robert T. Daland, "Attitudes toward Change by Brazilian Bureaucrats," *Journal of Comparative Administration* 4, No. 2 (1972): 167-203; Barry Ames, *Rhetoric and Reality in a Military Regime: Brazil Since 1964* (Beverly Hills, Calif.: Sage Publications, 1973); Bruce Drury, "Civil-Military Relations and Military Rule: Brazil Since 1964," *Journal of Political and Military Sociology* 2 (Fall 1974): 191-203; Georges-Andre Fiechter, *Brazil Since 1964: Modernisation under a Military Regime* (London: Macmillan Press, 1975); Henry H. Keith and Robert A. Hayes, eds., *Perspectives on Armed Politics in Brazil* (Tempe: Center for Latin American Studies, Arizona State University, 1976); and Kenneth S. Mericle, "Corporatist Control of the Working Class: Authoritarian Brazil Since 1964," pp. 303-38, in Malloy, *Authoritarianism and Corporatism in Latin America.*

135. Einaudi and Stepan, *Changing Military Perspectives*, p. 73.

136. Drury, "Civil-Military Relations and Military Rule," p. 191.

137. *Ibid.*

138. "A dramatic concentration of income occurred between 1960 and 1970. The top 5 percent of income earners increased their share of total income from 27.4 to 36.3 percent, while the share of the lower 80 percent fell from 45.5 to 36.8 percent." Mericle, "Corporatist Control of the Working Class," p. 306.

139. *Ibid.*, pp. 331-32.

140. Ames, *Rhetoric and Reality in a Military Regime*, p. 9.

141. C. Neale Ronning and Henry H. Keith, "Shrinking the Political Arena: Military Government in Brazil Since 1964," pp. 225-51, in Keith and Hayes, *Perspectives on Armed Politics in Brazil*, at pp. 226-27.

142. Daland, "Attitudes toward Change by Brazilian Bureaucrats," p. 199.

143. Ronning and Keith, "Shrinking the Political Arena," p. 235.

144. *Ibid.*, p. 242.

145. *Ibid.*, p. 243.

9
PARTY-PROMINENT POLITICAL REGIMES

The political party as an institution is pivotal in some manner in the operation of the political regimes in this broad grouping, although the party or parties involved may differ greatly in number, organization, ideology, membership, and other important respects, including relationships with the public bureaucracy. For our purposes, these political regimes are classified as polyarchal competitive systems, dominant-party semicompetitive systems, dominant-party mobilization systems, and Communist totalitarian systems.

As indicated by the last three of these four types, political regimes characterized by a dominant mass party of some kind have become quite common in the developing countries. They differ markedly in the kind and degree of political competition permitted. Various suggestions have been made for describing and analyzing these regimes, and for identifying specific varieties or subtypes. Tucker labels the general category as a "revolutionary mass-movement regime under single-party auspices," with a revolutionary ideology, a base of mass participation and involvement, and leadership by a militant centralized elite.[1] Apter speaks of a "mobilization system which has as its object the transformation of the society." It recognizes certain secular values, such as "equality, opportunity, and the unfolding of the individual personality in the context of the unfolding society" and downgrades others, such as "individual liberty, popular representation, pluralism and the like."[2] Esman prefers "dominant mass party" to identify the general type, with

341

varieties according to the degree of competitiveness permitted, and he distinguishes it as a type from Communist totalitarian systems.[3]

The three-way breakdown used here for political regimes with a dominant political party can be justified for other reasons as well, but the principal consideration in making this choice is that the role of the bureaucracy seems to differ in each of these kinds of political systems.

Polyarchal Competitive Systems

The states in this category have political systems that conform most closely to the models of Western Europe and the United States. As used here, the category does not require complete adherence to a model that assures regular free elections with an informed electorate, interest-oriented political parties, unrestricted political expression, and a balanced division of functions among representative institutions. The essential is political competition, in the sense that well-organized political groupings are engaged in an active rivalry for political power, with the probability of a significant shift in power relationships taking place without disrupting the system. The competing units need not be necessarily or exclusively Western-style political parties. Countries with viable competitive interest-oriented party systems are in the group, but it also includes other countries where in recent years temporary military intervention has occurred, or where there have been other interruptions to competition which can be considered as at least intended to be transitory. As Esman rightly points out, the more idealized model has been a fragile one, "tried in the majority of the transitional societies, abandoned in many, reinstated in few."[4] We are concerned here with the countries that still maintain, or have reinstated, it, or have only partially and temporarily modified it.

Even using this less restrictive definition, the number of nations with polyarchal competitive regimes has diminished since the early 1960s. The Philippines, Chile, Uruguay, Argentina, Brazil, and Nigeria are among countries which qualified in the early 1960s and no longer do. Lebanon has entered into what appears to be a prolonged period of social disorder which has disrupted a unique competitive system based on a complicated distribution of political power among religious sects. Greece, which until 1967 had a constitutional monarchy with a parliamentary government, succumbed to a military coup d'etat and was under the rule of a repressive military junta until civilian rule was restored in 1974 under a republican constitution which provides for a parliamentary system with a strong presidency. Other countries which currently appear to have substantial political competition include Jamaica, Costa Rica, Colombia, Venezuela, Israel, Sri Lanka (formerly Ceylon), and Turkey. Some of these countries have maintained polyarchal competition over a considerable period of time; others have only recently moved to such a condition.

Taken together, these polities have less clearly defined and cohesive political elites than the other regime types. Political power is dispersed. Urban merchants, landlords, military leaders, and representatives of other well-established interests share the stage with entrepreneurs, labor leaders, professionals, and other emerging leaders from newer interests in the society. Social mobility exists, and this permits and promotes competition.

Since participation in regular elections by the citizenry occurs in practice, or is at least recognized as the normal expectation, political leaders must direct appeals to public opinion and must make commitments in return for political support. This leads to a search for "the widest possible political consensus" and to political doctrine that is "pragmatic and melioristic."[5] It also makes politicians vulnerable to pressures from particular interest groups for special consideration. The resulting governmental programs emphasize short-range objectives in fields such as education, welfare, and health which can be easily understood and appreciated. Longer range goals involving major social and economic reform are less apt to be formulated and are much harder to effectuate. Mobilization of mass support for a developmental program is not likely to be attempted. For reasons such as these, the capacity of such a system to initiate and sustain government-sponsored measures for basic reform is doubtful; major transformation is more likely to come from entrepreneurial and allied professional groups acting primarily in the private sector. Political leadership determined to undertake far-reaching economic development measures or primarily concerned about maintaining public order and stability is tempted to abandon political democracy in favor of some alternative offering greater potential for decisive governmental intervention.

These prevailing conditions in polyarchal competitive systems indicate that the hand of government will be weak when it attempts to collect taxes, impose regulations, or otherwise exert pressures that affect private interests. Public administration must be carried on without consistent political support even from the political instrumentalities that have previously made the formal policy decisions being administered. The bureaucracy itself may become one of the focuses for competition among contending political groups in such a polyarchal system.

Two recent studies shed light on what seem to be typical bureaucratic behavior patterns in such circumstances. Both deal with Chile during the lengthy period of political competition prior to the ouster in 1973 of President Salvador Allende by the military junta which is now in power. Parrish explores the relationship between operation of the public bureaucracy and the selection and achievement of developmental goals in a setting such as Chile when it was "both economically underdeveloped and democratic."[6] Although the Chilean government was highly centralized geographically, he found it to be decentralized bureaucratically, with the bureaucracy having created a highly politicized informal system operating within the formal system. The bureaucracy fashioned what Parrish terms a "cartorial" political style, based on acceptance of the role of the state as basically the maintainer of the status quo, with support for the bureaucracy itself provided basically by patronage. Motivated primarily by a desire to reduce the level of threat to bureaucratic interests, the bureaucratic response is to accept a technique of cooptation for protective purposes. Such a cooperative strategy includes redefinition of goals as necessary to lower risks of danger to the bureaucracy. In the context of comprehensive national planning for development, this means that bureaucratic commitment is limited and incremental, becoming what Parrish refers to as "reformmongering," with the bureaucracy offering obstacles to the achievement of development objectives by redefining developmental goals to suit perceived group interests rather than wholeheartedly adopting such goals as received from nonbureaucratic policy-makers.

Also writing in the Chilean context, Cleaves examines how bureaucratic organizations "can be controlled, reinforced, or enervated for the implementation or thwarting of public policy."[7] Utilizing a political economy approach, he assumes that all organizations share resources, goals, and environment. By means of several policy-oriented case studies, he tries to link organizational behavior to concrete problems in such areas as agriculture, housing, public works, and finance.

Cleaves concurs with Parrish that newly elected regimes in Chile before 1973 usually chose to implement their policies through the public bureaucracy and had little difficulty in gaining its allegiance. "Almost all middle and upper administrative posts are spoils of the new government. Though protected from summary dismissal and salary cuts, the displaced administrators from the previous regime are delegated minor tasks in which they lose almost all influence. Their experience is not tapped; they are in a position neither to initiate policy nor to sabotage it, if such were their intention. When the ruling group is unified, the objectives of the regime can be dictated to the bureaucracy with very little slippage."[8]

Under such circumstances, bureaucratic politics must be accommodated to the realities of the environment. The rational response is for bureaucratic action to be aimed at an increase in access to political resources in order to reduce uncertainty as much as possible. According to Cleaves, bureaucratic behavior can be explained by two interlocking principles: "agencies attempt to reach their goals, and they try to expand their resource base to enhance their capabilities in their task environments."[9] To protect and further their goals, bureaucratic agencies are motivated to increase their access to political resources which can be exchanged for progress toward achievement of bureaucratic goals. In a setting such as democratic Chile, the congruence between national program goals set by the political regime and narrower bureaucratic goals varies with the status and authority of the political leadership. Popular support for elected Chilean presidents who could not succeed themselves after a six-year term in office tended to diminish with time in office. As support subsided, so did the degree of effective mobilization of the bureaucracy to achieve the regime's public policy goals. "Generally," as Cleaves says, "if leadership is articulate, receives continuing support from society, and can gain acceptance for its programs and compliance with the sacrifices it asks, the potential of bureaucracy is outstanding. On the other hand, it is evident that a regime lacking in status and authority cannot provide much assistance to a public administration carrying out unpopular programs."[10] Unfortunately, studies in depth similar to these on bureaucratic behavior patterns in Chile before 1973 are not available on most current polyarchal competitive systems, but the findings of Parrish and Cleaves appear to be relevant to other regimes of this type.

As case examples of polyarchal regimes, we will briefly review three countries presenting considerable variety in geographical location, cultural background, and political competition characteristics. The choices are Turkey, Sri Lanka (formerly Ceylon), and Venezuela.

Turkey is the nation-state remnant of the old Ottoman Empire, gradually emerging in recent years as a viable competitive polity following a period of rapid and pervasive modernization under the leadership of Mustafa Kemal Ataturk after World War I.[11] Modern Turkey is the product of a modernizing military leadership which surrendered power to civilian hands but has stood nearby to intervene as necessary. The Ataturk revolution, building on the Young Turk movement of early in this century, succeeded gradually in consolidating control over the power structure of the country. Until his death in 1938, Ataturk provided leadership which eliminated the political influence of the religious hierarchy, removed the military from direct participation in politics, and created the Republican People's Party as the vehicle for carrying out national modernization.

The political dominance of the Republican People's Party continued after Ataturk's death under his successor and associate Ismet Inonu. During the late 1940s, the Democratic party was organized in opposition and grew rapidly. In the 1950 election, it succeeded in ousting the Republican People's Party after twenty-seven years in office, ushering in a period of political competition which has been maintained with only one major interruption. During the decade of the 1950s, the ruling Democratic party embarked on a program of increased agricultural production, economic development, improved communication and transportation facilities, and other reforms designed to bring the traditional peasant masses more actively into the economic and political arenas. The changes which took place

. . . had profound consequences for patterns of elite composition and for inter-elite relationships. . . . An indication of the change is given by the transformation of the membership of Parliament, a critical and central institution of the political system. Heretofore, the Assembly had been dominated. . . by persons of military and bureaucratic background; now representatives of such occupational categories as "trade," "agriculture," and the "free professions" became dominant. . . . Unfortunately, the new political elite proved quite insensitive to the concerns and aspirations of its predecessors. It adopted policies that adversely affected the position of the military, the bureaucracy and the intellectuals. . . . Thus between 1954 and 1957 the tone and temper of Turkish politics deteriorated steadily and the stage was set for severe inter-elite conflict. The result was acute polarization.[12]

The outcome was military intervention in May 1960 and seizure of power by a junta called the National Unity Committee, which tried and convicted leaders of the Democratic party for misconduct in office. Former Prime Minister Menderes was hanged, and others were imprisoned. The military regime announced its intention to restore civilian rule promptly and actually did so late in 1961.

Political cleavages within Turkey have continued to be evident, however, in the subsequent record of civilian governance under the current constitution which was adopted when the military intervention ended.

In recent years, Turkey typically has had multiparty coalition governments. Although the Democratic party was outlawed, new parties were formed designed to appeal to its membership, particularly the Justice party and the New Turkey party. The Republican People's Party functioned as the leading party in a series of coalition governments, mostly under Inonu as prime minister, until 1965. In the general election that year, the Justice party won a major victory and was able to maintain a shaky unity within its ranks under Prime Minister Demirel until another crisis came to a head in 1971, resulting in the formation of "nonparty" governments during 1971 and 1972 after the imposition of martial law in several provinces. Following an inconclusive election in 1973, the Republican People's Party under Prime Minister Ecivit formed a coalition government with the Islamic National Salvation party, which lasted less than a year before being succeeded by a right of center coalition government headed by the Justice party. The political situation has continued to be stalemated, with the 1977 elections leading to capture by the Republican People's Party of a plurality, but not a majority, of the seats in the National Assembly. Currently, Turkey seems to have developed two major parties, the moderately left Republican People's Party and the moderately right Justice party, neither of which can form a government without working out a coalition involving one or more minor parties, and neither of which can maintain itself in a dominant position for long. However, political competition is a reality, and frequent shifts in party leadership have occurred in recent years as the result of choices by the electorate and negotiations among party groupings in the national legislature.

Turkey is unusual among developing countries in the solid bureaucratic base upon which the present-day nation-state could build. Modern Turkey inherited the centuries-old tradition of the Ottoman "ruling institution" comprised of the sultan's military and administrative establishments, as well as the benefits of a series of efforts during the nineteenth century to reform the civil bureaucracy, including a training school for the civil service, founded in 1859, which has been in almost continuous operation since. The Kemalist regime therefore was able to start after World War I with a bureaucracy which had been professionalized for generations. The public service continues to be attractive and prestigious for educated young Turks, although its appeal is no longer unchallenged; and the tradition of familial identification with the bureaucracy is still strong, son following in the father's footsteps.

Although the Turkish bureaucracy is not a by-product of colonialism, Western models have had an impact, with French influence being strongest. For example, Turkey has followed the French example in leaving management of the bureaucracy primarily to the individual ministries and agencies, subject to general policy guidelines, rather than relying heavily on a central personnel agency. The extent to which behavioral patterns in the Turkish bureaucracy deviate from performance norms is hard to measure accurately, but commentaries stress the prevalence of tendencies such as exceptional deference to persons with higher hierarchical status, reluctance to accept responsibility, centralization of authority, procedural complexity, emphasis on security and protection of civil service tenure, personalized value-premises underlying administrative action, and other "prismatic" or transitional characteristics.

In Turkey, the bureaucracy has been intimately involved in the policy-making process, and subject to relatively weak external controls. Political modernization can be accurately described as the joint handiwork of the civil and military bureaucracies. The new nation-state emerged under the leadership of a military officer, Mustafa Kemal, but he found support for his policies among the civil bureaucrats and he used them to put these policies into effect. As Chambers points out, the bureaucratic class and the military officer corps provided the major reservoir of talent available to him, and individuals with bureaucratic backgrounds provided a considerable proportion of the parliamentary leaders and cabinet ministers until they were substantially displaced following the free elections of 1950. He reports that at least until that time there was "considerable community of social, educational, and occupational background among parliamentary deputies and cabinet ministers on the one hand and the upper levels of the civil bureaucracy on the other," with a sort of closed corporation composed of "professional public servants who, acting as politicians, passed laws which they and their colleagues administered as bureaucrats."[13]

As already noted, during the 1950s the strength of both the civil and military bureaucrats within the national elite diminished markedly. The military intervention of 1960 reasserted the claim of the armed forces for a primary political role in case of necessity to maintain stability, a claim which was still understood as continuing after the restoration of civilian political control. The civil bureaucracy, on the other hand, has never regained its former key importance, although higher civil servants still are members of the governing elite. The process of political modernization in Turkey has brought in additional elements to the current elite mix, without eliminating earlier participants. The major impact of modernization "appears to have been the emergence of new groupings and concomitant pressures for greater political participation; in terms of individual mobility and changes in the composition of particular elites the pattern seems to be one of a gradually broadening base of recruitment and evolutionary changes over time."[14] As a consequence, the Turkish civil bureaucracy can be expected to retain its involvement in the exercise of political power but with a decreasing likelihood as time passes that it will regain its prerogatives of either the Ottoman or Kemalist periods. With somewhat less assurance, a similar prediction may be made about the future role of the military bureaucracy.

Sri Lanka represents another variant among polyarchal competitive systems. After more than four centuries of colonial domination under the Portuguese, the Dutch, and the British, Sri Lanka (then Ceylon) gained independent status within the British Commonwealth in 1948. During the three decades since independence, Sri Lanka has succeeded in maintaining a competitive political system, despite being a country of marked ethnic and religious diversity. The dominant racial group, making up approximately 70 percent of the population, consists of Sinhalese who originated in northern India. The Tamils, who have arrived more recently from southern India, constitute about 22 percent with the remaining 8 percent consisting of several smaller minority groups. Although two-thirds of the people of Sri Lanka are Buddhists, there are also sizable numbers of Hindus, Christians, and Muslims. Similar diversity exists in language and cultural patterns.

Even with these communal variations, Sri Lanka has been able to evolve as a nation-state without pronounced political instability or forceful usurpation of political power. Two political parties have alternated in control, under a parliamentary system patterned after the British model. The United National party governed from independence in 1948 to 1956, then briefly in 1960, again from 1965 to 1970, and was recently returned to power after a landslide victory in mid 1977 elections. During the intervening periods from 1956 to early 1960, from later that year to 1965, and from 1970 to 1977, the Sri Lanka Freedom party was dominant, led first by S. W. R. D. Bandaranaike and after his assassination in 1959 by his widow Sirimavo Bandaranaike. The practice of peaceful transfer of power after a shift in electoral support appears to be firmly established.

As in the case of other former British colonies in South and Southeast Asia, Sri Lanka began independence with the legacy of an ongoing administrative system which had been established under British rule. Although not the subject of much detailed analysis, apparently the bureaucratic apparatus has been able to transfer its services rather successfully from the colonial power to the political leadership of the new nation-state. Maintenance of the British parliamentary political pattern has facilitated also the continuation along orthodox British lines of relationships between the prime minister and cabinet on the one hand and the higher bureaucracy on the other.

Venezuela is one country among many in Latin America which has oscillated in its political history between authoritarian and democratic governments. During the twentieth century prior to 1958, short-lived periods of political competition occurred between the lengthy caudillo-type dictatorships of General Juan Vicente Gomez from 1908 to 1935 and General Marcos Perez Jimenez from 1952 to 1958. Early in 1958 Perez Jimenez was overthrown by a military junta which prepared the way for free elections which were held late that same year, ushering in two decades of political competition continuing to the present.

During this period, the major contenders for governmental power have been the Democratic Action and the Christian Socialist parties, with the former winning the presidency except in the elections of 1968 and 1978. Several minor parties have also been active, including one supporting former dictator Perez Jimenez, a Communist party and other left-wing parties, and splinter groups which have left the Democratic Action party. Kaufman labels the Venezuelan party system as "group-based," meaning that it has roots "in the group identifications and functional associations which emerged in the process of commercialization and industrialization." The defining characteristics of such a party system are that "at least one (and usually more than one) of the major parties was directly involved with middle-class, labor, and peasant protest against elite domination of the political system; that these parties continue to draw the bulk of their support from one or a few status groups within the population; and that they continue to predominate in organizing and representing the interests of these social sectors vis-à-vis other higher-status groups and institutions."[15]

In the Venezuelan case, the Democratic Action party has been populist in its orientation, drawing support primarily from labor union members and the peasantry. It was mainly responsible for building up the public pressure which led to the downfall of the Perez Jimenez regime, and has been able to muster sufficient political strength to dominate most of the time since 1958. Its long-time leader, Romulo Betancourt, was elected president in 1958, and was succeeded five years later by Raul Leoni. The third Democratic Action president, Carlos Andres Perez, was elected in 1973 for a five-year term.

The Christian Socialist party (COPEI), in contrast, has had a moderately conservative orientation based on social doctrines of the Roman Catholic church, and with links to similar parties in Chile and other Latin American countries. Competing regularly in recent elections and maintaining considerable strength in the national legislature, the party has succeeded in capturing the presidency during the term of Rafael Caldera Rodriguez from 1968 to 1973, and again in 1978 when Luis Herrera Campins defeated the Democratic Action candidate.

During this era of active political competition, Venezuela has also devoted considerable attention to reform of its administrative system. With the highest per capita income in Latin America, due to its vast petroleum deposits, the country has been able to make major investments in the development of human resources, including efforts to upgrade public service personnel by the establishment of national educational and training institutes in public administration and by sending large numbers of younger Venezuelans abroad for training at government expense.

Progress so far in these administrative reform and personnel improvement efforts seems only modest, with Venezuelan bureaucracy continuing to exhibit many "prismatic-sala" characteristics, according to available evidence. Although not as extensively studied, bureaucratic behavior patterns appear to be similar to those reviewed previously in democratic Chile prior to 1973, with comparable lapses in strong political support for programs of administrative action and with corresponding deficiencies in bureaucratic ability to meet public policy developmental goals. Political leaders have been primarily concerned with making plans for social and economic reforms and with husbanding and if possible extending their electoral support, and only peripherally with programs of administrative reform, despite the outlay of funds for this purpose.[16]

In summary of these examples of polyarchal competitive systems, we may generalize that although the professional caliber of their bureaucracies is of a relatively high order among all developing countries, these bureaucracies have internal weaknesses and suffer from inconsistent backing from political policy-makers. External controls over the bureaucracy are sufficient but sometimes work at cross-purposes. The danger is less of bureaucratic usurpation than of bureaucratic inadequacy to meet the demands placed upon it.

Dominant-Party Semicompetitive Systems

In a dominant-party semicompetitive system, one party has held a monopoly of actual power for a substantial period of time, but other parties are legal and do in fact exist. The dominant party has a record of overshadowing all other parties and is victorious in virtually all elections. It is nondictatorial, however, and a condition for classification in this regime type is the presumption that the dominant party can be displaced in competition at the polls by the successful challenge of a rival.

The number of qualifying polities is obviously small. The most clear-cut example of such a dominant party is Mexico's Partido Revolucionario Institucional (PRI). During most of the period since independence, India's Congress party (CPI) has been similarly dominant. Its displacement from power by defeat in the 1977 election, although confirming the presumption just referred to, does not necessarily mean that it will cease to be India's dominant party, in view of the ad hoc nature of the political coalition which was victorious in this particular election. A third example is Malaysia, where the Alliance, a "holding company" type of political party formed by communal organizations representing the country's three major ethnic groups, has dominated political life and controlled the government continuously since the first federal elections in 1955. Each of these instances is examined in more detail.

In Mexico, the Partido Revolucionario Institucional can be traced to the revolution of 1910 and it lays successful claim to be the official party of the revolution.[17] The PRI has been able, as a result, to monopolize the electoral process "by preempting and institutionalizing the revolutionary myth and by creating for itself an image as the key component of an indissoluble trinity composed of Party, government, and political elite."[18] The PRI controls all branches of the federal government and all state governments. Several other parties exist, but together they have been able to poll at most only about one-fourth of the votes in contested presidential elections, and in 1976 the PRI presidential candidate had no opponent at all. Only a handful of seats in the Mexican congress are not held by the PRI. The leading opposition party has been the National Action party, which is conservative, proclerical, and probusiness in its orientation. Other parties are more leftist ideologically than the PRI.

The strategy of the PRI as Mexico's dominant party is to seek a consensus that will avoid the splintering away of party factions on either the right or the left; it is a coalition party of the center. The Mexican political system has been described as "center-dominant,"[19] because the PRI embraces such a wide spectrum of the population, and "monistic," because it involves "the centralization and control of potentially competing interests."[20] As Stevens points out, "the sectors of the population whose consent is mobilized by the Party compose the overwhelming numerical majority of the nation. While the Party appeals to the populace in the name of the government, the aura of legitimacy conferred by majority consent is extended by inference to cover all policies promoted by the elite. This extension of legitimacy is facilitated by the inextricable intertwining of the Party, government, and elite roles held by the same persons. The Party has thus preempted a special and very privileged relationship with other important elements of the political system and has succeeded in preventing other parties from sharing in this privilege."[21] Although the situation is not identical, the PRI's role is obviously similar to that of the sole party in what are admittedly single-party systems.

In such a regime, the most significant political competition takes place among ideological, regional, and interest-oriented factions within the dominant party. This is officially recognized to some extent by the sectoral form of organization within PRI, put into effect by President Lazaro Cardenas when he reorganized the party in 1938. Currently the PRI organization is based on three distinct sectors—labor, agrarian, and "popular"—with an earlier separate military sector having being dissolved. The popular sector is a catchall category which includes representation for civil and military bureaucrats, among others. Policy interplay within the party structure stresses the objective of unanimity and consensus using a strategy of flexibility, with resulting difficulty in maintaining momentum toward developmental goals. The PRI, while retaining a strong revolutionary orientation in the lower echelons, exhibits more conservative conciliatory tendencies toward the top.

A secondary key feature of the Mexican regime is the preeminence of executive leadership in both the political and administrative spheres. Needler calls this "executivism," pointing out that the president is "by far the dominant figure in the Mexican political system,"[22] with other chief executives occupying somewhat comparable positions at the state and local levels. Legislative and judicial bodies do not operate in a way that can effectively check executive supremacy. The reins of control over the PRI, as well as the official governmental apparatus, are held by the Mexican president, subject to limits imposed by the requirements for protecting the centralist nature of the regime. In the opinion of Raymond Vernon, recent Mexican presidents, in their concern "to achieve unanimity, . . . to extend the reach of the PRI the full distance to both the right and the left," have been held to "a course of action which is zigzagging and vacillating when it is not blandly neutral."[23] The political process in this kind of dominant-party regime under executive leadership apparently tends over a period of time toward a policy orientation that stresses consensus at the price of boldness and decisiveness.

Turning to administrative capacities and performance, Mexican experience has been traumatic because of the almost complete breakdown of the administrative machinery during the revolutionary period of 1910–1917. Rebuilding has taken place on a gradual and piecemeal basis. The structure of the executive branch currently includes a bewildering complexity of units, ranging from almost a score of ministries to a myriad of interministerial committees, administrative commissions, and decentralized institutions in commercial, financial, and industrial fields.

Recruitment into the Mexican bureaucracy has been described as the outcome of "continuing struggle between the needs of the political system and the requirements for technically qualified personnel."[24] The formal personnel system does not include a central personnel agency. Each department has its own personnel office, with considerable variation in their operation. A basic personnel law, enacted in 1941, dealt primarily with the legal rights of employees. It divided them into two basic categories—"workers of confidence" and "ordinary workers"—with the former group corresponding roughly to an expanded administrative class and containing about one-third of the total number of employees. Our principal concern is with these "confidence" officials. Writing in the late 1940s, Wendell Schaeffer listed these factors as important in the selection of confidence personnel: personal and political relationships, family ties, contributions to the PRI, and expertise.[25] Greenberg asserts that the balance seems to have shifted in recent years from other considerations toward expertise because of technological developments which make professional training more important than before.[26]   Confidence personnel have been denied unionization and strike rights granted to the "ordinary" or "base" workers.   Official salary levels historically have been notoriously low, and only moderate progress has been made in raising salary rates. Multiple jobholding and "institutionalized" corruption are common consequences.   One observer refers to the continued practice of "undiluted, unambiguous corruption," sanctioned in part by an "enduring Mexican attitude of resignation and cynicism,"[27] and requiring fifteen Mexican terms to denote "graft."   Another states that the reasons for corruption can be found "both in the nature of the society and in the demands of the personnel system.   The prevalence in the society of personalism and *amistad*, with primary loyalties being directed toward one's family and friends rather than toward the government or administrative entity, has an important effect on the level of corruption. . . . In addition, the predicament of the bureaucrat, with no real union protection, no job security, and no guarantee of future income, causes him to turn to corrupt practices."[28]

Lack of information makes an assessment of the current level of performance of the Mexican bureaucracy risky, but some encouraging signs can be seen.   A political scientist says that the governing mechanism has developed a "cadre of career officials. . .to apply policy decisions through effective administrative techniques" and is providing "a predictable and constructive pattern to which the individual can adjust."[29]   An economist asserts that Mexico is a nation that has "a well-developed public sector, consisting of its government agencies and its government-controlled enterprises, which by now have acquired a sense of continuity and of effective performance. . . . The men who design the dams, roads, and factories of the country, direct its businesses and financial institutions, plan its educational system, provide its advanced training, and guide its agricultural research are principally Mexican nationals."   He goes on to state that "no one any longer doubts that Mexico has the internal human and physical resources, the social organization, and even the level of income which most other countries of the underdeveloped world would be content to achieve thirty or forty years hence."[30] Based on a case study of the Ministry of Hydraulic Resources, a student of public administration concludes that "government agencies *can* operate efficiently within a structure which on the surface appears to be inefficient."[31]

Significant participation by bureaucratic officials in policy-making is increasing, but apparently is confined to a secondary role. Scott has suggested the term "government by consultation" to describe the mechanism by which the Mexican chief executive uses "all of the formal and informal, legal and extra-legal agencies of the presidency" to hear and consider "the competing needs and desires of all the major functional interests concerned in any given policy decision."[32] The institution of the presidency provides a "monolithic facade" which obscures the extent to which actual political power is diffused in the system.[33] The arbiter in disputes over policy questions is the president. As Vernon puts it, "the ultimate authority of the president in Mexico must never be overtly questioned, and his freedom of action never overtly compromised by any member of the executive branch."[34] In actuality, constrained by the overriding requirement that he seek a national consensus and maintain the hegemony of the PRI, the president must engage in a complex consultative process. One of the groups consulted consists of the technicians within the bureaucracy, particularly the economic technicians who are integrally involved in decision-making related to development. The line between the *tecnicos* and the *politicos* is still reasonably clear, but the strength of the technicians is growing. It "lies not so much in their powers to shape policy directly as in their capacity to choose the technical alternatives which are presented to their political masters."[35] However, this range of proposals is not likely to extend to a drastic refashioning of governmental programs.

The basic fact to remember in understanding the relationship between the political system and the bureaucracy in Mexico is the primacy of politics and the PRI. "In a country with a political system like that of Mexico," according to Greenberg, "it is politics in the form of party ties that become the dominant force in the lives of the bureaucrats. Since the Party has the power of appointment and removal, bureaucrats must spend an appreciable amount of time in fostering good relationships with leading Party functionaries. . . . Almost all administrators, with the exception of small groups of technicians with special expertise, engage in extensive political activity, while at the same time performing, to one degree or another, their administrative functions." The multiplicity of roles played by Mexican bureaucrats, often including also involvement in private financial and economic enterprises, means that "the decision-making process in the agencies must therefore cope with often conflicting needs engendered by the system, with the result that technical considerations often take a back seat to political and personally based economic factors."[36]

The Mexican bureaucracy, therefore, although playing an important role in the political arena, including institutional recognition within the PRI organizational structure, is effectively sealed off from mounting a challenge to the PRI's historically established claim to political dominance.[37]

India and Malaysia, as Asian examples of dominant-party regimes, show similarities between them and together offer some contrasts to the Mexican case. The similarities include a common British colonial past with its legacy of political and administrative institutions, dominant parties with many shared characteristics, comparable working relationships between political leaders and professional bureaucrats, and established effective external controls over the bureaucracy.[38]

During the lengthy period of British colonialism in these areas, the British institutional imprint was firmly fixed. "Gradually under British rule," according to Kochanek, "a model of government evolved which was ultimately to be accepted as the structure of government for independent India." One key element in this model was "the creation of a unified central administration based on the emerging principles of a modern bureaucracy recruited on the basis of open competition and merit."[39] Similarly, Means says that the British impact on Malaysia has been "so pervasive it is impossible to trace all its manifestations," but with one feature being the British administrative system representing "an institutional embodiment of the values of rational organization designed to provide certain social services for the benefit of society as a whole."[40] In both instances, the inherited administrative pattern has been retained relatively intact since independence.

More noticeable adjustments have been made in the British parliamentary and party systems, particularly in the substitution of a dominant party for the British dual-party tradition. Since being founded in 1885, the Congress (CPI) has had no serious rival for leadership in the campaign for Indian independence or after 1947 in the postindependence government until very recently. This record of dominance, much like that of the PRI in Mexico, has been based on "strong leadership, a long history marked by a high level of institutionalization, an ability to manage internal conflict generated by competing demands, an integrative political style, and an ability to pre-empt the middle ground of the Indian political spectrum."[41]

Until its decline in recent years, the Congress had regularly been able to secure massive majorities in Parliament and had also controlled nearly all of the state governments, despite the existence of several other major political parties, arrayed both to the right and to the left. Deterioration in the political situation led to the declaration of a state of emergency by Prime Minister Indira Gandhi in June 1975, and to a decisive defeat for the Congress party under her leadership in the general elections which she eventually called for in March 1977. The victorious Janata party is a coalition of even more disparate elements than had made up the CPI, consisting of splinters from the Congress party, and most of the non-Communist opposition parties, including the Socialist party and the Indian People's Union, a right-wing nationalist Hindu party. Whether this coalition can be held together remains to be seen, but is certainly in doubt. Should a government supported by the Janata party succeed in maintaining power for an extended period with the Congress party in opposition, classification of India as a dominant-party regime would of course have to be revised.

The dominant-party counterpart in Malaysia is the Alliance party, formed in 1952 by a coalition of groups representing the three major ethnic components of the population. The United Malays National Organization has occupied the leading role in this coalition because of Malay numerical superiority, with Chinese and Indian communal organizations in secondary roles. In continuous control of the government since independence, the Alliance (now renamed the Barisan National Front) won 70 percent of the vote in the most recent national elections in 1974. The only significant opposition party is the Democratic Action party, predominantly Chinese in membership, which won 20 percent of the vote but elected less than half that proportion of the seats in the national legislature because of the weighting of election districts to favor rural Malay areas. As Means points out, the Alliance has depended for political success

... upon its ability to preserve intact a political coalition which bridges the basic communal cleavage within the country. On the most important communal issues, the Alliance has worked out fairly moderate compromises, but with a distinct pro-Malay bias. ... Although the political power of the Alliance has rested with its ability to dominate the basic communal cleavage, its Achilles heel is also located along that cleavage, for serious communal differences have produced strains among Alliance parties, and communal compromises, when they are finally worked out, have not always been supported by the rank and file. ... To function smoothly, the Alliance needs communal moderates in leadership positions of the constituent communal parties, and it relies upon the support of communal moderates at the polls. When these conditions have not been present, the Alliance has been rocked by internal crises.[42]

Future dominance is dependent on avoiding crises serious enough to break up the unstable coalition.

Both India and Malaysia have benefited from unusually advanced higher public bureaucracies. Indeed, India could legitimately lay claim to producing the forerunner of the modern civil service in Great Britain itself, due to the influence of the British East India Company experience during the nineteenth century. The preindependence Indian Civil Service (ICS) has gradually been replaced by the new Indian Administrative Service (IAS) as the apex of this system, supplemented by a series of other service categories staffing the central government and the state governments. The emphasis continues to be on the very selective, annual recruitment of exceptionally intelligent young men from the universities; a system of competitive examinations is administered by the Union Public Service Commission, an independent body that is also responsible for training new recruits. There is no question that those selected for the IAS are able. Critics claim, however, that the recruitment policy is overly exclusive and that the IAS has a law and order orientation not well suited to a welfare state. The system as a whole was rated in the 1950s by an American observer, Paul H. Appleby, as among the dozen or so most advanced in the world, but he also pointed out that it was "designed to serve the relatively simple interests of an occupying power," was not adequate for an independent India, and required systematic improvement.[43] Similar comments continue to be made, including Kochanek's recent recommendation that the bureaucracy "must be made more innovative, less subject to rapid expansion as a way of creating employment and must exercise self-restraint in its demands for higher incomes."[44]

The higher civil service in Malaysia likewise has evolved directly from the colonial bureaucratic system, with little change in the institutional arrangements or the social status attached to membership. The most significant transformation has been the substitution of national for expatriate personnel by the process of Malayanization, which had been substantially completed by the early 1960s. Selection for entry continues to be made primarily from university graduates by an autonomous public service commission, based mainly on previous academic performance. A feature of the post-independence recruitment process has been a legally imposed quota approach favoring Malay over non-Malay applicants in the population at a four-to-one ratio. This preferential treatment for Malays has no doubt been at a price in terms of quality of recruits, but this ethnic dimension has been insisted upon by the Malay-controlled government. In general, the legitimacy inherited from colonial times by the bureaucracy has been retained, and its level of competence continues to be impressive. Writing in 1964, Tilman concluded that the administrative system was not working precisely as it had in the colonial environment, but that it was effectively serving the current needs of the society.[45] A few years later Esman reported that the Malaysian bureaucratic cadres had "maintained their integrity, discipline, and organizational coherence" and remained competent "in the discharge of routine service and control activities." Echoing the criticism made by others of the Indian higher bureaucrats, however, he contended that the "attitudes, role definitions, and operational capabilities" of Malaysian bureaucrats were not adequate to meet development administration requirements.[46] The problem again is adaptation from the needs of colonialism to those of nationalism.

A cherished part of the political tradition in both India and Malaysia is that there should be a separation between the politicians who make policies and the administrators who carry them out. In practice, working relations between the political leaders and the professional bureaucrats have generally conformed to the tradition, and have proceeded smoothly, but with Malaysian bureaucrats playing a more active policy role than their Indian counterparts.

In India, this cooperative pattern has no doubt been fostered by the lengthy political dominance of the Congress party, and by the similarity in background and outlook of leaders in the party and the higher bureaucracy. The policy role of the administrative officials seemed to be growing, however, as the CPI moved toward its proclaimed dedication to establish "the socialist pattern of society" and government programs tried to achieve welfare state objectives. Through the process of defining and explaining alternatives of social and economic reform, and giving advice for choosing among them, the expert tends to be brought into more active participation. The magnitude of the machinery for government planning, combined with the autonomous position of the Planning Commission as an advisory body to the central government, has given rise to criticism by some that bureaucrats have been too influential in the politics of planning and not answerable enough to Parliament. The IAS probably has had a policy role equal to that of the British administrative class and one of equally low visibility. The general impression, nevertheless, has been that the professional bureaucrats have been effectively subordinated to the political leadership in the cabinet and in Parliament. So far, no indication of a change in these relationships has appeared since the Janata party replaced the CPI as the majority party.

In Malaysia, according to Esman's analysis, high ranking bureaucrats form an integral part of the governing elite, which is composed of "two sections which maintain a symbiotic pattern of relationships: the Alliance Party politicians who head the political section and the senior administrators who operate the bureaucracy. Despite tensions between them, their relationships are mutually supportive."[47] Many of the senior politicians were formerly administrators, which helps explain the collaboration. In a polity where communal pluralism is the basic reality, the dominant political party is compelled to rely on the relatively neutral bureaucracy as a partner in keeping the system going. Indeed, Esman goes so far as to claim that Malaysia's senior officials "have been the indispensable steel frame which has held this precarious state together even when political processes failed."[48]

Dominant-Party Mobilization Systems

Important differences separate countries in this group from those just discussed. Permissiveness in politics is less; actual or potential coercion is greater. The dominant party is usually the only legal party. If other parties are permitted to operate openly at all, they are surrounded by restrictive controls designed to keep them weak and only symbolic of opposition. Ideology is more doctrinaire and more insistently proclaimed, although it may be adjusted for purposes of expediency. Greater stress is placed on mass demonstration of loyalty to the regime. The elite group tends to be relatively young, urbanized, secularized, and well educated, with a strong commitment to developmental nationalism. Often a single charismatic leader holds a commanding position dominating the movement he heads. Such a regime is likely to have acceded to power during the post-World War II period of independence from colonialism, and is most commonly found in new African nations. It may have replaced some earlier regime in a recently independent state, or it may have altered its own character markedly since taking over the government at the time of independence. Its own political future may be precarious, thus emphasizing the urgency of building a strong base of mass support and of assuring the loyalty of key groups in the society. The leadership may feel a strong tutelary obligation to a population not yet considered ready for self-government. For the national mobilization effort to succeed, the dominant party must insist on the allegiance and support of the public bureaucracy, while being dependent on it for adequate performance.

The viability of these dominant-party mobilization systems has not been as high as was generally anticipated a decade ago. Several countries formerly in this category now have bureaucratic elite regimes under military leadership, including Algeria since the 1965 coup which overthrew Ben Bella, Bolivia since 1969 when the National Revolutionary Movement leadership was ousted, Ghana since the downfall of Nkrumah, Mali, and some of the other new states carved out of former French West Africa in which one-party regimes have been replaced by military regimes. Numerous nations continue to have one-party regimes, with considerable variation, however, as to whether the party role in governance is really central or somewhat peripheral. Among them are Egypt, Gabon, Guinea, Ivory Coast, Liberia, Malawi, Mauritania, Senegal, Tanzania, and Zambia. Egypt and Tanzania offer contrasting examples of dominant-party mobilization systems, the former having derived from a military reformist regime which sponsored the party and harnessed it to support the regime, and the latter evolving as the dominant party after serving as the vehicle for winning independence under civilian leadership.

During the twenty-five years since the 1952 coup which ousted King Farouk, the Egyptian regime in power has had unusual continuity in leadership, first under Gamal Abdel Nasser and, since his death in 1970, under Anwar Sadat. Beginning as a radical interventionist military regime, this government has endeavored to enhance its legitimacy and mobilize popular support for its foreign and domestic programs by combining charismatic appeal with the buildup of a single broadly based mass political party.[49] The 1952 revolution was started by the "Free Officers," a group of young army officers who were able to depose an unpopular monarch but who were politically inexperienced and lacked a well-defined revolutionary program. Their coup was triggered as a protest against the support failures they believed had led to the defeat of Egyptian armed forces by the Israelis in the Palestinian conflict. Beyond that they aimed at elimination of the monarchy and the introduction of agrarian reform.

This initial uncertainty was reflected in various ways. For a brief period after the coup a civilian prime minister was installed in office before the Free Officer group took over directly, under the title of Revolutionary Command Council. General Muhammad

Naguib was nominal head of the group for a while before being replaced by Nasser, who had actually engineered the takeover, and emerged by 1954 as the strongman and regime leader. Gradually Nasser and his colleagues turned toward a program of "Arab socialism" encompassing a far-reaching program of social and economic reforms. This brand of socialism was defended as being in accord with Islamic principles; it rejected the Marxist belief in the inevitability of the class struggle, and in theory favored a mixed economy, although it has involved the nationalization of most major business enterprises. Major emphasis was placed on land redistribution, with 15 percent of Egypt's arable land being acquired by the government for this purpose.

In consolidating its power, the regime first abolished the monarchy, purged the military officer corps, and dissolved existing political parties. Then it undertook to create an official party as the vehicle for realization of its program of Arab socialism. The first two experiments along this line were unsuccessful, in 1953 with the National Liberation Rally and in 1957 with the National Union. Disappointment with both of these organizations in mobilizing mass support led in 1962 to establishment of the Arab Socialist Union (ASU), which continues as the dominant party. The intention was to develop a "socialist vanguard" which would mobilize Egyptian society behind the revolution, borrowing many features from the practices of Communist party regimes, such as a nationwide pyramidal form of organization which would parallel the official governmental structure, interlinking of party and governmental personnel culminating in designation of the president of the republic also as chairman of the party, and restriction of party membership to individuals considered completely loyal to the political regime. On paper the ASU has developed along the lines planned. By 1966 its membership had grown to nearly seven million people, and the various levels in the party pyramid had been staffed, from the "basic units" at the local level through provincial and other intermediate levels to the party's Supreme Executive Committee headed earlier by Nasser and now by Sadat. Although the actual role of the party is obscure, most commentators are skeptical that it in fact fulfills its proclaimed function as "the supreme popular authority which assumed the leadership role in the people's name," exercising "popular political control on the government organism."[50] However sincere the intent of the revolutionary military leadership to constitute the ASU as the vehicle for moving toward mass political participation, less has been accomplished than projected. Akhavi notes that "having purposefully chosen a rationalist, elitist model of rule and modernization from above, the military has been unable to achieve meaningful participation. In consequence, political integration in society has been weak and political mobilization artificial."[51]   At the village level, basic transformations have not been effected. "Party membership in the rural areas tends, unfortunately for the ASU, to ensure that a former traditional leader will be able to maintain his position of power and authority in the village or rural community."[52]   Welch and Smith sum up the situation this way: "The involvement and support of the peasantry . . . remain uncertain. The step of organizing a responsive political party, able to articulate and support the interests of the fellahin, has not yet fully succeeded. The ASU was built from the top down, not from the bottom up. The fellahin have not yet fully awakened from the acquiescence and torpor that have characterized them for centuries."[53]

Despite these setbacks, the Egyptian leadership continues to seek ways to utilize the Arab Socialist Union as a means of increasing political awareness and extending political competition within carefully controlled limits. When elections were held in 1976, President Sadat authorized the formation of three political groups or subparties within the framework of the ASU, each of which nominated candidates for the unicameral national legislature, the People's Assembly. An overwhelming majority of those elected came from the centralist ASU faction with which Sadat himself was identified, but a few members were elected from each of the other two groups, one to the left and the other to the right of the dominant ASU core segment.

With the future of party politics uncertain, for the present Egypt appears to be firmly in the hands of political leaders representing a variety of interests, but with military components deriving from the 1952 revolutionary cadre at the inner core. Analysis of the composition of government cabinets, of the ASU executive committee, of provincial governorships, and of other important posts during the period since 1952 indicates that military officers or former military officers have had a representation ratio high enough to assure their control,[54] although the percentages have been declining under Sadat. The regime in Egypt, in the judgment of Welch and Smith, "increasingly seems a civil–military coalition, one based on the middle-class technocracy, skilled workers, medium landholders, and (of course) officers."[55]   Another view as to actual political processes in Egypt is that "the ASU is a facade behind which the constituent groups in Egypt's elite may operate. These groups include the military, the civil bureaucracy, political party leaders, and, to some extent, leaders of economic interest groups such as trade unions. Competition among these groups is amorphous and difficult to discern. However, there is in Egypt . . . a difference of opinion over important policy among different groups within the elite. This leads to a kind of disguised factionalism, which constitutes the essence of politics in Egypt. . . . Decisions are made by an insulated elite behind closed doors and are enforced by a civil bureaucracy responsible to the elite and not to the public."[56] The Arab Socialist Union, as the dominant party in this complex and evolving political system, plays an ambiguous part but one which seems more likely to grow than to diminish.

The contemporary Egyptian civil bureaucracy, which plainly is one of the actors on the political stage, has impressive historical antecedents. In embarking on its national reform program, the Nasser–Sadat regime has benefited from administrative advantages derived from Egypt's past, going back to a system of large-scale administration existing as early as 1500 B.C., which Weber called the historical model of all later bureaucracies. More recent are the administrative traditions resulting from successive conquests of the country, beginning with the Ottoman Empire in the sixteenth century, the period of French influence following the Napoleonic invasion of 1798, and the seventy years of British control which ended in 1952. The Egyptian bureaucratic tradition is thus ancient, cumulative, and mixed.

In the 1880s, Lord Cromer initiated improvements in administration, but these did not include the recruitment in large numbers of Egyptians for the more responsible civil service posts. As late as 1920 only one-fourth of the higher positions were held by Egyptians, but this changed rapidly after 1922, when the Egyptians assumed control of the civil service. That same year a classification system was installed, relating rank to salary following a French format. It was not until 1951, just before the revolution, that a merit system based on open competitive examinations was adopted and a civil service commission created, following a survey by a British expert. This system was activated by the new regime as part of its program for administrative reform. It follows Western patterns of selection, conduct, and discipline of civil servants.

A career in the middle or upper levels of the bureaucracy has always had great attraction for the educated elite in Egypt, and the educational system is geared to this occupational expectation. Competitive outlets have developed, but the demand for civil service jobs far exceeds the number available, particularly in the case of university graduates in the fields of law and commerce. This creates heavy pressures for overstaffing in the higher ranks as well as in the lower levels of the service.

Modern Egypt has been described as inheriting from its long past "a highly personalized pattern of administration in which the inter-play of religious, class, and family interests was, and to a considerable extent still is, the most distinctive behavior trait." A sense of status insecurity, resulting from favoritism "related to family connections, religion, social position, or political belief" is reported to stifle initiative and induce fear of exercising discretion. "There is thus a high premium on rigid conformity to formal procedural rules. This psychology also tends to discourage delegation of authority down the hierarchy."[57]

Empirical evidence is scarce, even after more than two decades of bureaucratic remolding under a mobilization regime, concerning changes in traditions, attitudes, and work methods, but indications are that the bureaucracy has become somewhat more competent and effective, and that it has been made responsive to the political leadership. The appointment of army personnel to key administrative positions is one way in which this has been accomplished. Recognized opponents of the regime in the civil bureaucracy have long since been purged. A growing professionalism seems to be altering work habits and codes of conduct among middle-management officials. Senior officials in Egypt have not traditionally taken the initiative in policy-making and have been subservient to holders of political power. Certainly the present regime wants to confirm such a relationship, and it seems to have done so.

An unanswered question is how prepared the bureaucracy is in the long run to accomplish what is expected of it. The military leaders have recognized that their plans for social and economic reform depend on competent professionals, and have turned to technically trained civilians for help. "The bonds connecting the technocrats and the officers are strong and numerous. . . . They are dependent on one another and each can be secure in his own position only if the other is also firmly entrenched."[58] The caliber of civilians in key positions is reported to be excellent, but as individuals they are vulnerable unless they satisfy their superiors, who are likely to be military officers. "In many ways," according to Akhavi, "the individuals serving on the administrative staff are exceptional for their intelligence and their motivation for achievement. In examining the biographies of some of them, one comes away feeling that they embody a kind of Renaissance-man ideal. However, . . . the energies and capabilities of these persons seem to have been sublimated in the interests of compliance." Indications are that "the non-military members of the Egyptian political elite are a service bureaucracy," under an urgent obligation to supply "technical and managerial proficiency."[59] McLennan concurs that "these new modern bureaucrats have increased in influence," mainly because of their technical expertise, but also points out that "if they wish to climb the hidden hierarchy to power, they have to impress the modernizing segment of the Egyptian elite—the military and nationalist politicians."[60] This setting makes it difficult to emulate the Western rational model of administration; instead, since authority granted to these Egyptian administrators is "always conditioned on loyal service to the state," they have a tendency to administer "as though their respective domains of activity were fiefdoms."[61] Program initiative and interagency cooperation are difficult to achieve under these circumstances.

Probably a more serious problem is conversion of the rank and file in the civil service from a traditional to a revolutionary perspective. Historically, Egyptian bureaucrats were representatives of the king's authority, expected to be completely subservient to the ruler, and in turn taking advantage of their opportunities to extract from taxpaying subjects gains for themselves in the process of collecting the royal revenues. Many long-standing habits persist. "The Egyptian bureaucracy remains a generally conservative force within a regime that is outwardly revolutionary. Traditionally subservient and never a great source of legislative initiative, the civil service in Egypt has been slow to transform itself into a revolutionary force. . . . Egypt has really not attacked many old institutions (including the bureaucracy) because of a basic commitment of the leadership to Egyptian nationalism. . . . Similarly, the personnel of the bureaucracy has been 'Egyptianized' . . . , but the manner of business itself is not very different from before."[62]

The East African nation of Tanzania was formed in 1964 by the union of Tanganyika on the mainland and the island of Zanzibar, both of which had gained independence within the British Commonwealth early in the 1960s. The union is not a close one, and the mainland component is by far the senior partner. Colonialism for what is now Tanzania had included both German and British rule, with British control coming later and exerting a much greater post-independence influence. The Tanzanian population is mostly African, rural, and poor. The economy is primarily agricultural, with few natural resources to be exploited. With a low per capita income, a high rate of population growth, and only limited industrial development, economic prospects are not promising. On the other hand, the nation does not have serious internal rivalries among racial or tribal groups, or great disparities between rich and poor. Its relative political stability has been a rarity among new African states.

Tanzania's successful campaign for independence and subsequent political development has taken place under a single political leader heading a single political party.[63] Julius Nyerere, who serves as president of both the republic and the party, came into political prominence during the 1950s as the chief advocate of freedom from British rule, using an organization then known as the Tanganyika (now Tanzania) African National Union (TANU), which had been originally an association of African civil servants before expanding into a vehicle for political action. After independence was peacefully obtained, there was a brief period of political competition between TANU and the much weaker United Tanganyika party before Tanzania became officially a one-party state in 1965.[64] Meanwhile, Nyerere was elected as the country's first chief executive, and has been re-elected at five-year intervals since. Nyerere's political program is one he describes as African socialism or *ujamaa* (meaning "brotherhood" in Swahili). Rejecting capitalism as a colonial inheritance exploitative in operation, Nyerere has advocated African socialism as an egalitarian concept based on traditional African views that society is an extension of the basic family unit. A one-party system is preferred, as part of this political philosophy, on the ground that two-party or multiparty systems foster divisive factionalism within society, whereas a single party can identify with the interests of the nation as a whole.

Unlike some other dominant parties, TANU is not highly centralized structurally. Building on local party cells, the levels of party organization extend through branch, district, and regional committees to a National Executive Committee, but detailed supervision from the center has not been attempted. The party's National Conference, held every two years, is mainly ceremonial. Neither the National Executive Committee nor the National Conference has major policy-making functions. "In fact," states Bienen, "policy for the TANU government is usually made by the President in consultation with key ministers.... TANU and government policy rarely originate in the NEC. Rather, TANU government leaders bring to it formulated policies for approval.... The chief function of the NEC, therefore, is to veto or approve proposals; it can also force leaders to postpone or modify their policies. But it does not propose and establish its own policies."[65] As in other single-party systems, individuals often simultaneously hold both party and governmental positions, but in contrast to the situation commonly found elsewhere, in Tanzania government posts are considered more powerful and prestigeful than party assignments.

In elections for the unicameral National Assembly, TANU has fostered a two-way competition in each of the single-member constituencies by having party agencies review the records of candidates and decide which two will be permitted to run. The two selected are both certified as acceptable to the party, and each is provided with equal access to campaign resources. Neither is supposed to claim to be favored by either the party or the president. This procedure has resulted in hotly contested elections in many constituencies, and a considerable turnover in membership at five-year intervals after each election. The level of popular political participation is relatively high for a country at Tanzania's level of development, indicating that TANU has functioned well as an instrument for building up a sense of national loyalty and identity. "TANU is the most important political structure in Tanzania," says Perry, "and its successes and failures, problems and prospects, are of vital concern to the country's political development. It has mobilized voters and party activists, organized the economic activities of Tanzania's peasantry, and served as a major recruitment source for governmental and quasigovernmental agencies as well as for more explicitly political positions."[66] Nyerere appears to have obtained considerably better results with TANU than Nasser and Sadat have with ASU in Egypt.

Although Tanzania after independence chose a constitutional system with an elected president and a single established party, it stayed closer to the British model in arrangements for executive organization and the civil service, and in subordinating the military to civilian control. A cabinet of about twenty ministries is headed by a prime minister appointed by the president. Within each ministry, a permanent secretary from the career civil service functions in the British tradition as chief aide to the minister. The civil service as an institution continues along much the same line as before independence, with the main change being the substitution of Africans for Britishers in the senior posts. Of about 3000 higher civil service positions in the early 1960s, less than one in six was filled by a Tanzanian. During the 1960s, Africans gradually replaced most of the Europeans, and now occupy nearly all of the important offices. Although civil servants can and do hold membership in TANU, the service has not been heavily politicized. Also, Nyerere has carried out a commitment to keep the civil service open to any

Tanzanian citizen, whatever the individual's racial background. Particularly with regard to specialized manpower needs for national planning programs, a central recruiting agency has been authorized to seek qualified personnel from any available source, pending the availability of qualified Tanzanian citizens. Technical competence has had high priority, and as a result the Tanzanian civil service seems to be functioning effectively. At the same time, Nyerere has tried to avoid the emergence of a civil service elite such as has happened in other African nations, by keeping firm control over salary levels and other benefits.

Also in sharp contrast to most new states in Africa, the military has not played a significant role in political affairs.[67] An antimilitary tradition before independence in Tanganyika led to serious consideration being given to the issue of whether or not a national army should be maintained at all after independence. The decision was to have an army, but it has been kept small and under tight rein. The only serious threat from the armed forces came in 1964, when a mutiny occurred reflecting discontent with status and pay, and with the rate at which British officers were being replaced by Tanzanians. This uprising was not politically motivated, and received little public support. It was quickly and decisively suppressed, with its leaders being imprisoned and many of the soldiers who took part being dismissed. "As with other cases of organized group dissatisfaction, the government decided on a mixture of co-optation and infiltration. Members of the army and police were admitted to TANU, and party members were given important posts in the army and police bureaucracies. Ordinary soldiers were ordered to take part in 'nation-building' projects (such as road construction and agricultural improvement) and to receive political indoctrination."[68]

The Tanzanian political experience to date, therefore, has resulted in the establishment of a one-party state under a political leader who has dominated the governmental scene since before independence. External controls are effectively in operation over both the civil and military bureaucracies. At least for as long as Nyerere remains politically active, Tanzania's prospects for a stable polity appear to be excellent.

Communist Totalitarian Systems

Aside from the USSR, all Communist regimes can be considered as falling within this group, although it is debatable whether all of them can be called developing in the same sense. Certainly the People's Republic of China, by virtue of its size and prominence in the Communist camp, deserves to be in a class by itself, despite its low rating on many indices of development. The Communist countries of Eastern Europe are no less developed than other European nations such as Spain and Portugal. Only North Korea, Vietnam, Laos, Cambodia, and Cuba clearly are developing countries like their non-Communist Afro-Asian and Latin American counterparts.

What they all have in common is commitment to Marxist-Leninist ideology, and a totalitarian political style. The ideology is central, although it ranges from Titoism to Maoism. In recent years, to enhance doctrinal appeal in the developing areas, anticolonialism and the advantages of totalitarian methods for rapid national development have been stressed.[69] Alienated intellectuals are drawn into Communist elites by the prospect of gaining power in a revolutionized society more to their liking. In the new states, according to Shils, Communist doctrine has the advantage of attracting "devoted educated persons, relentless in the pursuit of their goals in societies in which continuous purposiveness of effort is not common."[70] Coercion and terror are justified by the social transformation that is promised.

The totalitarian approach demands a monopoly of political power in the hands of a single party, and does not recognize the legitimacy of open opposition. It "seeks to dominate every sphere of life and to annul every center of previously independent authority."[71] Mobilization of the masses is diligently sought, but only for participation in approved activities, participation that will be secured to the extent necessary by coercion or the threat of coercion.

The administrative apparatus required by such a regime is enormously complex, and it must be subjected to reliable party supervision, which in turn calls for a control network responsive to the narrow circle of elitist leadership in the party. The state bureaucracy must be paralleled by an interlocking party bureaucracy. This is an arduous obligation in a society plagued by a shortage of skilled manpower, but it cannot be avoided without risking the security of the regime. These dual hierarchies are held together by the unquestioned right of the party to exercise control as it sees fit and by the common device of dual officeholding which makes most members of the state administrative hierarchy also subject to the party hierarchy and its discipline. It is not possible, as Carl Beck points out, "to pinpoint a formal state bureaucracy. . . . The course of administration is not determined by a bureaucracy in the sense of a formal state administrative system that is independent and instrumental; it is determined, instead, by the interplay between the leaders, the movement, and a series of administrative organizations."[72]

A perennial problem in staffing the state administrative apparatus is the relative stress put on the need to be "red" and to be "expert." Apparently the general tendency in China, Eastern Europe, and Cuba, as in the USSR, has been to emphasize class background and political loyalty while the regime is being installed and secured, and then to pay more attention to expert knowledge later on. Along the way there may be short-range alternations, as have occurred in both China and Cuba. Beck reports evidence that a new managerial class is being created and that representatives of this group are entering the administrative and political elites in countries such as Czechoslovakia and Hungary. Of course, the ultimate objective is to ensure that the system produces officials who will be both "red" and "expert." Hence, strenuous efforts are made to train a younger generation of industrial and technical intelligentsia and thus transform the party-versus-bureaucracy problem into more of a intraparty struggle.

Administration in these Communist countries encounters all of the problems faced in other societies urgently engaged in rapid industrialization and economic development that have inadequate resources for the scheduled pace of accomplishment. The insistent emphasis on responsiveness of the official state administrative machinery to the party apparatus introduces an additional set of complications. It leads in practice to continuous conflicts between party units and the official government agencies held accountable for the administration of particular programs, with resulting losses in organizational efficiency. It also poses problems of individual choice to the person who is both a public official and a disciplined party member, reducing his initiative and willingness to experiment because of apprehension about being caught between competing obligations.

Some speculation concerning administrative evolution in these countries holds that the impact of industrialization will be much as it was on Western political systems, with the growth of a professionalized bureaucracy that has a strongly hierarchical structure, intensive functional specialization, and tenure protection of status. Beck argues that the political environment in a Communist totalitarian regime is unlikely to allow this to happen. "In this setting," he concludes, "the creation of an independent bureaucracy, even of the instrumental type, would become a threat to the power position of the elite and the goal of maintaining revolutionary political zeal."[73] According to this analysis, the pattern of administrative change in these regimes in the future is likely to diverge sharply from that in the developed non-Communist countries and in the developing countries with polyarchal competitive political characteristics. It may, however, be paralleled much more closely in the dominant-party mobilization systems.

Available up-to-date reliable information on the state bureaucracies in these Communist totalitarian regimes is regrettably scarce. The most systematic analysis has been done on the Communist countries of Eastern Europe.[74] Some information is available on China and Cuba, providing an opportunity to compare the largest Asian Communist nation with the only one in Latin America.

From its establishment in 1949 to 1976, the People's Republic of China had a remarkable continuity in its top leadership. With the deaths of Mao Tse-tung, Chou En-lai, and other revolutionary veterans, changes in the political order are inevitable but what they will be is uncertain, so we must rely on what is known about Mao's China.[75]

The main political structures during the entire period since 1949 have been the Chinese Communist party (CCP), the official state institutions centering on the National People's Congress (NPC), and the People's Liberation Army (PLA). The CCP's highest formal organ is the National Party Congress, which elects the Central Committee, which in turn elects the Politburo and its Standing Committee. Theoretically, the Party Congress members are elected every five years and meet annually, but in practice meetings have been much less frequent. The actual decision-makers are the members of the Standing Committee of the Politburo, usually numbering fewer than ten individuals, including the chairman. The official state structure parallels this party structure, with the National People's Congress electing a Standing Committee and (until the position was abolished in 1975) the chairman of the People's Republic. The chief administrative organ in the state structure is the State Council, headed before his death by Chou En-lai, which brings together all ministry and commission heads. "In practice," according to Townsend, "the State Council has shared with the highest CCP bodies the ultimate responsibility for the government of China. It is subordinate politically to party leadership, but its role as translator of party decisions into state action has made it by far the most powerful of the various institutions established by the constitution. Its relative prominence has declined at times . . . but it has remained the authoritative organ within the state hierarchy."[76] The role of the People's Liberation Army as the third major political structure does not rest on any constitutional grant of special status, but on the intimate involvement of the PLA in the whole history of the Communist movement in China beginning in the late 1920s. Formally, the PLA is controlled by the Ministry of National Defense within the State Council, but actually direction over military policy has been closely held by the CCP Military Affairs Committee. This political chain of command is carried through at each level within the PLA hierarchy by means of a political commissar or officer who is stationed alongside the military commander of the unit. Thus, these three structures of party, state, and army "constitute three interlocking hierarchies of organization that dominate the Chinese political system. Elites within these hierarchies convert interests and demands into policy alternatives, and direct the implementation and enforcement of authoritative decisions."[77]

During its nearly three decades of existence, Communist China has gone through several stages in its political development, reflecting shifts in program objectives and power relationships. In the early years from 1949 to 1957, the emphasis was on reconstruction following the long years of warfare, and the launching of projects for rapid economic development with special stress on heavy industry. The Soviet model was influential, and the state apparatus was mainly relied on for results. During 1957 a complicated intraparty debate led to the movement known as the "Great Leap Forward," with what proved to be overly ambitious objectives for rapid movement on all fronts. The CCP took a more commanding role using the slogan "politics takes command," and the state apparatus was downgraded as overbureaucratized. Soviet-style economic planning was dropped in favor of a decentralized effort to stimulate agricultural production through rural communes without sacrificing industrial development. A breakdown in this campaign, resulting in a severe economic crisis from 1959 to 1961, ushered in a period of retrenchment and consolidation which lasted through 1965, and which involved extensive criticism of Mao's leadership because of his identification with the Great Leap Forward.

Mao resumed the political offensive again in 1966 by launching the "Great Proletarian Cultural Revolution," aimed at rectifying what were charged to be deviations by the CCP from Maoist policies. The widespread internal turmoil which was spearheaded by Red Guard revolutionary groups loyal to Mao had two important consequences on the institutional balance of power. The CCP leadership was purged and its organizational effectiveness vastly reduced; the People's Liberation Army emerged as the primary power center. By 1969 the Cultural Revolution had subsided. The CCP had been thoroughly revamped with military figures in a plurality on the CCP Central Committee, and with Mao's major opponents purged. From 1969 to Mao's death in 1976, an unstable equilibrium was maintained, during which military influence was sharply curtailed, and "moderate" and "radical" factions jockeyed for position within the CCP. Glorification of Mao increased as his actual participation in governance declined. The official state structure, which like the party had suffered during the Cultural Revolution, regained authority and responsibilities. The long anticipated power showdown triggered by Mao's death late in 1976 has apparently brought about at least a temporary victory for the more moderate and pragmatic elements in the CCP, as evidenced by the appointment of Hua Kuo-feng as premier and chairman of the CCP Central Committee, and the ouster of the so-called gang of four, one of them Mao's widow.

These systemwide political upheavals form a backdrop for an examination of the operation of the state bureaucracy, which has varied with changes in the political climate. In general, treatment of the official state bureaucracy in the Chinese Communist regime reflects a basic distrust of bureaucratic responsiveness and a desire to curb bureaucratic power, combined with reluctant acceptance of the inevitable need to maintain a state bureaucratic apparatus. The outcome of this ambivalence has been an alternating pattern of expansion and contraction, depending on general political conditions. Bureaucratic power peaked during the mid 1950s, rose again in the early 1960s, and in this decade has had another resurgence which seems to have increased substantially since Mao's death. The low points of bureaucratic status have coincided with the Great Leap Forward of the late 1950s and the Cultural Revolution a few years later.

Some consistent themes have persisted during the entire period since 1949. One is a determination to politicize the bureaucracy and make it responsive to party direction, using various devices. Most fundamental is the practice of putting party members in most of the important government positions. Another is to recognize a party "fraction" in each organizational unit, consisting of the leading party members in the unit, as the vehicle for making sure that party policies are being carried out. Backing up these measures is the existence of a hierarchy of party committees at each level of the state administrative hierarchy, with oversight functions designed to assure the supremacy of politics. As a consequence of these multiple controls, Barnett concludes that party dominance of the government bureaucracy "operates not only at the upper levels of leadership in the hierarchy, it also reaches effectively to the lowest levels of all organizations in the bureaucracy."[78]

The second theme is decentralization by the transfer of administrative powers to the lowest feasible level. This diffusion strategy is designed to prevent the buildup of a nonproductive administrative superstructure and at the same time strengthen local initiative and responsibility. Carried to an extreme during the Great Leap Forward, the central ministries essentially lost control over lower administrative levels, and local party committees became the effective decision-makers. A by-product of this involvement turned out to be a bureaucratization of politics as the CCP organs themselves became identified with administrative specifics, leading later during the Cultural Revolution to charges that the CCP itself had become overbureaucratized. Despite this and other problems, "members of the Chinese elite apparently remain committed to their pattern of diffused administrative responsibilities. This pattern has served as a check on bureaucratic expansionism, prepared the country for resistance to foreign attack, and compiled a creditable record of economic growth. Most significantly, perhaps, it has created an administrative system that is sensitive to the growth potential of localities and encourages them to maximize the use of their own resources."[79]

The product of this campaign to ensure subordination of the state administrative apparatus to CCP control is what Dittmer calls a "mass line" bureaucracy. The term is borrowed from Mao's "mass line" principle that there should be a pattern of reciprocal communication between citizens and party leaders, with the masses presenting ideas to the party for consideration and carrying out decisions rendered, but with the right of decision-making reserved to the party. Such a mass line bureaucracy is described by Dittmer as "neither as centralist as the Soviet administrative system nor as democratic as the quasi-autonomous workers' councils of the Yugoslav system, but a combination of an activist Central organization and extensive mass participation, the two coordinated by an evolving ideological consensus."[80] He rates it as an authority system having a high level of elite power combined with a high level of mass participation.

Criteria for recruitment into the Chinese bureaucracy, as in other Communist regimes, have varied in the stress placed on political loyalty versus competence, on being "red" as against being "expert." During mobilization and rectification campaigns, the former factor has been more important, with the latter gaining in times of comparative quiet and stability. Vogel points out that in case of direct conflict, the "red" or political considerations have taken priority, finding expression in the slogan "politics takes command." He also notes that bureaucratic career patterns "reflect the mixture of political and rational bureaucratic considerations." Generally career patterns have followed "a fairly regular progression much as one might expect in an ordinary bureaucracy, with some striking exceptions that have occurred for political reasons. The exceptions are concentrated at the time of rectification campaigns when political considerations take on greater primacy." In such circumstances, "the politically vulnerable are attacked and sacrificed. At the end of a rectification campaign, new openings are available as a result of the removal of the politically vulnerable, and the politically reliable . . . are promoted. In other words, under ordinary circumstances promotions within the apparatus are likely to be based on annual assessments when rational-bureaucratic considerations of competence are given greater weight, but at the time of rectification campaigns, promotions and demotions are more likely to be based on political considerations."[81] At all times, political reliability is a must. Disciplinary action to ensure it has been institutionalized in the "semipurge" rather than through resort to the violent purge methods of Russia in the 1930s, with offenders being sent away for study and labor and then returning to work but often at a lower level. "This practice tends to maintain a high degree of responsiveness to political pressures from above even if it derives more from anxiety than from spontaneous enthusiasm."[82] The overriding consideration is to make sure that the bureaucracy remains safely politicized.

Cuba under Castro has gone through several stages during the revolutionary period since the overthrow of the Batista regime in 1959, even though there has been no significant change in the top leadership.[83] After a couple of years devoted to consolidation of the regime and liquidation of prerevolutionary institutions, late in 1961 the system was avowed to be Communist, based on a claimed adaptation of Marxism–Leninism to Latin American circumstances. This led during the early 1960s to severance of diplomatic relations with the United States, increasing reliance on the Soviet Union, and vigorous efforts to export the revolution to other Latin American countries. Toward the end of the decade, emphasis shifted to

internal economic development based primarily on agriculture,
international revolutionary activity declined, and the strategic goal
became the "building of socialism in one island." Beginning about
1970, and culminating in the adoption of a new constitution in
1976, the dominant theme has become "institutionalization of the
revolution," leading to efforts at depersonalizing political leadership, strengthening the Cuban Communist party (PCC), and
revamping the governmental apparatus.

At least until recently, political leadership in Cuba has been
highly concentrated. Fidel Castro, his brother Raul, and a limited
group of associates from the revolutionary takeover have dominated
the regime. "Castro exerted a charismatic, personalistic type of
government characterized by the concentration of power in the
'Maximum Leader' and his inner circle of loyalists and by the lack
of institutionalization. . . . In practice, Castro and his small circle
occupied the top positions in the administration, the party, and the
army; he was the best example combining the jobs of prime minister,
first secretary of the party, and commander-in-chief of the armed
forces."[84] This pattern helps explain some unusual features of the
Cuban regime compared to other Communist systems: a relatively
weak Communist party; a high rate of participation by the military
in the top elite; and a lack of clear institutional differentiation
among the party, military, and administrative hierarchies. In
each of these respects, current reforms are intended to bring about
greater conformity to the prevalent practices among Communist
countries.

The PCC as it now exists is the descendant of a series of earlier
organizational manifestations going back to the 26th of July Movement which was formed to support Castro's opposition to Batista.
In its present form, the PCC was not established until 1965, and the
party as an entity has played a symbolic rather than a central role in
political affairs. With Fidel Castro as first secretary and a Central
Committee of about 100 members, the PCC has been tightly controlled despite an extensive organizational network. The party
membership has never been large; in 1969 it was only 55,000. The
party machinery has been relatively inactive. The first PCC party
congress was not held until 1975, following numerous postpone-
ments. In recent years, PCC membership has been increased considerably, reaching over 200,000 by 1975 (still only about 2
percent of the population). Despite these measures to enhance the
party's stature and expand participation in its activities, the PCC
remains peripheral as compared to other Communist polities.

On the other hand, the military role has been crucial. Castro's rebel army brought him to power, and veterans of the revolution have continued to occupy most of the important positions in both the party and the state administration. When the PCC was formed in 1965, two-thirds of the members of its Central Committee came from military ranks. Most cabinet ministers and heads of other central agencies continue to be drawn from those with military backgrounds. The army as an institution has been assigned a wide variety of nonmilitary as well as military duties, including active participation in the much publicized sugar cane harvest campaigns. As a consequence, Dominguez maintains that the key political role in Cuba is that of the "civic soldier." Cuba is largely governed, he asserts, by these civic soldiers—"military men who actually rule over large sectors of military and civilian life, who are held up as symbols to be emulated by all military and civilians, who are the bearers of the revolutionary tradition and ideology, who have civilianized and politicized themselves by internalizing the norms and organization of the Communist Party and who have educated themselves to become professionals in military, political, managerial, engineering, economic and educational affairs. Their civic and military lives are fused."[85] Unlike China, where the role of the People's Liberation Army has expanded and contracted over time and where party–military conflict has frequently surfaced, in Cuba military participation in central decision-making has been "more stable and institutionalized," without an alternative civilian elite available to replace the civic soldiers, who have "remained the top government elite and have turned the civic soldier concept into a dominant norm in civilian organizations."[86] Dominguez argues that this degree of reliance upon military personnel reflects failures in handling labor supply and economic production problems, and that the political use of the military "has stifled criticism from the bottom of the system, has shut off the upward flow of political communication, and has curtailed the adaptability of the political system."[87]

Perhaps in recognition of these consequences, a reorientation of the armed forces seems to have taken place in recent years, resulting in some reduction in size, more concentration on purely military activities, greater specialization, and more stress on hierarchical ranking within the officer corps. The trend has been away from the earlier political mission and more toward modernization and professionalization, with extensive help from the Soviet Union through providing weaponry and training military personnel.[88] Partly because of these measures, and partly because of the aging of the revolutionary generation, military prominence in the Cuban version of communism is on the decline although still a distinctive feature.

Institutionalization of the revolution has also brought a revamping of the official governmental structure, bringing it closer to the Soviet Union model. A new constitution, approved by the PCC congress in 1975 and adopted by a popular referendum early in 1976, established for the first time since the revolution a unicameral National Assembly whose members are indirectly elected for five-year terms from the membership of popularly elected municipal assemblies. The National Assembly now in turn formally designates from among its members a State Council, whose president serves as head of state. Executive and administrative responsibilities are assigned to a Council of Ministers. Fidel Castro serves both as president of the State Council and president of the Council of Ministers, in addition to continuing as first secretary of the PCC, so the institutionalization has not disturbed his undisputed place as "Maximum Leader." The Council of Ministers also currently includes Raul Castro as first vice-president, seven other vice-presidents, and twenty-three ministers heading up segments of the administrative structure.

These measures probably have not altered the actual pattern of political leadership much, although they may help to ease a later transfer of power from Fidel Castro to a successor. "The image projected in the second half of 1970 by Castro's promised reform was of a decentralized, democratic, independent, and mass-participation movement," according to Mesa-Lago, but in actuality "there has been an institutionalization trend characterized by central controls, dogmatism, and administrative-bureaucratic features resembling the Soviet system."[89]

In this milieu, civilian administrators have obviously not been in positions of crucial importance, and professional competence has been a secondary consideration. Administration in this revolutionary setting is carried out by what Petras calls "ambulating bureaucrats," who recognize that "decisions are made at the top and carried out on the bottom."[90] Most bureaucrats have been generalists who frequently change positions and rarely carve out a career in any particular area of administration. Political reliability has been the foremost criterion in recruitment and advancement, with little attention paid to professional preparation for administrative careers until recently. Petras asserts that although there is still an acute shortage of managerial personnel, the universities are now providing "an increasing flow of technically trained and politically reliable administrators. . . . The

Cubans are training administrators who are politically attuned to the revolution. The difficult period is passing; the administrators who were politically reliable but lacking in technical and managerial skills are being replaced."[91] Although he may be correct in predicting that a new technical intelligentsia is in the making, it is one that the revolutionary political leadership intends and should be able to keep firmly under control.

Notes

1. Robert C. Tucker, "Towards a Comparative Politics of Movement-Regimes," *American Political Science Review* 60, No. 2 (1961): 283. See also his "On Revolutionary Mass-Movement Regimes," *The Soviet Political Mind: Studies in Stalinism and Post-Stalin Change* (New York: Frederick A. Praeger, Inc., 1963), Chapter 1, pp. 3-19.

2. David E. Apter, *Ghana in Transition* (New York: Atheneum Publishers, 1963), p. 330.

3. Milton J. Esman, "The Politics of Development Administration," in John D. Montgomery and William J. Siffin, *Approaches to Development: Politics, Administration and Change* (New York: McGraw Hill Book Company, 1966), copyright © 1966, pp. 96-97.

4. *Ibid.*, p. 91.

5. *Ibid.*, p. 92.

6. Charles J. Parrish, "Bureaucracy, Democracy, and Development: Some Considerations Based on the Chilean Case," pp. 229-59, in Clarence E. Thurber and Lawrence S. Graham, eds., *Development Administration in Latin America* (Durham, N.C.: Duke University Press, 1973).

7. Peter S. Cleaves, *Bureaucratic Politics and Administration in Chile* (Berkeley, Calif.: University of California Press, 1974), p. 2.

8. *Ibid.*, p. 1.

9. *Ibid.*, p. 310.

10. *Ibid.*, p. 21.

11. Selected useful sources include Ersin Onulduran, *Political Development and Political Parties in Turkey* (Ankara, Turkey: Ankara University Press, 1974); Ilkay Sunar, *State and Society in the Politics of Turkey's Development* (Ankara, Turkey: Ankara University Press, 1974); Joseph S. Szyliowicz, "Elites and Modernization in Turkey," pp. 23-66, in Frank Tachau, ed., *Political Elites and Political Development in the Middle East* (Cambridge: Schenkman Publishing Company, 1975); Lynton K. Caldwell, "Turkish Administration and the Politics of Expediency," in William J. Siffin, ed., *Toward the Comparative Study of Public Administration* (Bloomington, Ind.: Department of Government, Indiana University, 1957), pp. 117-44; Richard L. Chambers, "The Civil Bureaucracy—Turkey," in Robert E. Ward and Dankwart A. Rustow, eds., *Political*

Modernization in Japan and Turkey (Princeton, N.J.: Princeton University Press, 1964), pp. 301-27; George L. Grassmuck, *Polity, Bureaucracy and Interest Groups in the Near East and North Africa* (Bloomington, Ind.: CAG Occasional Papers, 1965); Joseph B. Kingsbury and Tahir Aktan, *The Public Service in Turkey: Organization, Recruitment and Training* (Brussels: International Institute of Administrative Sciences, 1955); A. T. J. Matthews, *Emergent Turkish Administrators* (Ankara, Turkey: Institute of Administrative Sciences, Faculty of Political Science, University of Ankara, 1955); and Frederick T. Bent, "The Turkish Bureaucracy as an Agent of Change," *Journal of Comparative Administration* 1, No. 1 (1969): 47-64.

12.   Szyliowicz, "Elites and Modernization in Turkey," pp. 43-47.

13.   Chambers, "The Civil Bureaucracy—Turkey," pp. 325-26.

14.   Szyliowicz, "Elites and Modernization in Turkey," pp. 61-62.

15.   Robert R. Kaufman, "Corporatism, Clientelism, and Partisan Conflict: A Study of Seven Latin Countries," pp. 109-48, in James M. Malloy, ed., *Authoritarianism and Corporatism in Latin America* (Pittsburg, Pa.: University of Pittsburg Press, 1977), at pp. 117-19.

16.   For a detailed report on part of this record, see Roderick T. Groves, "The Venezuelan Administrative Reform Movement, 1958-1963," in Thurber and Graham, *Development Administration in Latin America*, pp. 47-80.

17.   For general treatments of Mexican politics, refer to William P. Tucker, *The Mexican Government Today* (Minneapolis: University of Minnesota Press, 1957); Robert E. Scott, *Mexican Government in Transition* (Urbana: University of Illinois Press, 1959); Raymond Vernon, *The Dilemma of Mexico's Development* (Cambridge: Harvard University Press, 1963); Martin C. Needler, *Politics and Society in Mexico* (Albuquerque: University of New Mexico Press, 1971); and L. Vincent Padgett, *The Mexican Political System*, 2nd ed. (Boston: Houghton Mifflin Company, 1976). More specialized studies dealing with Mexican administration include William Ebenstein, "Public Administration in Mexico," *Public Administration Review* 5, No. 2 (1945): 102-12, and Martin H. Greenberg, *Bureaucracy and Development: A Mexican Case Study* (Lexington, Mass.: D. C. Heath and Company, 1970).

18.   Evelyn P. Stevens, "Mexico's PRI: The Institutionalization of Corporatism?" pp. 227-58, in Malloy, *Authoritarianism and Corporatism in Latin America*, at p. 227.

19.   Kaufman, "Corporatism, Clientelism, and Partisan Conflict," pp. 120-21.

20.   Glen Dealy, "The Tradition of Monistic Democracy in Latin America," in Howard J. Wiarda, ed., *Politics and Social Change in Latin America: The Distinct Tradition* (Amherst: University of Massachusetts Press, 1974), pp. 73, 83.

21.   Stevens, "Mexico's PRI," p. 253.

22.   Needler, *Politics and Society in Mexico*, p. 42.

23.   Vernon, *The Dilemma of Mexico's Development*, p. 189.

24.   Greenberg, *Bureaucracy and Development*, p. 98.

25. Wendell Schaeffer, "National Administration in Mexico: Its Development and Present Status" (unpublished Ph.D. dissertation, University of California, 1949), pp. 183-84. Quoted by Greenberg, *Bureaucracy and Development*, p. 100.
26. Greenberg, *Bureaucracy and Development*, p. 98.
27. Vernon, *The Dilemma of Mexico's Development*, pp. 151-52.
28. Greenberg, *Bureaucracy and Development*, pp. 70-71.
29. Scott, *Mexican Government in Transition*, p. 293.
30. Vernon, *The Dilemma of Mexico's Development*, pp. 5-6.
31. Greenberg, *Bureaucracy and Development*, p. 138.
32. Scott, *Mexican Government in Transition*, p. 279.
33. For a fuller discussion, see Kenneth M. Coleman, *Diffuse Support in Mexico: The Potential for Crisis* (Beverly Hills, Calif.: Sage Publications, 1976).
34. Vernon, *The Dilemma of Mexico's Development*, p. 13.
35. *Ibid.*, pp. 136-37.
36. Greenberg, *Bureaucracy and Development*, p. 45.
37. "The Mexican political process is capped by a leadership apparatus under the guise of government in association with a single dominant political party (the PRI). One of that informal apparatus's key functions is control, in order to preserve the centralized national regime. Not only the general public but even members of the governing apparatus (elites themselves) find their political behavior closely regulated." William S. Tuohy, "Centralism and Political Elite Behavior in Mexico," pp. 260-80, in Thurber and Graham, *Development Administration in Latin America*, at p. 260.
38. Selected sources on India include Stanley A. Kochanek, "The Indian Political System," pp. 39-107, in Robert N. Kearney, ed., *Politics and Modernization in South and Southeast Asia* (Cambridge: Schenkman Publishing Co. Inc., 1975); Norman D. Palmer, *The Indian Political System* (Boston: Houghton Mifflin Company, 1961); Myron Weiner, *Party Building in a New Nation* (Chicago: University of Chicago Press, 1967); R. Dwardakis, *Role of the Higher Civil Service in India* (Bombay: Popular Book Depot, 1958); and A. R. Tyagi, "Role of Civil Service in India," *Indian Journal of Political Science* 19, No. 4 (1958): 349-56. On Malaysia, refer to Gordon P. Means, "Malaysia," pp. 153-214, in Kearney, *Politics and Modernization in South and Southeast Asia*; R. S. Milne, *Government and Politics in Malaysia* (Boston: Houghton Mifflin Company, 1967); David S. Gibbons and Zakaharia Haji Ahmad, "Politics and Selection for the Higher Civil Service in New States: The Malaysian Example," *Journal of Comparative Administration* 3, No. 3 (1971): 330-48; Milton J. Esman, *Administration and Development in Malaysia* (Ithaca, N.Y.: Cornell University Press, 1972); and Robert O. Tilman, *Bureaucratic Transition in Malaya* (Durham, N.C.: Duke University Press, 1964).
39. Kochanek, "The Indian Political System," p. 45.
40. Means, "Malaysia," p. 163.
41. Kochanek, "The Indian Political System," p. 69.

42. Means, "Malaysia," p. 181.

43. Appleby, quoted in Palmer, *The Indian Political System*, p. 132.

44. Kochanek, "The Indian Political System," p. 102.

45. Tilman, *Bureaucratic Transition in Malaya*, p. 137.

46. Esman, *Administration and Development in Malaysia*, p. 8. Esman's book is basically an account of a major effort at administrative reform designed to remedy such deficiencies.

47. *Ibid.*, p. 6.

48. *Ibid.*, Preface, p. v.

49. Selected sources on Egypt: Morroe Berger, *Bureaucracy and Society in Modern Egypt* (Princeton, N.J.: Princeton University Press, 1957) and *Military Elite and Social Change: Egypt Since Napoleon* (Princeton, N.J.: Center of International Studies, Princeton University, 1960); Grassmuck, *Polity, Bureaucracy and Interest Groups in the Near East and North Africa*; Walter R. Sharp, "Bureaucracy and Politics—Egyptian Model," pp. 145-81, in Siffin, *Toward The Comparative Study of Public Administration*; Amos Perlmutter, *Egypt: Praetorian State* (New York: E. P. Dutton and Co., 1973); Claude E. Welch, Jr. and Arthur K. Smith, *Military Role and Rule* (North Scituate, Mass.: Duxbury Press, 1974), Chapter 7, "Egypt: Radical Modernization and the Dilemmas of Leadership," pp. 178-204; and Shahrough Akhavi, "Egypt: Neo-Patrimonial Elite," pp. 69-113, in Tachau, *Political Elites and Political Development in the Middle East.*

50. R. Hrair Dekmejian, *Egypt under Nasir: A Study in Political Dynamics* (Albany: State University of New York Press, 1971), p. 284. Quoted in Welch and Smith, *Military Role and Rule*, p. 198.

51. Akhavi, "Egypt: Neo-Patrimonial Elite," p. 102.

52. James B. Mayfield, *Rural Politics in Nasser's Egypt: A Quest for Legitimacy* (Austin: University of Texas Press, 1971), pp. 118-19. Quoted in Welch and Smith, *Military Role and Rule*, p. 199.

53. Welch and Smith, *Military Role and Rule*, p. 201.

54. Refer to Akhavi, "Egypt: Neo-Patrimonial Elite," pp. 87-95.

55. Welch and Smith, *Military Role and Rule*, p. 202.

56. Barbara N. McLennan, *Comparative Political Systems: Political Processes in Developed and Developing States* (North Scituate, Mass.: Duxbury Press, 1975), pp. 259-60.

57. Sharp, "Bureaucracy and Politics—Egyptian Model," pp. 158-60.

58. Eliezer Be'eri, *Army Officers in Arab Politics and Society* (New York: Frederick A. Praeger, Inc., 1970), p. 432. Quoted in Welch and Smith, *Military Role and Rule*, p. 194.

59. Akhavi, "Egypt: Neo-Patrimonial Elite," p. 103.

60. McLennan, *Comparative Political Systems*, p. 261.

61. Akhavi, "Egypt: Neo-Patrimonial Elite," p. 103.

62. McLennan, *Comparative Political Systems*, pp. 260-61.

63. For available sources on the Tanzanian political system, refer to Henry Bienen, *Tanzania: Party Transformation and Economic Development*,

expanded ed. (Princeton, N.J.: Princeton University Press, 1970); Raymond F. Hopkins, *Political Roles in a New State* (New Haven, Conn.: Yale University Press, 1971); and Andrew J. Perry, "Politics in Tanzania," Chapter 13, pp. 405-40, in Gabriel A. Almond, gen. ed., *Comparative Politics Today: A World View* (Boston: Little, Brown and Company, 1974).

64. In Zanzibar, the Afro-Shirazi Party (ASP) is the counterpart single party of TANU on the mainland.

65. Bienen, *Tanzania*, pp. 175-76.

66. Perry, "Politics in Tanzania," p. 439.

67. For a detailed analysis, see Ali A. Mazrui, "Anti-Militarism and Political Militancy in Tanzania," pp. 219-40, in Jacques Van Doorn, ed., *Military Profession and Military Regimes* (The Hague: Mouton, 1969).

68. Perry, "Politics in Tanzania," pp. 426-27.

69. See Kautsky, *Political Change in Underdeveloped Countries: Nationalism and Communism* (New York: John Wiley & Sons, 1962).

70. Shils, *Political Development in the New States*, p. 75.

71. *Ibid.*

72. Carl Beck, "Bureaucracy and Political Development in Eastern Europe," pp. 268-300, in LaPalombara, *Bureaucracy and Political Development*, at pp. 281-82.

73. *Ibid.*, pp. 298-99.

74. Carl Beck is the best known specialist in this area. In addition to "Bureaucracy and Political Development in Eastern Europe," see his "Party Control and Bureaucratization in Czechoslovakia," pp. 437-55, in Fred W. Riggs, ed., *Frontiers of Development Administration* (Durham, N.C.: Duke University Press, 1970) [reprinted from *The Journal of Politics* 23, No. 2 (1961): 279-94]. Relevant studies of other East European Communist countries include Kenneth Jowitt, *Revolutionary Breakthrough and National Development: The Case of Romania*, 1944-1965 (Berkeley, Calif.: University of California Press, 1971), and Thomas A. Baylis, *The Technical Intelligentsia and the East German Elite* (Berkeley, Calif.: University of California Press, 1974).

75. For generalized treatments of the Chinese political system, refer to Harold C. Hinton, *An Introduction to Chinese Politics* (New York: Frederick A. Praeger, Inc., 1973); James R. Townsend, *Politics in China* (Boston: Little, Brown and Company, 1974); and Townsend, "Politics in China," Chapter 11, pp. 311-64, in Almond, *Comparative Politics Today*. More specialized studies of Chinese bureaucracy include Franz Schurmann, *Ideology and Organization in Communist China*, 2nd ed., enlarged (Berkeley, Calif.: University of California Press, 1968); Chalmers Johnson, "The Changing Nature and Locus of Authority in Communist China," pp. 34-76, in John M. H. Lindbeck, ed., *China: Management of a Revolutionary Society* (Seattle: University of Washington Press, 1971); A. Doak Barnett, "Mechanisms for Party Control in Government Bureaucracy in China," pp. 415-36, and Ezra F. Vogel, "Politicized Bureaucracy: Communist

China," pp. 556-68, both in Riggs, *Frontiers of Development Administration*; Lowell Dittmer, "Revolution and Reconstruction in Contemporary Chinese Bureaucracy," *Journal of Comparative Administration* 5, No. 4 (1974): 443-86; and Parris H. Chang, "The Dynamics of Party-Military Relations in China," pp. 123-48, in Welch, *Civilian Control of the Military*.

76. Townsend, *Politics in China*, pp. 86-87.

77. *Ibid.*, p. 100.

78. Barnett, "Party Control in the Government Bureaucracy in China," p. 429.

79. Townsend, "Politics in China," p. 358.

80. Dittmer, "Revolution and Reconstruction in Contemporary Chinese Bureaucracy," p. 480.

81. Vogel, "Politicized Bureaucracy: Communist China," p. 561.

82. *Ibid.*, p. 563.

83. Sources on the Cuban political system include Richard Fagen, *The Transformation of Political Culture in Cuba* (Stanford: Stanford University Press, 1969); James F. Petras, "Cuba: Fourteen Years of Revolutionary Government," pp. 281-93, in Thurber and Graham, *Development Administration in Latin America*; Jorge I. Dominguez, "The Civic Soldier in Cuba," pp. 209-38, in Kelleher, *Political-Military Systems*; and Carmelo Mesa-Lago, *Cuba in the 1970s: Pragmatism and Institutionalization*, rev. ed. (Albuquerque: University of New Mexico Press, 1978).

84. Mesa-Lago, *Cuba in the 1970s*, pp. 67-68.

85. This excerpt is reprinted from "The Civic Soldier in Cuba" by Jorge I. Dominguez in *Political-Military Systems: Comparative Perspectives*, Sage Research Progress Series on War, Revolution, and Peacekeeping, Volume IV, ed. Catherine McArdle Kelleher, © 1974, p. 210, by permission of the Publisher, Sage Publications, Inc. (Beverly Hills/London).

86. *Ibid.*, p. 234.

87. *Ibid.*, p. 236.

88. Mesa-Lago, *Cuba in the 1970s*, pp. 76-79.

89. *Ibid.*, p. 115.

90. Petras, "Cuba: Fourteen Years of Revolutionary Government," pp. 289-90.

91. *Ibid.*, p. 291.

10

AN OVERVIEW OF BUREAUCRACIES AND POLITICAL SYSTEMS

Now that we have surveyed the public bureaucracies in a wide variety of existing political systems, what can be said in summary about similarities and diversities among them, and about the relationship between the type of political system and the role of administration in the system as shown by bureaucratic traits and behavior? Let us start by considering basic expectations generally held concerning the proper character and conduct of bureaucracies, and move from that to more particularized treatment of variations associated with different kinds of polities.

Political Ends and Administrative Means

With few exceptions, there is common agreement transcending differences in political ideology, culture, and style, that bureaucracy should be basically instrumental in its operation, that it should serve as agent and not as master. It is almost universally expected that the bureaucracy be so designed and shaped as to respond willingly and effectively to policy leadership from outside its own ranks. The idea that bureaucratic officialdom, either civil or military, or both together, should for any extended period of time constitute the ruling class in a political system is generally rejected. The political elite may include members of the civil or military bureaucracies, but should not consist exclusively or even primarily of bureaucratic officials. Even in regimes in which a bureaucratic elite is clearly in a position of political dominance, it will rarely claim that this is the way things should be; instead, it will usually insist that such a situation can be justified only temporarily under unusual circumstances.

Of course, this is not the same as asserting that the bureaucracy can or should play strictly a passive role, uninvolved in policy-making and uncontaminated by exposure to the political process. Rather, it is an affirmation of the primacy of political control over the administrative system, whatever the character of the political leadership. This is a fundamental tenet of the doctrine held by advocates of widely variant political alternatives, including supporters of traditional monarchy, aristocratic oligarchy, representative democracy, mass-mobilization party rule, and totalitarianism of different varieties. All agree that the state bureaucracy should be responsible to the political leadership, however intimately it may be brought into the process of decision-making by the will of the political elite.

A consensus on the way things ought to be does not necessarily ensure that they will actually be that way. Of more importance to us than an idealized concept of what the role of bureaucracy should be is an accurate assessment of what it is in practice.

Bureaucracies—Usurpative or Instrumental?

A perennial concern relating to bureaucracies is the possibility that they may stray from their instrumental role to become the primary power-wielders in the political system. The political role of the bureaucracy has been a matter of continuing interest in the more developed nations, and has emerged as one of the principal issues in discussions about the political future of developing countries. The tendency in recent years for bureaucratic elite regimes to become more prevalent certainly enhances the relevancy of this issue.

The classic literature on bureaucracy does not ignore the problem but gives it relatively incidental attention. Weber himself has been criticized as not being sensitive enough to bureaucratic power considerations. Diamant considers this an unfounded view, and cites passages from Weber's writings to refute it.[1] He shows that Weber described the power position of a fully developed bureaucracy as "always overtowering," called for greater emphasis on political leadership, advised politicians to "resist any effort on the part of the bureaucrats to gain control," and warned that a nation "which believes that the conduct of state affairs is a matter of 'administration' and that 'politics' is nothing but the part-time occupation of amateurs or a secondary task of bureaucrats might as well forget about playing a role in world affairs.'' Weber recognized a dichotomy between policy and administration and wanted to draw a sharp distinction between the roles of the politician and the bureaucrat, but he also noted that "every problem, no matter how technical it might seem, can assume political significance and its solution can be decisively influenced by political considerations.'' Diamant's interpretation is that ambiguities in Weber's treatment of this matter reflect a dualism in his thinking, the severe rationality of his ideal-type constructs leading him to consider bureaucracy as a neutral tool, and his own political experiences teaching him that the power interests of the bureaucracy may threaten the mastery of political leadership.

Relating Bureaucratic and Political Development

A prolonged and vigorous debate in recent discussions of bureaucracy in developing countries has brought into sharp relief divergent opinions on this issue of the power role of the bureaucracy in the political system. The debate revolves around differing views as to the relationship between bureaucratic and political development, leading in turn to contrasting suggestions as to appropriate strategy for facilitating the attainment of political development.[2]

The importance of a competent bureaucracy in a developed political system is not in dispute. All commentators would agree with Almond and Powell as to the central role of bureaucracy in the process of political development, and concur with their statement that a political system "cannot develop a high level of internal regulation, distribution, or extraction without a 'modern' governmental bureaucracy in one form or another."[3] Also there is general agreement that in many developing nations the bureaucracy has gained ascendancy over other political institutions, and that the number of such cases is increasing, with a resulting current imbalance in bureaucratic and political development. At issue is the question of whether the presence of a bureaucracy that is relatively developed enhances or inhibits prospects for overall political development in the long run.

Stated simply, one argument is that the existence of a strong "modern" bureaucracy in a polity with political institutions that are generally weak presents in itself a major obstacle to political development. The main counterargument is that a high level of bureaucratic development can be expected to enhance rather than hinder prospects for future overall political development.

The best known spokesman for the first point of view is Fred W. Riggs. Others sharing similar judgments include Henry F. Goodnow, Lucian W. Pye, S. N. Eisenstadt, and Joseph LaPalombara, although they cannot all be lumped together because of differences in emphasis among them and, in some instances, what seems to be a shift in attitude over time.

Riggs has presented his analysis in several versions but with the same basic theme. One of the earliest, and still one of the best, expositions of this diagnosis is his "paradoxical view," reflecting a conviction based on the implications of his "prismatic-sala" model and his case study of Thailand, that transitional societies frequently lack balance between "political policy-making institutions and bureaucratic policy-implementing structures," the consequence being that "the political function tends to be appropriated, in considerable measure, by bureaucrats."[4] He surveys the power position of the transitional bureaucracies vis-à-vis other political institutions which exercise controls over bureaucracies in Western countries—such as chief executives, legislatures, courts, political parties, and interest groups—and finds the other institutions weak in contrast to the "burgeoning growth" of bureaucracies. In such circumstances, political direction tends to become more and more a bureaucratic monopoly, and as this occurs, the bureaucrats themselves are increasingly tempted to give preference to their own group interests. As the imbalance continues and increases, the prospect for attainment of a desirable mutual interdependence among competing power centers becomes more remote.

In a later formulation, Riggs has referred to regimes with these characteristics as "bureaucratic polities," or unbalanced polities dominated by their bureaucracies.[5] His underlying distinction between balanced and unbalanced polities rests on whether or not there is an approximate balance of power between the bureaucracy and extrabureaucratic institutions which he chooses to call the "constitutive system."[6] This term encompasses as subcomponents "an elected assembly, an electoral system, and a party system."[7] A polity is balanced if it maintains a reasonably stable equilibrium between the bureaucracy and the constitutive system, unbalanced if either dominates the other. The form of government found in nations generally regarded as modern is balanced, whereas most developing nations have unbalanced polities. Usually the latter have "bureaucratic polities," with the attendant tendency to inhibit political development, which Riggs has consistently argued results from "premature or rapid expansion of the bureaucracy when the political system lags behind."[8] Not only will a dominant bureaucracy have this adverse effect on the future of the political system, according to Riggs, but it also will be unlikely to meet its more immediate obligations, because it "will necessarily sacrifice administrative to political considerations, thereby impairing administrative performance."[9]

LaPalombara also called attention early to the difficulty of restricting bureaucracy to an instrumental role.[10] The risk, which is not sufficiently recognized in even the more advanced countries, is accentuated in developing nations, "where the bureaucracy may be the most coherent power center and where, in addition, the major decisions regarding national development are likely to involve authoritative rule making and rule application by governmental structures."[11] The result is the emergence in many places of "overpowering bureaucracies," with the growth in bureaucratic power inhibiting, and perhaps precluding, the development of democratic polities. In instances in which the military rather than the civil bureaucracy has the upper hand, the prospect is even more dismal. If democratic development is to be encouraged, a separation of political and administrative roles is required; and this calls for deliberate steps to limit the power of the bureaucracies in many of the newer states. He makes some specific suggestions, including a de-emphasis on goals of economic development, a shift in demands on the political system from economic to social and political realms, and a massive program of education, all designed in part to reduce the responsibility of the bureaucracy for goal-setting and goal implementation.

Henry Goodnow, generalizing about the power position of the bureaucratic elite in new states from his study of the civil service in Pakistan, reached the conclusion that the occupants of the higher civil service posts do indeed exert such predominant influence as to make the climate unfavorable for the development of democratic institutions.[12] He attributes this to the fact that they "fell heir to the instrumentalities of power" vacated by the colonial administrators, and were able easily to convert governmental institutions created to permit rule by a foreign bureaucratic elite to the service of a native bureaucratic elite. They had at their disposal the means "to coerce, to propagandize, to reward, to incarcerate." Most important, there were "seldom any effective countervailing forces."[13] He does not say that this trend was started by a lust for power on the part of the bureaucratic officials. He concedes that they have usually taken over with some reluctance, have often been sincere in blaming the shortcomings of politicians for making this necessary, and have regarded themselves as guardians of democracy as an ultimate goal; but he feels that the urge to hold and consolidate power is deceptively strong. Therefore, he is skeptical about the prospects of a gradual transition from bureaucratic elite rule to democratic government, and foresees as more likely a power struggle between an increasingly rigid governing bureaucracy and an increasingly revolutionary opposition, which will destroy prospects for evolutionary change.

Lucian Pye has taken much the same stance in discussing the political context of national development.[14] He argues that the greatest problem in nation-building is how to relate "the administrative and authoritative structures of government to political forces within the transitional societies," in the face of the usual imbalance between "recognized administrative tradition and a still inchoate political process."[15] Both external and internal factors are responsible for the situation. The nation-building efforts of the West have been almost exclusively devoted to upgrading administrative capabilities, with the creation of political capabilities left to chance. Even where nationalist movements have gained popular acceptance, they have "settled on the easy alternative of preserving their power by crowding in on the administrative structure rather than striving to build up permanent and autonomous bases of power."[16] To Pye, such tactics indicate weakness rather than strength, and do not offer grounds for encouragement even in countries with dominant national parties. His pessimistic conclusion is that there has been an unmistakable decline in both political party vitality and administrative effectiveness in most of the new states. He apparently does not agree with those who cite the countries with dominant mass parties as showing a capacity to control the bureaucracy without hamstringing it. Pye agrees closely with Riggs in saying that "public administration cannot be greatly improved without a parallel strengthening of the representative political processes. In fact, excessive concentration on strengthening the administrative services may be self-defeating because it may lead only to a greater imbalance between the administrative and the political and hence to a greater need of the leaders to exploit politically the administrative services."[17]

Pye also has explored the psychology of institutionalization in relation to the building of bureaucracies in new states,[18] leading him to disagree with those who consider new states fortunate if they inherit colonial administrative structures intact. Institutionalization of colonial authority came about through introducing the role of the clerk to indigenous civil servants. Imbued with "the spirit of the clerk," colonial civil servants were trained to give infinite attention to details, stress legalism in the extreme, and function with minimal discretion or imagination. Independence and nationhood meant that the old pattern of institutionalized behavior was no longer adequate. Ritualized relationships were replaced by power relationships. Technical skills became insufficient. Most civil servants "were suddenly compelled to adjust not to a disciplined order of role relationships but to the tensions of a political arena."[19] In this environment of politicized tension, "the members of bureaucracies often see themselves as a specific community ... whose status has been threatened by the universal search for power."[20] Bureaucrats in the new states therefore turn to participation in power conflicts, calling for traits such as competitiveness, creativity, and political skills.

S. N. Eisenstadt likewise has reviewed the extensive involvement of bureaucracies in the political process of new states, and has noted that they tend to fulfill functions that would more normally be carried out by legislatures, executives, and political parties, thereby impeding the development of more differentiated political institutions.[21] He appears to share the view that bureaucracies which become dominant retard the potential growth of other sectors needed to bring more balance to the political system.

These appraisals are representative of the prevalent negative judgment regarding the implications of what is taken to be the most typical bureaucratic role in developing polities. Other equally informed commentators express considerably more sanguine views. Usually they do not deny the tendency for the bureaucracy to occupy what seems to be an inordinately strong position relative to other political organs, but they are inclined to regard this as inevitable, perhaps desirable, and at any rate not easily susceptible to external manipulation. Ralph Braibanti has supported this position most extensively. Others with similar views include Milton J. Esman, Bernard E. Brown, Fritz Morstein Marx, Leonard Binder, Lee Sigelman, Edward W. Weidner, and myself; LaPalombara in his more recent writing also seems to share these views to some extent.

Braibanti, like Riggs, has addressed this problem on various occasions since the early 1960s. Given the high priority assigned to economic development in the new nations, he has pointed out that during the early stages of nation-building "what virtue there is seems to reside in the bureaucracy. Economic development must be achieved in the matrix of constructing an equilibrium of bureaucratic power and political control. This must be done even though development requirements are inherently antagonistic to the political results of the very equilibrium which will eventuate. The achievement in disequilibrium of a condition of development which the logic of popular sovereignty demands be achieved in an unattainable equilibrium is the crucial problem in political development."[22] During the interim period when there is no possibility of vigorous political activity in general in the society, an elitist bureaucracy with a guardianship orientation must be the principal initiator of change. The educative role it can play should be reassessed, and the problem of how such a bureaucracy "can with good grace relinquish its power and transform its function when a mature, viable political system begins to operate as the source of polity," should be studied.[23] Under some circumstances, the military bureaucracy may be more effective than the civil bureaucracy, since it sometimes "embodies nationalist and revolutionary ideals and manifests a zeal, sense of sacrifice, and devotion to duty greater than any other element in society."[24] Braibanti also has held out the theoretical possibility that either civil or military bureaucracy may develop representativeness and responsiveness to the public comparable to that provided by a popularly elected legislature, so that "a bureaucracy in which democratic patterns have been extended and fortified may not be the worst fate which might befall a developing nation."[25]

Braibanti has consistently maintained that a primary requisite for development is a competent bureaucratic system, and has assumed that "the strengthening of administration must proceed irrespective of the rate of maturation of the political process."[26] He argues that administrative reform does not occur autonomously, but "has a permeative effect on other institutions and structures and . . . may serve as a generant in the growth of these sectors." What is desirable is "the strategic strengthening of as many institutions, sectors, and structures as possible."[27] Pursuit of this strategy does not preclude "the further strengthening of already strong bureaucratic institutions, for the existence of a viable bureaucracy is held to be a paramount need of developing states."[28]

Esman and Brown also belong among those who acknowledge the centrality of administration in developing systems but advocate that it be strengthened further rather than downgraded. Although

Esman stresses the central and growing role of administrative institutions in carrying out action programs, he does not think that bureaucrats as a group can often afford to be political risk-takers, or that they are likely to contest for political leadership. He acknowledges that the efforts of political elites "must often be invested in gaining and maintaining effective control and direction over administrative agencies, civil and military, counteracting their tendency to achieve autonomy and independent power positions or to enhance their group interests." Nevertheless, he believes that bureaucrats, when under pressure, "usually opt for safety in order to protect their careers. When challenged by powerful opponents who themselves dispose of political power and influence, bureaucrats without strong political protection feel helpless."[29] Brown mentions tendencies for political power to shift to the executive sector of government, and within the executive, from political officials to professional civil servants; he recognizes that this raises a serious question concerning the future of democratic government, but nevertheless feels that the pressing need is to strengthen the executive branch. The dangers of a bureaucracy that is not adequately controlled are real. They cannot be eliminated but may be reduced by trying to make the bureaucracy more representative of the society, to provide built-in checks and balances.[30]

Fritz Morstein Marx credits the merit bureaucracies which emerged in the modern nation-states of the West with having contributed to the viability of constitutional government by accommodating demands made upon the body politic, participating in giving certain demands priority over others, discharging government responsibilities expeditiously, and in general, working toward stability and continuity. He mentions the possibility, although not the assurance, of similar contributions from the higher civil service in the new nations, with the observable growth of a nucleus of trained administrators, "usually relatively young, responsive to modern ways, and simultaneously aroused partisans of the new order" who "contribute to a professional outlook to the everday conduct of governmental activities," and who "are leaving a visible imprint." Since he believes civilian career officials to be primarily motivated by "prudential neutrality" rather than by an urge to take over direct political power, he is not much concerned about the prospect of bureaucratic elite rule, and he sees the civil servants in developing countries as heavily dependent on support from political leadership in various kinds of "strongman" government, rather than sitting in the driver's seat themselves.[31]

In analyzing prospects for transition to democracy, with particular reference to countries in the Middle East, Leonard Binder refers to the views held by others that democratic institutions have succeeded in non-European countries only when imposed from above, and suggests that in the Middle East the transition "depends upon the willingness and the ability of the military and bureaucratic elites . . . to reject their own institutional orientations and to decide rationally and consciously to establish and work certain democratic institutions to some extent." He expresses "only moderate" pessimism regarding the possibility, giving several reasons why it may happen, including "the fact that the military in these countries are neither professionally, ideologically, nor socially clearly differentiated from civil servants, professional intellectuals, and other members of the thin middle class."[32] The sequence of development being attempted in the Middle East is the reverse of that which took place in the West, with administrative development preceding both economic and political development, in an application of the "reversed democratic faith" of Middle Eastern leaders.[33]

Various other writers can be identified with the general proposition that the risk of jeopardizing a more balanced political equilibrium in the future does not justify a deliberate policy of stifling further bureaucratic development whenever current imbalance exists favoring the bureaucracy. Lee Sigelman has argued that evidence is substantial that "the presence of a relatively modern national administrative system is a necessary precondition of, not a hindrance to, societal modernization, including political development."[34] Hence he would favor efforts to build up such administrative capabilities where they do not currently exist. I have subscribed elsewhere to the basic view that "bureaucratic upgrading is apt to be beneficial rather than disadvantageous."[35] Weidner, in evaluating technical assistance programs in public administration, has acknowledged the desirability of maintaining a competitive balance between the political and administrative elements in the political system, but at the same time he asserts that "those responsible for technical assistance programs cannot wait for political systems, of whatever form, to mature before extending help."[36] Unwilling to concede that a strengthening of the bureaucracy will necessarily deter parallel growth elsewhere, he says that another possibility may be that an enlightened and capable bureaucracy may be willing and able to take leadership in bringing along the lagging sectors in order to meet developmental objectives. His inclination, therefore, is not to advise abandonment of bureaucratic improvement as a legitimate objective in external aid programs. LaPalombara, who earlier voiced considerable skepticism about the wisdom of attempting to help bureaucracies already tending toward dominance, has since moved toward a more discriminating approach in discussing alternative strategies for developing administrative capabilities in emerging countries. Given the overwhelming demands of crisis management which commonly burden developing nations, he has now taken the position that whatever bureaucratic apparatus a developing country may have inherited should generally be strengthened rather than weakened.[37]

External Inducement of Balanced Development

As might be expected, the ongoing debate just summarized is closely paralleled by a related divergence of opinion as to strategy for achieving balanced political development, particularly focusing on the role of external sources that may intervene in the process.

Those alarmed about bureaucratic imbalance understandably urge that aid should be forthcoming from outside only if it is realistically designed to bring about better balance in the political system. Riggs has presented the most extensive arguments for such an aid-giving strategy, under which decisions to extend or withhold aid would be dependent primarily on anticipated consequences in movement toward a more balanced polity in the recipient country. On the assumption that the imposition of control over a bureaucracy by the constitutive system is a difficult task in any event and will become more difficult as the bureaucracy becomes relatively more powerful, he recommends that deliberate measures be taken to curtail bureaucratic expansion and to strengthen potential control agencies. This would call, among other things, for a drastic re-evaluation of the objectives of technical assistance programs which have tended, he believes, to assist bureaucratic proliferation and to neglect the growth of strictly political institutions. The outcome in most but not all instances is that he advocates a reduction in efforts to provide aid to bureaucracies and a corresponding augmentation of externally supplied programs to strengthen elements of the constitutive system, such as legislatures, political parties, and devices for interest group representation.

According to Riggs,

... the administrative doctrines which have shown their usefulness in the United States and other Western polities are of limited utility in many non-Western countries where an imbalance exists between the power of bureaucracy and the power exercised by constitutive systems. In other words, our administrative principles may prove helpful in bringing about some improvement in administrative performance in balanced polities. By contrast, they may further undermine administrative performance in unbalanced polities. In these systems priority needs to be given to efforts to achieve balance, either by strengthening the constitutive system or the bureaucracy, depending on which of these key institutions is relatively less powerful.[38]

This statement would seem to discount the efficacy of external efforts at bureaucratic improvement except in the relatively few instances among developing countries in which a balance already exists between the bureaucracy and the constitutive system. In the case of imbalance favoring the bureaucracy, which is by far the more likely situation, Riggs seems to be saying that external aid to the bureaucracy would have the dual adverse results of adding to the degree of imbalance by further building up bureaucratic power while simultaneously detracting from the quality of administrative performance. Even in polities in which the imbalance is due to bureaucratic weakness, Riggs' position seems to be that external aid may indeed be able to enhance the political power stance of the bureaucracy but at the price of a lowered operational record, since he maintains that in unbalanced polities, no matter what the form of imbalance, efforts by Western polities to strengthen the bureaucracy are likely to "further undermine administrative performance." His conclusion seems to restrict very narrowly the beneficial prospects of external inducement of bureaucratic improvement.

In bureaucratic polities in which the imbalance is due to weaknesses in the constitutive system, on the other hand, Riggs apparently is optimistic about the possibilities for successful intervention to build up the strength of these elements in the political system. He makes a number of suggestions about courses of action which might strengthen nonbureaucratic institutions, but does not indicate how these steps might feasibly be taken in the absence of a request from the political leadership of the country concerned. The need for launching "soundly conceived programs for political development"[39] is mentioned, without any practical indication as to how this is to be done. The closest he seems to come is in the suggestion that "attention be given to intensive study of the political ecology of administration as a necessary prerequisite to the formulation of effective technical assistance and a realistic foreign policy concerned with developmental goals."[40]

In addition to his basic position that assistance to bureaucracies in unbalanced polities should be withheld, Riggs also argues that as a matter of American foreign policy such aid should be declined in balanced political systems which are not democratic. In other words, one form of balance may be found in a polity in which the constitutive system is dominated by a single party rather than offering opportunities for competition among two or more parties. According to his general analysis, "our administrative doctrines are relevant to the needs of these governments, as well as to those which are democratic. However, if one goal of American foreign policy is to encourage democratic regimes, then it may well be desirable to withhold assistance to undemocratic governments, even those which could use such assistance."[41] Riggs invokes Woodrow Wilson in support of this view, arguing that Wilson weighted democratic values more highly than administrative efficiency, and therefore would be shocked to find Americans exporting administrative doctrines and practices that might be of aid to authoritarian governments.[42]

The Riggsian strategy for external inducement of balanced development thus calls for the deliberate withholding of administrative technology transfer except in the relatively few instances in which developing countries have balanced polities that are also democratic in the sense of having competitive party systems, while simultaneously adopting an aggressive posture of promoting various aid programs intended to strengthen the constitutive system, especially in its competitiveness, except in the rare instances in which imbalance exists because of dominance by the constitutive system.

Ralph Braibanti and I, among others, have vigorously questioned key features of this strategy for inducing balanced political development from external sources. The issue is not the desirability, from the point of view of a country such as the United States, of contributing as much as possible to realization of whatever prospects may exist for movement toward a more balanced political system with democratic characteristics. Rather, the question is how this can be best accomplished, within the options actually available to aid-giving countries. One major consideration, of course, is the position taken on the point as to whether or not, in bureaucratic polities, further strengthening of already strong bureaucracies will reduce future prospects for movement toward greater balance. Riggs views such an outcome as almost axiomatic. Braibanti, on the other hand, as we have seen, believes that bureaucratic reform has a permeative effect on other institutions and structures, and that external aid for this purpose should never be withheld solely on the basis that a desirable political balance from the perspective of the donor country must be achieved first. I concur with this view.

Of course, this attitude toward providing external assistance for upgrading the bureaucracy does not preclude a similar willingness to assist in efforts to improve the capabilities of other elements in the political system. Instead, Braibanti's assumption, as already noted, is that "the strategic strengthening of as many institutions, sectors, and structures as possible is desirable."[43] However, foreign assistance to institutions in the constitutive system can be made available only subject to serious practical limitations.

Braibanti examines several aspects of this problem, including external aid programs to strengthen political parties, legislatures, community development institutions, and citizen consultative or advisory bodies.[44] For example, with regard to proposals made by Samuel Huntington and others that the United States try to strengthen political parties as part of its foreign assistance effort, Braibanti points out difficulties for both the donor and recipient countries. If the support goes only to a single dominant mass party, this would surely seem to run counter to the foreign policy goal of fostering political competitiveness. Where a two-party system is functioning, support for both parties might be possible, but on the other hand the fact of two-party competition would appear to lessen the policy motivation for intervention.

But in new states in which there are more than two parties or in which there are two parties very unevenly balanced in power, active support of party organizations by the United States seems especially dangerous. If all parties were supported equally, this might encourage a proliferation of new parties, the very condition ... which is conducive to instability. Moreover, indiscriminate support of all valid parties would place the United States in the untenable position of supporting party organizations which actively oppose crucial principles of American foreign policy. Some, ironically, even oppose American foreign assistance.... On the other hand, if only certain parties were "certified" by the United States and selected for assistance, difficult situations would arise. The mere act of selection would interfere in the natural evolution of creative, orderly political renovation which can best be provided by unfettered creation of parties arising from legitimate needs for articulating shifting interests.[45]

As far as the country on the receiving end of political party support is concerned, reasons for resistance also exist. In some instances, as in Pakistan, a clear legal prohibition against the support of political parties by foreign sources is in effect. In the background, whether or not such a law has been enacted, is the pervasive feeling that deliberate foreign support of parties, whether all of them or a few that are "certified," would require "probing in the most delicate tissues of the social system. Such probing is not and cannot be consistent with postcolonial sensitivities regarding sovereignty."[46]

Strengthening of legislative bodies is another frequently mentioned way of controlling bureaucratic power and improving political balance. This presents somewhat similar but fewer problems, particularly if attention is concentrated on improvement of the legislative infrastructure by providing staff services in areas such as research and bill-drafting. Transfer of parliamentary technology of this type might be successfully undertaken more frequently than has been attempted in the past.

Braibanti proposes, then, what he describes as a "somewhat eclectic" general strategy for the external inducement of political development, which concentrates on the strengthening of as many institutions as possible, including bureaucratic institutions that may already be strong. Acceptability on the part of the political leadership of the recipient nation is a necessary condition for success in external aid programs, no matter what the target may be. Arguing that "it is beyond the capability of an aid-giving nation to directly and deliberately accelerate politicization," he points out that "manipulation of the larger social order . . . is no longer politically feasible and is becoming less feasible. . . . The stimulation of the political process or the deliberate strengthening of counter elites implies internal interference with domestic politics" which is unacceptable to the leaders of newly independent states.[47]

I have likewise tried to stress the utmost importance of providing an opportunity for the political leaders of new nations to choose among options as to external aid programs. More specifically, these options might include requesting assistance only for purposes of strengthening the bureaucracy and improving the level of administrative performance, combining this with external help in building up nonbureaucratic institutions, or concentrating exclusively on the latter objective. My view, as expressed elsewhere, is that "for countries that we are generally willing to aid, as a matter of national policy, we should not discontinue technical assistance efforts in administration because of a judgment that the political system does not at the moment conform to our specifications for a working political democracy, or even because of concern that this kind of assistance may lessen the prospect for achieving such a political system in the future."[48] Certainly leaders in today's developing nation-states can legitimately claim that they should be able to pick and choose among possibilities for foreign assistance in whatever combination suits their own political predilections. Given this understandable attitude, prospects for success are poor for a policy of extending aid only under circumstances judged by the donor country to contribute positively to desirable political development. A combined package deal under which assistance for administrative improvement efforts will be made available only when accompanied by programs to strengthen political instrumentalities deemed to have the potential for exerting suitable controls over the bureaucracy is likely to be rejected. It almost certainly will be by an entrenched bureaucratic elite regime of the type for which the strategy is presumably most directly designed.

In short, an aid-giving country is not in a favorable position to insist on such conditions for providing help, as a method for successful stimulation of balanced political development. No blueprint for external guidance of the course of political development in emerging countries is likely to be drafted by donor country planners.

As a matter of common sense, why should this be expected? Is there anything concerning which the sensitive national leaders of new states should be expected to show more touchiness than to have foreigners tell them what they must do to achieve political development adjudged suitable by someone else's standards? ... A crucial point to bear in mind, whatever the judgment as to balanced versus unbalanced social growth strategies, is the relative impotency of external as compared to internal political decision-makers. Short of subversion or open coercion, the providers of foreign aid are severely limited in what they can accomplish in the absence of cooperation from the domestic political leadership. One of the reasons for disillusionment with the results of past technical assistance projects in administration has been that earlier we held overly optimistic expectations as to what could be accomplished where local political support was lacking or lukewarm. Disappointment on the part of the aid-giver and resentment on the part of the recipient would in all likelihood be much greater as a consequence of externally initiated programs of assistance to achieve a balance in political development not voluntarily recognized as desirable by the political elite of the country concerned.[49]

Testing the Imbalance Thesis

The prolonged debate about the relationship between bureaucratic and political development and about related strategies for achieving balance in development has been conducted until recently with very little reference to available cross-national data which might shed light on the matter. Lee Sigelman has tried to remedy this deficiency by undertaking two separate tests of the so-called imbalance thesis.[50]

According to the imbalance thesis, as already noted, the presence of a bureaucracy that is highly developed reduces the likelihood of attaining political development in Third World countries. As stated by Sigelman, "the chief components of the argument that bureaucratic development hinders the prospects of political development are the propositions that: (1) the relatively high level of bureaucratic development in new nations fosters overparticipation by the bureaucracy in the performance of governmental and political functions; and (2) such bureaucratic overparticipation stunts the growth of viable representative institutions."[51]   On the basis that data are lacking for testing the second proposition, but are available for testing the more central first proposition, Sigelman sets out to do this. He starts by stating more precisely the hypothesis to be investigated, as follows: "In politically underdeveloped nations, there is a positive correlation between (1) level of bureaucratic development and (2) extent of bureaucratic overparticipation in governmental and political functions."[52]   Confirmation of this hypothesis would support the imbalance thesis; rejection would cast doubt upon it.

To operationalize the key concepts of bureaucratic development and bureaucratic overparticipation in terms of available data, Sigelman turns to two different sources. From Banks and Textor,[53] he makes use of the variable "Character of Bureaucracy" which separates national bureaucracies into four categories, three of them relevant to developing countries. In his analysis, Sigelman equates the category "semi-modern" with a higher degree of bureaucratic development, and the categories "post-colonial transitional" and "traditional" with a lower level of bureaucratic development, producing an approximately equal division among the nations considered by using this dichotomy. From Almond and Coleman,[54] he relies on the judgments expressed by the area experts involved, in terms of the model proposed by Coleman in the concluding chapter of the volume, in classifying nations as to whether their bureaucracies are "overparticipant" or "not overparticipant" in the performance of "political" functions and of "governmental" functions, considered separately.

According to Sigelman's criteria as to what nations should be considered politically underdeveloped, fifty-seven such nations in Latin America, Asia, and Africa were common to the Almond-

Coleman and Banks-Textor analyses. Using this pool of politically underdeveloped nations, Sigelman's conclusion is that the comparison shows an inverse rather than a positive relationship between bureaucratic development and overparticipation. "The bulk of the relatively developed bureaucracies do *not* overparticipate: only six of the thirty developed bureaucracies overparticipate in political functions, only ten of thirty overparticipate in governmental functions. On the other hand, the vast majority of the underdeveloped bureaucracies *do* overparticipate: nineteen of the twenty-seven underdeveloped bureaucracies overparticipate in political functions, and fully twenty-two of twenty-seven in governmental functions."[55]

Claiming that this study effectively undercuts the argument that modern bureaucracies inhibit political development on overparticipation grounds, but recognizing that such findings run counter to commonly held views, Sigelman has more recently replicated his first study, utilizing alternative data for re-examining the relationship between bureaucratic development and bureaucratic dominance. In retesting the imbalance theory, he substituted for the Banks-Textor classification scheme to measure bureaucratic development a variable labeled "Degree of Administrative Efficiency," used by a pair of economists to separate national bureaucracies into three categories.[56] This measure of bureaucratic development groups countries as to those with systems of public administration characterized by: (1) reasonably efficient bureaucracies without widespread corruption or instability of policy at higher administrative levels; (2) considerable bureaucratic inefficiency with corruption common and moderate policy instability; or (3) extreme bureaucratic inefficiency probably combined with widespread corruption or policy instability or both. Sigelman considers this variable an improvement on the Banks-Textor measure because it is explicitly ordinal and is less ambiguous as to the criteria used for grouping nations.

For measuring bureaucratic dominance, he uses in the retest the classification scheme employed by me in the original version of this study for highlighting the political role of bureaucracy in a variety of developing nations. Of the six categories in that classification plan, he groups the traditional-autocratic and the bureaucratic elite political regime types together and scores the nations in these two groups as having "high dominant" bureaucracies, on the basis that these bureaucracies "are squarely at center stage in the play of political power." Nations in the remaining four categories, where the regimes have polyarchal competitive or dominant-party systems which keep the bureaucracy's power position relatively restricted, are scored as having "low dominant" bureaucracies. Again, Sigelman believes that he has found for the retest a better means of measuring bureaucratic dominance than the "overparticipation" ratings used in his first study, since such ratings are "an imperfect indicator of dominance, in that politicized bureaucracies do not necessarily dominate their political systems," whereas the political regime type of approach measures bureaucratic dominance "directly in terms of political-bureaucratic power arrangements."[57]

The retest sample is composed of thirty-eight developing nations common to the Adelman-Morris and Heady analyses. Cross-tabulation of the two variables reveals, as in the previous study, that the cases are arrayed in precisely the opposite pattern from that predicted by the imbalance thesis. "Bureaucracies which are highly developed do *not* dominate less developed polities. Of all the bureaucracies which have attained a 'high' level of development, . . . not a single one is politically dominant. It is rather bureaucracies at a 'low' and, to a lesser extent, 'medium' developmental level which dominate their political systems—the former by a whopping margin (11–2), the latter by a bare majority (9–8). The findings . . . thus present new and striking evidence that the hypothesis of positive relationship between bureaucratic development and dominance cannot withstand empirical test."[58]

Sigelman's assertion as to the significance of his findings seems to be justified, and to date nobody has challenged his claim that these two studies warrant an attitude of "extreme skepticism toward the hypothesis that modern bureaucracies dominate less developed polities."[59] Although I concur that the arguments on behalf of the imbalance thesis have been greatly weakened by these studies, and welcome Sigelman's findings because they lend support to my own previously expressed views, I believe that it should be pointed out that recent political regime shifts do reduce the margin by which his findings are supported, although the basic pattern in his array of cases is not altered. Between 1966 and now, at least six of the nations classified as "low dominant" in his second study have had earlier competitive or dominant-party regimes replaced by bureau-cratic elite regimes of some kind. As a consequence, these nations would now have to be scored as "high dominant." Included in this retabulation would be Chile, Argentina, Brazil, Ghana, Nigeria, and the Philippines. All of these countries except one fall within the group considered "medium" as to level of bureaucratic develop-ment. Hence the main impact would be a redistribution converting the number of cases in which bureaucracies at a "medium" level of development are "high dominant" from a bare majority (nine versus eight) to an obvious preponderance (fourteen versus three). The huge margin (eleven versus two) by which bureaucracies at a "low" developmental level dominate their political systems would be undisturbed. Similarly, there would be only a slight shift (from none versus eight to one versus seven) in the low incidence of cases in which bureaucracies at a "high" developmental level are also "high dominant" politically. It is these two latter sets of relationships, of course, that are most important as evidence of an inverse rather than a positive correlation between bureaucratic development and bureaucratic overparticipation or dominance in the political system.

In discounting the imbalance thesis, Sigelman emphasizes that he is not denying the adverse effect of dominant bureaucracies on the emergence of vigorous political institutions. Granting that political development is likely to be hampered by bureaucratic dominance, his findings indicate that political development may be facilitated rather than thwarted by bureaucratic development, because "cross-sectionally, the higher the level of bureaucratic development, the lower the level of bureaucratic dominance. . . . Far from inhibiting the growth of political institutions, then, bureaucratic development is quite consistent with, and may well play a significant role in the promotion of, political development."[60] Certainly his analyses have increased doubt as to the validity of the imbalance thesis, although the debate about the relationship between bureaucratic and political development is sure to continue.

The Significance of System Variation

Certain questions were posed in Chapter 2 (see page 61) concerning higher public bureaucracies in various kinds of polities. The comparative study of public administration has not yet advanced far enough to provide satisfactory answers to these questions in the full range of existing political systems. The problem is due in part to a lack of consensus regarding what and how to compare, but it is both more basic and more elementary than concern over conceptualization and methodology. The absence or inadequacy of reliable information on bureaucratic structures and behavior in a large majority of the nation-states of the modern world continues to be a major handicap. Despite the gradual accumulation of relevant studies, the rate of progress has been disappointing, access to much valuable work is difficult, and too little systematically organized cross-national research has been carried through to completion.

What has become more and more obvious is the extreme importance of variation among political regimes as an explanatory factor for variation among public bureaucracies, making it crucial that efforts be intensified to remedy the existing gaps in reliable information. Meanwhile, the general state of affairs is that we know much more about the developed nations than the developing, and among them, much more about the United States, Great Britain, France, and Germany than about Japan or the USSR. Similarly, within the ranks of the developing nations, our knowledge, skimpy enough at best, is relatively greater in quantity and superior in quality for countries with long colonial histories prior to independence, such as India or the Philippines, or for countries that gained independence early or maintained national identity without interruption, such as the Latin American countries or Thailand, than it is for newly created Middle Eastern or African states with arbitrary boundaries marked on the map or for countries that have turned to communism during the last three decades.

Our ability to answer these questions also varies from one question to another. We are least ready to compare the internal operating characteristics of national bureaucracies. A few Western civil service systems have been studied in depth, and reassessments of their operations continue to appear. In only a scattering of non-Western systems has similar research been done. More often, if reports on the workings of these systems are available at all, we are apt to have only impressionistic and incidental comments to go on. We know little about internal behavioral patterns in individual bureaucracies, or about degrees of consistency or variation among them. This is an area that still urgently calls for systematic attention.

To the second question, concerning the extent to which the bureaucracy is multifunctional, we have a somewhat sounder basis for response. At a minimum we can say that there is a relationship between political modernity and bureaucratic specificity of function. The bureaucracies in developed countries resemble the diffracted model, with its more restricted functional activity for the bureaucracy; the bureaucracies in the developing countries are more likely to be multifunctional, participating actively in policy- or rule-making and even in interest articulation and aggregation. Still lacking are detailed case studies on the range of bureaucratic activity in most of the developing and some of the developed countries.

We are best prepared to respond to the third question, on the means for exerting external controls over the bureaucracy and the effectiveness of these controls. These matters have long been of concern in developed polities, and they have more recently been explored in treatments of developing political regimes.

The principal issue here is not whether political development is unbalanced to date in numerous emerging nations when judged by standards of balance in a modernized polity that is not totalitarian. This is acknowledged, and the explanation is not hard to find. It is a combination of two basic factors—the colonial heritage of bureaucratic rule which has been carried over into the fledgling nation after independence, and the unavoidable requirement of a minimal level of administrative competence for sheer political survival. It would be political suicide for a struggling nation with inchoate nonbureaucratic political institutions to insist for the sake of balance that the bureaucracy deliberately be brought down to the same level of inadequacy.

Rather, the issue, as already discussed, is whether a bureaucratic bid for power is so predictable, and bureaucratic rule so inevitable, unless resisted, that this outcome must be countered whenever possible by constraints on bureaucratic development and by continuous and systematic upgrading of nonbureaucratic potential sources of political power. A secondary but important issue is the feasibility of such a strategy on the part of external forces which may be trying to shape the future course of a developing polity.

Admittedly, the data for a definitive response to this question are not at hand, but what we do know points toward caution rather than assurance in the use of any analytical scheme to fit developing bureaucracies into a single mold. As Morstein Marx has pointed out, "the higher civil service, viewed as an action group exerting influence upon a country's political development, usually leaves quite indistinct tracks. Its role is neither easily assessed nor predictable. Aside from institutional variables, we must allow for differences not only between countries but also between stages in each country's evolution."[61] The alternatives open to the bureaucracy range from unquestioning defense of the status quo to ardent advocacy of basic reform, with one of the possibilities being simply quiescent non-involvement in matters of political policy. Weidner has suggested that the role of the bureaucracy, as compared with the roles of other parts of government or society, "ranges widely from country to country in regard to the original formulation and later modification and refinement of development values. Variations in its role in securing these values are equally great."[62]

Joseph LaPalombara has suggested that political and bureaucratic evolution be viewed "within a context of challenge-and-response, or as a process over time whereby political systems respond to changes in the kinds of demands they encounter." No particular pattern of adaptation is considered optimal for development. Recurring kinds of challenge or crisis can be identified, but they vary from one political system to another in the sequence in which they occur, their frequency, the ease or difficulty of resolution, and so forth. Transitional political systems commonly face the dilemma that they "must telescope into years the crisis management which was accomplished over generations in older nations." This makes it especially important that the tasks to be performed are identified and that priorities be established among them. "It is only after one has understood the relative priority assigned to the goals of the system that discussions about what kinds of administrators and administrative organization are best attuned to reaching them in a given situation make much sense." Despite their shared burden of crisis demands, the developing countries "present a wide variety of crises configurations and of administrative resources that might be made to deal with them."[63]

These reminders warn of the pitfalls in grouping together all bureaucracies, or even all bureaucracies in developing countries, and point toward the necessity of considering the role of the bureaucracy in relation to the political system and its goals. Such considerations have led to efforts to classify bureaucracies into types that take into account basic orientations and operational characteristics. The best known general classification is that proposed by Morstein Marx in his fourfold division of historical and current systems into guardian, caste, patronage, and merit bureaucracies.[64] Fainsod's classification, based on the criterion of the relationship of bureaucracies to the flow of political authority, is most pertinent here.[65] As reviewed earlier, this scheme distinguishes five forms of bureaucracy: representative, party-state, ruler-dominated, military-dominated, and ruling. In only the first two of these categories are officials clearly responsible to, and generally responsive to, political forces outside the state officialdom. Ruler-dominated bureaucracies present a more ambivalent situation, with the bureaucracy being the subservient personal instrument of the ruler, but with individual bureaucrats likely to be influential if they enjoy the confidence of the ruler, and with the regime highly dependent on adequate bureaucratic performance. In the remaining two categories, the political regimes are controlled by ruling elements dominated by officials of military background in one case and civilian in the other. If military men have seized power, they soon face nonmilitary problems that cause them to turn to civilian administrators for advice. If the civil bureaucracy is itself the ruling element, it must find legitimization from some other source, such as a colonial power or a figurehead monarchy, and the loyalty of the armed forces is usually essential.

Both Fainsod's categories and the groupings used in this study are based on a recognition that there is an intimate relationship between political system characteristics and bureaucratic system characteristics in all polities, including those that share the designation "developing" but are far from identical either in their political regimes or their bureaucracies. The categories chosen, however, coincide only in part. Fainsod's party-state category is subdivided into three groupings, and his two types of official-dominated regimes are also further subdivided and analyzed from a somewhat different perspective.

Put in terms of the classification system we have used, the following tentative statements summarize briefly what now seems to be known about the efficacy of external controls over the bureaucracy and the risks of bureaucratic power dominance in different types of political regimes.

1.   In the developed nations, both democratic and totalitarian, sufficient devices for political control exist to give significant direction to the bureaucracy and to minimize the likelihood of bureaucratic dominance while permitting substantial participation in political decision-making. The devices and methods show decided contrasts, however—for example, between the United States and the USSR. The long-term trend, even in Japan where bureaucratic centrality is most prominent, does not indicate a threat of transition to a bureaucratic elite regime.

2.   Among the developing countries, the variation is greater. Controls over the bureaucracy are weakest and the risks of indefinite bureaucratic power dominance are greatest in the various kinds of bureaucratic elite systems—civil and/or military. The number of these regimes is definitely on the rise, and they have received special attention from scholars, providing much of the basis for generalized models of developing polities, as is made evident by a comparison of the prismatic model of Riggs and his case study of Thailand, or of the general views of Goodnow and his case study of Pakistan. In these systems, the military bureaucracy normally will occupy a position of primacy and the civil bureaucracy will play a secondary

role. Although the civil bureaucracy is less likely than the military
to initiate a takeover of power, its cooperation is vital to the continued success of most bureaucratic elite regimes. The staying
capacity of these regimes is debatable. Janowitz and others who
have investigated the political record of the military conclude that
such regimes are often transitory; however, many of them have
been able to maintain themselves in power for considerable periods
of time. More polities have been moving into than out of this basic
configuration, but the possibility of transition from bureaucratic
elite status to some other regime type has already been demonstrated
in countries such as Turkey and Greece, where the movement has
been toward greater political competition. In other cases, such as
Egypt and Tanzania, the growth of a mobilizing mass party has
reduced the earlier direct influence of a military or civil bureaucratic
elite.

   3. Traditional-autocratic regimes produce what Fainsod has
called ruler-dominated bureaucracies. The usual expectation is that
these regimes are vulnerable and likely to undergo transformation.
The most usual shift possibility is to a bureaucratic elite regime, as
occurred some time ago in Thailand and more recently in Afghanistan
and Ethiopia, and may happen in Iran, Morocco, Jordan, or Saudi
Arabia. Other alternatives for transition, of course, are also present
but less probable.

   4. In polyarchal competitive systems, the trend is toward less
rather than more bureaucratic involvement in the exercise of political
power, toward a better balance between the bureaucracy and other
political institutions in regimes that resemble those of developed
democratic polities. However, these are volatile systems, and their
number has been declining. The most common direction of change
has been toward bureaucratic elitism. In a number of instances, as
in Pakistan, Burma, Indonesia, and Nigeria, this is what happened
soon after independence. In other instances, such as Chile, Uruguay,
and the Philippines, bureaucratic elite regimes of some variety have
replaced polyarchal competitive regimes of long standing in countries
which gained independence earlier.

   5. Among the dominant-party political systems, the prospect
that a preponderance of political power will be transferred to the
hands of officials in the state bureaucracy, civil or military, is
generally low. This eventuality becomes increasingly remote as we
move across the spectrum from dominant-party semicompetitive to
dominant-party mobilization to Communist party totalitarian
regimes. In terms of Western democratic standards, the imbalance

that can be expected in these systems is not one that overweighs but one that underweighs the bureaucratic element in the political equation. A decade ago, the most frequent prediction as to trends in political evolution among developing countries was movement toward a higher proportion of dominant-party regimes of some kind, but this has not materialized. Instead, except for newly established Communist party regimes such as those in Southeast Asian countries, the actual trend has been away from dominant-party systems, most often toward military regimes.

For the present, considerations such as these point toward a multiple rather than a uniform appraisal of the present status and future prospects of the role of administration in the political regimes of the developing countries. The actual role will depend on the type of political regime, and beyond that, the specialized circumstances in the particular country. In the commendable effort to identify central tendencies, we should avoid relying too greatly on experience in a few countries and on too easy an assumption that there is any clear-cut tendency at all that has shown up so far.

This survey of bureaucratic behavior in different types of developing political systems indicates that a categorical response to the issue of whether bureaucracy is usurpative or instrumental in developing countries is inappropriate and risky, particularly if it leads to prescriptive recommendations regarding the propriety of efforts toward bureaucratic upgrading which are to be applied generally. A more realistic approach is to relate the issue of the risk of bureaucratic domination to political system subtypes among the developing nations. When this is done, the threat of bureaucratic monopolization of political power becomes much less menacing, despite the frequency of imbalance between bureaucratic and non-bureaucratic political institutions among developing nations.

A Concluding Comment

The subject of comparative public administration has many ramifications. It can be studied from a number of different, although not necessarily mutually exclusive, perspectives. Our choice has been to use the public bureaucracy of the modern nation-state as the focus for comparison. Further, we have concentrated on the higher bureaucracy rather than on the whole bureaucratic apparatus, and on its external working relationships with other parts of the political system rather than on its internal operating characteristics. We have, however, deliberately elected to include a wide variety of existing nation-states in order to explore the role of bureaucracy in diverse settings that show marked contrasts in political system characteristics. We have found that the modern nation-state is sure to have as one of its political institutions a public service that meets the minimal structural requirements for bureaucracy as a form of organization, but that there is no standard pattern of relationships between public bureaucracy and the political system as a whole. Factors of crucial importance that affect these relationships include the stage of political development of the nation-state, its political regime characteristics, and the nature of the program goals it has chosen for accomplishment through administrative instrumentalities. Recognition of the existence of such diversity is the first step toward both a fuller understanding of particular national systems of administration and more meaningful comparisons among them.

Notes

1. Alfred Diamant, "The Bureaucratic Model: Max Weber Rejected, Rediscovered, Reformed," in Ferrel Heady and Sybil L. Stokes, eds., *Papers in Comparative Public Administration* (Ann Arbor, Mich.: Institute of Public Administration, The University of Michigan, 1962), pp. 79-81, 84-86.

2. The most comprehensive source is Ralph Braibanti, ed., *Political and Administrative Development* (Durham, N.C.: Duke University Press, 1969). Copyright 1969 by Duke University Press. For summaries of different points of view, refer also to Warren F. Ilchman, "Rising Expectations and the Revolution in Development Administration," *Public Administration Review* 25, No. 4 (1965): 314-28; and Ferrel Heady, "Bureaucracies in Developing Countries," pp. 459-85, in Fred W. Riggs, ed., *Frontiers of Development Administration* (Durham, N.C.: Duke University Press, 1970).

3. Gabriel A. Almond and G. Bingham Powell, Jr., *Comparative Politics: A Developmental Approach* (Boston: Little, Brown and Company, 1966), pp. 158, 323.

4. Fred W. Riggs, "Bureaucrats and Political Development: A Paradoxical View," pp. 120-67, in Joseph LaPalombara, *Bureaucracy and Political Development* (Princeton, N.J.: Princeton University Press, 1963).

5. Riggs, "Bureaucratic Politics in Comparative Perspective," in Riggs, *Frontiers of Development Administration*, pp. 375-414.

6. This concept and the related term "head of state," with derivative classification systems, are discussed in great detail by Riggs in "The Structures

of Government and Administrative Reform," pp. 220-324, in Braibanti, *Political and Administrative Development.*

7. Riggs, "Bureaucratic Politics in Comparative Perspective," p. 389.

8. Riggs, "Bureaucrats and Political Development," p. 126.

9. Fred W. Riggs, *Administrative Reform and Political Responsiveness: A Theory of Dynamic Balancing* (Beverly Hills, Calif.: Sage Publications, 1971). Safe Professional Papers in Comparative Politics, Volume 1, Series No. 01-010, p. 579.

10. LaPalombara, "An Overview of Political Development," pp. 3-33, and "Bureaucracy and Political Development: Notes, Queries, and Dilemmas," pp. 34-61, in LaPalombara, *Bureaucracy and Political Development.*

11. LaPalombara, "An Overview of Political Development," p. 15.

12. Henry Goodnow, "Bureaucracy and Political Power in the New States," in *The Civil Service of Pakistan* (New Haven, Conn.: Yale University Press, 1964), Chapter 1, pp. 3-22.

13. *Ibid.,* p. 10.

14. Lucian Pye, "The Political Context of National Development," in Irving Swerdlow, ed., *Development Administration: Concepts and Problems* (Syracuse, N.Y.: Syracuse University Press, 1963), pp. 25-43.

15. *Ibid.,* p. 31. He makes the same point in *Aspects of Political Development* (Boston: Little, Brown and Company, 1966), p. 19.

16. Pye, "The Political Context of National Development," p. 32.

17. *Ibid.,* p. 33.

18. Pye, "Bureaucratic Development and the Psychology of Institutionalization," pp. 400-26, in Braibanti, *Political and Administrative Development.* Refer particularly to pp. 408-22.

19. *Ibid.,* p. 414.

20. *Ibid.,* p. 419.

21. S. N. Eisenstadt, "Problems of Emerging Bureaucracies in Developing Areas and New States," pp. 159-75, in Bert F. Hoselitz and Wilbert E. Moore, eds., *Industrialization and Society* (The Hague: Mouton, 1963).

22. Ralph Braibanti, "The Relevance of Political Science to the Study of Underdeveloped Areas," in Ralph Braibanti and Joseph J. Spengler, eds., *Tradition, Values, and Socio-Economic Development* (Durham, N.C.: Duke University Press, 1961), p. 143.

23. *Ibid.,* p. 173.

24. *Ibid.,* p. 174.

25. *Ibid.,* p. 176.

26. Braibanti, "External Inducement of Political-Administrative Development: An Institutional Strategy," pp. 3-106, in Braibanti, *Political and Administrative Development,* at p. 3.

27. *Ibid.,* p. 79.

28. *Ibid.,* p. 105.

29. Milton J. Esman, "The Politics of Development Administration," pp. 59-112, in John D. Montgomery and William J. Siffin, *Approaches to Development: Politics, Administration and Change* (New York: McGraw-Hill Book Company, 1966), copyright © 1966, at pp. 81-82.

30. Bernard E. Brown, *New Directions in Comparative Politics* (New York: Asia Publishing House, 1962), pp. 49-51.

31. Fritz Morstein Marx, "The Higher Civil Service as an Action Group in Western Political Development," in LaPalombara, *Bureaucracy and Political Development*, pp. 65, 92-95. See also his "Control and Responsibility in Administration: Comparative Aspects," in Heady and Stokes, *Papers*, pp. 145-71.

32. Leonard Binder, *Iran: Political Development in a Changing Society* (Berkeley, Calif.: University of California Press, 1962), p. 54.

33. *Ibid.*, p. 58.

34. Lee Sigelman, "Do Modern Bureaucracies Dominate Underdeveloped Polities? A Test of the Imbalance Thesis," *American Political Science Review* 66, No. 2 (1972): 528. See also his *Modernization and the Political System: A Critique and Preliminary Empirical Analysis* (Beverly Hills, Calif.: Sage Publications, 1971). Sage Professional Papers in Comparative Politics, Volume 2, Series No. 01-016.

35. Ferrel Heady, "Bureaucracies in Developing Countries," in Riggs, *Frontiers of Development Administration*, p. 483.

36. Edward W. Weidner, *Technical Assistance in Public Administration Overseas: The Case for Development Administration* (Chicago: Public Administration Service, 1964), p. 166.

37. LaPalombara, "Alternative Strategies for Developing Administrative Capabilities in Emerging Nations," pp. 171-226, in Riggs, *Frontiers of Development Administration*, at p. 206.

38. Riggs, "The Context of Development Administration," pp. 72-108, in Riggs, *Frontiers of Development Administration*, at pp. 81-82.

39. Riggs, "Bureaucrats and Political Development," p. 166.

40. Riggs, "Relearning an Old Lesson: The Political Context of Development Administration," *Public Administration Review* 25, No. 1 (1965): 70-79, at p. 79.

41. Riggs, "The Context of Development Administration," pp. 82-83.

42. Riggs, "Relearning an Old Lesson," pp. 70-72.

43. Braibanti, "External Inducement of Political-Administrative Development," p. 79.

44. *Ibid.*, pp. 79-103.

45. *Ibid.*, p. 80.

46. *Ibid.*, p. 81.

47. Braibanti, "Administrative Reform in the Context of Political Growth," pp. 227-46, in Riggs, *Frontiers of Development Administration*, at pp. 229, 232.

48. Heady, "Bureaucracies in Developing Countries," p. 476.

49. *Ibid.*, pp. 478, 480. LaPalombara also believes that "the evidence is strongly persuasive that very little can occur by way of increasing or improving administrative capacity unless those in favor of such changes secure the overt, continuous, and single-minded support of central political leadership." "Strategies for Developing Administrative Capabilities," p. 192.

50. Lee Sigelman, "Do Modern Bureaucracies Dominate Underdeveloped Polities? A Test of the Imbalance Thesis," *American Political Science Review* 66, No. 2 (1972): 525-28; and "Bureaucratic Development and Dominance: A New Test of the Imbalance Thesis," *Western Political Quarterly* 27, No. 2 (1974): 308-13.

51. Sigelman, "Do Modern Bureaucracies Dominate?" p. 525.

52. *Ibid.*, italics in original removed.

53. Arthur S. Banks and Robert B. Textor, *A Cross-Polity Survey* (Cambridge: M.I.T. Press, 1963), pp. 112-13.

54. Gabriel Almond and James S. Coleman, eds., *The Politics of the Developing Areas* (Princeton, N.J.: Princeton University Press, 1960).

55. Sigelman, "Do Modern Bureaucracies Dominate?" p. 528.

56. Irma Adelman and Cynthia Taft Morris, *Society, Politics, and Economic Development: A Quantitative Approach* (Baltimore, Md.: Johns Hopkins Press, 1967), pp. 77-78.

57. Sigelman, "Bureaucratic Development and Dominance," pp. 310-11.

58. *Ibid.*, p. 312.

59. *Ibid.*, p. 313.

60. *Ibid.*, pp. 312-13.

61. Fritz Morstein Marx, "The Higher Civil Service as an Action Group in Western Political Development," pp. 62-95, in LaPalombara, *Bureaucracy and Political Development*, at p. 75.

62. Edward W. Weidner, "Development Administration: A New Focus for Research," pp. 97-115, in Heady and Stokes, *Papers*, at p. 99.

63. LaPalombara, "Public Administration and Political Development: A Theoretical Overview," pp. 72-107, in Charles Press and Alan Arian, eds., *Empathy and Ideology: Aspects of Administrative Innovation* (Chicago: Rand McNally & Co., 1966), at pp. 98-103.

64. Fritz Morstein Marx, *The Administrative State* (Chicago: University of Chicago Press, 1957), Chapter 4, pp. 54-72.

65. Merle Fainsod, "Bureaucracy and Modernization: The Russian and Soviet Case," pp. 233-67, in LaPalombara, *Bureaucracy and Political Development*, at pp. 234-37.

AUTHOR INDEX

417

SUBJECT INDEX

Acheampong, I. K., 321
Adenauer, Konrad, 185
Administration
  in Byzantium, 150
  defined, 2
  in Imperial Rome, 147-149
  in individual countries (*see* names
    of countries)
  medieval, 153, 157
  in Prussia, 159, 160
  as related to civilization, 128, 129
Administration and Society, 23
Administrative studies, central
    concerns in, 3
Administrative systems
  "classic," 67, 68, 170
  common patterns in developed
    countries, 168-170
  common patterns in developing
    countries, 270-275
  models of, 66-74
Afghanistan, 137, 243, 255, 284,
    307, 411
Africa
  arbitrary national boundaries in,
    407

[Africa]
  CAG committee on, 16
  colonies in, 106
  and comparative politics, 6
  as dependent area, 105, 112
  dominant-party mobilization
    regimes in, 361
  emergence of new nations in, 243,
    246
  military regimes in, 249, 254,
    256, 258, 259, 261, 268,
    291-294
  modernization in, 81, 244
  political development in, 85, 98
  politically underdeveloped nations
    in, 403
  political systems in, 265, 269
  traditional-autocratic regimes in,
    284
Afrifa, Akwasi, A., 321
Akuffo, Fred W., 321
Alexander the Great, 137
Algeria, 294, 362
Allende Gossens, Salvador, 303, 344
American Political Science Associa-
    tion, 10, 11